# THE
# TRAVELING
# CYCLIST

# THE TRAVELING CYCLIST

## 20 FIVE-STAR CYCLING VACATIONS

### ROY M. WALLACK

DOUBLEDAY

NEW YORK
LONDON
TORONTO
SYDNEY
AUCKLAND

PUBLISHED BY DOUBLEDAY

a division of Bantam Doubleday Dell Publishing Group, Inc.
666 Fifth Avenue, New York, New York 10103

DOUBLEDAY and the portrayal of an anchor with a dolphin are trademarks of
Doubleday, a division of Bantam Doubleday Dell Publishing Group, Inc.

Library of Congress Cataloging-in-Publication Data
Wallack, Roy M.
The traveling cyclist : 20 five-star vacations / Roy M. Wallack.—1st ed.
p. cm.—(The Traveling sportsman)
1. Bicycle touring—Guide-books. I. Title. II. Series.
GV1044.W35 1991
796.6'4—dc20 90-43208
CIP
ISBN 0-385-41373-4

BOOK DESIGN BY SIGNET M DESIGN, INC.
MAPS BY JACKIE AHER

MAY 1991
1 3 5 7 9 10 8 6 4 2
FIRST EDITION

*To my brother Marc
and
the late Martin Swart
who taught me all I know
about bike touring*

*Special thanks to my advisors, Larry Lawson, Kevin Mireles, and Bob Winning, and to my travel agent, Tops In Travel of Santa Monica, California.*

# CONTENTS

## THE BIG ADVENTURE:
### Pacific to Atlantic

## ROLLIN' ON THE RIVER:
## *The Mighty Mississippi*

# FOREWORD

**B**IKE TOURING LEADS TO REVELATIONS. TO TAKE A VACATION BY *bicycle is to change the way you see the world. The scenery—not filtered by glass or altered by speed—is raw, real. Unlike other modes of travel, there's nothing vicarious about bicycle touring. On a bike, you don't view a destination—as a moviegoer views a film. You experience the place. The bike's human scale makes you a part of every scene. You don't whiz through towns and countries. You pass homes and yards, porches and storefronts, trees and churches.*

*As you ride, your legs are transformed from Jell-O to marble. You burn calories like never before. A 170-pound man riding at a moderate pace (fifteen miles per hour) expends 570 calories an hour. A 120-pound woman burns 400 an hour. This gives you license to guiltlessly eat whatever you want as you travel. In this book the average day's ride is 68 miles, which at a moderate pace means 1,800 to 2,565 calories burned a day.*

*On a bike tour you touch the breezes, the raindrops, the warmth of the sun. Unprotected by life's usual cocoons, you feel nature's peace, its power. Unencumbered by an exhaust pipe, you do nature no harm.*

*But the best part of bike touring is the people you meet. In this book, you'll meet a funky guitar player from Venice, California; a pinkie-less tall-tale teller from Alaska; a respectable, upper-class couple from Michigan who once a year put on leather jackets and take a trip posing as hippie motorcyclists; a stout woman offering food and arm-wrestling in the Polish countryside; and many more. These characters are real. Like most people, they're fascinated by bike travelers, and quick to offer food, accommodations, and—best of all—conversation.*

*This is the enchantment of bike touring. People trust you. As South Dakota's Ernest L. Mudd explains to his cycling guests in Chapter 3, "If you stole something from me, you're still on bikes. How far could you get before I caught you?"*

*Ol' Ernest has a point. Maybe that's why people are so friendly to traveling cyclists. Whatever the reason, a bike tour does allow you to get close to people, to swap stories and ideas, to understand a little more about the town, the region, the country, the world. It's a type of learning that simply can't happen at fifty-five miles per hour.*

*The person who showed me that is Roy Wallack. I met him on the first bike tour ever into the Soviet Union. Both of us were writing stories on the historic trip, Roy for* California Bicyclist, *and I for* Bicycling *magazine. As a senior editor at* Bicycling, *I was already familiar with Roy's work. He had done some of the most interesting travel writing our magazine had ever published. His unique style—earthy, honest, often outrageous—is well suited to the subject of bike tours. It's like getting a letter from a friend who's on the road.*

*On the day I met Roy in Poland in '88, we saw many sights. But none is as memorable as meeting the desperate young Polish protesters who would soon topple their government. Later in the same trip (Chapters 14–16) we pedaled into Red Square, a place that had always seemed more mythical than real. At that moment, as the orange glow of a setting sun bathed the Kremlin, I remember thinking that the true power of a bicycle isn't how fast it can go, but where it can take you.*

*Roy's bike, as you'll see, has taken him all over the world. It's also helped change him from a frustrated MBA graduate who felt miscast in the business world to a successful writer who's finally spending life the way he wants. It's a transformation many people dream about. On these pages, you'll see it happen.*

*This book might not cause a career change for you, but it will inspire you to bike tour. Even now, fresh from bike trips in Finland and Long Island, I read about all these places Roy has experienced, and all the people he has met, and it gets me in the mood to pull out the atlas again. Revelations await.*

—NELSON PENA

# INTRODUCTION:

## The Principles

## of Cycle-ology

"THE FAMOUS STINKWATER PARADE OF CODY, WYOMING, WOULD like you all to give a big Fourth of July welcome to four California bike riders," the announcer's voice boomed. "They're riding their bicycles across the continent—from west to east!"

Well, that wasn't quite right. Our trip was also to stretch all the way to the Gulf of Mexico, six thousand miles in total. But no matter—we had some entertaining to do.

We had already carried Miss Wyoming on our shoulders, walked on our hands, and posed for pictures with Wyoming senator Alan Simpson, Cody mayor Dorse Miller, and the parade's grand marshall, actor Merlin Olsen. One member of our group, Crazy Martin, even kissed a horse on the lips.

So now we broke into figure-eight formation. We rode "sidesaddle." We stood on our handlebars. We waved to the crowd as if we were Rose Parade queens. And the locals and tourists who jam this town every July Fourth responded with rousing cheers. The Cody Stinkwater Parade, named in honor of the sulfur-laden local river, was certain to smell sweet in our memories.

After the parade was over, a reporter ran over and interviewed us. Then we were swarmed by dozens of locals, who started us on an hour-long session of yarn spinning and joke telling—a ritual we were to repeat dozens of times across the continent.

Amid the chuckling and gabbing, two other bike riders pedaled up. They too were riding across country, from Portland, Oregon, to Portland, Maine. They had witnessed our spectacle from the sidelines and quickly blended into the crowd surrounding us.

Like us, they were equipped with the standard touring regalia: panniers, sleeping bags, and waterbottles. But they had spent the previous evening at the KOA campground outside of town, while we had been in town at Cassie's Bar, the gargantuan "Gilly's" of Cody. They'd read a couple of chapters of *The World According to Garp* while we traded wit and wisdom with the locals, who led us to the parade organizers. The next day, the other cyclists watched the Stinkwater Parade. We rode in it.

And now, of course, we told tales about the unusual and funny experiences of our trip for an hour. They could only laugh—and listen.

As we traveled on, this became typical. We not only saw all the traditional Big Sights—Old Faithful, Mount Rushmore, the Sears Tower, and Niagara Falls—but also accumulated dozens of unique episodes like the Stinkwater Parade that we ended up telling all the other bikers about.

The difference, I think, was that while others simply *observed* America from their bicycle seats, we *participated*. We took an active role in making things happen. And things almost always did. We went out of our way to go to interesting places, and when we got there, we went out of the way to get close to the people. In doing so, we ended up meeting many interesting folks, getting dozens of stories to tell, and having the adventure of our lives.

Our "system" boiled down to three simple, yet critical steps. We called them the Principles of Cycle-ology:

1) *Go out of your way to see the sights, including the big cities.*

2) *When possible, stay in towns, not campsites, for contact with locals.*

3) *Visit taverns, bars, and other local hangouts.*

I know these principles work. When I got home, I was so excited by our adventure that I wrote a story about it. Since I wasn't a writer at the time, I was pleasantly surprised when *Bicycling* magazine published "The Principles of Cycle-ology" in its July 1983 issue. Even more surprising, when I took a bike ride down the California Coast in the fall of 1984, I met a half-dozen cyclists at a rest stop who were talking about the story—a year and a half after it came out.

Three of them claimed my article had taught them "the joy of bike touring." One heavy-set man, an accountant from Encino, California, even said that he had lost 105 pounds in the last year by bike riding—an activity he began after reading my article.

That was too much for me. I revealed my authorship, and although they reacted with disbelief, they'd already reaffirmed my thoughts about bike touring: there's no better way to take a vacation. If done right, you can see more, learn more, meet greater challenges, have more adventures, talk to more people, and gather more stories on a bike than by traveling any other way. And on top of that, you get in shape and pick up a nice tan. What a bargain!

For some people, like the fat man, bike touring leads to more than a great vacation: it can change your life. It sure changed mine.

A confirmed tour-aholic even before my 1982 trip across country and down the Atlantic Coast to Florida, I had by 1990 ridden down the West Coast, pedaled the length of the Mississippi River, down from Alaska, and along numerous other routes in North America and Europe, including the landmark first-ever bicycle tour into the U.S.S.R. Each trip seemed to lead to the next. And by the time I'd toured sixteen countries, thirty-eight states, six Canadian provinces, one territory, and twenty-eight thousand miles, what started off as a simple love for adventure had shaped my life. Due to my love of bike touring, I was fired from a job, developed deep friendships, lost a girlfriend, and gained an entirely new career. It truly is a case of My Bike Trips, Myself.

Most of the twenty routes I describe here are jammed with enough history and sightseeing to provide you with goals for nearly every day of the tour. Of course, you can sightsee by watching a *National Geographic* special, but the slow, methodical bike forces you to stop every twenty miles for food and drink, and will turn you into a roving anthropologist. You can't help but notice changes of accents, regional concerns, and priceless tidbits of American, Canadian, or European culture.

The average daily mileage on these trips is sixty-eight—with some longer, some shorter. If this seems like a lot, don't worry. At a normal pace on moderate terrain, cycling doesn't make the heart pound and the lungs wheeze. Riding a bike today is a lot easier than it was pedaling to school with an armful of school books. Not only can you ride a modern touring bike all day long without getting exhausted, but you can comfortably ride a hundred miles a day—no matter what age or what sex. I saw two sixty-eight-year-old men, both badly out-of-shape when they began, pedal their way from London to Moscow.

Anybody can ride a bike and do it on their own—without a tour—which is what this book is all about. Why should you pay for a tour? You can go to better places on your own, with the freedom to do what you please. All you need is an independent spirit, a good route, and a good list of sights to see and places to stay—all included here.

Wherever you decide to ride, your tour will go more smoothly if you have the right equipment, clothing, and riding technique. Starting as a beginner bike tourist, I learned some of the basics—like carrying a pump and spare tube—the hard way. Over a decade of touring, I've learned subtle lessons as well, such as how to get a room in a hotel claiming "no vacancy." In fact, on my most recent trip, to Hawaii, I even had to relearn the most common-sense lesson of them all: carry money and look at a map. Failure to do these turned a moderate four-hour hill climb into a grueling all-day ordeal.

Obviously, I'm a slow learner. But so it doesn't take you a decade of bike touring to become enlightened, as the chapters progress, you'll learn "Rules of the Road." A Bike Touring Checklist, condensing this advice, follows below.

Be realistic, however. The best equipment in the world alone won't give you a great voyage of discovery. All you really need is a decent bike—and the right attitude.

I met a guy at the end of my cross-country ride who had been with an organized tour group. He listened silently for two hours as I babbled on about my group's adventures at the Stinkwater Parade, in Chicago, Niagara Falls, Montreal—you name it.

When he finally spoke, he looked as if he wanted to cry. "We went right through the middle of the country, mainly through cornfields, and more cornfields, and more cornfields," he lamented. "Our big night out on the town was Pueblo, Colorado. Not Toronto, not Montreal. We avoided all the big cities. I wanted to see the Arch in St. Louis, but our route was fifty miles south of there."

I was appalled. The Arch is one of the most famous things in the whole country! Being so close and *not* seeing it was a crime. I love bike touring, but if I wanted to pedal through corn, I'd get a stationary bike, paint my walls yellow and watch old reruns of "I Love Lucy."

So before you take your bike tour, certainly study the checklist. And on the trip, never forget one more thing: a strong dose of Cycle-ology.

## THE BIKE TOURING CHECKLIST

### Attire

* ★ Gloves
* ★ Cycling shorts with crotchpad
* ★ Helmet
* ★ Non-attaching, hard-soled cycling shoes (better comfort, transfer of power than tennis shoes; better off-the-bike walking than clipless)
* ★ Additional clothes: two bike shorts, underwear, T-shirts, tank tops; one sweatshirt, windbreaker, set of "good" clothes—jeans, nice shirt/blouse

### Bike Setup

* ★ Clip-on aerobars (less air resistance and stress on back and arms)
* ★ Strong rack (Bruce Gordon model among best)
* ★ Universal-fitting rear panniers
* ★ Triple front chain ring, including Granny gear
* ★ Strong wheels (triangular "aero" wheels among best)
* ★ Mr. Tuffy tire liners
* ★ Toe clips
* ★ Several waterbottles

### Equipment (For each person)

* ★ Map
* ★ Money
* ★ Pump and patches
* ★ Spoke tightener and freewheel remover
* ★ Adjustable wrench
* ★ Screwdriver
* ★ Spare brake cables
* ★ Needle-nose pliers with cable cutter
* ★ Two extra tubes, especially if French Presta valve type
* ★ One spare tire for every 1,000 miles
* ★ Allen wrenches to tighten rack, waterbottle cage, gooseneck

★ *Rain poncho*
★ *Sunscreen*
★ *Rubber booties in high-rain areas*

## For the group
★ *Screened window tent for ventilation and mosquito protection*

## General Strategy

★ *Don't go all-out at first if you aren't in shape.*
★ *Don't ride at night.*
★ *Use Granny gear up long hills—saves wear on bike and body.*
★ *Leave early in the day—especially while climbing hills.*
★ *Try to ride with partners of similar abilities.*
★ *Pedals come off in the opposite direction as the pedal stroke. For taking pedals off, turn right one counterclockwise, left one clockwise.*
★ *Know how to true a wheel and fix a flat.*
★ *Know how to use a good camera.*
★ *Drink at least a waterbottle an hour.*
★ *Don't leave bike unattended long, even if locked.*
★ *Put belongings in plastic bags; no panniers are waterproof.*
★ *Use extra bungie cords to secure belongings on rack.*
★ *Travel light, especially clothing.*
★ *In a lightning storm, get off and away from the bike.*
★ *Set a goal for the day. If you lose one another, meet at the goal.*
★ *Have a telephone contact to relay messages if separated.*
★ *Continually stretch calves, quads, and hamstrings—before, after, and during the ride.*

## Miscellaneous:

★ *Enquire about a damaged room if a hotel posts a no-vacancy sign.*
★ *Campers should bring along youth hostel information book for cities.*
★ *Carry a sleeping bag even if hoteling it, in case of no vacancies.*
★ *Hitchhiking, if necessary, is easy: see truck, put out thumb.*
★ *Don't take pictures at Indian bars.*
★ *Never ignore posted signs in Wisconsin.*
★ *Avoid drinking beer during the day.*
★ *Don't be unshaven, unkempt, or smart-alecky to Canadian Customs.*
★ *Don't lean on a wheel with perpendicular force. It could bow.*
★ *Don't bike in Alaska out of season.*
★ *Cover hands, feet, and head in cold weather.*
★ *Join a tour only if prepared to compromise.*
★ *Airlines owe you a hotel room if they lose your bike.*
★ *Going solo is better than: 1) not going at all or 2) with a partner who hates touring.*

# CHAPTER 1

## BREAKING
## THE BARRIER
## THE FIRST
## OVERNIGHTER

**A**NYTHING'S SCARY UNTIL YOU DO IT ONCE.

If somebody had told me in 1978 that I'd ride all over the world for weeks, even months, at a time during the next decade, I'd have thought he was nuts. At twenty-two, I hadn't done much traveling of any kind, and none without some kind of support group.

Think of all the unknown factors: route, weather, wind, your body condition, mechanical breakdowns, finding accommodations. A book like this helps remove some of that fear. Physical fitness will remove some more. But even after all is taken care of, one thing remains: the psychological barrier of taking an overnight trip into uncharted territory on a fragile bicycle.

My brother Marc and I broke this barrier in the fall of 1978. Our route, from Santa Monica to San Diego, was far from exotic and practically in our own backyard. The distance was only 135 miles, which some would hardly consider a trip at all. But, for us, it was a grand adventure that changed forever how we looked at our bikes.

Of course, we didn't just decide to ride to San Diego on a lark one day, either. Getting to that point was a gradual process. In the fall of 1978 Marc, having no car, rode over twelve miles with a duffle bag full of clothes strapped to his back from Whittier College to my parents' home in Lakewood, a Los Angeles suburb. Then he rode back, completing a twenty-five-mile loop and astounding my parents and his dorm-mates.

That gave Marc an idea: a bike ride to and from Santa Monica, thirty-five miles away.

When he called me, it seemed improbable. But after we'd done it, we were ecstatic. Though we rode around an area where we grew up, we saw things we'd never seen before, like the Compton ghetto, most of Wilshire Boulevard, Los Angeles's main business street, and the barrio of East Los Angeles. On top of that, we logged over seventy miles.

Seventy miles! We were amazed that human beings could go that far.

The next day, Marc called me up. "This weekend, how about San Diego? It'll take two days."

"Okay," I replied quickly. Though leery of an overnighter, I couldn't hesitate. Marc, eighteen, was my little brother.

This isn't a full-fledged bike tour, like those in the rest of this book. In fact, the mostly-flat route through Southern California's beach towns could easily be used as a southern extension of the trip in Chapter 7.

But it is symbolic. What we achieved can be accomplished by any overnight bike trip anywhere: breaking the psychological barrier. Once we broke it, the great potential of bike touring opened up before us—an activity as big as the world itself, and one that has given us much pleasure since.

---

*ROUTE SLIP*
*Total of 137 miles in 2 days*

| Day | Ending Point | Terrain* | Sights | Mileage |
|---|---|---|---|---|
| 1 | San Clemente, California | Easy/Moderate | Santa Monica Pier, Venice Beach, Queen Mary**, San Juan Capistrano** | 72 |
| 2 | San Diego, California | Easy/Moderate | Scripps Aquarium, Sea World | 65 |

*Easy = flat to rolling; moderate = hilly; difficult = repeated miles of hills and climbing
**Require brief detours

★

---

# DAY 1

Santa Monica to San Clemente
Terrain: Flat plus a few rolling hills
Sights: Venice Beach, Queen Mary
72 miles

Starting at the Santa Monica Pier at 10:00 A.M., Marc and I rode on the boardwalk for one mile into Venice Beach, where we stopped dead in our tracks. It was impossible not to gawk.

There was a teeming hodgepodge of weird characters, roller skaters, body builders, circus acts, and thousands of "regular" people looking at them. One guy was juggling a running chainsaw. Another was balancing objects, including my bicycle, on his head. Three or four women were reading palms and Tarot cards. A light-skinned, blue-eyed black man named Harry, wearing a Sikh turban and robe, a baseball catcher's shin guards, and carrying an electric guitar and an amplifier on his back, roller skated up and began serenading us with an airy, meditational rock 'n' roll song.

Wow, man. Venice Beach. What a show! Neither of us had ever seen anything like it. As I handed Harry a dollar, I knew I was going to have to come back here someday.

More new sights followed: a parade of flesh on the Strand in Hermosa Beach, a unique U-shaped pier in Redondo Beach, even smelly oil wells in West Long Beach. We'd never seen any of this before, even though we grew up just a few miles away.

The revelation continued down Pacific Coast Highway at Huntington Beach, home of the annual world surfing championship and the beach we'd gone to every weekend as teenagers. As we checked out the skateboarders and teenybop bicycle free-stylers doing tricks at the pier, I was stunned to realize that I'd never been to the pier before. We'd always parked at a lot several miles to the south—too far away to walk!

A few miles south in Newport Beach, we stopped for chocolate-dipped Beach Bars at Balboa Island. The proprietor, seeing our sleeping bags, assumed we were on a lengthy journey, so we didn't let him down, telling him we'd begun two weeks earlier in San Francisco. Awestruck, he gave us the bars for free.

By late afternoon, we'd conquered the hilly terrain in and out of chic Laguna Beach and paused in San Clemente, where our family had watched the Fourth of July fireworks since 1966, before Richard Nixon's Western White House arrived. But, until I rode a bike there, I didn't know about the Thrifty Drug Store, since the freeway bypasses it. Now I picked up a triple scoop of my favorite ice cream, chocolate mint flake.

That should have been the last stop of the day, but we both felt strong and decided to shoot for a hundred miles. It'd be dark by then, but the night was warm. Maybe, we thought, we could make it all the way to San Diego.

We headed past the San Onofre nuclear power plant and got on the old coast road of San Onofre State Beach. Campers on the concrete strip were setting up lanterns as darkness fell. A couple miles further, it grew very dark. There was no moon out. I could barely see the outline of the road.

Suddenly I slammed into a pile of broken concrete.

I couldn't see how badly I was cut up, but every part of me hurt. My head. My knees. Especially my gloveless, bloody hands. My front tire was punctured and the wheel bent. I learned my first rule of the road: don't ride at night.

Crossing through a tunnel under the San Diego freeway, we walked in pitch blackness for about an hour before coming to a small hut, where a big, burly man shined a light on us.

"My god, what happened to you?" said the marine. This was Camp Pendleton.

I stayed at the guard shack while Marc hitched into the base to inflate my wheel, since neither of us had a pump. Before we left for Oceanside, we took a slew of joke pictures with the cooperative marine, who alternatively pretended he was choking me, hitting me with his baton, and stepping on my face. The photos, I figured, would make the pain of the ninety-three-mile day, our longest ever, worth it.

**DIRECTIONS:** South 2 miles on bike path thru Venice. Turn east ¾ miles on Washington Blvd. South 14 miles on bike path thru Marina del Rey to Redondo Beach. East ¼ mile on Avenue I, merge with Pacific Coast Highway, ride south 22 miles to Bolsa Chica State Beach. 9 miles south on bike path to Newport Beach. South 23 miles on Pacific Coast Highway to San Clemente.

**ACCOMMODATIONS: San Clemente North TraveLodge,** 1301 N. El Camino Real, San Clemente, (800) 843-1706 or (714) 361-0636. Amenities: saunas. Rooms: 32 units, double $40–$69. AMEX, MC, VISA.

**CAMPING: San Clemente State Beach,** 225 Avenue Calafia, (714) 492-3156. Amenities: beach access, showers.

# DAY 2

San Clemente to San Diego
Terrain: Flat, some hills
Sights: Scripps Aquarium, Sea World
65 miles

The terrain is almost pancake-flat through the pretty, eucalyptus-lined seaside towns of Carlsbad, Leucadia, Solana Beach, and Encinitas, places I'd never even heard of. In the latter, we stopped at the Taj Mahal-like golden dome and lush tropical gardens of the Self-Realization Fellowship, where the faithful sat on little stone benches, meditating in peaceful silence. Marc picked up some literature before we left, probably, I thought, to pray for a miracle. Because soon we looked in horror at the steepest, longest hill we'd ever seen: Torrey Pines Road.

In reality, Torrey Pines is only about a 350-foot climb, chicken feed as far as real hills go. But Marc and I hadn't much to compare it against. We had crossed a few short hills in the previous fifty miles, but nothing like this. After straining in slow motion, we found it impossible to climb and soon were walking.

After a couple of minutes, a woman on an old-fashioned three-speed bike passed us. She flew by, whizzing up the hill.

We looked at each other like idiots. She had gray hair and was at least fifty.

Several minutes later, she went barreling down the hill on the other side of the road. Soon after, she was coming up it again. This woman was working out on Torrey Pines Road!

This time, I ran alongside her. "Is there a trick to this?" I asked.

"Yes, there is," she said, breathing lightly. "It's called switching gears."

No wonder we couldn't make it up the hill. She explained that spinning in a lower gear keeps you moving without torqueing your knees.

So for the first time all trip, I downshifted into what I'd previously considered a "sissy" gear. And I flew up that hill after her.

Riding through the University of California at San Diego, we stopped briefly at the renowned Scripps Institute Aquarium-Museum in La Jolla, an affluent section of San Diego that has been a longtime resort. Further south, as we looked out over the blue waters from the La Jolla seacliffs, a couple of guys carrying snorkeling gear asked how far we'd ridden.

"San Francisco," we said in unison. Their jaws dropped.

We joined them for some underwater sightseeing and back on the cliffs an hour later, headed south. We crossed over Mission Bay near Sea World, home of Shamu, and kept heading south on the wind-blown Point Loma penninsula, where the view was striking. On our left lay San Diego Bay, one of the finest natural harbors in the world; on the right was the Pacific. At land's end was a monument to Juan Cabrillo, the first Spaniard to visit California, in 1542. Seeing this spot for the first time myself, my guess was that Juan had been impressed.

Though there was plenty more of San Diego to be impressed about, like Old Town, Coronado Island, and of course, the zoo, they would have to wait for another day. We had a train to catch. On the ride home, we were abuzz with all the things we'd learned in the past two days. We'd seen many new things; we'd seen old things in a new way. We learned a lot about bike riding, like the value of switching gears, of carrying a pump, of wearing cycling gloves, and of not riding at night.

A few days later, I even learned a lesson about photography. I hadn't threaded the film properly on my new 35-mm camera, so we didn't have one picture to remember our great adventure by. The scenery would al-

---

**DIRECTIONS:** South 4 miles on roads and bike path to San Onofre State Beach, 8 miles under I-5 into Camp Pendleton. Right 7 miles after checkpoint, right 2 miles on Vandenberg Boulevard into Oceanside. South 20 miles on SR 21 (Torrey Pines Road), pass Univ. of Cal. at San Diego, right 2 miles on La Jolla Shores Drive to aquarium. South 4 miles on Mission Boulevard. South 8 miles on Sunset Cliffs Boulevard, SR 209 (Catalina Boulevard and Cabrillo Memorial Drive) to Cabrillo National Monument. Backtrack 5 miles on SR 209, 3 miles on Harbor Drive to airport. It's 4 miles on Harbor Drive to downtown and Amtrak.

**ACCOMMODATIONS: Mission Bay Motel,** 4221 Mission Boulevard, (½ block from beach), San Diego, (619) 483-6440. Amenities: pool. Rooms: 30 units, double $45–$65. AMEX, VISA, MC.

**CAMPING: Campland on the Bay,** 2211 Pacific Beach Drive (on Mission Bay), San Diego, CA, (619) 274-6260. Amenities: pool, gameroom, café, showers.

ways be there, but some things we'd surely never see again—like the marine choking me in Camp Pendleton.

But photos or no photos, our little weekend ride had been a great adventure. Over the next few months, we made more trips—to the Spanish mission of San Juan Capistrano to see the swallows depart for South America, to the Rose Bowl in Pasadena, to the J. Paul Getty Museum in Malibu, and on Mulholland Drive at the ridge of the Hollywood Hills.

Driving back from the train station after that first ride, we laughed about how we'd told everyone we'd ridden from San Francisco. Suddenly, it didn't seem so unlikely. "Next Easter vacation," Marc said, "we ride to the Golden Gate."

As Chapter 7 will tell you, we did the San Francisco trip. And after that, we knew that Canada-to-Mexico, or Pacific-to-Atlantic, or even around-the-world was within our grasp.

## SIGHTSEEING INFORMATION

LAGUNA BEACH, CALIFORNIA
**Festival of Arts,** Irvine Bowl Park, 650 Laguna Canyon Road; mid-July–Aug; $9. (714) 494-8971.

LA JOLLA, CALIFORNIA
**Scripps Institute Aquarium-Museum,** 8602 La Jolla Shores Drive; $3; 9:00–5:00. (619) 534-6933 (feeding time at 1:00 P.M.).

LONG BEACH, CALIFORNIA
*Queen Mary* and *Spruce Goose,* south of Long Beach harbor; from Pacific Coast Highway, turn right on L.A. River bike path, ride to end: One of the largest passenger liners ever built; Howard Hughes—built all-wood airplane is largest in history; $14.50. (213) 435-3511.

SAN DIEGO, CALIFORNIA
**Cabrillo National Monument,** overlooks harbor at end of Cabrillo Memorial Drive: Where Spanish explorer Juan Cabrillo landed in 1542.
**Sea World,** 1720 S. Shores Road: "Oceanarium" on Mission Bay has shows, Shamu, dolphin petting zoo, penguins; $20; 9:00 A.M.–11:00 P.M. (619) 226-3901.

SAN JUAN CAPISTRANO, CALIFORNIA
**Mission San Juan Capistrano,** 3.5 miles east of Doheny State Beach, just before Highway 1 merges with I-5, 4 miles north of San Clemente: Dates to 1776; swallows arrive March 19 and leave October 23; $2. (714) 493-1424.

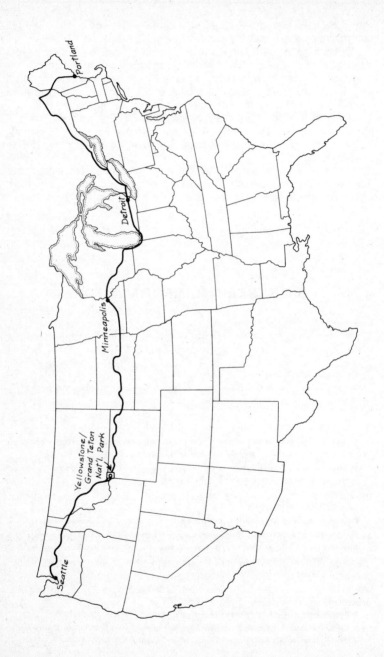

# THE BIG ADVENTURE

## Pacific to Atlantic

★

"I WISH I'D DONE SOMETHING LIKE THIS." NO MATTER WHERE WE went in the summer of 1982, from Wenatchee, Washington, to Waukegan, Illinois, to Waterville, Maine, there wasn't a day that went by without that comment. It came from people of all ages, of all occupations. It came wrapped in admiration and envy. It was the romantic notion of going ocean to ocean.

The trip was my brother's dream. By that time, Marc had become a car-less bicycling fanatic who was commuting between Long Beach and San Diego twice a week—almost two thousand miles a month. He had huge legs. He had planned on doing the transcontinental trip by himself in the summer of 1981 until my mother—not normally the emotional type—literally broke out in hives.

Stymied, Marc planned for the future. During the next year, he tried to sell his friends on the idea, persuading them to buy bikes and cajoling them into taking longer and longer preparatory bike trips with him—up to the mountains, out to the desert, and up the coast to Santa Barbara.

By that summer, Marc had it together. His friend Bob took a leave of absence from his job to go on the trip. Another, Martin, left his floor-waxing business in the hands of his teenaged brother and joined up.

I was just out of grad school, unemployed and frustrated. I paid fifteen dollars for a used pair of panniers and signed on the day before they left.

Marc's idea was to ride across the country in a straight line as fast as he could, stopping only for food, doing two hundred miles a day at a minimum. But since I'm a history-reading, picture-taking sightseeing machine and figured I'd never have the time to do a ride as grand as this one again, I decided that we were going to do it right. That meant we would see everything—from Old Faithful to the Sears Tower to the Miller Brewery to the citadel of Quebec City.

And that's how a 3,000-mile trip became 4,356 miles.

The trip we did went from northwest to northeast—from the west to take advantage of the prevailing winds, and in the north to avoid the stifling southwestern deserts. Passing through eleven states and two provinces, the tour started in Seattle,* wrapped around the bottom of Lake Michigan, headed up the St. Lawrence Seaway and ended in Portland, Maine. And as it rolled east, the tenor of the journey changed.

In the dry, underpopulated West, we were amazed by the grandeur of the natural sights; of the mountains and mountain passes; of the rocky solitude of craggy canyons; of natural wonders like the Devils Tower, Yellowstone Park, and the Badlands; and of man's alteration of nature, like Mount Rushmore and the Grand Coulee Dam. We saw a culture of mining and logging; a culture that wasn't much more than one hundred years old.

In the humid, crowded, older Midwest and East, where the river-crossed and lake-dotted prairie terrain is much flatter, there was more farming, more manufacturing, and more big cities, like Minneapolis, Milwaukee, Chicago, Detroit, Toronto, and Montreal. Then, at the very end, it was back to nature, across the rugged face of Maine before reaching the Atlantic. We not only got two different countries in the bargain, the United States and Canada, but also two languages—English and French.

This was an awesome trip across monumental geography, crossing the Rockies, the Plains, the mighty Mississippi, the Great Lakes, the St. Lawrence Seaway, and the Appalachians, but it was also an odyssey across time. As we crossed the land west to east, I felt like we were riding backwards through North American history, like Lewis and Clark in reverse.

By the time Los Angeles had its first paved streets, Chicago was a bustling metropolis that had already been burned down and rebuilt. And one hundred years before Chicago was even an idea, Quebec City was the thriving capital of New France. Seeing the sites of Indian battles and three-hundred-year-old forts from the seat of a bicycle gave me a vastly better eduction than I had gotten from books.

Although I've taken bike trips in a dozen countries since this one, nothing else has matched it for sheer variety—of history, scenery, terrain, and sightseeing. To this day, my tourmates and I simply refer to the trip as "the Big Adventure."

For you, the Big Adventure has been broken up into five contiguous segments, none of which are joyrides. To go the distance and see all the sights, you've got to move sixty to one hundred miles per day over often-difficult terrain, especially in the rocky West.

Therefore, get in shape. Then get psyched up for the ride(s) of your life.

---

*If I have one regret about this trip, it is that it doesn't technically start at the Pacific Ocean. Seattle is a Pacific port city, but actually sits on Puget Sound, nearly one hundred miles inland from the Pacific. Another potential starting point, Portland, Oregon, is over seventy miles from the ocean. The first big city actually on the Pacific is San Francisco, which is far, far to the south and requires a frightening journey to the east across deserted, blazing-hot Nevada atomic testing grounds. Even if you don't get radiation poisoning, you could die of dehydration. So we decided to start from Seattle.

## SEATTLE TO YELLOWSTONE

**T**HERE WEREN'T A LOT OF MAN-MADE TOURIST ATTRACTIONS ON this challenging section of the Big Adventure—but the ride went through 984 miles of some of the best natural scenery in North America, topped off by one of the crown jewels of Mother Nature, Yellowstone Park.

Heading southeast through Washington, Idaho, and Montana into the northwest corner of Wyoming, we rode over two mountain ranges— the Cascades and the Rockies—and rose from sea level to almost nine thousand feet. Though the mountainous route crossed the Continental Divide three times, I-90 and the smaller highways are well-graded and well-shouldered, so the ride was a workout, but not difficult or unsafe. Traveling on river-grade roads much of the way, we rode over and along the mighty Columbia River, saw vast wheat fields, forests and cattle-grazing lands, and met some of the friendliest people in the country.

That may be because nearly all the people are small-town folks. Other than Seattle and Spokane, the "big" cities like Missoula and Butte have populations only in the mid-thirty thousands. Most of the tiny mining, logging, and cattle towns along the way make those two look like giants by comparison.

Summer temperatures range from cool in the higher elevations to sweltering in the middle of the day. The beauty of riding in this section of the country is that you can always hop into one of the ubiquitous mountain streams to cool off. Heck, you could take a full-blown siesta in the afternoon if you want to; the long hours of sunlight in the northern latitudes allow comfortable riding as late as 9:30 P.M. With that kind of leeway, this route is manageable for bicyclists of all abilities.

## ROUTE SLIP
Total of 984 miles in 15 days

| Day | Route End Point | Terrain* | Sights | Mileage |
| --- | --- | --- | --- | --- |
| 1 | Seattle, Washington | Easy | Museum of Flight, Space Needle, Pioneer Square | 11 |
| 2 | Skykomish, Washington | Easy | Scenic ride | 62 |
| 3 | Wenatchee, Washington | Difficult | 4,061-ft. Stevens Pass, scenic ride | 75 |
| 4 | Grand Coulee, Washington | Difficult | Rocky Reach Dam | 96 |
| 5 | Spokane, Washington | Easy | Grand Coulee Dam Tour, Riverfront Park | 87 |
| 6 | Kellogg, Idaho | Difficult | Lake Coeur d' Alene, Fourth of July Pass | 71 |
| 7 | St. Regis, Montana | Difficult | 4,680-foot Lookout Pass, scenic highway | 61 |
| 8 | Missoula, Montana | Easy | Scenic highway | 71 |
| 9 | Deer Lodge, Montana | Easy | Towe Ford Museum | 77 |
| 10 | Three Forks, Montana | Difficult | Continental Divide, Homestake Pass | 84 |
| 11 | Big Sky, Montana | Easy | Scenic highway, rafting, gondola ride | 71 |
| 12 | West Yellowstone, Montana | Easy | Scenic highway | 47 |
| 13 | West Thumb, Wyoming | Moderate | Old Faithful, Paint Pots, Continental Divide | 48 |
| 14 | Mamth Hot Springs, Wyoming | Difficult | Artist Point, Lookout Falls, Grand Canyon | 74 |
| 15 | West Yellowstone, Montana | Difficult | Norris Geyser Basin | 49 |

*Easy = flat to rolling; moderate = hilly; difficult = at least one major hill climb

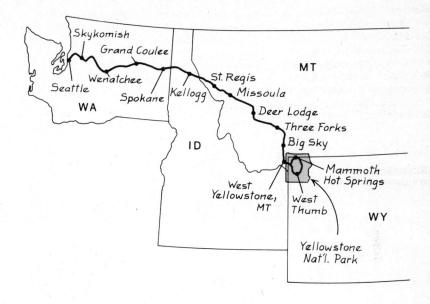

## DAY 1

Seattle
Terrain: Flat
Sights: Museum of Flight, Space Needle, Pioneer Square
11 miles

Marc not only had been riding two thousand miles a month to prepare for this monumental trip, but also had taken a massage class and
was studying the teachings of Maimonides, Gandhi and Carlos Casta-
neda. I, however, carried the maps. So on June 21, 1982, he followed me
as we pedaled out of the airport and set off to meet Bob and Martin, who
were waiting for us at the landmark Space Needle in downtown.

Our first act together as a group was to take the requisite 605-foot
journey up to the Needle's observation deck, getting a panoramic view of
the city, Puget Sound and the Olympic and Cascade mountains, including 14,410-foot Mount Ranier.

We shared a telescope with a University of Washington professor,
who quickly delivered an impromptu lecture. Seattle, he explained, was
first visited by British Captain George Vancouver in 1792, founded in
1851 as a logging and fur-trapping center, destroyed in 1889 by the Great
Fire, then revived as the jumping-off point for the 1898 Klondike Gold
Rush in Canada's Yukon. It became an aircraft manufacturing center in
the 1950s due to Boeing and gained a world-class downtown and the
famed Space Needle with the 1962 World's Fair.

Properly educated, we then rode randomly around town, discovering in the process that Seattle is as good a transition to a bike trip as any big port city of half a million could be. The air is fresh and crisp; nature seems to hold its own against the concrete. Situated on a narrow strip of land bordered by the Sound to the west and Lake Washington to the east, the city is a green and glorious mixture of hills, water, mist and rain (thirty-seven inches a year, but with summers generally sunny). It was a super day of climbing and descending.

---

**DIRECTIONS:** From Sea-Tac International Airport, Highway 99 2 miles north. Left on Marginal Way 4 miles. Right on 4th Avenue, 5 miles north to Seattle center.

**ACCOMMODATIONS: Best Western Executive Inn,** 200 Taylor Avenue N. (near Space Needle), Seattle 98109, (206) 448-9444. Rooms: 123 units, doubles $70–$80. AMEX, VISA, MC.
**Days Inn Town Center,** 2205 7th Street, Seattle 98121, (206) 448-3434. Rooms: 92 units, $49+. AMEX, DINERS, MC.

**CAMPING: Lake Pleasant RV Park,** 24025 Bothell Highway SW, Bothell, (206) 487-1785. (14 miles north of Seattle) From SR 522 (see Day 2 instructions), turn left (north) on SR 527 (Bothell Highway).

---

## DAY 2

Seattle to Skykomish
Terrain: Flat, rolling
62 miles

I was filled with a mixture of excitement and fear on the early afternoon of June 22, 1982, our official day of departure. Looming ahead was incredibly long mileage—made even more daunting since I'd only previously bike toured a total of six days in my life. There were so many unanswered questions: Who were these guys I was riding with? (Bob and Martin were Marc's friends. I didn't know them.) Where were we going? (No one had planned a route.) What if I got a flat? (I hadn't brought a pump, figuring I'd just ride ahead of everyone and use theirs when they caught up to me.) Was I carrying enough stuff? (Everyone else had both front and rear panniers. I only had rears, and didn't even know how to pronounce them. Panny-ears? Pan-yays?) Could our legs handle the strain of riding thousands of miles? What if we were cut off by killer bears in the wilderness, out of reach of a phone, with salivating eagles circling overhead? What if we ran into those mountain men from the movie *Deliverance*? As we left Seattle heading north and west, I felt like a member of Columbus's crew sailing for the Indies, probing blindly at the edge of the world.

By the end of the day, however, the fear was gone. Not only was the ride easy and trouble-free, but the cool, crisp air and evergreen splendor of western Washington gave me the best first day of riding I'd ever had on any tour. After getting out of town, US 2 is a beautifully scenic, river-grade cruise past a half-dozen tiny towns into the lush green forest and mountains of the Cascade Range and the Snoqualmie National Forest.

After commemorating the beginning of our adventure with a picture of the city sign at the town of Startup, we stopped in Zekesville, popula-tion six. There we met sixty-two-year-old Zeke himself, who served as police chief, town mayor, fireman, dog catcher, and a myriad of other important government posts. He gave each of us a Zekesville bumper sticker before he released us from custody.

At about mile thirty into the day came the logging town of Gold Bar, population eight hundred. Once a prospectors' camp, Gold Bar was such a hotbed of anti-Chinese bigotry during the building of the Great North-ern Railroad a century ago that some frightened Chinese laborers fled town hidden in coffins.

As we continued east, the scenery seemed to get even more beauti-ful. That night in tiny Skykomish, while Marc massaged his legs, tinkered with his bike and read some Zen, Martin, Bob, and I visited the only bar in town. We met Gus, the one-eared logger (yes, a chainsaw accident), and a couple of long-haired Vietnam vets, then had some rousing dis-cussions about the domino theory, Reaganomics, and life in the boonies. Martin talked about his floor-waxing business, Bob about his women, me about my job hunt. Martin taught us an old Tennessee Ernie Ford song: *You load sixteen tons and what do you get? Another day older and deeper in debt. Saint Peter, don't you call me 'cause I can't go, I owe my soul to the company store.* I went to bed with a good buzz and very satisfied. Yes, I thought, this was going to be a great way to spend the summer. I woke up humming "Sixteen Tons" and sang it several times the next day—as I have on every bike trip since.

---

**DIRECTIONS:** From Space Needle, Broad Street ½ mile to Naval Reserve Train-ing Center. Name changes to Valley for 3 blocks. Bearing left as street splits, take Eastlake Avenue 2 miles north across University Bridge to University of Washington. From University, 12th Avenue north for 2½ miles to intersection of SR 522 (Lake City Way NE, changing to Bothell Way), which loops around Lake Washington thru Bothell for 25 miles east to US 2. Take US 2 33 miles to Skykomish.

**ACCOMMODATIONS: Skylark Motel,** south end of Skykomish River Bridge, PO Box 117, Skykomish, (206) 677-2261. <u>Amenities</u>: on riverfront. <u>Rooms</u>: 17 units, doubles $40. DINERS, MC, VISA.

**CAMPGROUNDS: Breckler River,** 1 mile east on US 2 and 1 mile north on FR 65, (206) 677-2414. No facilities.

★

## DAY 3

Skykomish to Wenatchee
Terrain: 4,000-foot climb at Stevens Pass
75 miles

One thing stands out about this day: the Climb. Though 4,061-foot-high Stevens Pass is not high in sheer elevation, its base is very low, so it is the second biggest climb—next to Wyoming's Granite Pass—on the entire Big Adventure. It was by far the biggest climb of our lives and came long before our legs had become *cycling* legs.

Luckily, however, the Climb started just seventeen miles from Sky-komish, so the air was cool. When I finally ended it after two hours, then saw vendors selling cherries, peaches, pears, plums, and apples at the top of the pass, I thought I'd died and gone to high-fiber heaven.

This produce came from the rich, volcanic soil of the Wenatchee Valley, one of the world's largest producers of apples. Gradually descending into the valley for the rest of the day, we paralleled the Wenatchee River for four striking miles through Tumwater Canyon, stopped at Der Markt Platz in tiny, Bavarian-style Leavenworth, and ended with a feast of apples, apple cider, and apple butter sandwiches at a roadside stand in Wenatchee.

---

**DIRECTIONS:** 71 miles on US 2 to Wenatchee exit, 4 miles south into town.

**ACCOMMODATIONS: Red Lion Inn,** 1¾ miles north on US 2, 1225 N. Wenatchee Avenue, Wenatchee, WA, (509) 663-0711. Amenities: pool, whirlpool. Rooms: 149, doubles $56–$67. AMEX, MC, VISA.

**CAMPING: Lincoln Rock State Park,** Take US 2 east across Columbia, ride north 2 miles past Rocky Reach Dam, (509) 884-3044.

---

## DAY 4

Wenatchee to Grand Coulee Dam
Terrain: Climb, then flat
Sights: Rocky Reach Dam
96 miles

With our cycling legs far from ready, all of us—except Marc—were in pain after this day. There was a *lot* of riding—made even tougher by the heat of eastern Washington. The Oz-like greenery of the rainy, tree-lined Cascade Mountains disappeared as we crossed into the dryer, eastern half of the state, where the average annual rainfall, thirteen inches, is less than half Seattle's. The land is part of a vast basaltic tableland known as the Great Northern Desert, a barren landscape of wheat fields and fruit trees—all of it dependent on the mighty Columbia River, which cuts down through Washington from Canada in a massive arc known as the Great Bend.

When US 2 suddenly bent east at Orondo after a flat ride along the Columbia and a pit stop at the Rocky Reach Dam, our jaws dropped. Out of nowhere, there was a wall—a seven-mile climb up to the town of Waterville. After that, it got even worse: a fifty-mile-long stretch of townless, flesh-baking asphalt all the way to Dry Falls Dam and Banks Lake. It was impossible not to take a dip and relax after doing a half-century ride in the world's largest microwave oven.

When Marc and I arrived at Banks Lake, exhausted, sunburned, and dehydrated by the hundred-degree heat, we were surprised to find Bob and Martin waiting for us there, looking fresh and relaxed. This didn't make sense, since they were slower than us and had left later in the morning, but they calmly claimed to have found a short-cut around Waterville, avoiding the hill. As an inveterate map reader, I found that questionable.

After the lake, the day's last twenty-six miles north along Banks Lake had better scenery, but no access to food and drink. We arrived hungry and beat at the Coulee House Motel, which has a great view of a nightly laser light show on the dam wall. Next door at a restaurant bar, Bob had one too many beers and, to Martin's chagrin, admitted they'd hitchhiked all the way to Banks Lake.

---

**DIRECTIONS:** Cross Columbia River, 16 miles north on US 2 to Orondo. Turn east with US 2 50 miles to Banks Lake. Left on Sr 155 for 26 miles.

**ACCOMMODATIONS: Coulee House Motel,** 110 Roosevelt Way (on SR 155, pass Electric City and Grand Coulee, cross river bridge), Grand Coulee, WA, (509) 633-1101. Amenities: laundry, sauna, suites with kitchens, restaurant, view of spillway. Rooms: 61 units, doubles $44–$62. AMEX, DINERS, VISA, MC.

**CAMPING: Spring Canyon,** south on SR 174 at Grand Coulee for 3 miles, on lake. No phone or showers.

---

# DAY 5

Grand Coulee Dam to Spokane
Terrain: Flat, rolling
Sights: Grand Coulee Dam Tour
87 miles

By now, everyone except Marc was hurting *bad*. There was some grumbling about the mileage we were doing—ninety-six miles yesterday,

eighty-seven miles today—all in the frying heat. You may rest easy knowing that these are the two longest consecutive days on this tour. But all
Martin and Bob heard from Marc was that we were working our way up
to two hundred miles a day. Since Marc is my brother, I would never
admit I couldn't hack it. And anyway, I figured the pain would eventually
disappear as we rode into shape. As long as Marc didn't get in the way of
my sightseeing, I'd do his miles.

On this day, the sightseeing came early: a two-hour tour of the Grand
Coulee Dam, the world's largest hydroelectric facility. Then it was a day
of unbroken riding over rolling-to-flat country of more wheat fields and
blazing heat, ending with a long downhill coast into Spokane, the second
largest city in Washington with 175,000 people and the first Northwest
trading post set up after Lewis and Clark's 1805 expedition.

Our first stop in town was the gym at the Gonzaga University, where,
during my third or fourth shower, I was startled by a loud *thunk!* on the
tile floor next to me. It was Marc and Martin fighting! All day long, Martin
had been calling Marc a "robot" while Marc countered with, "You're a
weak-minded, lazy slob." In the shower, they both snapped. Martin was
angry that we weren't stopping enough, jumping in the rivers, meeting
the people. Marc said Bob and Martin were slowing him down. It was the
classic conflict of bike touring. In the end, they cooled off and agreed
that we needed a day off to wash clothes, make repairs, and recuperate.

At a laundromat, we met some girls who put us up in their apartment and showed us the city the next day. Between the city-bisecting
Spokane River, the illuminated Spokane Falls, the view of the city from
nearby Cliff Park off of 13th Avenue and the pseudo-hippies at Riverfront
Park, Spokane made for a beautiful and interesting pit stop. I hung out
at the river by myself and just sort of *gazed* for a while at the trees, the
stars, and the lights reflecting off the gurgling waters.

Ultimately, the feuders agreed to disagree. Martin would do it his
way and Marc would do it his, and if they had to, they'd split up. I hoped
they wouldn't. Neither realized it, but we had been doing this trip *my*
way—both Martin's partying and Marc's distance (so far). If forced to
choose between them, I'd be the loser. I was having a great time the way
it was.

---

**DIRECTIONS:** From Grand Coulee, south on SR 174 for 20 miles to Wilbur.
East on US 2 62 miles to outskirts of Spokane. At downhill, bear left to Sunset
Boulevard, paralleling US 2/I-90 freeway. Merge with 2nd and Sprague ave-
nues.

**ACCOMMODATIONS: Cavanaugh's Inn at the Park,** W. 303 N. River Drive,
Spokane, WA, (509) 326-8000. Amenities: river view, sauna, whirlpool, exercise rm., pool. Rooms: 266, doubles $95–105; VISA, MC, AMEX, DINERS, DIS.

**CAMPING: Riverside State Park,** northwest end of city, by river, (509) 456-
3964. Amenities: showers.

★

# DAY 6

Spokane to Kellogg, Idaho
Terrain: Flat-rolling, climb at Fourth of July Pass
Sights: Lake Coeur d'Alene
71 miles

Crossing your first state border by bike is a thrill. For us, the big, colorful "Idaho Welcomes You" sign was the scene of a half-hour picture-taking orgy that has become a ritual at every border I cross. A photo of a welcome sign is hard proof that you are truly a bike-touring stud.

Idaho is located twenty-three miles east of Spokane on I-90. It seemed odd to bike on an interstate highway, but out in the hinterlands it's not exactly an eight-lane rush-hour freeway—more like a well-graded four-lane country road. Our directions from this point were simple: stay on I-90, angling south and east, virtually all the way to Yellowstone.

Idaho didn't last long—about seventy miles. Crossing it just below the thinnest part of the panhandle, we passed through a mix of forested mountains, large lakes, grain fields, pastureland, and the narrow canyons of the Coeur d'Alene mining district.

Coeur d'Alene contains vast quantities of silver, zinc, and lead, minerals in which Idaho ranks first, second, and fourth among the states. Its nickname is "The Gem State," which doesn't make sense since none of these are gems.

But Lake Coeur d'Alene, fifteen miles inside the border, truly is a gem. Called one of the five most beautiful lakes in the world by *National Geographic,* it is one of Idaho's most popular tourist destinations for boating and fishing. Not for swimming, however. I shot out of that ice-cold mountain water like Baby Shamu.

After a run-of-the-mill thousand-foot climb over 3,081-foot-high Fourth of July Pass, we came to rest in the mining center of Kellogg, one of many "population-equals-elevation" towns on this route: 2,800 to 2,300. Then our normal routine began.

While Marc read and watched the bikes, Martin, Bob, and I spent the evening in a bar, talking with some bitter, out-of-work copper miners. Martin said he had plenty of work for them waxing floors in San Diego. I encouraged them to do what I did: try a bike trip.

---

**DIRECTIONS:** From Spokane, Broadway Street 2 to 3 miles to I-90.

**ACCOMMODATIONS: Silverhorn Motor Inn,** 699 Cameron Avenue, (exit 49 to Bunker Avenue), Kellogg, ID, (208) 783-1151. <u>Rooms</u>: 40, double $44. VISA, MC, AMEX, DINERS.

**CAMPING: KOA,** 701 N. Division. 3 miles before Kellogg on I-90, exit 45, ½ mile south, (208) 682-3612. <u>Amenities</u>: running stream, showers, groceries, laundry.

★

## DAY 7

Kellogg, Idaho, to St. Regis, Montana
Terrain: Climb at Lookout Pass
61 miles

The ride into Montana was no piece of cake. Lookout Pass sits on the border at 4,738 feet—2,350 feet higher than Kellogg. We definitely earned our photo of the state border sign, as well as the long, enjoyable descent down from Lookout.

On the cruise down, we set our watches forward one hour for the change from Pacific to Mountain Time. Montana means "mountain" in Spanish, reflecting the mountainous western half of the state that we were traveling in. Ironically, the fourth biggest state in the United States (after Alaska, Texas, and California) is nicknamed "Big Sky Country" after its eastern half, mostly prairie.

Though we were in the Rockies, the riding generally stayed easy all the way to Yellowstone. For the next few days, I-90 paralleled the St. Regis River, with fairly easy river-grade highway, no major climbs, crisp mountain air and excellent riding.

On the way into St. Regis, we met a thirty-five-year-old (an old man to us) touring alone from Georgia with just a sleeping bag and a gallon jug of water on his rack. His ripe odor and three-speed clunker bike, on which he claimed to ride a hundred miles a day, sobered us up. Until now, everyone had been so impressed with us that we'd begun feeling superhuman, despite riding a third of Marc's two hundred-miles-per-day goal. But Marc now had evidence that a hundred per day was doable, and the tension returned.

---

**DIRECTIONS:** From Kellogg, I-90 all day.

**ACCOMMODATIONS: St. Regis Super 8;** 1 block east off I-90, exit 33, (406) 649-2422. <u>Rooms</u>: 32, doubles $38. VISA, MC, AMEX, DINERS, DIS.

**CAMPING: Campground St. Regis,** 1 and ¾ miles west of exit 33 (Camel's Hump Road); follow signs; (406) 649-2470. <u>Amenities</u>: showers, laundry, pool, rec room.

---

## DAY 8

St. Regis to Missoula
Terrain: Flat to rolling
71 miles

We awakened at 9:00 A.M. on the porch of a general store to find customers tiptoeing over us. Soon the owner came out with some free coffee and donuts. "I didn't want to wake you guys up," he explained. "You looked so comfortable."

We decided we liked it here in Montana.

Marc, however, apparently didn't like the slow pace. Rubbing the sleep from our eyes, we noticed that he'd already packed up and left! As we passed through each tiny little town along the easy, rolling highway, we figured he'd be waiting for us—but he wasn't. By the time we came to a big white "M" etched into a mountain—for the University of Montana at Missoula—we figured we'd never see him again.

Missoula, a regional hub of 33,400, has a lot of history, mostly derived from its location at the edge of Hell Gate Canyon. In the 1600s, the Blackfeet Indians ambushed the Salish tribe here, which is why French trappers dubbed the site *Porte de l'Enfer,* "The Gates of Hell." A natural gateway, Missoula grew fast in the 1860s as a supply depot for the nearby goldmines and later as a lumber center.

We learned all this from a policeman at a 7-Eleven, who had driven up to us earlier, threatening to write us tickets for speeding. "I'm a little short on cash," he joked. That didn't mean a bribe, he explained. In Montana, the government was so anti-bureaucracy that the cops simply collect five dollars on the spot from the drivers they catch speeding. There's no paperwork. The police turn in the cash on an honor system.

---

**DIRECTIONS:** From St. Regis, I-90 all day.

**ACCOMMODATIONS: Holiday Inn,** 200 S. Pattee Street; exit on Orange Street off I-90; river view, scenic valley; (406) 721-8550. <u>Rooms</u>: 200, double $62–$71. VISA, MC, AMEX, DINERS, DIS.

**CAMPING: El Mar KOA,** 3695 Tina Avenue; 1 mile south off I-90 via Reserve Street; (406) 549-0881. <u>Amenities</u>: groceries, laundry, showers, pool.

---

# DAY 9

Missoula to Deer Lodge
Terrain: Easy
77 miles

Well, not every day can be a scenic wonder. There aren't even any tough hills to mark this easy, dull day, which ended in the old gold-strike town of Deer Lodge, another population-equals-elevation city (4,000 at 4,519) and the second-oldest in Montana.

The only thing that stands out in my mind, aside from wondering where Marc was, is mile forty-five and the town of Drummond, the self-proclaimed "World's Largest Bullshipping Capital." Hiding from the world's largest raindrops, Bob and I spent a couple of hours in the coffee shop getting to know each other, which was a good thing. Since Martin had hitchhiked to Great Falls to visit a friend earlier in the day, we were now the only two left on the trip.

---

**DIRECTIONS:** I-90 all day.

**ACCOMMODATIONS: Super 8 Motel,** 1150 Main Street; exit 184, north 1 mile; (406) 846-2370. <u>Amenities</u>: scenic valley, indoor pool. <u>Rooms</u>: 54, double $36. VISA, MC, AMEX, DINERS, DIS.

**CAMPING: Deer Lodge KOA,** 330 Park Street; exit 184 or 187; (406) 846-1629. <u>Amenities</u>: laundry, groceries, showers.

---

# DAY 10

Deer Lodge to Three Forks
Terrain: Rolling to flat, one climb
Highlight: Continental Divide
84 miles

Butte, whose copper gained it the reputation as "the richest hill on earth," is where we patched things up. After forty-one miles, just before town, I got my first flat, which normally wouldn't be a problem. But since it happened the only time during the entire trip that I—with no pump—rode at the back of the pack, I had to walk a mile and a half to the edge of the city. Bob awaited with logical advice: buy one. Everybody rides at his own pace on a bike trip, so you have to carry all your own tools.

After repairs, we entered Butte to see a lone figure silhouetted at the top of a hill. It was Marc. He didn't say it, but he was lonely. Marc didn't even complain when we spent the afternoon waiting for Martin to show up.

Getting out of Butte entailed a 700-foot climb over 6,393-foot Homestake Pass—the first of three crossings of the Continental Divide on the tour. Sure, a measly seven hundred feet shouldn't have been as tough as Stevens Pass back in Washington or even Lookout Pass at the Idaho border. But it seemed to come right in the hottest part of the day—and right after we ate. I felt like a human cup-of-soup—with my lunch cooking inside me.

The remaining miles dropped us 2,300 feet into the tiny town of Three Forks, where the Jefferson, Madison, and Gallatin rivers meet. Lewis and Clark identified this spot as the headwaters of the Missouri River, which stretches 2,500 miles to the Mississippi from here. A plaque in a small park downtown explained that Three Forks was a favorite Indian hunting ground and childhood home of Sacajawea, "Birdwoman" in Blackfoot, who guided Lewis and Clark through this area.

Speaking of Indians, Martin entertained us all night with stories about bar-room brawls, loose women and general mayhem in Great

Falls' many Indian bars. Though we spent many nights in them thereafter, we couldn't find an Indian bar in Three Forks, which is far from a reservation. Instead, we settled for a cowboy bar, The Frontier, and an "Indian" hotel, the Sacajawea Inn, a restored 1862 wood-framed motel stuffed with elegant antiques and a mural of the famous Birdwoman herself.

---

**DIRECTIONS:** From Deer Lodge, I-90 all day.

**ACCOMMODATIONS: Sacajawea Inn,** 5 N. Main, Three Forks, MT, (406) 285-6934. Amenities: B & B, lounge, full breakfast; historical landmark. Rooms: 50, doubles $25–$50. VISA, MC, AMEX.

**CAMPING: Three Forks KOA,** just before town, 1 mile south on US 287 from I-90 exit 274, (406) 285-3611. Amenities: laundry, groceries, heated pool, showers.

# DAY 11

Three Forks to Big Sky
Terrain: Flat to rolling
Highlight: Rafting, gondola ride
71 miles

Since we didn't know about highly scenic US 191, we took US 287, a peaceful cattle-ranching valley road that isn't as pretty. It also lacked 191's other amenities: white water rafting, a long gondola ride with beautiful views, and excellent lodgings at Big Sky, a famous ski resort founded by the late TV newsman Chet Huntley.

---

**DIRECTIONS:** East 22 miles on I-90. Turn south on US 191 for 44 miles. Turn west on SR 64.

**ACCOMMODATIONS: Huntley Lodge at Big Sky,** 7 miles west of US 191 on SR 64, Big Sky, MT, (406) 995-4211. Amenities: golf, tennis, sauna. Rooms: 298, doubles $72–$139. VISA, MC, AMEX, DINERS, DIS.

**CAMPING: Three sites within 10 miles of SR 64 on US 191, (406) 587-5271. No showers.**

## DAY 12

Big Sky to West Yellowstone
Terrain: Flat to rolling
47 miles

Given the easy ride from Big Sky, it may be possible to combine Day 12 and Day 13. Unfortunately, we got caught in a rain storm and were marooned in hotel-jammed West Yellowstone, the main jumping-off point for the Park.

Stopping early in the day for nearly the first time all trip, we had time to take inventory. Other than the "good" clothes we put on that night, jeans and polo shirts, half the clothing we brought along had gone unworn. In fact, other than a fresh pair of sneakers or sandals for the evenings, all anyone really needed was a windbreaker, a sweatshirt, a couple of tank tops and T-shirts plus two pairs of socks, underwear, and bike shorts—what I happened to be carrying. Because we routinely rinsed off the sweaty items and hung them out to dry on our bikes like rolling clotheslines, everything else was dead weight. The next morning my three partners mailed home all their excess plus their front panniers (however they're pronounced).

Incidentally, Martin's load had already been lightened considerably, which is why he'd been adamant about stopping at a hotel. His sleeping bag fell off his bike the day before because he didn't strap it down tightly. He didn't want to buy another one.

---

**DIRECTIONS:** US 191 all day.

**ACCOMMODATIONS: Stage Coach Inn**, 209 Madison Street (3 blocks northwest of park entrance), West Yellowstone, MT, (406) 646-7381. Amenities: sauna, two indoor hot tubs. Rooms: 95 doubles $53–$59. VISA, MC, AMEX, DIS.

**CAMPING: Yellowstone Park KOA**, 6½ miles west of entrance on US 20, (406) 646-7607. Full facilities.

★

---

## DAY 13

West Yellowstone, Montana, to West Thumb, Wyoming
Terrain: Moderate with hill climbs
Sights: Paint Pots, Old Faithful, Continental Divide (twice)
48 miles

Today we achieved our first big goal of the trip: the Old Faithful geyser. It turned out to be just one of many sights we'd see in our three days of riding in bigger-than-Rhode Island Yellowstone Park, established in 1872 as the nation's first national park. But watching scalding bursts of water jump hundreds of feet in the air wasn't all the excitement in store for us. We crossed the Continental Divide—twice. We saw elk, deer, antelope, moose, bears, and buffalo, who almost came close enough to label this place a petting zoo. We passed thousands of steaming, bubbling, and spitting pools of water that compose the world's largest thermal basins. And we wondered if Martin would be thrown in jail.

Having no sleeping bag, Martin left West Yellowstone with two of the hotel's blankets strapped to his rack. After paying the four-dollar bicycle entrance fee at the main gate and riding to the Visitors Center, we were informed by a janitor that the park rangers were looking for a red-haired bike rider carrying stolen blankets. That was Martin.

We urged him to dump the blankets and buy a bag, but instead he wrapped them in a trashbag and covered his hair in a ski cap. It wasn't the money. Martin simply liked the adventure of finishing the trip with blankets.

That was going to be an accomplishment in chilly Yellowstone. The elevation climbs from West Yellowstone's lofty 6,667 feet up to the park's central volcanic plateau of 7,000 to 8,500 feet. On July 1, we still saw patches of snow on the ground.

Heading south from the Visitors Center, we stopped at the Paint Pots, multicolored caldrons of bubbling hot clay, before seeing Old Faithful.

After the geyser popped off, so did Marc. He didn't want to be associated with Martin when he got caught. But by the time we arrived in West Thumb after crossing the switchbacking Continental Divide twice in the next eighteen miles, Martin was still free, having ducked into the woods several times, out of view of approaching ranger trucks.

It was getting very cold by dusk, but Grant Village was all booked and Canyon Village, thirty-seven miles away, was too far to ride. After a great day of riding and sightseeing, we slept under the stars. Martin put on every piece of clothing he owned and bundled between us under his blankets.

---

**DIRECTIONS:** US 20 all day.

**ACCOMMODATIONS: Grant Village,** 2 miles south on US 191 out of West Thumb Junction, (307) 344-7311. <u>Rooms</u>: 299, doubles $48—$59. VISA, MC, AMEX, DINERS, DIS.

**CAMPING: Grant Village Camp,** <u>Amenities</u>: showers, groceries, laundry. (307) 344-7381. **Bridge Bay,** 16 miles north, (307) 344-7381.

★

# DAY 14

West Thumb to Mammoth Hot Springs
Terrain: Mixture of flats and challenging climbing
Sights: Artist Point, Lookout Falls, Dunraven Pass
74 miles

In the middle of the night, I dreamt that I was shivering. I also dreamt that I saw Martin doing jumping jacks.

Well, when we got up, Martin told us that he'd almost died last night. He awoke at 4 A.M. with no blankets on him—and wasn't even cold. In fact, he felt so warm and comfortable that he almost went back to sleep before realizing it was hypothermia. He didn't want to die, so he got up and did jumping jacks until he got cold again.

Just as he finished the story, a ranger walked up. "How'd you all sleep? It was twenty degrees last night," he said. Then he saw the blankets and the red hair. "These are stolen blankets!" he shouted, grabbing Martin and hauling him and the loot away.

A half an hour later, Martin returned without the blankets, but with another sleeping bag. After he entertained the rangers with some jokes and stories, they dropped the charges and sold him an old, used bag for five dollars.

That was lucky, because there still was a lot more of Yellowstone to see. And the nights were all below freezing.

After a fast, exhilarating ride along the largest high-altitude body of water in the world, 7,731-foot-high Yellowstone Lake, we headed north in a big loop around the Park. Our first stop, just before Canyon Village, was Artist Point, for the brilliant reds, yellows, and oranges of the Grand Canyon of the Yellowstone and Lookout Falls.

After a thousand-foot climb over 8,859-foot Dunraven Pass, we put on some extra warm clothes. The switchback road dropped a blood-rushing 2,600 feet to the village of Tower, the home of Tower Falls. The beautiful scenery almost proved deadly, as I became entranced by Mount Washburn and almost flew over the side. The final stretch of climbing and descending past rivers, canyons, and waterfalls into Mammoth Hot Springs was a super ending to a great day.

---

**DIRECTIONS:** US 20 north 21 miles to Fishing Bridge. North on US 89 35 miles to Tower. West 19 miles to Mammoth Hot Springs.

**ACCOMMODATIONS: Mammoth Hot Springs Hotel & Cabins,** 1 mile south of Lake Junction, (307) 344-7311. <u>Rooms:</u> 94, 126 cabins, double $35—$125. VISA, MC, AMEX, DINERS, DIS.

**CAMPING: Mammoth Campground,** (307) 344-7381. No showers.

★

# DAY 15

Mammoth Hot Springs, Wyoming to West Yellowstone, Montana
Terrain: Big climb, then up and down
Sights: Norris Geyser Basin, Gibbons Falls
49 miles

Our last day in Yellowstone was no leisurely ride in the park. First, we climbed twelve hundred feet out of Mammoth. After following some walking trails through a bubbling and simmering collection of geysers, hotsprings, and mudpots in the Norris Geyser Basin, another climb led to a white-knuckle descent on a steep, potholed road past Gibbon Falls. This put us at the Visitors Center, where we saw a familiar face.

"Hey, I heard the rangers finally caught you," said the janitor to Martin, laughing. "That was the most exciting thing to happen around here in years."

For you, however, the excitement's over—just fourteen familiar miles from the Visitors Center to West Yellowstone and the airport.*

But for us, it was just the beginning. For the last two weeks, by the power of our own legs, we had argued, laughed, drunk, and shivered our way across one of the most rugged and beautiful sections of America. We learned some lessons to be used on all future bike tours: that climbing hills goes quicker when it's cool, that you learn a lot about a town in a bar, that having partners of vastly different abilities creates tension, that you'd better have a good sleeping bag and your own tools along at all times.

After hitchhiking past Old Faithful to Fishing Bridge, we did what had become almost instinctive: kept pedaling east.

---

**DIRECTIONS:** South on US 89 35 miles to Madison. West 14 miles on US 20 to West Yellowstone.

---

## SIGHTSEEING INFORMATION

BIG SKY, MONTANA
**Whitewater Rafting** trip on the Gallatin; half-day fare $30; trips at 9:30, 1:30 and 4:30. (406) 995-4613.

BUTTE, MONTANA
**Historic District and Mineral Mansion,** (406) 494-5595, (406) 496-4414.
**Virgin Mary Tour:** Ninety-foot statue atop Continental Divide. (406) 782-1221.

*Seasonal summertime flights in and out of West Yellowstone are available from Delta Airlines (1-800-221-1212) and other carriers.

DEER LODGE, MONTANA
**Towe Ford Museum of Classic Cars,** 1106 Main Street; Exits 184 or 187 off I-90: One of world's best Ford collections; 90+ vintage Fords, Lincolns. (406) 846-3111.
**Grant-Kohrs Ranch National Historic Site:** One-time hub of a million-acre range; free tours explain Montana's cattle ranching history; open daily 9:00—7:00 (406) 846-2070.

GRAND COULEE, WASHINGTON
**Grand Coulee Dam:** World's largest concrete structure, 550 feet high, 500 feet wide at base, 5,223 feet long; visitors center open 8:30 A.M.—10:00 P.M., summer. (206) 633-0320.

LEAVENWORTH, WASHINGTON
**Der Markt Platz,** Front and 8th streets: Thirty-minute film describes city's rise and fall as rail town and modern-day rebirth as resort.

MISSOULA, MONTANA
**Historical Museum at Fort Missoula;** open 10:00—5:00. (406) 728-3476.
**Western Montana Fair,** August. Call Visitors Bureau at (406) 543-6623.

SEATTLE, WASHINGTON
**Museum of Flight,** 9404 E. Marginal Way: Exhibits document the history of aviation technology from the thirteenth century through the late 1930s; 10:00—5:00 daily, 10:00—9:00 Thursday and Friday; admission $4. (206) 764-5720.
**The Space Needle,** in Seattle Center; open daily until 1:00 A.M. in summer, 12:00 A.M. other seasons; $3.50 elevator ride free with dinner. (206) 443-2100.
**Pike Place Market,** 2nd & Pike streets: Marketplace that opened as fish market in 1907.
**Pioneer Square Historic District:** A 30-block area of restored historic buildings, art galleries, and cafés, is just south and west of Pike Place on Yesler Street.

SPOKANE, WASHINGTON
**Riverfront Park:** Site of Expo '84, still retains some original attractions— IMAX theater, Japanese Garden, planetarium—big local gathering place. (509) 456-5511.
**Manito Park,** Grand Boulevard between 17th and 25th avenues: Conservatory and gardens—rose, lilac and others. (509) 456-4331.
**Cheney Cowles Memorial Museum,** W. 2316 First Street: Northwest settlement history. (509) 456-3931.

# CHAPTER 3

## GRAND TETONS TO MINNEAPOLIS

RIDING EAST FOR 1,394 MILES, THIS SEGMENT TOOK US FROM mountain to prairie, from West to Midwest, from western Wyoming to eastern Minnesota. There were many similarities to what we'd seen before: big elevation changes, from 8,500 feet in Yellowstone way down to 695 feet at the Mississippi River; relative newness, as settlement didn't begin throughout the region until the 1850s; and small-town America, anchored by a major-league city at the end.

On the way to Minneapolis, we rolled down out of the Rockies and up a smaller neighboring range, the Bighorns, for the biggest climb of this trip and the scariest of our lives—Granite Pass. Halfway through the trip, the scenery changed from grazing land of mountain and rock to the rich farmland of the Great Plains. When we crossed the Missouri River in Pierre, South Dakota, the difference was startling.

Although the terrain is rough (especially in the west) and the summertime heat stifling, the route is jammed with attractions. Everyone knows about Mount Rushmore, but there are many lesser-known and worthwhile tourist spots along the way—like the Mitchell Corn Palace in Mitchell, Pierre's flaming water fountain, Wall Drug Store, the Devils Tower, the Badlands, the Buffalo Bill Historical Center in Cody, Jewel Cave and others. In fact, there's something interesting to see nearly every day—including Day 1, featuring one of the continent's most striking natural wonders: the Grand Tetons.

## ROUTE SLIP
### Total of 1394 miles in 16 days

| Day | Stopping Point | Terrain* | Sights | Mileage |
|---|---|---|---|---|
| 1 | Jackson, Wyoming | Easy | Tram ride, Tetons | 33 |
| 2 | Grant Village, Wyoming | Easy | Tetons, Scenic ride | 77 |
| 3 | Cody, Wyoming | Difficult/Easy | 3,500-foot descent, Cassie's Bar | 101 |
| 4 | Shell, Wyoming | Easy | Buffalo Bill Historical Center | 70 |
| 5 | Sheridan, Wyoming | Difficult | Incredible 6,000-foot climb at Granite Pass | 83 |
| 6 | Gillette, Wyoming | Moderate | | 107 |
| 7 | Sundance, Wyoming | Moderate | The Devils Tower | 92 |
| 8 | Custer, South Dakota | Easy | Jewel Cave, Flintstones Museum | 94 |
| 9 | Rapid City, South Dakota | Moderate | Mount Rushmore, Needles Highway | 72 |
| 10 | Cedar Pass, South Dakota | Easy/Moderate | Wall Drug Store, the Badlands | 84 |
| 11 | Pierre, South Dakota | Easy | Missouri River, D&E Cafe, state capitol | 121 |
| 12 | Chamberlain, South Dakota | Easy | Riverboat ride | 83 |
| 13 | Mitchell, South Dakota | Easy | Mitchell Corn Palace, doll museum | 69 |
| 14 | Worthington, Minnesota | Easy | | 125 |
| 15 | Mankato, Minnesota | Easy | | 98 |
| 16 | Minneapolis, Minnesota | Easy | Minnehaha Park, Mississippi River | 85 |

*Easy = flat to rolling; moderate = hilly; difficult = at least one major hill climb

★

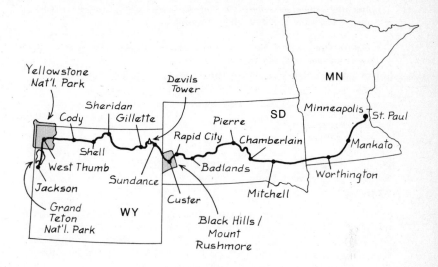

## DAY 1

The Grand Tetons: Airport to Jackson or Teton Village
Terrain: Flat to rolling
20 miles to Teton Village or 33 miles with a return to Jackson

Since we couldn't find an efficient loop south on our continuous journey across the continent, my group didn't see the awesome peaks of the Tetons. But stepping off the plane in Jackson Hole, you'll be a little luckier—facing a murderer's row of sixteen majestic mountain peaks, all ten- to thirteen-thousand feet high. The best panorama of the Teton Range and Jackson Hole Valley is said to be from 10,450-foot Rendezvous Mountain, reached by an easy ride south on John D. Rockefeller, Jr., National Parkway (Rockefeller used to *own* the Tetons) through the ski resort/Old West town of Jackson to Teton Village and the Jackson Hole Aerial Tram.

---

**DIRECTIONS:** From airport: 8 miles south on US 89 to Jackson. Turn 4 miles west on SR 22. North 8 miles on SR 390 to Teton Village. Into park: 8 miles north on dirt road.

**ACCOMMODATIONS: Alpenhof Resort Lodge,** Teton Village, WY, (800) 732-3244 or (307) 733-3242. Rooms: 40, doubles $80–$150. VISA, MC, AMEX, DINERS, DIS.
**Teton Motel,** 165 W. Gill, Jackson Hole, WY, (307) 733-3883. Rooms: 14, $45–$58. VISA, MC, AMEX. Jackson Hole Visitors Information: (800) 782-0011, ext. 215.

**Colter Bay Village,** in Grand Teton Park, (307) 543-2855. Rustic resort cottages. <u>Rooms</u>: 209; $47–$89; VISA, MC, AMEX.

**CAMPING: Village KOA,** between Teton Village and Jackson, 6 miles south of Tram on SR 390, (307) 733-7078.
**Tent Village,** in Colter Bay, Grand Teton Park, (307) 543-2855. Only site with showers.

## DAY 2

Jackson to Grant Village, Yellowstone Park
Terrain: Easy gradual rise
77 miles

Going north will take you past a great view of the Tetons as well as a museum and visitors center before linking with the main highway to Yellowstone Park's Grant Village. Fishing Bridge is twenty-one miles further (the only miles of overlap from the previous trip), but has no hotels, no campgrounds with showers, and hungry bears.

**DIRECTIONS:** From Jackson, 13 miles north on US 89. Left across Snake River. North 20 miles on Teton Road. North on US 89/191 to Grant Village.

**ACCOMMODATIONS: Grant Village,** 2 miles south on US 191 from West Thumb Junction, (307) 344-7311. <u>Rooms</u>: 299, double $48–$59. VISA, MC, AMEX, DINERS, DIS.

**CAMPING: Grant Village Camp,** (307) 344-7381. <u>Amenities</u>: showers, groceries, laundry.

## DAY 3

Grant Village to Cody
Terrain: Climb, then descent and tailwinds
Highlights: 3,500-foot downhill, Cassie's Bar
101 miles

One hundred miles might seem like a lot so early in the trip, but today's ride is mostly downhill and tailwinds—100 percent exhilaration. It features what my group refers to as "The World's Greatest Downhill."

Starting with an easy cruise along the flat shoreline of Yellowstone Lake, we turned right at Fishing Bridge and stayed on US 14 for eighty miles all the way to Cody. But it wasn't all easy. We still had one final climb, an eight hundred footer over 8,530-foot Sylvan Pass, which made for a good warm-up in the nippy mountain air. At the top, we threw on a couple of layers of clothes, then held on tight—because in the next fifteen miles, we barreled downhill for three and one-half *thousand* feet!

And I'm not talkin' delicate, brake-squealing switchback roads here. The road makes grand sweeps around whole mountainsides, soaring over beautiful vistas that go on for miles. The curves are gradual and the decline isn't steep, so we could really let loose. We zoomed inches away from rock fences—and certain death—but didn't seem to care. We thought about applying the brakes, but none of us did—because the feeling was too incredible to stop. I wanted to pause for a minute, just to drink it all in, just to take a picture, but I couldn't, because I was already drunk on nature, on speed, on the feeling that I might never again feel this high.

You'll feel like a great bird soaring down those mountains. So when you climb the final feet of Sylvan Pass, get ready to spread your wings. Every time I think of this ride down the mountain, I feel that I became kind of immortal back there. I'd felt the timelessness of nature, and I knew I'd take a little bit of it with me forever.

And I felt like a bicycle was the greatest instrument ever created on this earth.

The rest of the day only added to the feeling, as we had a twenty-five mile-per-hour tailwind and striking multicolored rock formations all the way. Teddy Roosevelt was so impressed he called this stretch the "most scenic fifty-two miles in America."

Our first stop in Cody, named after famous Pony Express rider "Buffalo Bill" Cody, was Cassie's Bar, two miles before the main part of town. Cassie's is the Gilly's Bar of Wyoming—as big as a football field and jammed stool to stool with locals, tourists, and rodeo riders. It was swelled with people who'd come to see next day's Fourth of July parade, the state's biggest. About 1:00 A.M., we stumbled out arm-in-arm with some locals who bid us farewell with what they called Cassie's Code: "See you later—when your legs are straighter."

Before we rode off, we asked if they knew of any cheap places to stay. "How will free do ya?" one said. And that's how we ended up sleeping in the teepees on the lawn of the Buffalo Bill Center.

---

**DIRECTIONS:** 21 miles northwest to Fishing Bridge. East 80 miles on US 14.

**ACCOMMODATIONS: Best Western Sunset Motor Inn,** ¾ mile west on US 14 at 1601 8th Street, Cody, WY, (307) 587-4265. <u>Rooms</u>: 82, double $64. VISA, MC, AMEX, DINERS, DIS.

**CAMPING: Ponderosa Campground,** next to Best Western, 3 blocks west of Buffalo Bill Center, (307) 587-9203.

# DAY 4

Cody to Shell
Terrain: Flat, some rollers
Sights: Buffalo Bill Historical Center
70 miles

We were awakened at 6:00 A.M. by the sounds of people milling around our teepee. It turned out to be the renowned Fourth of July Stinkwater Parade, forming up just a few feet away on Sheridan Avenue.

As you know from reading the Introduction, we met all the dignitaries and parade organizers by 8:00. And in what has proved to be *the* highlight of all my tours, we actually rode in the parade!

Pedaling behind the Moose Club, we did our best to entertain. I gallantly carried a teen-aged girl on my handlebars. Bob pedaled his bike backwards. Marc kissed Miss Hospitality. Being mobbed afterward by dozens of people and interviewed by a local reporter made the rest of the day feel like pedaling on air.

But we wouldn't have needed to ride in a parade to enjoy Cody. We did a little Old West sightseeing at our "hotel," the Buffalo Bill Historical Center, then stopped at Old Trail Town to visit the grave of "Jeremiah" Johnson and a hideout used by Butch Cassidy, the Sundance Kid, and other members of the Wild Bunch.

Four hours after leaving Cody, we arrived in Greybull, a small mining/oil town where we stocked up on food for our assault on the Bighorn Mountains. That would come soon at the tiny town of Shell, where we began a mind-boggling climb of twenty-two miles and six thousand feet—the longest, highest continuous climb of this tour and of the entire cross-continental journey. It's a climb we almost didn't live to tell about.

---

**DIRECTIONS:** From Cody, 54 miles east on US 14 to Greybull, 16 miles east to Shell.

**ACCOMMODATIONS: K-Bar Motel,** Greybull, WY, (307) 765-4426. <u>Rooms</u>: 18, double $30, VISA, MC, AMEX, DINERS, DIS.
**Kedesh Ranch,** 1940 Shell Road, log cabins at base of Shell Canyon, Shell, WY, (307) 765-2791. Mountain view. <u>Rooms</u>: 16 units, $42–$52. VISA, MC, AMEX, DINERS.

**CAMPING: KOA,** Greybull, WY, (307) 765-2555.

---

# DAY 5

Shell to Sheridan
Terrain: 6,000-foot climb
Sights: The Bighorn Mountains
83 miles

Our strategy for 8,950-foot-high Granite Pass was to begin at dusk, to climb comfortably in the cold night air and sleep at the top. Everything went perfectly at first. The sky was a cloudless blanket of black velvet, embroidered with tiny, glistening pearls. It was like a dream up in these remote mountains, looking out twenty-five, fifty, maybe a hundred miles and seeing no cars and no city lights—only stars. Off in the distance, tiny silent lightning bolts flashed every ten seconds. It was a storm, but so far away that I got out my camera, set the shutter open, and shot pictures. What a concept—to photograph a storm like it was a tourist sight, to gaze at it as if it were a movie.

In minutes, we were actors in that movie. Because with shocking speed, the clouds turned and raced closer and closer, until we were in the middle of the most ferocious thunderstorm I've seen in my life.

Howling winds blew us sideways. Rain drenched us. Lightning splattered on the ground just inches away. Paralyzed with fear, afraid of becoming rolling lightning rods, we threw our bikes down, ran away, and huddled in our flimsy rain tarps on the side of the road for two hours, watching the electric-light show around us with amazement and horror. After the lightning passed, under black skies of drenching rain, we trudged blindly up the hill—cold, soaked to the bone, and scared, not knowing when the night would end.

Finally we came to a light. It was the Shell Falls Interpretive Site, a simple nature display with an attached restroom. But to us it was a miracle, an oasis of safety that appeared when all seemed hopeless. You may think of it simply as a toilet nine miles up the mountain. But for the rest of my life, that toilet shall remain a luxury hotel.

---

**DIRECTIONS:** From Greybull, 74 miles west on US 14, 9 miles southeast on I-90 to Sheridan.

**ACCOMMODATIONS: Holiday Inn,** 1809 Sugarland Drive, Sheridan, WY, (307) 672-8931. Amenities: pool, sauna, racquetball. Rooms: 212, double $53–$69. VISA, MC, AMEX, DIS.

**CAMPING: Big Horn Mountain KOA,** 63 Decker Street (I-90 exit 20, ⅛ mile south to Main Street, right to SR 338, ½ mile north to Decker), (307) 674-8766.

★

By the next day, resting in the flea-speck town of Ranchester, we'd ridden sixty-six mountainous miles from Shell and dropped 4,200 feet from Granite Pass. The descent was no thrill, though, as it was pouring rain. It didn't let up until Sheridan, this tour's biggest city so far with 16,000 people.

In honor of Calamity Jane, Red Cloud, and Crazy Horse, all of whom called the Sheridan area home, we located an Indian bar and spent the evening recovering from our frightening night on the mountain.

## DAY 6

Sheridan to Gillette
Terrain: Flat, rolling
107 miles

This day wasn't real pretty or difficult; just a big boring hunk of sun-baked real estate. We loaded up with food and drink in Buffalo, because there wasn't much of anything on the long ride to Gillette. To handle it, I aimed at the white line on the shoulder of I-90, put it on auto-pedal and sang my theme: *"You move sixteen tons, and what do you get . . . Another day older and deeper in debt."*

Ironically, that song fit Gillette, a hard-hit oil town of 20,600. A lot of them were unemployed—at least, in the bar we went to. Oil prices had tumbled; wells were capped off. Riggers once making $40,000 a year were now getting $166 a week—an unemployment check. Again, Martin told them he'd put them to work in San Diego doing floors. My advice to them? Take a bike ride.

---

**DIRECTIONS:** I-90 all day.

**ACCOMMODATIONS: Best Western Tower West Lodge,** 109 North Highway 14-16 (north of exit 124 off I-90), Gillette, WY, (307) 686-2210. Amenities: pool, sauna. Rooms: 190, double $50–$60. VISA, MC, AMEX, DINERS, DIS.

**CAMPING: Greentree Campground,** 1001 2nd Street, Gillette, WY, (307) 682-3665.

---

## DAY 7

Gillette to Sundance
Terrain: Hilly
Sights: The Devils Tower
92 miles

Ah, the value of looking at a map! Set to power out of Wyoming directly to South Dakota's Mount Rushmore, the name "Devils Tower" caught my eye.

"Why, that's that funny-shaped mountain in *Close Encounters of the Third Kind*," a guy at a gas station told us. Despite the extra riding required, there was no way we could bypass this flat-topped mountain that looks like a giant tree stump. If you arrive early enough (we didn't), you can climb up to the top of the freakish volcanic monolith, 867 feet high.

Riding over hilly terrain on a day of blazing heat, we arrived for our own close encounter with the Devils Tower totally drained. From our campsite, I gazed at its eerie moonlit silhouette, reminiscent of a nuclear reactor cooling tower.

The closest hotels are located in Sundance, famous for providing Harry Longbaugh, who spent eighteen months in the Crook County jail for horse stealing, with his famous nickname: "The Sundance Kid."

---

**DIRECTIONS:** I-90 28 miles east to Moorcroft. North 22 miles on SR 14. North 6 miles on SR 24 at Devils Tower Junction, then west 1 mile into Devils Tower. After 7-mile backtrack, turn east on SR 14 for 21 miles to Sundance.

**ACCOMMODATIONS: Bear Mountain Motel,** 218 Cleveland (near junction of SR 14 and I-90 bus loop), Sundance, WY, (307) 283-1611. Rooms: 32, double $38–$40. VISA, MC.

**CAMPING: Reuter Campground,** West Sundance (take Road 838 north 2¼ miles), (307) 283-1361. No showers.

**KOA Devils Tower,** at entrance, (307) 467-5395. Amenities: showers, laundry.

---

# DAY 8

Sundance, Wyoming, to Custer, South Dakota
Terrain: Flat, rolling
Sights: Jewel Cave, Flintstones Bedrock City
94 miles

After fifty-eight miles of unmemorable, drab country, we crossed into South Dakota and came to the Black Hills, which abruptly rise 3,500 feet from the surrounding prairie flatlands. A retired miner we met later in Custer told us that the Black Hills were named so by the Indians for their dark appearance (caused by a thick covering of Ponderosa pines). Later legend insists that the eroded mountains were formed by the burial of Paul Bunyan's blue ox, Babe.

The miner had come to the Black Hills for the same reason that the first white settlers arrived in 1874: gold. He had worked at one of the largest working gold mines in the Western Hemisphere, Homestake Mine, about seventy miles north in the town of Lead.

We mined some gold that day, too—bike-touring gold. The first nugget was the Jewel Cave National Monument, one of the longest caves in the world—so long that part of it is still unexplored. Two more came on the way into Custer: the National Museum of Woodcarving, a giant col-

lection of animated woodcarvings; and Flintstones Bedrock City, a repro-
duction of the set and characters of the popular TV cartoon show.

---

**DIRECTIONS:** From Sundance, 27 miles southeast on SR 585/285 to Four
Corners. South 22 miles on US 85 to Newcastle. 9 miles southeast on US 16
to border, 29 more to Custer.

**ACCOMMODATIONS: Dakota Cowboy Inn,** 208 W. Mount Rushmore Road
(½ mile west of junction of US 16 and 385), Custer, SD, (605) 673-4659.
Rooms: 23, double $52–$55. VISA, MC, AMEX, DINERS, DIS.

**CAMPING: Black Hills KOA,** 3 miles west of town, (605) 673-4304.
**Big Pine Campground,** 2 miles east, (605) 673-4054.

---

# DAY 9

Custer to Rapid City
Terrain: Hilly
Sights: Mount Rushmore, Crazy Horse, Needles Highway
72 miles

Today was another gold rush—a riding and sightseeing dream. Every
road was a scenic one. Every sight was bigger than life, with the final
foursome—the immense Mount Rushmore faces of four American pres-
idents—capping off an amazing forty-nine miles of riding.

Our first stop was the colossal, incompleted memorial to Crazy
Horse, the Indian chief who led the defeat of General Custer at Little Big
Horn. When done, the sculpture will be 563 feet high and 641 feet long,
the largest in the world. Blasting was visible from the museum, which
displayed a scale model of the Indian.

Going directly to Mount Rushmore from there would have been
quicker, but would have meant missing Needles Highway, which has
scenery almost as striking as Rushmore itself: fourteen miles of hairpin
turns that weave in and out of striking granite spires, or "needles."
Threading the Needles, we took a shortcut over gravel road (see directions) past the Black Hills Playhouse, then went face to face with the fab
four.

Each sixty-foot-high head on Mount Rushmore represents a mile-
stone in American history: Washington, the nation's founding; Jefferson,
the Declaration of Independence and the great expansion west; Lincoln,
the preservation of the Union; and Teddy Roosevelt, final expansion into
the Pacific and conservation of nature. We stood there for a good hour to
soak it all in—a truly heady experience.

A fast, slightly downhill ride led to Rapid City, the biggest city of this
tour so far with 49,000 people, half of them Indian and many of those

where we hoped to find them: Indian bar central. After getting ugly stares from three places, we finally visited a seedy joint called D's Place. ("You went in *there?*" the deskman at our hotel, the Castle Inn, asked incredulously. "You're nuts.") But it wasn't that bad until I brought out my camera. Some of the Indians were appalled, saying the film would "steal a piece of their soul" and suggesting that it was a good idea that we leave. We did, and, though I had a nagging feeling that they were just joking, I never brought out my camera at an Indian bar again.

---

**DIRECTIONS:** From Custer, north 5 miles on US 385/16 to Crazy Horse. Continue 5½ miles. South onto Needles Highway (SR 87) for 14 miles. Right at US 16 Alt. for 25 miles. Left on SR 244 1 mile to Rushmore. (Note: To shorten US 16A, turn left on gravel road after 12 miles of Needles Highway. Ride 5 miles to US 16A, turn left.) Continue 4 miles on US 16A, northwest 16 miles to Rapid City.

**ACCOMMODATIONS: Castle Inn,** 15 E. North Street, 5 blocks west of K-Mart, Rapid City, SD, (605) 348-4120. Amenities: pool, kitchenettes. Rooms: 20, double $39–$63. VISA, MC, AMEX, DIS.

**CAMPING: Berry Patch Campground,** 1860 N. East Street, near I-90 exit 60, (605) 341-5588.

# DAY 10

Rapid City to Cedar Pass
Terrain: Flat, then hilly
Sights: Wall Drug Store and the Badlands
84 miles

We couldn't miss the 800-person town of Wall if we tried. The roadside was covered with hundreds of signs—some corny, some hokey, and all alerting us to the ever-closer bottomless pit of ice water at the "World's Largest Drug Store."

It's one of those only-in-America sagas: twenty years ago, Wall Drug was a tiny storefront in a dusty, ignored, one-store I-90 town. One day, store owner Ted Hustead put a sign out on the interstate offering "free icewater" to any passersby who wanted to take a break from the sweltering highway. When a few came in for ice water, Ted put up more signs in each direction. A lot more came in. Soon, wacky signage stretched for hundreds of miles, not only "Free Ice Water," but "Free Map of the Badlands at Wall," "Have You Dug Wall Drug?" even "Would You Believe Wall Drug?"

Believe it. Today, Wall Drug is a gargantuan hodgepodge that practically covers the entire town, and an attraction in its own right. Tourist trap or not, we needed that ice water. Riding through stifling heat, we arrived in Wall in a state of delirium—a state matched by the town, which was celebrating its seventy-fifth anniversary. We decided to stay overnight for the rodeo and parade.

Wall is also the jumping-off point for Badlands National Park, a spectacular mini-Grand Canyon of irregular ravines, fantastic ridges, iridescent sedimentary layers, and craggy cliffs. The next morning, we roller coastered through the scenery in searing heat until we hit the Badlands Visitors Center at Cedar Pass, where we collapsed asleep near the entrance door—to the amusement of all of the "motorized" tourists.

---

**DIRECTIONS:** I-90 east 54 miles. North 1 mile on SR 240 to Wall. Then south on SR 240 28 miles to Badlands Visitors Center/Cedar Pass.

**ACCOMMODATIONS: Cedar Pass Lodge,** Cedar Pass, SD, (605) 433-5460. Rooms: 24 cabins, double $32. VISA, MC, AMEX, DINERS, DIS. **Badlands Inn,** 1 mile south on SR 377, Cedar Pass, SD, (605) 433-5401. Rooms: 24, $38. VISA, MC.

**CAMPING: Badlands Interior Campground,** 2 miles south on SR 377 at SR 44, (605) 433-5335. **KOA,** 4 miles east on SR 44, (605) 433-5337.

---

## DAY 11

Cedar Pass to Murdo or Pierre
Terrain: Initial climb, then flat to rolling
Sights: State capitol, D & E Cafe, Flaming Fountain
69 or 121 miles

The long ride today was uneventful—until we got to Pierre, where we were stuffed with food for under three bucks, saw a beautiful state capitol building and actually watched water burn.

Of course, 121 miles is a long way, which is why microscopic Murdo, a town of 700, comes in handy as a way station. We took an alternate route that had the same mileage but went over virtually abandoned, hotel-less backroads nearly all the way.

A major landmark on our route was the 100-degree meridian line. A sign on US 14 describes how this line became the historic dividing line between "The Civilized East" and "The Great Western Desert." Insurance companies "would not lend a shiny dime west of that line," which led South Dakota into the farm loan business.

The irony of the 100-degree meridian is that it speaks the truth. The line roughly bisects the state—and a good part of the nation—into two distinct personalities: Mountain/ranchland on the left and the Midwest prairie on the right. South Dakota becomes more crowded with people and corn, oats, sunflowers, flaxseed, rye, and barley east of the Missouri River. The word "crowded" may be misleading; there are only 700,000 South Dakotans. A higher percentage of them earn livelihoods through agriculture than in any other state.

South Dakota also becomes flatter on the east side of the Missouri. From Pierre to the Minnesota border, the elevation drop is only eighty-four feet, just enough to keep the river flowing. We were on the Great Plains now—riding flat-out all the way to Minneapolis.

Although a population of just 12,400 makes Pierre (pronounced *peer* by the locals) America's tiniest capital city, it's the site of some very big memories for us. When Martin asked people where the "hot spot" in town was, nearly everyone replied, "The D & E Cafe." Soon stuffed with a half-chicken, soup, salad, fries, toast, and a scoop of vanilla ice cream each, all for only $2.35 ($2.95 in 1990), we found out why. I even splurged on two extra scoops of ice cream at ten cents each and an iced tea for twenty cents. As you can imagine, the place was jammed.

We also got good value out of the state capitol building, where you can walk in unannounced and talk to the governor if he's in (Monday to Friday, eight to five). Although he wasn't there when we stopped by the next morning, we hung around and posed for pictures at his desk, anyway. After that, we were amazed by the flaming water fountain at the edge of geese-filled Capitol Lakes. Yes, that's right—water is actually on fire, and if those geese get too close, their goose is cooked. Apparently, natural gas somehow got mixed in with the fountain pipes, and somebody got the bright idea to light it. Who said life was dull on the Prairie!

---

**DIRECTIONS:** 9 miles north on SR 240. East on I-90 for 60 miles to Murdo. Then 20 miles east and north on US 83 for 32 to Fort Pierre. Cross US 14 bridge to Pierre. Alternate from Cedar Pass: 9 miles north on SR 240, then 12 miles east on I-90. North 15 miles on SR 73 to Philip, then east on US 14 for 98 miles to Pierre.

**ACCOMMODATIONS: Anchor Inn,** ¼ mile west of US 83 on I-90 bus loop, Murdo, SD, (605) 669-2322. <u>Rooms</u>: 29, double $39. VISA, MC, AMEX, DIS. **State Motel,** 640 Euclid Avenue, ½ mile north on US 14, Pierre, SD, (605) 224-5896. <u>Amenities</u>: pool, sauna. <u>Rooms</u>: 48, $36–$40. VISA, MC, AMEX, DINERS, DIS.

**CAMPING: Tee Pee Campground,** Murdo, SD, (605) 669-2629. **Griffin Park,** 222 E. Dakota Avenue, at bridge, Pierre, SD, (605) 224-5921. <u>Amenities</u>: Missouri beach, nearby municipal pool with showers.

★

---

## DAY 12

Pierre to Chamberlain
Terrain: Flat, rolling
Sights: Missouri riverboat
83 miles

Since our next sightseeing goal, the famous Mitchell Corn Palace, was too far to ride (154 miles), we settled on Chamberlain, a tiny Missouri River town. Once a way station for Black Hills gold miners, it is now a ferrying point between the farm territory of the east and the ranch territory of the west. We experienced the Missouri for ourselves by taking an hour and a half sightseeing cruise on the *Missouri Trader* riverboat, which follows the Lewis and Clark Trail into the local Indian reservations.

We spent the evening in a malt shop with a bunch of high school kids, who told us all the local gossip. They didn't really care about our trip, which seemed incomprehensible to them, anyway. Like everybody we seemed to meet, they only wanted to hear about California.

"Do you surf?" they all asked. None of us did, but we didn't want to ruin the illusion. "Of course," we nodded. "Doesn't everybody?"

---

**DIRECTIONS:** SR 34 for 48 miles thru Crow Creek Indian Reservation. South at Mac's Corner, 12 miles to Fort Thompson. East for 6 miles, then south on SR 50 for 20 miles.

**ACCOMMODATIONS: Oasis Inn,** on US 16 and I-90 bus loop, ½ mile east of I-90 exit 260, Chamberlain, SD, (605) 734-6061. <u>Rooms</u>: 86, double $40–$50: VISA, MC, AMEX, DINERS, DIS.

**CAMPING: Familyland Campground,** (605) 734-6959. <u>Amenities</u>: laundry, pool.

---

## DAY 13

Chamberlain to Mitchell
Terrain: Flat
Sights: The Corn Palace, Doll Museum
69 miles

Corn was everywhere in eastern South Dakota—even on buildings! Yes, the Moorish-style Mitchell Corn Palace is redecorated every year with thousands of bushels of various colors of corn and grasses. And by the time we arrived at this cornographic wonder, we'd discovered a major kernel of truth.

It came from the lips of Ernest L. Mudd, a talkative seventy-eight-year-old great-grandfather whom we met at a supermarket. Inviting us to stay in his home, he told us that his parents had moved out here from Massachusetts in the 1890s *because* of the Corn Palace, built in 1892 specifically to attract settlers to South Dakota. It seems people thought the state was a desert, and the Palace proved crops could be grown.

Ernest also gave us an insight into bike touring. That night, over a few beers, we asked him why he trusted us after only a five-minute conversation.

"Well, it's not often I see something unique around here," he said. "And who said I trust you? If you stole something from me, you're still on bikes. How far could you get before I caught you?"

---

**DIRECTIONS:** I-90 all day.

**ACCOMMODATIONS: Anthony Motel,** 1518 W. Haven (2 miles east and north of Corn Palace), Mitchell, SD, (605) 996-7518. <u>Amenities</u>: pool, mini-golf. <u>Rooms</u>: 34, double $40. VISA, MC, AMEX, DINERS, DIS.

**CAMPING: Dakota Campground,** ¼ mile south of I-90 exit 330, (605) 996-9432.

---

## DAY 14

Mitchell, South Dakota to Worthington, Minnesota
Terrain: Flat, some rollers
125 miles

Today was typical Minnesota—a flat highway through cornfields. And that's a good thing, too, because our effort focused on the 125-mile day—this tour's longest.

My strategy on long rides is to break it up into small goals. Then I reward myself with a root beer when I hit each.

Root beer number one came at Sioux Falls, South Dakota's largest city with a population of 87,800. The next root beer came twelve miles

---

**DIRECTIONS:** I-90 all day.

**ACCOMMODATIONS: Holiday Inn,** junction of I-90 and US 59, Worthington, MN, (507) 372-2991. <u>Amenities</u>: sauna, whirlpool. <u>Rooms</u>: 118, double $50–$60. VISA, MC, AMEX, DINERS, DIS.

**CAMPING: Adrian Campground,** just off I-90 and SR 91, Adrian, MN, (507) 483-2820.

later at the boundary of Minnesota, the third and last of the states on this tour. Then, three more root beers remained: at the towns of Luverne, Adrian (where campers should stop, since there are no campgrounds in Worthington), and finally in Worthington. It was a lot of miles, but it got us to Minneapolis a half-day early—and also made us experts on root beer. We all liked a regional brand named Barq's, mainly because it gave us the opportunity to mistakenly ask waitresses for a nice, cold—you guessed it—Barf's.

Such are the sublime pleasures of being four men on a bike trip.

# DAY 15

Worthington to Mankato
Terrain: Flat, a couple of rollers
98 miles

Leaving I-90 for a lightly trafficked, generally flat ride northeast to Mankato, we saw vintage Minnesota. That means lakes, which increased in number as we headed toward Minneapolis. Though the license plates call Minnesota "the Land of 10,000 Lakes," there are actually more than 15,000, each one formed, legend has it, when melting snows filled in the hoofprints of the Bunyanesque blue ox, Babe.

All that water not only keeps the corn green, but also gives Minnesota its incredible summer humidity and serves as a breeding ground for mosquitos. When they weren't stinging, millions of black micro-gnats were—motivating us to move fast.

When I did stop, it seemed like Minnesota had more friendly people, and more elderly ones, than I'd ever seen, all asking the same question in their quasi-Scandinavian accents: "Where 'er ya from and where 'er ya goin'?" The accent is a remnant of a massive influx of Swedish, Norwegian, and German immigration following the Civil War. Before then, though explored by the French from 1660, Minnesota largely remained Chippewa and Sioux Indian country.

We ended up running into three Chippewas at the two large waterfalls and deep gorge of Minneopa State Park, six miles south of Mankato. They informed us that Mankato is Indian for "Blue Earth," the color of the

---

**DIRECTIONS:** SR 60 all the way.

**ACCOMMODATIONS: Holiday Inn,** 101 E. Main Street, Mankato, MN, (507) 345-1234. Amenities: pool, sauna, putting green. Rooms: 151, double $54—$64. VISA, MC, AMEX, DINERS.

**CAMPING: Minneopa State Park,** 6 miles south of city, (507) 625-4388.

clay that lines the banks of the local Blue Earth River. After they and Martin drove into town for a case of beer, we camped and talked all night, hearing their sadness over both the destruction of their culture and their alienation from modern American society.

## DAY 16

Mankato to Minneapolis
Terrain: Flat, rolling
85 miles

We barreled toward Minneapolis going faster and faster, pulled by the excitement of the biggest, funkiest city since Seattle. Awaiting us were a couple of luxurious days of rest at Martin's dad's home and a nonstop party planned for us by his boyhood friends.

We arrived during Minneapolis's "Aquatennial," a midsummer, waterfront party that celebrates the thousand lakes within city limits with trick waterskiing, log-rolling contests, and soapbox boat races. it was a great time to ride around this beautiful place of big lakefront homes and vast stretches of park. (The next chapter has more about Minneapolis/St. Paul, including an all-greenbelt loop beginning at Minnehaha Park.)

After two days of nonstop sightseeing and bar-hopping, we clinked beer mugs one last time in a Minneapolis Indian bar on July 18, 1982, with a combination of happiness and sadness. Happiness, because we were hard, tough veterans of the road now, the toughest miles behind us, and the mother lodes—the Chicagos, the Torontos, the Montreals— sighted and ready to be mined.

And sadness, because no matter how much fun we were going to have on the rest of the Big Adventure, it surely wouldn't be as much fun without Martin. Growing paranoid over leaving his floor business in the hands of his teenaged brother, he was flying home to San Diego the next day.

---

**DIRECTIONS:** US 169 north 55 miles to Shakopee. Continue east 21 miles, as US 169 changes to SR 101 and SR 13 along the Minnesota River (some campsites along here) to SR 55. Cross river, pass through Veterans area near airport, thru Minnehaha Park for 8 miles to downtown, or take Mississippi River Parkway.

**ACCOMMODATIONS: Best Western Normandy Inn,** 405 S. 8th Street, Minneapolis, MN, (612) 370-1400. <u>Rooms</u>: 228, double $58–$70. VISA, MC, AMEX, DINERS.

**CAMPING: Town and Country Campground,** 12630 Boone Street, (look for signs just before change from SR 101 to SR 13) Savage, MN, (612) 445-1756.

★

Marc was actually kind of relieved; he and Martin had battled the whole trip. "Now we can do some miles," he said under his breath. But I had come to rely on Martin's instincts—following him into Indian bars, meeting the locals, *living* the adventure rather than just *observing* it.

So far as I was concerned, there was only one thing to do in his absence: keep on living it.

## SIGHTSEEING INFORMATION

BLACK HILLS, SOUTH DAKOTA
**Jewel Cave National Monument:** One- to three-hours tours; three-hour spelunking tour, mid-June to mid-August, thru unimproved passageways—only for hardy. (605) 673-2288.
**National Museum of Woodcarving,** 2 miles west of Custer: One of world's largest collections of animated woodcarvings. (605) 673-4404.
**Flintstones Bedrock City,** 1 mile west of Custer. (605) 673-4079.

CHAMBERLAIN, SOUTH DAKOTA
**Missouri Trader Riverboat:** Follows Lewis and Clark Trail into Indian reservation; last cruise at 7:30 P.M.; $7. (605) 734-6225.

CODY, WYOMING
**Old Trail Town:** Reconstruction of Old Cody frontier town. (307) 587-5302
**Buffalo Bill Historical Center,** 720 Sheridan Avenue: Four museums devoted to the American West. (307) 587-4771.

JACKSON, WYOMING
**Jackson Hole Aerial Tram,** 12 miles north on SR 390: 2½-mile tram to top of Rendezvous Mountain; sweeping vista; $9. (307) 733-2414.

MINNEAPOLIS, MINNESOTA
**Walker Art Center,** Hennepin and Vineland Place: Late twentieth-century American, European paintings, sculpture. (612) 375-7600.
**Hennepin County Historical Society Museum,** 2303 3rd Avenue S: History of Minneapolis, including "From Moccasins to Microchips." (612) 870-1329.
**Aquatennial Festival:** Minneapolis's ten-day celebration with parades, music, log rolling contests, waterskiing races; late July.

MITCHELL, SOUTH DAKOTA
**Corn Palace,** Sixth and Main streets: Inside murals designed by famous prairie artists; free guided tours until 10:00 P.M. (605) 996-7311.
**Enchanted World Doll Museum:** Four thousand dolls from all over the world; open until 8:00 P.M.; $2.50. (605) 996-9896.

PIERRE, SOUTH DAKOTA
**State Capitol Building,** Capitol and Nicollette avenues: Free tours Monday

through Friday, 9:00 to 3:00; flaming fountain on Capitol Lake. (605) 773-3688.

**D & E Cafe,** 115 Dakota Street. (605) 224-7200.

ST. PAUL, MINNESOTA

**State Capitol Building,** Aurora Avenue between Cedar and Park: Forty-five-minute tours. (612) 296-2881.

**Science Museum of Minnesota,** 30 E. 10th Street: Science, space programs. (612) 221-9454.

**St. Paul Hall of Justice,** between St. Peter Street, Kellogg Boulevard, Wabasha and 4th streets: Monstrous thirty-six-foot-high onyx statue, "Left-handed Indian God of Peace." (612) 298-4131.

# CHAPTER 4

## MINNEAPOLIS
## TO
## DETROIT

THE HEARTLAND HOP? THE RUST BELT ROLL? AS WE DISCOVERED during our easy, mostly flat, 769-mile, two-week tour through five states from Minnesota around Lake Michigan to Michigan, the Midwest defies simple characterization.

It could be the Tour of the Big Cities, including Minneapolis–St. Paul (625,000 total), Milwaukee (650,000), Chicago (2.9 million), and Detroit (1 million). There's a lot of personality in these cities, and each would normally require at least a full day of exploration to do it justice.

It could be the Tour of the Small Cities, since there are more of them on this tour than any other stretch of the transcontinental route, though it is by far the shortest. It's also loaded with small farms, as opposed to the huge spreads of South Dakota and western Minnesota.

It could be the Tour of the Breweries, as we sampled Leinenkugel beer in Chippewa Falls, Miller in Milwaukee, and Stroh's in Detroit.

It could be the Tour of the Lakes. Minnesota has 15,000. Wisconsin has 9,000, including the striking Devils Lake near Baraboo and lakeside rides in Madison. Riding along Lake Michigan from Milwaukee to Michigan City, Indiana, we headed across Michigan, with 11,000 lakes within its borders and four of the Great Lakes shaping it. From the Mississippi River to Detroit, which sits on a short river just between Lake Erie and Lake St. Clair, this tour is all wet.

That's why it could be the Tour of Humidity. There's no cool mountain air or hot, dry desert air here. It's just water-drenched prairie land— flat and green with only an occasional rolling hill. The terrain would be ideal for riding—if the incredible summertime heat and humidity didn't make you feel a hundred pounds heavier. If we felt microwaved in Wall, we were stir-fried in Sturgis.

That leads to the Tour of the Mosquitos. Residents in each state told us that the blood-sucking pest is their unofficial "state bird." Some people claimed they'd seen them "this long," holding their fingers eight inches apart.

Historically, it's the Tour of the Northwest Territory, the land the United States gained from Britain following the Revolutionary War in 1783. By then, it had already been traversed for 150 years by French explorers and trappers, who left behind names like Eau Claire, Prairie du Sac, and Detroit (d' etroit). Since American settlement began after 1800, these states are older than the West, but much younger than the East.

Sometimes it was the Tour of the Rust Belt. Regional manufacturing centers for steel, cars, farm equipment, and other big-ticket products thrived for a century, then cooled off in recent decades, wracked by obsolescence and foreign competition. We saw both idle plants and raging smokestacks throughout the trip.

If this trip is nothing else, it is the Tour of the Backroads. Bring a detailed map, because this route, especially through Wisconsin, makes highway changes five or six times a day. We lost each other several times on the small country farm roads. And that often meant it became a Tour of the Snarling Dogs. Get your pump ready!

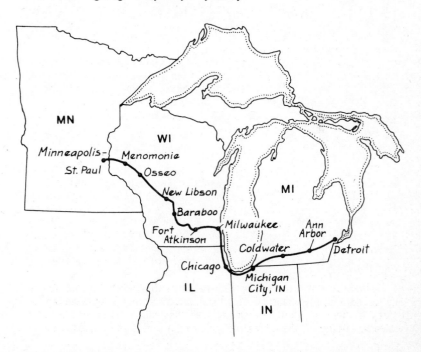

## ROUTE SLIP
### Total of 769 miles in 14 days

| Day | Route End Point | Terrain* | Sights | Mileage |
|---|---|---|---|---|
| 1 | Minneapolis–St. Paul, Minnesota | Easy | Twin Cities Park Loop, state capitol, Left-handed God of Peace | 30 |
| 2 | Menomonie, Wisconsin | Easy | | 61 |
| 3 | Osseo, Wisconsin | Easy | Leinenkugel, Hibernia breweries | 59 |
| 4 | New Lisbon, Wisconsin | Easy | | 82 |
| 5 | Baraboo, Wisconsin | Easy | Wisconsin Dells, Ringling Circus Museum | 43 |
| 6 | Fort Atkinson, Wisconsin | Easy | Devils Lake, state capitol | 73 |
| 7 | Milwaukee, Wisconsin | Easy | Miller Brewery, lakefront statue | 50 |
| 8 | Chicago, Illinois | Easy | Lakeshore Drive, Sears Tower | 87 |
| 9 | Chicago city tour | Easy | Historical Society, Old Water Tower, Art Institute, Board of Trade, Field Museum, Shedd Aquarium, Adler Planetarium | |
| 10 | Michigan City, Indiana | Easy | Museum of Science & Industry, Indiana Dunes | 55 |
| 11 | Coldwater, Michigan | Easy | | 101 |
| 12 | Ann Arbor, Michigan | Easy | University of Michigan, Gerald Ford Library | 76 |
| 13 | Detroit, Michigan | Easy | Henry Ford Museum, Greenfield Village, Renaissance Center | 33 |
| 14 | Detroit, Michigan | Easy | Airport | 19 |

*Easy = Flat to rolling; moderate = hilly; difficult = at least one major hill climb

★

# DAY 1

Minneapolis Airport to St. Paul
Terrain: Flat
Sights: City park loop, state capitol, Left-handed Indian God of
    Peace
30 miles

Marc slammed my bike to the ground. "Learn to fix your own wheels!" he shouted, throwing down the new spokes and spoke-tightener he was using to repair my out-of-true wheel.

Damn jerk! So what if he'd repaired my broken spokes umpteen times already in the month we'd been on the road? We each had our roles. Where would he have been without me? I read the maps, plotted out the course. Take, for example, our trip that day: the Twin Cities Park Loop. A perfect thirty-mile warmup for the longer rides ahead, it took us on a nearly all-greenbelt grand tour of the highlights of *two* cities: Minneapolis, on the west bank of the Mississippi River, and east-bank St. Paul. There we visited the state capitol building, the Science Museum, and the St. Paul City Hall and Courthouse, featuring a monstrous thirty-six-foot-high onyx statue called the Left-handed Indian God of Peace.

Minnehaha Indian lore has it that left-handed people have magical powers, incredible sexual prowess, and the gift of supreme wisdom. Hand-carved left-handed icons were often given to French traders as symbols of peace. They were also given to young warriors to enhance

---

**DIRECTIONS:** Park Loop Route: From Minnehaha Park, go west on Minnehaha Parkway, north on Lake Harriet Parkway around Lake Harriet. North on William Berry Parkway, north to East Lake Calhoun Parkway, north on E. Lake of the Isles Parkway to Kenwood Park. Go north on Morgan Avenue, east on Kenwood Parkway, through park northeast to Hennepin Avenue, past Walker Art Center and Historical Society Museum to downtown Minneapolis and Mississippi River. Cross to St. Paul on Hennepin, right on University over 35W freeway, right to river bank, follow Mississippi River Boulevard/Shepard Road 15 miles around riverbend to downtown St. Paul.

**ACCOMMODATIONS: Radisson St. Paul,** 11 E. Kellogg Boulevard, St. Paul, MN, (612) 292-1900. River view. Rooms: 489, double $56–$99. VISA, MC, AMEX, DINERS.

**CAMPING: St. Paul KOA East,** 568 Cottage Grove Drive, (612) 436-6436 (9 miles east of capitol; from I-94, turn ½ mile southwest on CR 15, follow signs ¼ mile).

★

their sexual potency and technique. Unfortunately, I couldn't find where to buy one of these icons for myself.

I was about as successful in getting Marc to fix my wheel. "You gotta learn sometime," he growled. So I got out the spoke tool and began tightening a spoke myself. A minute later, we heard a loud *hissss*. I had turned the spoke so much that it punctured the tube from the inside.

## DAY 2

St. Paul, Minnesota, to Menomonie, Wisconsin
Terrain: Flat to rolling
61 miles

With my rear wheel wobbling like a boxer in the twelfth round, I led the charge across the Wisconsin state line.

This was our last ride on an interstate, even though we'd be shadowing I-94 nearly all the way to Detroit. We'd gotten used to the easy grades and wide shoulders of the interstates out West, but there was obviously now a lot more traffic. More important, as we were soon to discover, it's illegal to ride a bike on an interstate in Wisconsin.

Wisconsin is known for many things—the Green Bay Packers; producing cheese, milk, and butter; and beer, which made Milwaukee famous and turned a half-dozen other Wisconsin cities into bustling brew towns. But what I think of first about Wisconsin is a piece of wood—a big, beautiful twenty-foot-high wooden welcome sign greeting after the St. Croix River. Shaped like the state, hanging from a giant wooden crossbar, it is easily the fanciest state sign in the country.

It figures that our stop, Menomonie, is a famous old lumber town with giant mansions built by nineteenth-century wood barons. We arrived there by jumping back and forth under I-94, something we weren't used to doing. Marc wanted to risk riding the interstate, tiring of the inefficient, indirect route, but we held him off. The small roads had a lot more personality, anyway.

---

**DIRECTIONS:** Northeast on 7th Street 1½ miles. Bear right onto Minnehaha Avenue 3 miles east. Right on any street to I-94 for 13 miles to stateline. From border, north on SR 35 1 mile to Hudson. Turn right at Route A for 10 miles to Roberts, right on SR 65 3 miles under I-94. East on Route N for 32 miles until merge with SR 29 for last 7 miles.

**ACCOMMODATIONS: Best Western Holiday Manor Motor Lodge,** 1815 Broadway, Menomonie, WI, (715) 235-9651. Amenities: pool, whirlpool. Rooms: 140, double $40–$50. VISA, MC, AMEX, DINERS, DIS.

**CAMPING: Menomonie KOA,** 3 miles on SR 25, past I-94, (715) 235-0641. Amenities: laundry, groceries, pool.

★

# DAY 3

Menomonie to Osseo
Terrain: Flat
Sights: Two beer breweries
59 miles

From the time we entered Wisconsin, all we heard about was Leinenkugel. That is the tongue-twisting name of a German family that stopped in Chippewa Falls around 1900, where they tasted a very pure ground water they thought would make an excellent beer. Apparently, they were right. "You've got to try it," everybody raved to us, "it's the best beer in the country."

Leinenkugel was good—too good. Semi-drunk after an hour in the tasting room, we cooled out for a couple of hours at the nearby Chippewa Falls Dam and Lake Wissota before heading on to Eau Claire, just southwest of the brewery. Translated as "Clear water" in French, Eau Claire is also a brew town, home of the Hibernia brewery. Late already, we kept riding this time.

In hindsight, maybe we should have stopped for another beer. Instead of taking US 53 to Osseo, Marc surged onto I-94 and was soon out of sight. The fool! He knew the interstates were illegal! Bob and I had no choice but to try and chase him down. In minutes, of course, we heard a siren behind us.

"But officer," I pleaded, "we're only trying to catch my brother."

"Don't worry about that," he said, instructing us to take apart the bikes and put them in the trunk of his highway patrol car, "we already got him."

Back at the station in Eau Claire was a surly Marc. I suggested that things might go more smoothly if he did all the repairs and left the route-leading to me. The arresting officer wrote us warnings, posed for a picture with us, then suggested we sleep on the lawn. "I don't want you boys stinking up the cells," he explained.

---

**DIRECTIONS:** 26 miles east on SR 29, under I-94, to Chippewa Falls. Route 124 leads to 1-3 Jefferson Avenue and Leinenkugel. Go southwest on US 53 across Chippewa River for 8 miles to Eau Claire, then southeast on US 53 for 19 miles to Osseo.

**ACCOMMODATIONS: Friendship Inn Alan House,** just west of I-90/US 10 junction, Osseo, WI, (715) 597-3175. <u>Rooms</u>: 50, double $40. VISA, MC, AMEX, DINERS, DIS.

**CAMPING: Osseo Exit Campground,** southeast of I-94 on US 10, (715) 597-2102. <u>Amenities</u>: laundry, groceries, pool.

## DAY 4

Osseo to New Lisbon
Terrain: Flat to rolling
82 miles

Waiting on the side of the road at midday, I knew something was wrong. I'd read a hundred pages of a novel sitting there. Marc and Bob were lost.

God, I hated this waste of time. A lot of the country roads that cross and recross I-94 through flat, occasionally rolling farm country aren't well-marked—and, of course, Bob and Marc didn't pay attention and were now off in Outer Mongolia.

Finally, I decided to ride on another ten miles to the next town, then call the cops. On the way, I ran into a massive downpour. Hiding in a barn, I was attacked by two giant farm dogs, which I fought off with my pump. When I arrived in the tiny town of Millston, I was raving mad. Yes, said the cops, they had reports of Marc and Bob about twenty miles north and would redirect them.

Two hours later, I gave them a piece of my mind—and they told me to go to hell. "He's still playing the know-it-all big brother—as if he never makes mistakes," I heard Marc whisper to Bob. "That's why he screwed up all his job interviews."

That made me reflect a bit. You learn a lot of unexpected things on a bike trip.

---

**DIRECTIONS:** From Osseo, south on US 53 11 miles to Pigeon Falls. Straight on Route P 22 miles thru Taylor. Turn north at SR 54 2 miles, south on SR 27 a few hundred feet. Go southeast on US 12 51 miles through Millston, crossing and recrossing I-94, to Tomah. Then cross I-90 in Oakdale to New Lisbon.

**ACCOMMODATIONS: Rafters Motor Inn,** north on SR 80 near I-94, New Lisbon, WI, (608) 562-5141. <u>Rooms</u>: 72, double $44. VISA, MC, AMEX, DIS.

**CAMPING: Fischer's Campground,** N 7989 Highway 80, 4½ miles north on SR 80, (608) 562-5355. <u>Amenities</u>: laundry, groceries.

---

## DAY 5

New Lisbon to Baraboo
Terrain: Flat, plus rollers
Sights: the Wisconsin Dells and Ringling Brothers Circus
   Museum
43 miles

At the beginning of our day in Millston, Marc, Bob, and I said just two things to each other: "Madison" and "US 12." Behind schedule, we were going to shoot for a 140-mile day, the biggest of the trip.

Unfortunately, that wouldn't allow time for the Wisconsin Dells, the most popular natural attraction in the state. For fifteen miles, the Wisconsin River has carved the sandstone into striking "dells"—towering 150-foot-high cliffs, caverns, and rock formations.

But as I rode through a few miles of man-made tourist madness in the early afternoon, passing a wax museum, an auto museum, Waterworld, Familyland, Crossroads, Noah's Ark Bible World, and even Tommy Bartlett's Robot World, I got the Dells bug. Maybe I could slip in a two-hour Dells boat tour, I thought. I was already ahead of my partners, and would just catch up later.

While looking for the Dells, I ran into three beer-drinking Winnebago Indians at a lakeside park. "Winnebagos?" I exclaimed. "I thought those were motor homes." "Yes," one replied, offering me a beer, "we are indeed happy campers."

During the next few minutes, they explained that their name isn't the only thing the Americans stole from them; this used to be their land. They made a point of differentiating between Americans and other white men. "The French landed in Green Bay in 1634, looking for a northwest passage to China," the historian of the trio said. "And we got along with them fine for a hundred and fifty years—trading fur and such. But the Americans kept trying to kick us out when they got control." When the United States beat the Indians in the Black Hawk War of 1832, American immigrants rolled in.

After a few beers, I dozed off. When I woke up three hours later, the Winnebagos were gone without a trace. It was already 6:30 by then, and long miles to Madison awaited. With no more clowning around, I blew by Baraboo's Circus World Museum and Devils Lake at twenty miles per hour. I had roughly forty more miles to go before the sun went down— and I actually believed I'd make it.

That is, until the hills began. Or what I thought were hills. When it was flat, I thought it was hilly, and vice versa. My carbohydrate-deprived mind was playing tricks on me. I was getting dizzy. I was out of gas; I craved sugar. So I stopped in a bar and, to stares from the patrons, loaded up on seven bags of M & Ms. After twenty minutes, that seemed to get me back to normal.

On my way into town as the sun was setting, I realized that bikes were supposed to get off US-12 back at Middleton. I was now riding illegally on a freeway. But I couldn't get off it because a highway patrolman was posted at the next exit, pulling cars over for driving on the shoulder of the road. I ditched myself in the bushes and lay low, agonizingly watching for an hour and a half as he pulled about twenty cars over.

When I finally reached the state capitol building in Madison, it was 11:00 P.M. "Roy," a shout came from behind a statue, "what happened to you?" It was Bob. He and Marc had been there for four hours already.

They'd met several people while they waited, including a sixty-year-old, long-haired Japanese bookbinder and his twenty-six-year-old University of Wisconsin grad student girlfriend, who took us to a bar to celebrate. For the first time, I politely declined a beer. Two cans had been enough already.

---

**DIRECTIONS:** Southeast 30 miles on US 12 to Dells. Southeast 12 miles on US 12. East on SR 3 for 1 mile to Baraboo.

**ACCOMMODATIONS: Spinning Wheel Motel,** 809 8th Street on US 33, 2 miles east of US 12, Baraboo, WI, (608) 356-3933. Rooms: 25, double S–Th $42, Fri–Sat $49. VISA, MC, AMEX, DIS.

**CAMPING: Hefty's Skillet Creek Farm,** 3 miles south on US 12, ½ mile east on SR 159, adjacent to Devils Lake State Park, (608) 356-4877.

---

# DAY 6

Baraboo to Fort Atkinson
Terrain: Flat, few rollers
Sights: State capitol
73 miles

The Japanese bookbinder told us that Madison was just like Washington, D.C., to him. Like D.C., it existed only on paper when it was selected as the Wisconsin territorial capital. Like D.C., it has one of the most striking capitol buildings in the entire country. But even better than D.C., he said, it has four beautiful bike path-lined lakes, which we pedaled around before leaving for Milwaukee.

If we had been able to pause at Baraboo the day before, as this route suggests, we'd have seen what I hear is an even more beautiful body of

---

**DIRECTIONS:** US 12 south 32 miles to Middleton. East ½ mile on SR M. Southeast 5 miles on Allan Road/Lake Mendota Drive to Picnic Point. Merge to University Drive to capitol building. Then do half-loop around Lake Monona, go east on Washington Avenue 2 miles. Right on Atwood Avenue 2 miles through Olbrich Park, name change to Winnequah Drive 3 miles around the lake to Broadway (US 12), 27 miles east on US 12 to Fort Atkinson.

**ACCOMMODATIONS: Best Western-Welcome Inn,** 225 S. Water Street, Fort Atkinson, WI, (414) 563-8444. Rooms: 40, double $41.00; VISA, MC, AMEX, DINERS, DIS.

**CAMPING: Pilgrim's Progress Outpost.** Stop 2½ miles before city, 1 mile west on Route C, (414) 563-8122. Amenities: groceries, pool.

water: quartz-surrounded Devils Lake at Devils Lake State Park. When you get to Madison, look for a great view of the city from Picnic Point, a narrow spit jutting into Lake Mendota, and another view from the capitol dome.

# DAY 7

Fort Atkinson to Milwaukee
Terrain: Flat to rolling
Sights: Miller, Pabst breweries
50 miles

Milwaukee, an industrial city of 600,000 on Lake Michigan, gave us a choice of two of the country's biggest brewers, Miller and Pabst. Starting from Madison, we pedaled like mad past the Milwaukee County Zoo into the city, where we could smell our way to the Miller brewery. Though Bob and I missed the last tour at 3:30, we did find the outdoor tasting garden, and quickly celebrated our arrival with a dozen cups of Lite and Lowenbrau.

Naturally, we fell asleep. Marc shook us awake several hours later, telling us we'd been invited to stay in the home of a young couple whose bikes he had fixed coming into the city. We were treated to a big barbeque bash featuring bratwurst, or as our hosts called it, "the Midwest's national food."

---

**DIRECTIONS:** SR 26 7 miles north to Jefferson. Right on US 18 past Milwaukee County Zoo, changes name to Blue Mound Road and later Wells Street.

**ACCOMMODATIONS: Marc Plaza,** 509 W. Wisconsin Avenue, Milwaukee, WI, (414) 271-7250. Rooms: 500, double $90–$100. VISA, MC, AMEX, DINERS, DIS.
**Budgetel Inn,** 5110 N. Port Washington Road, north of Miller Brewery, (414) 964-8484. Rooms: 150, double $37. VISA, MC, AMEX, DINERS, DIS.

**CAMPING: Yogi Bear's Jellystone Park Camp,** 20 miles south, (414) 835-2565. Amenities: pool, showers.

---

# DAY 8

Milwaukee, Wisconsin, to Chicago, Illinois
Terrain: Flat
87 miles

Some of the best miles I've experienced on a bike started at the Lake Michigan waterfront, where we picked up the Milwaukee County 76-Mile Bike Tour at McKinley Marina. Then we headed south along a dream bike path—a winding, slightly rising and dipping path through forested shore-line parkland. By the Illinois border, the dream was over. I'd lost my partners.

Stopping to run into a bathroom, I subsequently waited for an hour before deciding they must have passed me by. Alone, I rode Sheridan Highway through the manicured, tree-shaded Chicago North Shore suburbs, passing the ornate, diamondlike dome of the Baha'i Temple in Wilmette, heading into Lincoln Park, and watching the beach's ethnicity change from all-white in the north, to all-Mexican in the middle, to all-black south of downtown Chicago.

I rode five miles south to the Museum of Science and Industry, which we'd all discussed visiting, and waited. And waited. And read until the sun was gone. Then I called our emergency contact in Los Angeles, my dad, and left him the number of the gas station phone booth I was at.

I spent the next three hours talking with the attendant, who told me about the deep racial divisions in the city. When I asked him about a local hotel, he shook his head. "You'd be commitin' suicide bein' a white boy on a bike at night around here," he said. "Just hide."

Just then, the phone rang—it was Bob. There was music and female giggling in the background. He said they'd meet me tomorrow at the Chicago Historical Society in Lincoln Park. "But I'm in the *South Side* right now," I began to beg.

*Click.*

I found a bench in an enclosed courtyard at the University of Chicago and slept uncovered in the boiling humidity. It wasn't a good sleep. I snapped awake, ready to fight or flee, at the slightest rustle of a grasshopper's legs.

---

**DIRECTIONS**: From McKinley Marina, follow bike path signs south to SR 32. South 40 miles to Illinois border, south on Sheridan Highway 37 miles. South 6 miles on Lakeshore Drive, 3 miles past beaches to Jackson Boulevard in downtown Chicago.

**ACCOMMODATIONS: Ohio House Motel,** 600 N. La Salle Street at Ohio Street, 1 block north of Sears Tower, Chicago, IL, (312) 943-6000. <u>Rooms</u>: 50, double $59–$74. VISA, MC, AMEX, DINERS.
**Grove Motel,** 9110 Waukegan Road, Morton Grove, IL, 12 miles northwest of city, (708) 966-0960. <u>Rooms</u>: 40, $31–$33. VISA, MC, AMEX, DISC.

**CAMPING:** none.

---

# DAY 9

## A Day in Chicago

Next day, I turned my attention to learning about Chicago at the Chicago Historical Society. Though reached by French explorers Marquette and Jolliet in 1673, this area wasn't developed for nearly 160 years. Finally founded in 1830 as the start of a proposed waterway linking Lake Michigan with the Mississippi River, centrally located Chicago became the largest city in the central United States in forty years, being close to farmlands, iron ore deposits, and the Mississippi and Great Lakes. Even the Great Fire of 1871, which burned down nearly the entire city, couldn't slow the growth.

Not to be slowed ourselves by the Art Institute of Chicago, an all-day affair, we headed next for the Chicago Board of Trade. There we watched a jam-packed room of buyers and sellers scribbling on paper, shouting prices, and making wild hand gestures as they made split-second bids for grains and minerals. From there it was on to the Sears Tower, the world's tallest building at 1,454 feet and 110 stories, which gave us a sweeping overview of the entire city, a beautiful sight at dusk.

Our last Chicago stop came on the next day's ride out of town, back at the massive Museum of Science and Industry. Among other things, it housed a cutaway view of a modern toilet, a captured Nazi submarine, a moon-orbiting *Apollo 8* space capsule, and a Tiffany glass exhibition. Everything, it seems, but a bicycle.

# DAY 10

Chicago, Illinois, to Michigan City, Indiana
Terrain: Flat
55 miles

The ride around the bottom of Lake Michigan was a mixed bag. First, the hideously rundown remnant of an old steel town, Gary, Indiana, then the pretty oceanlike sand dunes of the Indiana Dunes National Lakeshore. Hugging US 12, the main route for nearly the rest of the way to Detroit, we stopped in the summer resort town of Michigan City for a memorable evening.

After watching several believers become "healed" at a screaming, gasping, hallelujah-rich, tent-city revival meeting (but it sure didn't help *my* aching thighs any!), we headed over to the town's Dunkin' Donuts, where the manager loaded us up with a dozen free donuts. As if that wasn't enough, we also picked up some good advice from a policeman. "If

---

**DIRECTIONS:** US 41 (S. Lake Shore and other names) south 17 miles to Indiana border. East on US 12 (Indianapolis Boulevard and others) 38 miles.

**ACCOMMODATIONS: Al & Sally's Motel,** 3221 Dunes Highway, Michigan City, IN, (219) 872-9131. Rooms: 16, double $36. VISA, MC, AMEX.

**CAMPING: Michigan City KOA,** 1601 N. US 421, 7-mile detour south from US 12 down US 421, (219) 872-7600. Amenities: laundry, groceries, pool.

★

you need a cool place to sleep," he said, on that hot, muggy night, "just go down to the station and ask for Laverne."

Laverne was quite accommodating, locking us into a clean, comfortable, air-conditioned cell in the Michigan City jail.

## DAY 11

Michigan City, Indiana, to Coldwater, Michigan
Terrain: Flat
101 miles

Just outside the city limits of Michigan the City came Michigan the State. After our traditional picture at the border, we rode an easy century, despite incredible humidity and Bob's getting lost for two hours. Hand-shaped Michigan is nearly dead-flat down here in the "wrist" area.

US 12, the route of the old Chicago–Detroit Turnpike, hugs the Indiana border and finally angles northeast into Coldwater, originally built as a station on the CDT.

Hanging out at a Coldwater donut shop, we were approached by an admiring Hell's Angel-like motorcyclist wearing a week-old stubble, a coat of dust, a bandana, and black leathers. His name, he said, was Slick. After buying us coffee, he introduced Chick, his similarly attired wife, then showed us their Harleys and told us all about their two-week trip to the West Coast and Canada. Before leaving, Slick invited us, as fellow "roadies," to "crash in my pad" in Ann Arbor the next night.

Bob, the most skeptical of us, was worried about stepping into a drug den. "Naw," I reminded him, "this is what bike touring is all about."

---

**DIRECTIONS:** US 12 all day.

**ACCOMMODATIONS: Little King Motel,** 847 E. Chicago Road (1 mile east of US 12/I-69 junction), Coldwater, MI, (517) 278-6660. Amenities: pool. Rooms: 18, double $38–$48. VISA, MC, AMEX.

**CAMPING: Waffle Farm Campground,** 779 Union City Road, north of city at Craig/Morrison Lake; take Union City Road five miles north past Jonesville Road, (517) 278-4315.

---

## DAY 12

Coldwater to Ann Arbor
Terrain: Some hills
76 miles

Green, rolling hills made for a picturesque and fun ride. We refueled in Irish Hills, unknowingly skipping the wondrous Mystery Hill, where objects supposedly defy gravity. We then cruised easily into Ann Arbor, a college town of pizza shops, bookstores, movie theaters, and 110,000 people.

In town, as we passed the University of Michigan and the Gerald R. Ford Library, Bob again questioned our going to Slick's. But the couple had been very friendly to us, and I was curious to see how these biker people lived. We prepared to see a hovel.

Therefore, I was surprised as the directions led us through a prim, middle-class neighborhood. Riding further, the homes got bigger and more luxurious until we arrived at a mansion with a Cadillac Eldorado and a Mercedes coupe parked on a horseshoe driveway. Something was screwy here.

The front door opened to reveal an immaculately coiffed, clean-shaven man in a navy dinner jacket. Up rushed a gorgeous blonde in a body-hugging blue satin evening gown. It was Slick and Chick!

"This is what we're really like," John (Slick's real name), a videogame entrepreneur, explained over our catered dinner of Peking duck and champagne. "Joan [Chick] and I take one big motorcycle trip a year. We are amazed at how differently we are treated in our other identities."

Through much conversation and a dozen rounds of Pac-Man, I remained in a daze of disbelief until John later took us down to his four-car garage. There were the Harleys, all polished and cleaned—and ready for Slick and Chick's next adventure.

---

**DIRECTIONS:** From Coldwater, take US 12 45 miles to Irish Hills. Continue 26 miles northeast. Turn north 2 miles east of Saline on State Street, north 5 miles to Ann Arbor.

**ACCOMMODATIONS: Knights Inn,** 3764 S. State Street (on south side of I-94), Ann Arbor, MI, (313) 665-9900. <u>Rooms</u>: 105, double $40. VISA, MC, AMEX, DINERS, DIS.

**CAMPING: Detroit-Greenfield KOA,** 6680 Bunton Road, south of Ypsilanti, 7 miles east of junction US 12 and I-94 (cross I-94, turn south on Carpenter Road, east on Textile Road to Bunton Road, then south). <u>Amenities</u>: Lakeside, laundry, groceries. (313) 482-7722.

---

# DAYS 13 & 14

Ann Arbor to Detroit to airport
Terrain: Flat
Sights: Henry Ford Museum, Greenfield Village, Renaissance
   Center
33 plus 19 miles

After passing the airport, we stopped in Dearborn at the Henry Ford Museum and Greenfield Village, then moved on to the Historical Museum in Detroit. In doing so, we picked up a good understanding of why Detroit is, in a way, one of the most significant places in world history: the birthplace of modern industry.

Named Fort Pontchartrain du Détroit by the French in 1701 because it is "of the Straits" (on a river between two lakes), Detroit had grown from a Revolutionary War fortress to a steamboat boomtown. Still, it remained a small town at the turn of the twentieth century.

Then, due to men like Henry Ford, the auto industry exploded. Immigrants from Europe and the south jammed Motown's bustling mass-production factories. Detroit ballooned to over a million people and its port became one of the world's busiest.

By 1982, however, as we rode from Dearborn to downtown Detroit, we saw a city that had turned to slum. Like so many other middle-class folks, our relatives had escaped to the suburbs. They met us at the refurbished waterfront area that hoped to lead the city's rebirth: the Renaissance Center.

As we ate dinner on the seventy-third story of the gleaming, glass-paneled, five-tower RenCen, I was struck by two things: the view across the Detroit River into Windsor, Ontario, the only stretch along the border where the United States is due north of Canada; and the view of the depressed surroundings. RenCen or not, it seemed Detroit's renaissance would be a long time coming.

---

**DIRECTIONS:** From University of Michigan campus, turn east on Huron Street (soon Huron River Road) 6 miles into Ypsilanti. Cross river on East Michigan Avenue US 12. Ride 27 miles through Dearborn into Detroit to RenCen.
**To Detroit Metro Airport:** West 14 miles on US 12 (Michigan Road/Avenue), south 3 miles on Merriman Road.

**ACCOMMODATIONS: Shorecrest Motor Inn,** near RenCen, Detroit, MI. (313) 568-3000. Rooms: 54, double $52–$68. VISA, MC, AMEX, DINERS, DIS.
**Budgetel,** 9000 Wickham Road, (opposite airport, 19 miles southwest on US 2, south on Merriman), Romulus, MI, (313) 722-6000. Rooms: 50, double $38. VISA, MC, AMEX, DINERS, DIS.

**CAMPING:** none.

---

We ended this part of the Big Adventure almost the way we'd begun—by touring a brewery (Stroh's, now closed). But things seemed different as we pedaled off toward Canada, as though the warmth from relatives and friendly strangers had brought us closer together.

As we pedaled up to the Detroit River, another one of my spokes broke. "I'll get that," said Marc. "Here's a spoke tool," offered Bob.

"Naw—thanks anyway, you guys," I said. I'd learned how to fix my own wheel since Minneapolis. And in that time I learned other things, too: not to drink a beer in the middle of the day; each person should carry a map; have a telephone contact and a planned meeting place; and never ignore posted highway signs—especially in Wisconsin.

# SIGHTSEEING INFORMATION

ANN ARBOR, MICHIGAN
**Gerald R. Ford Library;** 100 Beal Street; closes 4:45 P.M. (313) 668-2218.

BARABOO, WISCONSIN
**Circus World Museum,** SR 113 at 426 Water Street: First "Greatest Show on Earth" in 1882; live performances, elephant rides, illusions; open 9:00 A.M. to 10:00 P.M. July 22 to August 9; restaurant open 9:00 to 6:00; $7.95. (608) 356-8341.

CHICAGO, ILLINOIS
**Alder Planetarium,** 1300 S. Lake Shore Drive: Time and astronomy museum; solar telescope; Sky Show, $3. (312) 322-0300.
**Art Institute of Chicago,** Michigan and Adams in Grant Park; $5. (312) 443-3500.
**Chicago Board of Trade,** 141 W. Jackson: One of the world's largest futures exchanges; free. (312) 435-3590.
**Chicago Historical Society,** in Lincoln Park at Clark Street and North Avenue: Exhibits include 1880 locomotive, Mayor Daley's first campaign posters, maps of Great Fire; $1.50. (312) 642-4844.
**Field Museum of Natural History,** Lake Shore Drive in Grant Park: World famous; over ten acres of natural science exhibits; $2. (312) 922-9410.
**Museum of Science and Industry,** S. Lake Shore and 57th Street in Jackson Park: Fourteen acres of exhibits; free. (312) 684-1414.
**Old Water Tower,** Michigan and Chicago: Features "Here's Chicago" film of Chicago's gangster past; only area building to survive Great Fire; $4.75. (312) 467-7114.
**Sears Tower,** Jackson and Franklin streets: Skydeck, 9:00 A.M. to midnight; $3.75. (312) 875-9696.
**Shedd Aquarium,** 1200 Lake Shore Drive: Eight thousand fish and other sea and fresh water animals; $2. (312) 939-2438.

CHIPPEWA FALLS, WISCONSIN
**Leinenkugel Brewery,** 1–3 Jefferson Avenue on Highway 124: Free tours, Monday through Friday, every half hour. (715) 723-5557.

DEARBORN, MICHIGAN
**Henry Ford Museum,** Oakwood Boulevard and Village Road, 1 mile south off US 12 at Oakwood: Fourteen-acre museum, tours of three hundred years changing technology; $9.50. (313) 271-1620.

**Greenfield Village:** Near museum; Industrial Revolution exhibits including work of the Wright Brothers, Thomas Edison, young Abe Lincoln; $9.50. (313) 271-1620.

**Fair Lane,** Evergreen Road off US 12, University of Michigan Dearborn campus: Henry Ford's estate; $5. (313) 593-5590.

DETROIT, MICHIGAN

**Detroit Historical Museum,** Woodward and Kirby avenues; Wednesday through Sunday to 5:00 P.M. (313) 833-1805.

**Historical Fort Wayne,** 6325 W. Jefferson Street at Livernois: Exhibits, costumed guides to Detroit's military history. (313) 297-9360.

DEVILS LAKE, WISCONSIN

**Devils Lake,** 3½ miles south of Baraboo on SR 123: Underground-spring fed, surrounded by iridescent quartz rock walls; programs explain glacial history. (608) 356-8301.

EAU CLAIRE, WISCONSIN

**Hibernia Brewery,** 318 Elm Street: Tours Monday through Friday at 10:00 and 2:00. (715) 836-BEER.

IRISH HILLS, MICHIGAN

**Mystery Hill,** on US 12: Gravity-defying objects. (517) 467-2517.

**Stagecoach Stop,** east of city: Eighteenth-century theme park; saloon, blacksmiths, glassblowers; sawmill; $6. (517) 467-2300.

MADISON, WISCONSIN

**Capitol Building:** Free guided tours on the hour. (608) 266-0382.

MENOMONIE, WISCONSIN

**John Holy Knapp House,** (circa 1868) & **Wilson Place** (circa 1846): Near Lake Menomen, stately Victorian mansions built by lumber barons.

**Wilson Place,** at Wilson Circle: Museum of early settlement era.

MILWAUKEE, WISCONSIN

**Milwaukee County Zoo,** on US 18: One of nation's largest with four thousand animals. (414) 771-3040.

**Miller Beer Valley,** 4251 W. State Street: Last tour 3:30 P.M. (414) 931-2153.

**Pabst Brewery,** 915 W. Juneau Street: Last tour at 3:00 P.M. (414) 223-3709.

**Milwaukee County Historical Center Museum,** 910 N. Old World Street: Slide shows of city history; Monday through Friday, 9:30 to 5:00. (414) 273-8288.

MINNEAPOLIS, MINNESOTA

**Walker Art Center,** Hennepin and Vineland Place: Late twentieth-century American and European paintings, sculpture. (612) 375-7600.

**Hennepin County Historical Society Museum,** 2302 3rd Avenue S.: History of Minneapolis, including "From Moccasins to Microchips". (612) 870-1329.
**Aquatennial Festival:** Minneapolis' ten-day celebration with parades, music, log rolling contests, waterskiing races; late July.

ST. PAUL, MINNESOTA
**State Capitol Building,** Aurora Avenue between Cedar and Park: Forty-five-minute tours. (612) 296-2881.
**Science Museum of Minnesota,** 30 E. 10th Street: Programs on space and science. (612) 221-9454.
**St. Paul City Hall and Courthouse,** bounded by St. Peter, Kellogg, Wabasha, and 4th streets: Including monstrous thirty-six-foot-high onyx statue, "Left-handed Indian God of Peace." (612) 298-4131.

WISCONSIN DELLS, WISCONSIN
**Dells Boat Tour,** follow signs across Wisconsin River from US 12/SR 16 at Rocky Arbor State Park: Striking rock formations; four-hour trip, upper and lower Dells, $13.50; shorter trips, $9.50. (608) 254-8555.

# CHAPTER 5

## DETROIT
## TO
## OTTAWA

HE QUESTION LOOMED: SHOULD THE LAST LEG OF THE BIG AD-
venture be short and boring, or long and interesting?

The answer is on the map: our route, which began and ended in the
United States but went almost entirely through Eastern Canada, was not
the most efficient way to get from Detroit to the Atlantic. Yet it looked far
more interesting than the alternative: a beeline from Motown to Bean
Town that included Niagara Falls and Boston, but would go through the
humdrum midsection of upstate New York.

The trip through Canada has been split into two trips here: English
and French. The English part, the province of Ontario, may not seem very
foreign to Americans at first. The language, the food, the customs, all
seem the same. But as we traveled 636 miles along the "South Coast" of
Canada, following the virtually flat northern shores of Lake Erie and Lake
Ontario, we enjoyed discovering the differences—in the character of the
people and in national history.

To most Americans Niagara Falls is just scenery, but to Canadians it
also represents the scene of a military battle against the country's long-
ago enemy: the United States. Toronto, Canada's giant financial and cultural center, somehow seemed a little more civilized than most compa-
rable American cities. Old Fort Henry in Kingston, complete with functioning eighteenth-century cannon and a changing of the guards, was
actually built to defend against Americans. By the time we reached the

## ROUTE SLIP
*Total of 636 miles in 8 days or 654 miles in 9 days*

| Day | Route End Point | Terrain* | Sights | Miles |
|---|---|---|---|---|
| 1 | Leamington, Ontario | Easy | Point Pelee | 58 |
| 2 | St. Thomas, Ontario | Easy | | 105 |
| 3 | Niagara Falls, Ontario | Easy | Niagara Falls at night | 112 |
| 4 | Hamilton, Ontario | Easy | Niagara Falls, Goat Island, Fort George Historical Park | 56 |
| 5 | Toronto, Ontario | Easy | Ontario Place, CN Tower, City Hall, Yorkville | 40 |
| 6 | Brighton, Ontario | Easy | Ontario Parliament Building | 92 |
| 7 | Kingston, Ontario | Easy | Old Fort Henry | 75 |
| Option: | Gananoque, Ontario | Easy | 1000 Islands Boat Ride | 18 |
| 8 | Ottawa, Ontario | Easy | Parliament Hill, Rideau Canal; Parliament tour, Changing of the Guard, War Museum, National Gallery, Currency Museum, two-hour guided bike tour, Museum of Canadian Civilization | 99 |

*Easy = flat to rolling; moderate = hilly; difficult = extremely hilly

country's strikingly elegant capital, Ottawa, we'd gained an appreciation of what makes Canadians Canadian—and had a great bike tour to boot.*

## DAY 1

Detroit, Michigan, to Leamington, Ontario
Terrain: Flat
Sights: Point Pelee
19 miles plus 66 kilometers equals 58 miles

*All prices quoted in Canada are in Canadian dollars. Although the exchange rate fluctuates, use $1 Canadian = $.75 U.S. as a general guide.

Neither Bob, Marc nor I had been to Canada before, but our excitement was strangely muffled. Foreign intrigue? Ha! All we expected was a cleaner, safer, friendlier but duller version of the United States. After pedaling through the potholed battle zone of Detroit's ghetto streets, we found the Ambassador Bridge downstream of the RenCen and pedaled across the Detroit River.* Rolling up to Canadian customs, we anticipated a smile and a thumbs-up. We emerged three hours later ready to declare war.

Marc and Bob had beards and moderately long afros, and I was shirtless. We each carried only a couple of hundred dollars. When we told them we expected to be in the country for two weeks, the customs officer called a conference. They told us to strip everything off our bikes, and proceeded to search every item of clothing and every piece of paper; because we smarted off, they decided to search our bikes for drugs. In the next hour Marc gave me a first-class lesson in bike assembly—and disassembly. And I thought truing wheels was all I needed to know.

After finally clearing, we rode onto Riverside Drive and looked over Canadian car-carrying trains back across the river to Detroit's Renaissance Center, shimmering in the background. That view was fitting: Windsor, a highly industrialized city of nearly 200,000, is Canada's De-

---

*This was illegal, we discovered later. You must hitchhike across the bridge.

troit—although much cleaner. It typifies the province of Ontario, which has more people (9 million, 30 percent of the nation's population) and a higher percentage of the national income (40 percent) than any other Canadian province. It is Canada's second-largest province (next to Quebec), about one and a half times as big as Texas.

Since we were in the southernmost part of Canada, we figured it'd be nice to have a picture at the exact southernmost point, Pelee Island, in the middle of Lake Erie. So we headed southeast over easy, flat country toward Leamington and a Lake Erie ferry.

Unfortunately, we didn't make it. Just as the sun dropped below the horizon, we were pulled over by a policeman, who checked our IDs. "Take your bikes apart and put them in the trunk," he said. "It's illegal to ride bikes in the dark without lights."

But it was only four kilometers to town, we protested. It would take us longer to take the bikes apart than it would to ride. "I don't care— rules are rules," he lectured. "You Americans are going to have to learn that."

So that was it—*Americans*. Didn't this guy realize that the first English-speaking people to settle Canada were not Englishmen, but Loyalist Americans fleeing the Revolutionary War?

And that's when it hit me. The difference between Americans and Canadians dates back two hundred years! Those who stayed in the thirteen Colonies—the Americans—were the rebels, the law-breakers, whereas the future English Canadians preferred relocation to rebellion. Canadians have a stronger intolerance of deviant behavior.

When the cop dropped us off at an information booth that looked like a giant tomato (Leamington is the tomato capital of Canada, due to a hundred-year-old Heinz factory), I knew Marc and I would have to backtrack two miles the next day to keep our "ride every mile" goal intact. I also had gained a major cultural insight: no wonder everything looks so clean and there's so little crime. They obey the law in Canada.

---

**DIRECTIONS**: From Detroit Airport, north 3 miles on Merriman Road, east 15 miles on US 12 (Michigan Road/Avenue). Go right 1 mile to Grand Boulevard and bridge. From Windsor, go southeast 3 kilometers (2 miles) on Ouellette Street. Continue 4 kilometers (2.5 miles) after merge with Dougall Avenue. Turn onto CAN 3 for 42 kilometers (25 miles) to Leamington.

**ACCOMMODATIONS: Wigle's Colonial**, 133 Talbot Street E., Leamington, Ont., (519) 326-3265. <u>Rooms</u>: 21, double $38–$42. VISA, MC, AMEX.

**CAMPING: Seacliff Park at Lake Erie**, 154 Erie Street, 1.5 kilometers down Erie Street, then right on Highway 18 for 1 block, (519) 322-2337.

★

## DAY 2

Leamington to St. Thomas
Terrain: Flat to rolling
167.5 kilometers (104 miles)

I was obsessed with seeing Niagara Falls at night. And the only way to do that would be cycling over a hundred miles each of the next two days.

Fortunately, the terrain through tiny towns and farmland all day on Highway 3 was mostly flat and fast. This area, with the longest growing season and richest soil in Canada, produces half its agricultural output. We saw tobacco, corn, livestock, dairy products, fruit, and vegetables growing there, as well as hundreds of backpacking Quebecker migrant laborers looking for work in the fields.

We made good time, stopping at a movie theater in St. Thomas about 7:00. The owner was so impressed with our trip that he gave us free entrance to the movie *Best Little Whorehouse in Texas* plus free drinks and popcorn. After the movie, he invited us to sleep on the balcony, which we did.

Maybe Canada was all right after all, we mused—if you keep away from the authorities.

---

**DIRECTIONS:** Highway 2 all day.

**ACCOMMODATIONS: Hilltop Motel,** Highway 4 at exit 177A, St. Thomas, Ont., (519) 633-0501. <u>Rooms</u>: 16, double $42. VISA, MC.

**CAMPING: London-401 Campground,** 24 kilometers (15 miles) northeast at junction of highways 401 and 74, (519) 644-0222. <u>Amenities</u>: laundry, groceries, heated pool.

---

## DAY 3

St. Thomas to Niagara Falls
Terrain: Flat to rolling
Sights: The Falls at Night
180 kilometers (112 miles)

The task at hand, 112 miles, was formidable, especially considering the weather. We remained holed up in the theater until 11:00 because of rain. When it slackened, we blitzed Highway 3 for forty miles until more rain forced us into a Kentucky Fried Chicken (*North* America's Hospitality Treat, the sign says), then hammered another twenty-five miles until forced into a maple-leaf-adorned McDonalds. At this point, Bob urged me to give it up. Though Niagara Falls at night would be spellbinding, we had forty-seven miles to go and only two hours of rain-soaked daylight left.

Just then, however, the clouds parted. A few rays of sunlight popped through. This was our last chance! We hit Canborough at full speed and kept moving east. The sky was darkening fast, but was clear. By the time we hit Wellandport, there were only twenty-five miles to go. We were going to make it!

Then, ten miles before the fateful gaze, a deafening downpour began. Waiting in a hotel lobby as night fell, Bob and I began arguing. He wanted to get a room; I held him off. When he derisively called me a "junkie—a sightseeing junkie," I exploded.

"Listen. We are on a bike *tour,* and Niagara Falls at night has got to be one of the greatest sights in the world. We *will* see it!"

When the rain stopped, we pushed on. I drove Marc and Bob like cattle, singing the *Rocky* theme to keep their minds on the quest.

Boring in on the Falls on Ferry Street, we passed block after block of gaudy commercialism: wax museums, the Ripley's Believe It or Not Museum, Castle Dracula, Circus World, miniature golf courses, T-shirt shops, honeymoon specials, drive-through wedding chapels, and hundreds of hotels.

At 11:30, I led Bob to a viewing platform. There it was.

The Falls looked almost magical—brilliantly illuminated twin waves cascading off 180-foot-high ledges with a muted roar, great clouds of mist boiling above them. It was everything I'd hoped for.

I carefully removed my camera and took my time setting up several time-exposure pictures of the awesome sight. Bob, now caught up in the excitement, waited impatiently to use my tripod, the only way to get a good night photo. Just as I finished my last shot and an antsy Bob was ready to shoot his pictures of the spectacularly lit Falls, the lights unexpectedly flicked off. Startled, I glanced at my watch: midnight.

Bob looked at me as if he wanted to cry. I could only smile. Somehow, it seemed, justice had been done.

---

**DIRECTIONS:** East on Highway 3 77 miles to Canboro. East 20 miles on Highway 63 to Ridgeville. Straight 14 miles on Highway 20 over Welland Canal into Niagara Falls. Go up Lundy's Lane and Ferry Street to Falls.

**ACCOMMODATIONS: Marco Polo Inn,** 5553 Ferry Street (1 kilometer from Falls), Niagara Falls, Ont., (416) 356-6959. Rooms: 38, double $55–$75. VISA, MC, AMEX.

**CAMPING: Niagara-Glenview Park,** 3950 Victoria Avenue (3.5 kilometers [2 miles] north of Falls on River Road), (416) 358-8689. Amenities: laundry, groceries.

★

# DAY 4

Niagara Falls to Hamilton
Terrain: Flat to rolling
Sights: The Falls, Niagara-on-the-Lake
90 kilometers (56 miles)

Though the morning sky was clear, we were literally "rained on" by the clouds of mist from the Horseshoe Falls. We gazed at the Falls from different vantage points, just as the first European to see the Falls, France's Father Louis Hennepin, must have done in 1678, just as the first tourists, sideshow freaks, tightrope walkers, barrel-riding daredevils, and con artists did in the 1840s, and just as 12 million tourists and honeymooners a year do today. We considered going over to Goat Island on the American side for a trip down to the bottom—until we remembered that we'd have to pass back through Canadian customs.

Leaving town along the pretty Niagara River Gorge, we came to Niagara-on-the-Lake, once the capital of English Canada and now famous for the summertime plays of the George Bernard Shaw Festival. After stopping at Fort George National Historic Park, the scene of bloody British-American War of 1812 battles, we turned southwest on Lake Ontario, loaded up on peaches at St. Catharines, the hub of the Niagara fruit-growing region, and shot for Hamilton, one of Canada's biggest ports. Just as we were riding across Hamilton Harbor to Lakeshore Road, it started pouring rain again.

We ducked into the Venture Inn, only to find it all booked up. Not knowing where to go, Marc and I sat down while Bob stood at the counter telling the desk woman about our trip. Soon, he tapped me on the shoulder. "We've got a free room."

It seems most hotels withhold rooms if they are excessively dirty or damaged. Our room's carpet had been flooded, but no problem. The beds did just fine.

---

**DIRECTIONS:** North 16 kilometers (10 miles) on Niagara Parkway to Niagara-on-the-Lake. Southwest and west 32 kilometers (20 miles) on Lake Shore Road (Highway 87). Cut south to Highway 8. Ride west 42 kilometers (26 miles) to Hamilton, north 3 kilometers (2 miles) on Highway 20, 1.9 kilometers (5.6 miles) on Beach Boulevard across Hamilton Harbor to Lakeshore Road (Highway 2).

**ACCOMMODATIONS: Venture Inn Burlington-On-The-Lake,** 2200 Lakeshore, Hamilton, Ont., (416) 681-0762. Rooms: 122, double $68–$71. VISA, MC, AMEX, DINERS.
**Esquire Motel,** 1110 Plains Road W (Highway 2, back side of harbor), Hamilton, Ont., (416) 529-3915. Rooms: 22, double $36–$44. VISA, MC, AMEX.

**CAMPING:** none.

★

---

# DAY 5

Hamilton to Toronto
Terrain: Flat
64 kilometers (40 miles)

They say Toronto's the New York of Canada. Well, like the Big Apple, Big T is the biggest city in its country (2.5 million people), a financial center, industrial center, and cultural center. But it ain't no New York. Where's the dirt? Where are the rude, menacing people? Where's the excitement? It's "life in the big city" Canadian-style—neat and clean and hospitable urban sprawl for fifty miles.

Our first stop in town was Ontario Place, a waterfront entertainment complex built on pilings over Lake Ontario, where we watched water shows and wide-screen films about Ontario province. Next was the CN (Canadian National) Tower, the world's tallest free-standing structure at 1,815.25 feet and a panoramic view all the way to Niagara Falls. We could see our next stops, too: the Ontario Parliament building and Toronto City Hall.

The latter was striking: a two-story domed hall framed by two curving office buildings, fountains, modernistic sculptures, and a reflecting pool. We asked the locals where to find the city's best nightlife, getting answers ranging from "In Montreal" to "What nightlife?" When I asked a woman what made Montreal so good, she answered quickly: "It's French."

By contrast, Yorkville—the most-mentioned Toronto hot-spot—is English. Some claim it's a hip spot on par with Washington's Georgetown, New York's Greenwich Village, or Los Angeles's Westwood. Well, it may have chic boutiques, gentrified townhouses, high-tech yogurt shops, and well-dressed Yuppies, but Yorkville seemed lukewarm for a hot spot.

---

**DIRECTIONS:** Highway 2 (Lakeshore Road) all the way.

**ACCOMMODATIONS: Journey's End Hotel,** 111 Lombard Street (near waterfront) Toronto, Ont., (416) 367-5555. <u>Rooms</u>: 196, double $75. VISA, MC, AMEX, DINERS.

**CAMPING: Woodland Park Campgrounds,** 6.1 kilometers north on Highway 48 (Markham Road), then 4.4 kilometers east on Steeles Avenue at Ressor Road, Toronto, Ont., (416) 640-1700.

★

---

## DAY 6

Toronto to Brighton
Terrain: Flat
148 kilometers (92 miles)

Refreshed after a couple of easy days, our goal was to get as close as possible to Kingston, where some big sightseeing awaited at Old Fort Henry. Though the only sight today was the flat pavement, we were able to learn a lot about bike touring and human nature—at a McDonald's—when Bob walked up to me and slapped four "Free Big Mac" coupons on the table. He had just been given these by the owner.

I was amazed. Bob had gotten us into Ontario Place free, had been given free tickets to a Toronto Blue Jays game (which we didn't go to), gotten us into the movie theater in St. Thomas for free and that hotel in Hamilton. What was going on?

Bob scratched his head. "I don't know," he pondered. "When people ask me what the greatest part of our trip is, I tell them it's been the people. I tell them about the couple in Milwaukee who barbequed bratwurst for us, all the free donuts we got in Indiana, and the movie theater. Then, I guess that gives 'em the urge to do likewise."

People, we concluded, are basically good. All they need is a little encouragement.

---

**DIRECTIONS:** Highway 2 all day.

**ACCOMMODATIONS: Presque Isle Beach Hotel,** Highway 2 at 243 Main Street, Brighton, Ont., (613) 475-1010. Rooms: 20, double $42–$59. VISA, MC.
**Loyal Ramada Inn,** 11 Baybridge Road (junction highways 2 and 62, overlooks Bay of Quinte), Belleville, Ont., (613) 968-3411. Rooms: 125, double $80–$90. VISA, MC, AMEX.

**CAMPING: Presque Isle Provincial Park,** south of Brighton, lakefront campsites on Highway 30, (613) 475–2204. Amenities: groceries, visitors center.
**Carlton Cove Trailer Park,** 5 kilometers away from Belleville; turn north on Loyalist College Road; cross 401 freeway, east on Rural Route 1, north on Highway 62, down hill, (613) 962-6344.

---

## DAY 7

Brighton to Kingston
Terrain: Flat
Sights: Old Fort Henry
119 kilometers (75 miles)

We saw the enemy, and he was us. That is the lesson we learned at Old Fort Henry.

"The enemy would attack over here," an eighteenth-century uniformed guard said, pointing to the small choke point where the St. Lawrence River and Lake Ontario meet. In 1673, this point was part of New France, and the enemy was the English. In 1812, the English owned this point, and the enemy was the good ole U.S.A.

Old Fort Henry is a living museum. We saw a changing of the guards, booming salutes fired from authentic eighteenth-century cannon, and Buckingham Palace-style sentries who stood perfectly rigid. A nineteenth-century-garbed "captain" lectured us on military history, telling us that the United States had invaded Canada in the War of 1812, and that relations were tense for another fifty years.

But an American high school history teacher behind me snickered. "They're not telling the full story," he said. Before the invasion, the British had kidnapped American sailors at sea, supplied Indians on the frontier with arms, and occupied Detroit and other American forts.

In the light of history, our treatment at the border made a little more sense. And, in light of Bob's history, it wasn't surprising that we got in free at Old Fort Henry.

---

**DIRECTIONS:** Highway 2 to junction of Highway 15.

**ACCOMMODATIONS: First Canada Inns,** 1 First Canada Court, Kingston, Ont., (613) 541-1111. <u>Amenities</u>: coin laundry. <u>Rooms</u>: 73, double $40–$50. VISA, MC, AMEX.

**CAMPING: Lake Ontario Campground** on King Street, (613) 542-6574.

---

# OPTION

## Day in Gananoque

If only we'd known: Gananoque, eighteen miles northeast of Kingston, has three-hour boat cruises through the Thousand Islands (1,700 islands that jam the west end of the St. Lawrence) and to Boldt Castle, a never-finished hundred-year-old stone palace.

---

**DIRECTIONS:** 18 miles north on Highway 2. To return to the route to Ottawa, go inland (north) on Highway 32 for 21 kilometers (13 miles). Then continue on Highway 15.

**ACCOMMODATIONS: Carriage House Motor Inn,** junction Highway 2 and 1000 Islands Parkway, Gananoque, Ont., (613) 382-4781. <u>Rooms</u>: 67, double $50–$90. VISA, MC, AMEX.

CAMPING: Ivy Lea KOA, 11 kilometers east on 1000 Islands Parkway, 3 kilometers west of 1000 Islands International Bridge, (613) 659-2817.

## DAY 8

Kingston to Ottawa
Terrain: Gently rolling
Sights: Parliament Hill, Rideau Canal
160 kilometers (99 miles)

Ottawa is the capital of Canada, and no matter how humdrum we expected it to be, a bike touring maxim is that you must take a picture of all capitals.

Leaving the St. Lawrence River, we headed inland across flat and rolling farmland, forest, and rivers. By late afternoon, at the small town of North Gower, about twenty miles south of Ottawa, a downpour was upon us.

Ducking into a crowded little restaurant, I spent an hour talking to a young woman and her boyfriend, a Canadian information officer named Garnet. When he offered us shelter and a ride, Bob quickly accepted.

But Marc and I continued, trying to keep intact our goal of riding every mile of the tour. For the next twenty rainy, dark, traffic-packed miles, I hung onto Marc's rear wheel for dear life, drafting behind as he powered those tree-trunk legs into town in just forty-five minutes.

By the time we arrived, the rain had stopped; the city was still, the streets empty. Marc and I gazed in awe at the magnificent Gothic spires of the three green copper-roofed Parliament Buildings, whose ninety-meter-high (300-foot) tower dominates the city. We shot a picture of the eternal flame burning out front, then rode across the street to the National War Memorial arch, which honors the 66,000 Canadians who died in World War I. Then we saw the streetlight-lined Rideau Canal, which looked like a dreamy path of glittering pearls arcing into the silent black night. Indeed, this whole place seemed like a dream. Ottawa is no ordinary place, after all.

DIRECTIONS: North 89 kilometers (55 miles) on Highway 15 to Smiths Falls. Northeast on Route 4 and Route 6 for 41 kilometers (26 miles) through North Gower. North 30 kilometers (18.6 miles) to Highway 16 to Ottawa.

ACCOMMODATIONS: Parkway Motel, 475 Rideau Street, Ottawa, Ont., (613) 232-3781. Rooms: 60, double $62–$68. VISA, MC, AMEX, DINERS.

CAMPING: Cantley, (Quebec) Camp, on Highway 307, 12 kilometers north of Hull, Que., (819) 827-1056. Amenities: pools, laundry, groceries.

# DAY 9

A Day in Ottawa
Sights: Parliament Hill, Changing of the Guard, Two-hour guided
  bike tour

Touring the city with our host, Garnet, in the morning, it became
clear that Ottawa really isn't a city, but a giant park with an occasional
urban interruption. We rode past a unique forest called the Central Experimental Farm, where the Department of Agriculture has planted hundreds of varieties of trees for research. We rode through several of Ottawa's seventy municipal city parks, including the Rideau Canal, which
serves as a wintertime highway for commuting ice-skaters and a summertime highway for—get this—bicyclists. In fact, with 104 kilometers
of bike paths around the city, Ottawa is renowned to city bicycle planners
worldwide. It seemed like a marvelously livable meeting place of man
and nature, of French and English, of Ontario and Quebec.

And then it got better. We headed over to Parliament Hill to catch the
changing of the guards, red-coated, high-hatted, and lock-stepping.
Around the corner from Parliament Hill was a fascinating sight: the National Gallery of Canada, which is actually a building within a building—
a modern mostly glass exterior entirely housing the historic Rideau
Chapel.

We'd have needed an entire extra day to see the Canadian War Museum and the Royal Canadian Mint, and probably would have found
value in the Currency Museum, but it was time to forge on. We'd seen
enough of this fairy-tale place to keep us happy.

As pretty as it looks, Garnet explained that Ottawa didn't always have
a storybook quality about it. Its harsh cold-in-the-winter, hot-in-the-sum-
mer weather kept it unpopulated until the late 1700s, even though its
site at the confluence of the Rideau and Ottawa Rivers was a strategic
gateway to the interior. First seen by French explorer Samuel de Cham-
plain back in 1615, it wasn't until the 1831 completion of the Rideau
Canal, which allowed British warships to bypass potential American
bombardment on the St. Lawrence River, that the city finally sprouted.

Though unpopular when chosen as Canada's capital by Queen Victoria in 1857, Ottawa has become a truly national city. Due to its location
on the Ontario–Quebec border and the government's French-speaking
requirements, over a third of Ottawa's residents are bilingual.

Although we intended on knocking off some easy miles along the
Ottawa River, we never got out of town. When it started raining again,
we ducked into The Potato Villa, a little burger joint, and spent the next
three hours writing in our diaries and telling the owners, Rene and Ce-
cille Lavigne, about our adventures. Eventually, they brought out piles of
free hamburgers and fries for us and, in the end, took us home. Inviting
about twenty-eight family and friends over, they opened their liquor cab-
inet and threw a big party.

I'll never forget sitting around a dining room table telling jokes in
English with the peanut gallery guffawing in French. Partly because of

the Lavignes and Garnet, I'll never forget rye whiskey and ginger ale, the city of Ottawa, or the province of Ontario.

## SIGHTSEEING INFORMATION

GANANOQUE, ONTARIO
**1000 Islands Tour:** Three-hour boat tours through St. Lawrence islands, including a stop at Boldt Castle, uncompleted turn-of-century stone castle; hourly; $10. (613) 382-2144.

KINGSTON, ONTARIO
**Old Fort Henry,** Highway 2 and Highway 15: Features an hourly changing of guard, $5. (613) 542-7388.
**Marine Museum of the Great Lakes,** 55 Ontario Street: In waterfront area; exhibits and films of Great Lakes military, commercial history; $2.75. (613) 542-2261.

NIAGARA FALLS, ONTARIO
**Skylon Tower:** 160 meters high (500 feet) above Canadian Falls; $4.75.
**Table Rock House:** Elevator, three tunnels go to floor of gorge; $3.85.
**Whirlpool Aerocar:** Cable car across gorge and back; $3.35.
**Cave of the Winds Trip,** Goat Island: Walkway down to within twenty feet of falls' base; $3.00.

NIAGARA-ON-THE-LAKE, ONTARIO
**Historic Village:** Onetime capital of Upper Canada.
**Shaw Festival:** April to October performances of plays of George Bernard Shaw, others. (416) 468-2172.
**Niagara Historical Society Museum,** 43 Castlereagh Street: Town history, War of 1812 involvement. (416) 468-3912.
**Fort George Historical Park:** Reconstructed War of 1812 fort.

OTTAWA, ONTARIO
**City Bike Tours:** Guided, two hours; includes Central Experimental Farm; summer only. (613) 233-0268.
**Changing of the Guard,** on Parliament Hill lawn; 10:00 A.M., June 24 to August 28.
**Parliament Buildings:** Free tours, 9:00 A.M. to 8:00 P.M. July 1 to Labor Day; free. (613) 993-1811.
**National Gallery of Canada,** 380 Sussex Drive: Modern, mostly-glass exterior entirely houses Rideau Chapel; works of Rembrandt, van Gogh, others; $4. (613) 990-0570.
**Canadian War Museum,** 330 Sussex Drive: Exhibits on Canada history from first French explorers. (613) 992-2774.
**Royal Canadian Mint,** 320 Sussex Drive: Coin-manufacturing tour; 8:30 to 2:30. (613) 992-2348.

**Currency Museum,** 245 Sparks Street: Guided tours; Chinese gold coins to beaver pelts to dollars; free. (613) 782-8914.

**Museum of Canadian Civilization,** on Rue Laurier directly across the Ottawa River from Parliament in Hull, Quebec: Canadian history from prehistoric times to present; $2. (819) 992-3497.

POINT PELEE, ONTARIO

**Pelee Point National Park:** Marshland, bird sanctuary, naturalist talks, historical sites; 12 kilometers (7.4 miles) south on Route 77 and Route 33; Visitors Center 8 kilometers (5 miles) from gate; open 10:00 to 6:00. (519) 322-2365.

TORONTO, ONTARIO

**CN (Canadian National) Tower,** 301 Front Street: Tallest free-standing structure in the world at 1,815.25 feet (553.33 meters); $8, observation deck; Space Deck, $2 extra; open 9:00 A.M. to 11:00 P.M. (416) 360-8500.

**Ontario Parliament Buildings,** Queens Park: Guided tours of assembly rooms, statues, and painting exhibits; free. (416) 965-7711.

**Ontario Place,** 955 Lakeshore Road: On pilings over Lake Ontario; hodge-podge of exhibits, restaurants, water shows, musical performances, films honoring Ontario; $6; open 10:00 A.M. to 1:00 A.M. (416) 965-7711.

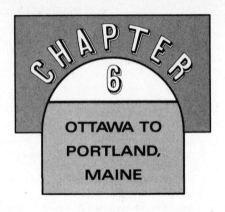

# CHAPTER 6

## OTTAWA TO PORTLAND, MAINE

**W**HETHER QUEBEC BECOMES AN INDEPENDENT NATION OR stays a Canadian province, it'll always be a great place for Americans to tour. Its French culture and language gave it an aura of excitement we didn't find in the rest of Canada or the United States. Montreal* and Quebec City, whose fall in 1763 changed the course of Canadian and American history, are beautiful places jammed with sights to see. Add the general perfection of Canada's roads, pretty countryside, and tailwinds, and Quebec was exceptional.

The terrain on this tour was easy—until the very end. Following flat-to-rolling roads along the Ottawa and St. Lawrence rivers, we turned south at Quebec City to a different ride altogether: a strenuous but exhilarating Appalachian Mountain rivergrade roller coaster across the American border to Portland and the Atlantic Ocean.

In the end, after crossing two distinctly different "worlds"—sensual Quebec and mountainous Maine, we sat down in Portland in front of two big Maine lobsters each. It was the perfect ending to an excellent trip—the 573 miles of this tour and the 4,356 miles of the entire Big Adventure.

*A special treat awaits those riding in Montreal in the first weekend of June: the biggest amateur cycling event in the world, Le Tour de l'Ile de Montréal, takes enthusiasts on a seventy-kilometer tour of seven cities on Montreal island. The 1988 Tour made the Guinness Book of World Records with 32,000 riders. Call (514) 251-6955 for information.

**ROUTE SLIP**
*Total of 573 miles in 9 days*

| Day | Route End Point | Terrain* | Sights | Miles |
|---|---|---|---|---|
| 1 | Rockland, Ontario | Easy | | 25 |
| 2 | Montreal, Quebec | Easy | Rue St. Denis, Mount Royal | 91 |
| 3 | A day in Montreal | | Parc Olympique, Olympic Tower, Botanical Garden, History Centre, Old Montreal, The Old Fort | 12 |
| 4 | Trois-Rivières, Quebec | Easy | | 79 |
| 5 | Quebec City, Quebec | Easy | Quebec Parliament tour, Citadel, Fort Museum, Château Frontenac, Dufferin Terrace | 74 |
| 6 | A day in Quebec | Easy | Montmorency Falls | 19 |
| 7 | Jackman, Maine | Moderate | | 109 |
| 8 | Waterville, Maine | Difficult | | 91 |
| 9 | Portland, Maine | Moderate | State capitol in Augusta, lobster dinner | 73 |

*Easy = flat to rolling; moderate = hilly; difficult = extremely hilly

# DAY 1

Ottawa, Ontario, to Rockland, Ontario
Terrain: Flat to rolling
40 kilometers (25 miles)

**DIRECTIONS:** East 40 kilometers (25 miles) on Highway 17.

**ACCOMMODATIONS: Best Western Riviera Hotel,** 2950 Laurier, Rockland, Ont., (613) 446-7121. <u>Rooms</u>: 81, double $53. VISA, MC, AMEX.

**CAMPING: Plaisance (Quebec) Camp.** <u>Different route</u>: cross Ottawa River to Hull, Quebec. Take Highway 148 east for 67 kilometers. (819) 427-6974.

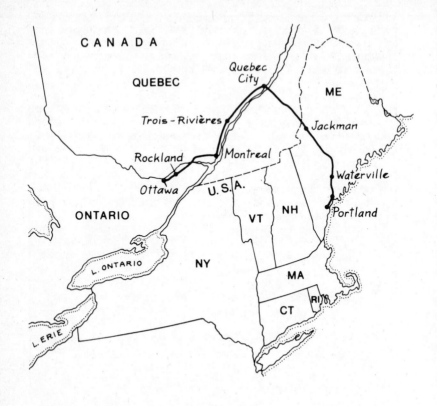

## DAY 2

Rockland, Ontario, to Montreal, Quebec
Terrain: Flat to rolling
Sights: Rue St. Denis, Mount Royal
146 kilometers (91 miles)

Starting the day in Ottawa, we were excited. Everyone in Ontario said the French really know how to party, or, as one guy said, "the Gallic really frolic." All the guys said the women were sexy, and we knew why: the accent. In Ontario, as the population became progressively more French as we went north and east, it seemed to turn plain-Jane women into sexy ones. Our hormones were racing as we headed toward the epicenter of sensuality—Montreal, the biggest French-speaking city in North America.

Crossing the Hawkesbury bridge, we were greeted by a sign reading *"Québec vous souhaite la bienvenue!* Quebec welcomes you." That was the last time English was equal with French for five days, until we rode into Maine, U.S.A. Unlike Ontario, where all signs are in French and English, those in Quebec, Canada's oldest and biggest province, appear only in French. Eighty percent of its 6.5 million people use the language of Jacques Cartier, the French explorer who sailed to eastern Quebec in 1534. Though Britain defeated France 230 years later, the French language stayed.

Just as the sun set, we rode into Montreal's Latin Quarter, a jumble of low-cost ethnic restaurants, sidewalk cafés, reggae bands, students, street people, and an occasional prostitute. The streets were not antiseptically clean like Toronto's; the atmosphere was foreign, exciting, alive.

For a spectacular nighttime view of Montreal, we followed Garnet's advice and climbed up 765-foot-high Mount Royal, our only real hill in weeks. We passed through a ritzy English-Canadian neighborhood on the way up to Parc du Mont-Royal, a beehive of activity hosting Israeli folk dancing, a rock concert, and a soccer game. I spent an hour hunting for a good view of the city lights below.

Unfortunately, I lost Marc and Bob in the process. Heading back to Rue St. Denis alone, I spent the rest of the night in a croissant shop drinking cappuccino with a left-wing radical named Pierre. His main purpose in life, he said, was to seduce English-Canadian women (who, he said, can't resist French men) and to become president of a one-world government ruling over "Planet Love."

---

**DIRECTIONS:** East 56 kilometers (35 miles) on Highway 17 to Hawkesbury. Cross bridge into Quebec, east 62 kilometers (38 miles) on Highway 148 to St. Eustache. Cross bridge onto Laval island. Take Boulevard Sauve and Boulevard St. Martin 19 kilometers (12 miles) in 90-degree arc around half the length of the island to Boulevard des Laurentides. Cross bridge to Île de Montréal. Ride 9 kilometers (5.5 miles) on Rue Berri and Rue St. Denis to Montreal's Latin Quarter.

**ACCOMMODATIONS: Le Montfort,** 1975 Boulevard de Maisonneuve Ouest, corner of Fort Street, Montreal, Que., (514) 934-0916. Rooms: 200, double $54–$89. VISA, MC, AMEX.

**CAMPING: Camping Alouette,** 13 kilometers (8 miles) across Pont Victoria, Highway 20 to exit 105, (514) 464-1661.

---

# DAY 3

A Day in Montreal
Terrain: Flat
Sights: Parc Olympique, Olympic Tower, Botanical Gardens, History Centre, Old Montreal, The Old Fort
Est. 20 kilometers (12 miles)

While I was sitting in my café reading the *Montreal Times,* who pulled up but Marc and Bob. They'd met a family last night who took them to an Expo baseball game, then home. Great—they get a shower and a bed, and I get coffee stains and Planet Love.

They took me to Parc Olympique to see the velodrome, swimming pool, and 72,358-seat, retractable-roofed Olympic Stadium where the Expos play. Then it was back to the riverfront for a walking tour of Vieux Montréal (Old Montreal), the city's first permanent settlement dating to 1642, and the Old Fort on Île Ste.-Hélène (St. Helen's Island). The fort was built in 1820 to protect Montreal against—guess who?—the aggressive Americans. We wolfed down giant balls of brown bread at the historically accurate medieval-style restaurant, whose meals included no forks and spoons.

We were planning on a night out on the town to meet some of the fabled Montreal women, but after climbing Mount Royal again, Bob lost control on the steep descent when he paid too much attention to some teenaged girls trudging up the hill. About to hit a parked car, he jammed on his brakes and did a three-quarter flip over the handlebars.

We spent our last Montreal night in a sterile waiting room, while Bob had his two broken fingers bandaged.

## DAY 4

Montreal to Trois-Rivières
Terrain: Flat to rolling
128 kilometers (79 miles)

Planet Love Pierre had told me that "Quebec City makes Montreal look like Toronto." But Bob's bandaged hand put French Canada's historical and spiritual mecca, 155 miles away, out of the question this day.

Constant tailwinds and flat to rolling countryside made it easy on Bob all the way to Trois-Rivières (Three Rivers), the second-oldest city in Quebec. Founded in 1634 at the junction of the St. Lawrence and the three channels of the St.-Maurice River, Trois-Rivières was a vital way-station halfway between Montreal and Quebec.

It served the same function for us. We got dinner and hit a bar, but soon left when we found no one who spoke English. For the first time, Canada seemed like a foreign country.

**DIRECTIONS:** Highway 138 all day.

**ACCOMMODATIONS: Motels Journey's End,** 6255 Rue Crobell, 2 kilometers north of Laviolette Bridge, Trois-Rivières, Que., (819) 371-3566. Rooms: 100, double $50–$52. VISA, MC, AMEX.

**CAMPING:** None nearby.

★

# DAY 5

Trois-Rivières to Quebec City
Terrain: Rolling and flat
Sights: Quebec Parliament tour, Citadel, fort museum, Chateau
  Frontenac, Dufferin Terrace
120 kilometers (74 miles)

A beautiful, sun-drenched, semi-hilly, tailwind-blowing ride led us to a latter-day Jerusalem—the walled city of Quebec. Though a modern town of 170,000, its old walled section goes back 350 years, when Quebec was the heart of New France. It's a unique world of seventeenth-century Europe—stone walls and gates, old churches and narrow streets, with ancient cannons mounted around its perimeter. We arrived with plenty of time for a walking tour of this once-strategic site.

Perched 350 feet above the smallest choke point of the St. Lawrence River, French defenders would rain cannon fire on enemy ships. But after decades of British attacks, the city fell in 1759 in just half an hour. British general James Wolfe sent his troops up steep cliffs to the Plains of Abraham above Quebec, where they surprised the Marquis de Montcalm and the French—effectively ending French rule in Canada and changing the course of North American history. If the French had prevailed, all of Canada and much of what is now the United States might be speaking French today. And we might have been on a *tour de biciclette*.

Quebec City remains the capital of Quebec Province. After shooting a picture of the ornate Parliament Building, Bob and I walked on the walls (rebuilt after 1820 to defend against *American* aggression), posed with old cannons at the famous Château Frontenac, where Roosevelt and Churchhill met during World War II, then walked up to the highest point on the hill, the Citadel, to catch the changing of the guard. For us, the view was needlessly romantic. Hitting several discos in town that night, we partied till 2:00 A.M., then stumbled back alone to the youth hostel.

---

DIRECTIONS: Highway 138 all day.

ACCOMMODATIONS: **Au Manoir Ste-Geneviève** (Victorian stone mansion behind Château Frontenac overlooking St. Lawrence River), Quebec City, Que., (418) 694-1666. Rooms: 12, double $70–$90. No credit cards.
**Motels Journey's End**, 10 du Vallon (across the St. Lawrence via the Lévis Ferry, 5 kilometers to junction of Route 173 and CAN 20), Lévis, Que., (418) 835-5605. Rooms: 100, $52. VISA, MC, AMEX, DINERS.

CAMPING: **Canadien Camping**, 4030 Boulevard Hamel, 7 kilometers west on Highway 138, (418) 872-7801.

★

## DAY 6

A day in Quebec City including Montmorency Falls
Terrain: Flat to rolling
30 kilometers (19 miles)

After visiting Musée du Fort (Fort Museum) for the history of Quebec, I took a short road trip to the 83-meter-high (265 feet) waterfalls of Chute Montmorency, one and a half times higher than Niagara). I could see how the St. Lawrence River narrowed at Quebec—and why this point was so strategic from a military point of view.

---

**DIRECTIONS:** East 15 kilometers (9.3 miles) on Highway 360 to waterfalls of Chute Montmorency.

---

## DAY 7

Quebec City, Quebec to Jackman, Maine
Terrain: Flat to rolling, then hilly
152 kilometers plus 16 miles equals 109 miles

This day we saw a couple things we hadn't seen since Detroit: the U.S.A. and hills. Though scenic, the rolling, then hilly, country made a long day much longer.

The population thinned out after we ferried across the St. Lawrence to Lévis and headed south down Highway 173 to the border. No one spoke English. On the previous day, lost from my partners during a heavy rain and hiding under a carport, I was invited to spend the night with a family that knew only *one* English word. The bachelor father showed me some mirrors above his bed, laughed, and said, "*Playboy.*" That was better than me; I spoke no French. But his kids stayed up the whole night and taught me *C'est bon!* (This is good), *Quel est ton nom?* (What is your name?), and *Plaisir rencontre vu* (Pleasure meeting you). I even finally learned how to pronounce *pannier:* It's "pan-yer," old-style French for "breadbasket."

International understanding had greatly increased by breakfast. Riding off, I shouted, "*Vive la Québecois!*" as they hummed the *Rocky* theme—my song the last few weeks.

Reunited with my partners a few miles later, we all remarked on what a great time we'd had in Canada—French or English. The sights—both natural and historic, the people, the roads—all were superb. Ah, yes . . . the roads. We all noticed a change—from seamlessly smooth in Canada to cracked and warped on Route 201 of Maine. At least we weren't hassled on the way in. It was good to be home!

After shooting a picture of the unique Peter Max border sign, a painting of mirror-image twins proclaiming "*Bienvenue aux États-Unis*" (Welcome to the United States), we hustled up a big hill about four miles inside the border and toughed out the next rainy dozen miles to tiny Jackman before darkness fell. As luck would have it, in a store we met the son of the owner of the no-vacancy Briarwood Mountain Lodge. A fellow bike rider, he saw to it that we were comfortable in the laundry room.

---

**DIRECTIONS:** Ferry across St. Lawrence to Lévis, south 152 kilometers (94 miles) on Highway 173 to border. South 16 miles on US 201 to Jackman.

**ACCOMMODATIONS: Briarwood Mountain Lodge,** on US 201, Jackman, ME, (207) 668-7756. <u>Rooms</u>: 20, double $110. VISA, MC, AMEX.
**Hillcrest Motel,** 3 miles north of Briarwood, Jackman, (207) 668-2721. <u>Rooms</u>: 13, $34–$37. VISA, MC, AMEX, DINERS, DIS.

**CAMPING: Moose River Campground,** ½ mile north on US 201, 1½ miles east on Nichols Road, (207) 668-3341.

# DAY 8

Jackman to Waterville
Terrain: Extremely hilly
91 miles

Yesterday's rolling hills were just the beginning. The ride today was the hilliest since the Rockies, with constant headwinds to boot. However tough it was, though, it was beautiful—all trees, rivers, and mountains, a branch of the Appalachians called the Longfellows.

Even though over half of the ride is alongside the Kennebec River, the Longfellows pump US 201 up and down like a roller coaster. By the time we reached 18,000-strong Waterville, we were exhausted.

---

**DIRECTIONS:** 71 miles on US 201 to Skowhegan, south 16 miles on SR 104.

**ACCOMMODATIONS: Atrium Motel,** 332 Main, Waterville, ME, (207) 873-2777. <u>Rooms</u>: 102, double $60–$70. VISA, MC, AMEX, DINERS, DIS.

**CAMPING:** Closest is in Skowhegan, **Two Rivers Campground,** 2 miles east on US 2, (207) 474-6482. <u>Amenities</u>: laundry, groceries.

# DAY 9

Waterville to Portland
Terrain: Very hilly
Sights: State capital, lobster
73 miles

The final day was not going to be easy.

More hills. More headwinds. But just when I began getting too depressed, I read an historical sign telling of people who did this route by foot—without paved roads.

In the fall of 1775, 1,100 rebels led by Colonel Benedict Arnold, the notorious turncoat American who later fought for the British in the Revolutionary War, launched an attack on British-held Quebec City across 600 miles of wilderness. After two months of tramping through the rapids, woods, and swamps that are now known as the Benedict Arnold Trail, the surviving 500 were easily beaten back by the British. Maybe Benedict and his boys should have gone by bicycle.

Later, taking a lunchtime siesta at the state capital in Augusta, we were approached by an old man. He told us he was a "maniac."

Huh?

"Like Maine: *Maine-iac,*" he laughed, pronouncing it in that goofy backwoods accent that sounds like Ted Kennedy with too much taffy in his mouth. He then launched into a torrent of Maine trivia—that Maine wasn't one of the original thirteen colonies, since it was actually part of the state of Massachusetts until 1819; that Portland is the largest (61,000) and oldest (founded 1632) city in Maine; that Maine has the biggest and cheapest lobster; that Maine . . .

Wait a minute. Did he say cheap *lobster?* I swear I could still hear the Maine-iac spewing facts and figures forty miles away in Freeport, when we were slowed by hordes of outlet store shoppers hunting for deals at L. L. Bean.

Finally, at 4:14 P.M. on August 16, 1982, on our fifty-third day on the road from Seattle, we saw it—a sign on the right that told us our 4,356-mile odyssey was over: "Entering Portland." And on the left, there was the object of our desire, the goal that had pulled us, day in, day out: the Atlantic Ocean.

Two hours later, a waitress at John Martin's Restaurant put two giant red lobsters each in front of us for $7.95 plus tax.* This was just the beginning of our celebration. After gawking at our cycling shorts, many of the other customers came over and bought us drinks.

That may have been the main lesson we'd learned on our journey: that people become incredibly friendly and generous when they are impressed by something. And, fortunately, many consider a cross-country bike trip to be a most impressive thing.

---

*When I returned to Portland on a tour of Nova Scotia in 1986, John Martin's had closed down. But right on the waterfront, on the long wharf on Commercial Street, is DiMillo's, where two one-pound lobsters go for $16.95 (as of January 1990).

When we went to pay the bill, the owner waved us off. "Congratulations," he said to the two of us.

The *two* of us?

Well, we hadn't seen Marc since Jackman. He was waiting for us in Boston.

---

**DIRECTIONS:** South 21 miles on SR 104 to Augusta (cross river to capitol). South 29 miles on SR 201 to Brunswick. South 23 miles on US 1.

**ACCOMMODATIONS: Budget Traveler Motor Lodge,** 1 Riverside Street, Portland, ME, (207) 775-0111. Rooms: 130, double $42. VISA, MC, AMEX, DINERS, DIS.

**CAMPING: Wassamki Springs Campground,** 855A Saco Street, Westbrook (near airport), (207) 839-4276.

---

# SIGHTSEEING INFORMATION

AUGUSTA, MAINE
**Maine Statehouse and Museum,** on SR 201 (State Street): Free tours 9:00—11:00 A.M., 2:00—5:00 P.M. (207) 289-1110.

MONTREAL, QUEBEC
**Parc Olympique,** Rue Sherbrooke: Velodrome; swimming pool; Olympic stadium, including 77-meter-high (254 feet) Olympic Tower, world's highest inclined tower; fifty-mile panorama; $5. (514) 252-4737.
**Botanical Garden of Montreal,** across from Parc Olympic: World's third biggest; over 26,000 species of plants, 30 gardens, 10 greenhouses; minitrain rides; $3. (514) 872-1400.
**Centre d'histoire de Montréal** (History Centre), 335 rue St.-Pierre: Film, exhibits of Montreal history; Tuesday—Sunday 10:00 to 4:00. (514) 845-4236.
**Vieux Montréal** (Old Montreal), near river between rues McGill and Notre-Dame: City's first permanent settlement in 1642; walking tour brochure free; includes Basilica of Notre Dame, one of North America's largest churches. (514) 871-1595.
**Old Fort on Île Ste-Hélène** (St. Helen's Island), middle of St. Lawrence River via Cartier Bridge: Fort includes 150-year-old maps, barracks, an armory, cannons; daily military parade; $2; a medieval-style restaurant, reservations needed. (514) 879-1141.

PORTLAND, MAINE

**Portland Museum of Art,** 7 Congress Square $3.50. (207) 775-6148.

**Wadsworth-Longfellow House,** 485 Congress Street: Poet's childhood home; $2.50. (207) 774-1822.

QUEBEC CITY, QUEBEC

**Parliament,** Grande-Allée, just outside walls: Thirty-minute tours; 10:00 to 5:30. (418) 643-7239.

**Battlefields Park,** Plains of Abraham, Grande-Allée: Tablets explain the historic battles; Martello Towers have also exhibits. (418) 648-3506.

**Musée du Fort** (Fort Museum), 10 rue Ste-Anne: Exhibits and narrations describe the six sieges of Quebec from 1629 to 1759; $3.50. (514) 692-2175.

**Château Frontenac:** Ornate 1893 hotel where Churchill, Roosevelt, and other World War II allies met twice. (418) 692-3861.

**The Citadel:** Highest point in city; active troops; official residence of Canadian Governor-General; changing of guard, 10:00 A.M., 7:00 P.M., July and August; fifty-minute guided tours; $3. (418) 648-3563.

# CHAPTER 7

## THE CURSE OF
## THE COAST
### SAN FRANCISCO
### TO
### SANTA MONICA

THE COAST.

In bike touring circles, those words usually conjure up dreamy memories of a blissful week touring what the League of American Wheelmen calls "probably the most popular long-distance bike route in the world": the beautiful, uncrowded 486-mile* California coastline from the Golden Gate Bridge in San Francisco to the Santa Monica Pier in the Los Angeles area.**

The Coast has a little bit of everything: cool and favorable ocean breezes and super sightseeing, featuring the charms of San Francisco, the world-class aquarium and scenic seventeen-Mile Drive in Monterey, the old Spanish missions in Carmel and Santa Barbara, the opulent Hearst Castle in San Simeon, and the biggest attraction of them all—Big Sur.

While Big Sur is actually the name of a small river and a contiguous state park, the term has come to represent a stretch of mountainous coastal road south of Carmel that swoops up and down continuously for an astounding *seventy-five miles*. While there are some other notable hills along the rest of the mostly flat-to-rolling route, the biggest chal-

---

*Though it includes the Monterey 17-Mile Drive, 486 is a minimum figure, to be increased by additional riding in San Francisco. It does not include a seven-mile ride to Los Angeles airport.
**Some people extend this trip south another 135 miles to San Diego. The Mexican border is another 20. See Chapter 1.

lenge and real heart of the ride is Big Bad Sur. If you can get through it intact, you can do *any* bike trip. This may be why the Coast is often the first destination that comes to mind for people who are planning their first "serious" bike trip—and also the reason why the Coast often seems like a bicyclist freeway. It is truly the Mecca of bike touring; some of the faithful visit it again and again.

I, for one, have attempted the Coast *four* times, first in the spring of 1979, when Marc and I departed from Los Angeles on our maiden major bike trip. Two weeks earlier, I'd plunked down $168 to buy the "dream" bike I was to use for the next nine years, an orange Schwinn Le Tour III. I outfitted it with a rack and some new contraptions I'd just heard about called toe-clips, which make pedaling more efficient. We strapped down our sleeping bags and headed north up the Pacific Coast Highway.

That was our big mistake.

Heading north, Marc and I had prevailing northerly winds in our face the whole time. We struggled past Santa Barbara at less than ten miles per hour, then almost had to walk through the forty-mile-per-hour head-winds in Gaviota Pass. As we crawled along at five miles per hour about thirty miles north of Lompoc, two fully packed bikers sped by us the other way at *thirty miles per hour*—riding *without* their hands. Marc and I looked at each other with the same thought: this is it. This is no fun. This is bike-touring hell.

We boarded a Greyhound bus in Santa Maria. Disembarking 160 miles later in Salinas, we climbed over to the coast at Carmel on our own power and finished out the last 100 miles to San Francisco. But the ordeal wasn't over yet. Unable to get our pedals off at the airport (they come off in the opposite direction as the pedal stroke), we missed our flight to L.A.

Back home, we told everyone we'd made it, even though we'd cheated. We hadn't done Big Sur. We hadn't done the Coast. We had failed. And in doing so, we'd learned the one major lesson of this route: always ride from north to south.

In the summer of 1983, I left from San Francisco with my other Big Adventure partners, Bob and Martin. All went well until we got to Carmel, where we learned that the great winter storm of 1982–1983 had wiped out several of the Big Sur bridges. Detouring into the blazing Central Valley on US 101, we were fried by temperatures reaching 105 degrees, and finally decided to hitch the 150 miles to Santa Barbara. Back in the cool air of the Coast, we easily finished the ride into Los Angeles. Failure Number Two.

In the fall of 1984, with the bridges repaired, I decided to tackle the Coast on my own. Scraping together a few comp days and a three-day Labor Day weekend gave me five days, so I had to average roughly ninety miles a day. I'd hardly ridden my bike in six months, but I'm never out of shape, and I'd been running and swimming daily. I landed in San Francisco, touched base at the Golden Gate, and headed south.

After three days, I had faced the endless, up-and-down challenge of Big Sur for the first time with gritty determination. Powering up those twisty-turny mountain roads like a man possessed, I passed other bikers

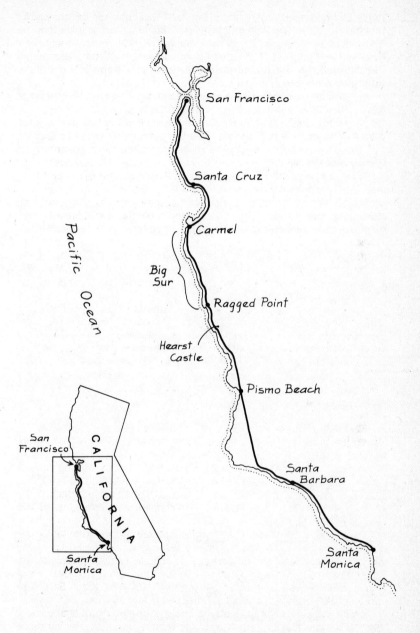

Pacific Ocean

San Francisco

Santa Cruz

Carmel

Big
Sur

Ragged Point

Hearst
Castle

Pismo Beach

Santa
Barbara

Santa
Monica

San
Francisco

CALIFORNIA

Santa
Monica

right and left. I was making great time, and was on schedule, but unfortunately had developed a minor problem: I could no longer walk. And on the bike, it wasn't so good, either. I could not pedal without emitting a horrible moaning sound. Worried about permanent physical damage, I hobbled into the Greyhound station in San Luis Obispo and bought a ticket to Los Angeles.

I had failed a third time—and learned another lesson: don't start off a bike trip at ninety miles a day without warming up.

A month later, I got a new job. Although there were plenty of other places I wanted to tour, I felt that I couldn't pursue them until I'd cast off this albatross, until I'd awakened from this unrelenting nightmare of *coastus interruptus*.

Taking a week off, I flew up to San Francisco yet again. It was colder now; there were few other cyclists on the road. But as long as the bridges were up, I was determined to conquer the Coast—mileage, sightseeing, everything. Once and for all, I was going to exorcise my bike-touring demon. This time, there would be no failure.

### ROUTE SLIP
**Total of 486 miles in 7 days**

| Day | End Point | Terrain* | Sights | Mileage |
|---|---|---|---|---|
| 1 | San Francisco, California | Up to You | Fisherman's Wharf, Lombard Street, Cable Car Museum, Golden Gate Park | 18** |
| 2 | Santa Cruz, California | Easy/Mod. | | 79 |
| 3 | Carmel, California | Easy | Monterey Bay Aquarium, 17-Mile Drive | 67 |
| 4 | Ragged Point, California | Difficult | Big Sur | 71 |
| 5 | Pismo Beach, California | Easy | Hearst Castle, Morro Rock | 66 |
| 6 | Santa Barbara, California | Easy plus Climb | Mission Santa Barbara, County Courthouse | 98 |
| 7 | Santa Monica, California | Easy/Mod | Getty Museum | 87 |

*Easy = flat to rolling; moderate = hilly; difficult = repeated miles of hills and climbing
**Minimum miles from airport to Golden Gate Bridge

★

# DAY 1

### A day in San Francisco

Stepping off the plane on October 8, 1984, for the second time in a month, I felt optimistic about breaking the jinx. Body, bike, and byway were in perfect health. The key was to warm up correctly, *not* to do the big miles right out of the Golden Gate. San Francisco was ideal for this plan. With its modern skyscrapers, eighty-year-old Victorian row houses, cable cars, massive bridges, and million polyglot people perched atop a compact, hill-laden peninsula, the City by the Bay demands to be looked at from every angle.

Two flat tires at the airport delayed me for half an hour, an occurrence I viewed as good luck. "I'll get all the bad stuff out of the way in the first hour," I told myself.

Soon, the sights were coming at me left and right: black kids break-dancing at Pier 39 on Fisherman's Wharf, Chinese guys catching crabs on the Municipal Pier, old Italian men playing boccie ball in Marina Green, Alcatraz Island from the top of Russian Hill, and the Cable Car Museum.

After lurching down the sharply-raked switchbacks of Lombard Street, I trekked north over the two and a quarter-mile-long Golden Gate Bridge to Marin County and climbed up Conzelman Road, the big hill west of US 101. Up was a spectacular vista: the gleaming, white skyscrapers of San Francisco framed perfectly between the Golden Gate's partially fog-enshrouded, 746-foot-high orange bridge towers, the world's tallest. Another view lay half an hour north at Sausalito, where the City's ivory-tinted downtown seemed to be floating on a rolling carpet of gray fog.

After dinner in Chinatown and a cup of Irish coffee at the Buena Vista Café, I made my final checks. The weather was clear, no storm fronts for a thousand miles. My legs felt good, loosened up by the fifty-odd non-stressful miles. The entire day had been perfect.

I'd forgotten completely about those two flat tires.

---

**DIRECTIONS:** From Airport: 13 miles north on Airport Boulevard to Bayshore Boulevard to Third Street. Then take Embarcadero to Fisherman's Wharf.

**ACCOMMODATIONS: Phoenix Inn,** 601 Eddy Street (at Larkin), San Francisco, CA, (415) 776-1380. Amenities: cable car access, pool, massage. Rooms: 44, double $65–$80. VISA, MC, AMEX, DINERS.
**Pensione San Francisco,** 1688 Market Street, near San Francisco Civic Center, (415) 864-1271. Rooms: 36, $45+. VISA, MC, AMEX.

**CAMPING: San Francisco International Hostel,** Building 240 at Fort Mason Center, Bay and Franklin streets, San Francisco, (415) 771-7277.

★

# DAY 2

The Golden Gate to Santa Cruz
Terrain: Flat, one climb and gentle hills
79 miles

By now, having ridden the entire route one way or another, I knew the way by rote. Of course, there wasn't much to know: ride south on Highway 1 virtually all the way. I passed Golden Gate Park, made a 600-foot climb in Daly City, rounded Half Moon Bay, and put it on Santa Cruz-control for the rest of the gloriously sunny day on the gently rising and dipping road. When I arrived in the seaside city, originally a 1791 Spanish mission, it was still warm out. Windsurfers dotted the ocean as I stretched and massaged. My legs felt great; my plan was working.

But emerging from a supermarket after an hour and a half of magazine reading, I flew into a panic. The nightmare of all bike-touring nightmares had happened: my half-inch cable had been cut! My bike, my sleeping bag, my clothes—everything but the camera, keys, and wallet in my hand—was gone!

Stunned, I dropped my groceries and scanned the parking lot, just in time to see a guy lifting my orange Le Tour into a pickup truck!

Luckily, the scrawny teenager was struggling to hoist my cumbersome sixty-pound house-on-wheels into the cargo bed. Running like a wild-eyed pit bull, I slammed into the kid and tackled him to the ground. The truck squealed and the kid ran, leaving me and my bike in a heap on the pavement.

Hobbling back to the store, I noticed that the back tire was flat. What luck! No wonder the thief couldn't ride it away.

As I picked up my severed cable and spilled groceries, fixed the flat, then slowly pedaled to a hotel on my precious Le Tour, I couldn't help but wonder about me and the Coast. Maybe I shouldn't have left my bike unattended so long. And maybe there really was a curse.

---

**DIRECTIONS:** 4 miles to ocean from Golden Gate parking lot. Lincoln Boulevard south under US 101, out of Presidio into Lincoln Park. Left on Legion of Honor Drive, right (west) on Geary/Point Lobos. From Seal Rock: pass Golden Gate Park on Great Highway for 4 miles. Merge with SR 35, Skyline Boulevard. After Daly City hill, go parallel with SR 1 freeway until traffic ends.

**ACCOMMODATIONS: Dream Inn,** 175 West Cliff Drive, Santa Cruz, CA, (408) 426-4330. Amenities: ocean view, on the wharf, pool, Jacuzzi, sauna. Rooms: 164, double $90–$180. VISA, MC, AMEX, DINERS.
**National 9 Motel,** 130 Plymouth Street, (408) 426-4515. Amenities: pool, coffeeshop. Rooms: 17, $57. VISA, MC, AMEX.

**CAMPING: New Brighton State Beach,** SR 1, 4 miles south of Santa Cruz, on bluffs, ocean view, (408) 475-4850.

★

# DAY 3

Santa Cruz to Carmel
Terrain: Flat to rolling
Sights: Monterey Bay Aquarium, State Historical Park, 17-Mile
  Drive
67 miles

New cable in hand, ribs still aching from the parking-lot tackle, I looked forward to an easy ride and sightseeing—exactly what was in store in Monterey.

Monterey State Historical Park taught me that the Spanish, under Sebastián Vizcaíno, landed here in 1602. Father Junípero Serra established a chapel here in 1770, the first European settlement in Northern California. After looking at the barking seals at Fisherman's Wharf and visiting the famed Monterey Bay Aquarium, I fueled up with a frozen yogurt and readied myself for a ride to Carmel on the renowned 17-Mile Drive.

Then I discovered that my bike had been violated yet again. Though still cabled around a tree, its front wheel was smashed—five or six broken spokes, mangled rim, totally unfixable. A parking car must have sideswiped it. The couple who came out to their car soon said it was like that when they pulled in.

Yeah, sure it was.

Did someone say something about a curse?

---

**DIRECTIONS:** 45 miles south on SR 1 to Monterey. Right on Del Monte Avenue to Cannery Row and 17-Mile Drive. In Carmel: Carmel Way, San Antonio Drive.

**ACCOMMODATIONS: Carmel River Inn,** at SR 1 and Carmel River Bridge, Carmel, CA, (408) 624-1575. Amenities: pool. Rooms: 43, double $50. VISA, MC, AMEX.
**Rancho Monterey Motel,** 1200 Munras Avenue, Monterey, CA, (408) 372-5821. Amenities: pool. Rooms: 27, $55–$75. VISA, MC, AMEX.

**CAMPING: Vet's Memorial Park,** Jefferson Street at top of hill, Monterey, (408) 646-3865.

---

# DAY 4

Carmel to Ragged Point
Terrain: Very hilly
Sights: Point Lobos
71 miles

New wheel installed, forty-four dollars and ninety-three cents gone, I did some thinking. Since trouble started whenever I stopped, I decided to limit my pauses to the necessities: photos, water, and *healthy* food. After the 17-Mile Drive, I blitzed through the Carmel art-and-yogurt colony, skipped Carmel Mission, said to be the most beautiful of California's twenty-one Spanish missions, glanced at the strikingly rocky coast and wind-twisted cypress trees, shot a quick picture of sea lions at Point Lobos, then headed for the hills.

And I mean hills. A sign on SR 1 just south of Carmel read "Winding Hilly Road Next 75 Miles." It was Big Sur—a narrow, two-lane highway burrowed into the ocean-plunging, redwood-covered Santa Lucia Range, dangling 200 to 1000 feet above the sea, relentlessly dipping up and down. It would often swoop inland onto majestic canyon-spanning, concrete-arched bridges, some of which were the highest in the world (up to 270 feet) when built in the 1930s.

I remember the day as an epic struggle to build momentum, a struggle for "Big Mo," the term then-Vice President George Bush used to describe his last-ditch victories over Reagan in the 1980 primaries. Big Mo was my goal on the descents, as I plunged into the bottom of the U between the hills at full speed, then barreled out in big gears in hope of topping the successive rise without breaking stride. I'd never quite make it, though, ignoring the spectacular seascapes while furiously switching into lower gears and slowly grinding over the next peak.

After a pit stop for food at Pfeiffer Big Sur State Park, twenty-eight miles south of Carmel, I ran into a hill that all the Big Mo in the world couldn't dent—a 750-footer. Still, after a long descent and another series of climbs had brought me twenty-five miles to a store/lodge at Lucia by the late afternoon, I felt invincible. Despite the hard work, my legs were painless; my plan had worked. So I decided to shoot for the whole enchilada. Blowing by the Kirk Creek Campground, I attacked the last twenty Big Sur miles with everything I had.

Just before sunset, I stopped on the crest of a long hill to see an amazing vision spread out below me: as if by magic, the mountains had dropped away, revealing a lush grassy carpet of gently rolling, wide-open country. My god—I had done it: conquered all of Big Sur in one day!

Flushed with victory, San Simeon just twenty miles away, and a long downhill awaiting, I donned my windbreaker, crouched into an aerodynamic tuck, and streaked downward like a kamakazi skier—a maniacal juggernaut not to be stopped by any force on earth.

Except a golf ball.

I don't really remember if it hurt. All I know is that I suddenly was jerked off my bike by a mighty blow to the temple—and sent wildly sprawling, tumbling, skidding on the highway. Blinded with terror, wondering what had happened, I frantically groped my way off the road. As I lay there in shock, a thirtyish guy ran up. He was out of breath. And he had a golf club in his hand.

"God I'm sorry, God I'm sorry," he babbled. "Are you all right?" Except for a bloody left knee, it turned out I was; my cycling gloves had protected my hands, which had absorbed most of the impact. A helmet might have mitigated the throbbing pain in my temple, which this guy seemed to feel so guilty about. I understood why after he helped me to my feet and walked me down the hill to a small, level bluff. At our feet lay dozens of old golf balls. This idiot was hitting drives off the cliff!

And he was doing it on his honeymoon, no less. He and his bride were staying at the Ragged Point Lodge, just a few hundred feet down the road. Probably due to guilt, he invited me to stay for the night.

Gazing at the awesome view, the three of us sat up talking for hours. He was amazed that I didn't even yell at him. "It doesn't surprise me," I said wearily, describing the curse of the Coast.

---

**DIRECTIONS:** From Carmel: Ocean Avenue to SR 1.

**ACCOMMODATIONS: Lucia Lodge,** 26 miles south of Big Sur, 10 hand-split wood cabins with ocean view, Lucia, CA, (408) 667-2391. <u>Amenities</u>: groceries. <u>Rooms</u>: 10, double $55–$93. CASH ONLY.
**Ragged Point Inn,** 15 miles north of Hearst Castle, (805) 927-4502. <u>Amenities</u>: ocean view, beach access. <u>Rooms</u>: 19, double $84–$94. VISA, MC.
**Big Sur Lodge,** in Big Sur State Park (26 miles south of Carmel), (408) 667-2171. <u>Amenities</u>: cottages, rustic, wooded grounds. <u>Rooms</u>: 61, double $80–$100, deposit needed. VISA, MC.

**CAMPING: Pfeiffer Big Sur State Park,** (408) 667-2315. <u>Amenities</u>: groceries.
**Kirk Creek Campground.** <u>Amenities</u>: water, no showers, no phone.

---

# DAY 5

Ragged Point to Pismo Beach
Terrain: Rolling to flat
Sights: Hearst Castle, Morro Rock
66 miles

Rubbing the knot on my head in the morning, beat up after ninety-two almost-deadly miles yesterday, I wondered what would come next. Attacked by the cows grazing on the hillside?

Fortunately, a gentle cruise over rolling grasslands took my mind off the curse and my aching body. After a few hours of touring William Randolph Hearst's monument to his own grandiose decadence, I soft-pedaled it to Morro Bay for the less ornate Morro Rock, a volcanic plug that pops 580 feet out of the sandy shore like a giant pimple.

When I arrived in San Luis Obispo, the unofficial beginning of Southern California and scene of Failure Number Three a month earlier, I was elated. Despite the bruises and scabs, my legs felt great. Better yet, no big crisis had happened that day—not even a flat. Continuing uneventfully over the last easy miles, passing the wind-sculpted sand dunes of Pismo Beach, I was sure the curse had been broken.

---

**DIRECTIONS:** 57 miles on SR 1 to Morro Bay exit. 4 miles on Main and State Park Road back to SR 1 for 13 miles to San Luis Obispo. Take sideroads in, out of town, 14 miles to Pismo Beach.

**ACCOMMODATIONS: Edgewater Motel,** 280 Wadsworth Avenue, Pismo Beach, CA, (805) 773-4811. <u>Amenities</u>: on beach, pool, laundry, jacuzzi. <u>Rooms</u>: 97, double $55–$80. VISA, MC, AMEX, DINERS, DIS.
**Blue Sail Inn,** 851 Market Avenue, Morro Bay, CA, (805) 772-2766 or (800) 336-0707. <u>Amenities</u>: view of Rock and Bay, fireplaces, whirlpool. <u>Rooms</u>: 48, double $65–$95. VISA, MC, AMEX, DINERS.

**CAMPING: Pismo State Beach,** 2 miles south of city on SR 1, (805) 489-8655.
**Morro Bay State Park,** 1 mile south of SR 1, (805) 772-2560.

---

# DAY 6

Pismo Beach to Santa Barbara
Terrain: Flat to rolling, with one tough climb
Sights: Mission Santa Barbara
98 miles

Heading inland in fog, I glided south through lightly trafficked, level farmland, until hitting a narrow, twisting, climbing road that yanked me onto my toes and pumped my lungs like bellows. The 900-foot climb was only three miles long, but seemed like a lot more. The top, however, made it worth it, as the view of the patchwork-quilt farmlands of the Lompoc Valley below made me feel like Julie Andrews in *The Sound of Music.*

---

**DIRECTIONS:** take SR 1 49 miles to Lompoc. Continue 49 miles to Santa Barbara on SR 1/US 101. Exit on Hollister Street to State Street.

**ACCOMMODATIONS: King's Inn,** 128 Castillo Street, 3055 De La Vina (at State), Santa Barbara, CA, (805) 963-4471. <u>Amenities</u>: pool, free breakfast, jacuzzi, sauna, block from beach. <u>Rooms</u>: 45, double $58. VISA, MC, AMEX, DINERS.

**CAMPING: Carpinteria State Beach,** 12 miles south of Santa Barbara on Palm Avenue, (805) 684-2811. <u>Amenities</u>: groceries, swimming.

A long downhill into Lompoc led to a twisty, 1000-foot climb out of it, but the fourteen-mile rise was so gradual and the tailwinds so perfect that I flew up to the summit at full speed. Following a wild, wind-whipped five-mile downhill joyride through Gaviota Pass to the Pacific Ocean, I streaked over the last thirty miles of rolling shoreline into Santa Barbara in time to stop at the old Spanish mission, grab a nice dinner, and see a movie.

Despite the tough climb and another flat tire, the day was great—free of accident or theft and leaving me within striking distance of Los Angeles. Nothing could keep me from finishing the Coast now.

# DAY 7

Santa Barbara to Santa Monica
Terrain: Flat plus a few hills
87 miles

Driven by anticipation of impending victory and a noon meeting in Ventura with my Big Adventure partner Bob, who was joining me for the final stretch into Santa Monica, I skipped the County Courthouse and its renowned view of the mountain-framed, palm-tree-dotted Santa Barbara area, and blazed down State Street.

Just as I turned south at the beach, a scream of "Watch out!" came from above. It was a hang glider—ready to crash into the tall palms lining Cabrillo Boulevard! At the last second, he caught an up-draft, turned, and landed across the street in a baseball field. Unfortunately, while watching all this, I crashed into a palm tree.

Rubbing the knot on my helmetless head, I didn't feel like crying until I saw my wheel. It looked like a pretzel. The curse was back.

Luckily, Santa Barbara is a bike-crazy town with more bike shops per capita—over twenty in an area of 100,000 people—than any other city in the United States. A quick hitchhike brought me to a bike mechanic who said that the wheel probably wasn't worth saving. Heck, what was another forty-five dollars?

With only forty-five minutes elapsed, I turned south on Cabrillo with the new wheel and saw the hang glider across the street having lunch. I couldn't resist going over, eventually telling him the entire story of the curse of the Coast.

Before I left, he offered me a free hang-gliding lesson if I was ever in Santa Barbara again. "Thanks, anyway," I said, "but hang gliding seems a little too dangerous."

"Oh yeah?" he replied, "After what you told me about your trip, it sounds a hell of a lot safer than bike touring."

I met Bob thirty-five miles later in Ventura, and we rode the last forty-three miles across the Los Angeles County line and the Malibu hills. We celebrated with an hour of peanuts and beer at Gladstone's 4 Fish, a hip oceanfront restaurant at the base of Sunset Boulevard, before finishing the long-awaited four miles to the Santa Monica Pier.

At sight of the famous neon sign arching over the entrance to the pier, I raised my hands in triumph. The curse was over! The Coast, after four tries, was finally conquered. Nothing else could possibly happen, for I lived two blocks from there.

Hopping on the bikes after a half-hour of picture taking, I busted out laughing. My back tire was flat—for the sixth time in a week! "You know," said Bob, "you ought to try Mr. Tuffy, a plastic strip you put on the inside of the tire. I haven't had a flat in years."

As we walked home, I noted this advice—along with the other lessons of the Coast: bring sun block, don't leave your bike unattended too long, get in shape before a trip, take pedals off by turning them the opposite way as the crank, and never ride south to north along the Pacific Ocean.

I knew they had to be valuable lessons. It had taken me four trips and six years to learn them all.

---

**DIRECTIONS:** Down State Street to the beach, south on Cabrillo Boulevard. Right 2 miles on Channel Drive. Go over, then parallel to, US 101 1½ miles on Olive Mill Road. Cross US 101, then bear right 6 miles on Jameson Road, Ortega Hill Road and others. Cross 101, south 4 miles on Carpintaria Avenue. Continue 11 miles south on US 101 shoulder/old highway. Bear right 3 miles on bike path through Ventura. Go 8 miles south on Harbor Boulevard, 1.3 miles on Channel Islands Boulevard, right 2 miles on Ventura Road, 1.2 miles on Hueneme Road, right 5 miles on Naval Air Road, south 36 miles through Malibu on Pacific Coast Highway. Pick up Los Angeles bike path just south of Sunset Boulevard. Ride 4 miles to Santa Monica pier.

**ACCOMMODATIONS: Holiday Inn Bayview Plaza,** 530 Pico Boulevard, Santa Monica, CA, (213) 399-9344 or (800) HOLIDAY. Amenities: pool, sauna, airport shuttle.* Rooms: 310, double $109. VISA, MC, AMEX, DINERS, DIS.

**CAMPING: Leo Carillo State Beach,** 28 miles north on Pacific Coast Highway in Malibu, (818) 706-1310. Amenities: swimming, store.

---

*To ride to Los Angeles Airport, seven miles south of Santa Monica, take the bike path south into Marina Del Rey, then cut south on Lincoln Boulevard.

# SIGHTSEEING INFORMATION

CARMEL, CALIFORNIA
**Mission Carmelo,** 3080 Rio Road: Last home of Father Serra. (408) 624-3600.

MALIBU, CALIFORNIA
**J. Paul Getty Museum,** 17985 Pacific Coast Highway (just north of Sunset Boulevard): Facsimile Roman villa houses Greek and Roman art, American and European art, photos; free. (213) 458-2003.

MONTEREY, CALIFORNIA
**Monterey Bay Aquarium,** 886 Cannery Row: One of biggest in world, with sharks and over 600 other species; total of 5,500 marine creatures, many rarely seen; $7. (408) 375-3333.
**Monterey Jazz Festival,** Monterey County Fairgrounds: In September. (408) 373-3366.
**Monterey State Historic Park,** 20 Custom House Plaza: Eight nineteenth-century buildings that played impressive roles in early California history. (408) 649-2836.
**17-Mile Drive:** Famous Pebble Beach and other golf courses; million-dollar estates; maps available; special bike permit may be required. (408) 624-9585.

SAN FRANCISCO, CALIFORNIA
**Cable Car Museum,** Washington and Mason streets: Functioning power-house, cable car parking lot, exhibits free; 10:00 to 6:00. (415) 474-1887.

SANTA BARBARA, CALIFORNIA
**Mission Santa Barbara,** E. Los Olivos and Laguna streets: Best-preserved of state's twenty-one Spanish missions; $1. (805) 963-4364.
**County Courthouse,** 1100 Anacapa Street: View from top has best view of entire Santa Barbara area; free. (805) 962-6464.

SAN SIMEON, CALIFORNIA
**Hearst Castle (San Simeon State Historical Monument):** Grandiose hilltop palace newspaper mogul William Randolph Hearst began building in 1919; contains sprawling buildings, grand artwork, and gardens; $10; tours on the hour; reservations recommended. (805) 927-3500; (800) 446-7275 in California.

# THE FINAL FRONTIER

## Alaska, the Yukon, and British Columbia

★

FIRST, THERE CAME CHEAP AIRLINE TICKETS. THEN, THERE WAS A forty-five-year-old chain-smoking, potbellied, bald-headed, red-bearded, alcoholic carpenter named Willie.
Those two together produced three chapters of my most adventurous travels by bike: a moderately challenging bicycle-train-ferry loop around the state of Alaska and a two-part 2,200-mile mega-trip from Alaska to Vancouver, British Columbia.

It all started in May of 1984, when my stewardess sister got me two thirty-dollar round-trip tickets.

Knowing a good deal when we saw one, my roommate, Bob (of Big Adventure fame), and I took our bikes to Alaska—for the *weekend*.

On the train to Denali National Park, we met Willie—slurping down his fourth of sixteen screwdrivers—who cycled with us to Fairbanks and was then off on a 500-mile loop around the state. His plan was to make it to the Alaska Pipeline terminal in Valdez, take a ferry cruise past the giant Columbia Glacier, then ride the final fifty miles back to Anchorage. He said that the scenery was so pristine, so beautiful, so remote that it could very well be the most nature-filled route in the world. And he was so excited about the trip that he decided to go "on the wagon."

Therefore, when the airline offered a similar deal the next year, I knew exactly where to go. I grabbed my brother Marc and flew north to complete Willie's Loop.

It was early May of 1985, and it was *cold*. The snow hadn't melted yet, even though it was light until midnight in Fairbanks. If I had to do it again, I'd wait until the summer. In a way, though, the harsh weather lent an already exciting trip an aura of danger that made it even more memorable.

Riding half the time in valleys and half over mountains, we were treated to a bike-riding spectacular: snow-covered ranges, wild animals, the famous pipeline, and the awesome glacier. Although we traversed isolated, empty country, we were actually never more than a day's ride away from civilization, even if it was only a lodge and a gas station. It was a super ride, everything Willie said it would be.

I thought that was it for Alaska until I got a late August phone call from Marc, who had stayed and worked there for the summer. Over the objections of my boss, who threatened to fire me, Marc and I embarked on a once-in-a-lifetime trip—from Anchorage to Vancouver.

This would be no mere tour through cornfields. In Alaska, there are barely a handful of towns on the highways and hardly any people at all outside Anchorage. There are long stretches of nothing, save a telephone pole or two. There are virtually no bike shops from which to get spare parts. There are no 7-Elevens in the entire Yukon Territory, which, as big as Texas, has only 25,000 people—17,000 in Whitehorse. The northern two-thirds of British Columbia is just as sparse. It would just be us, animals, trees, some Indians, and logging trucks. There'd be no room for error. It would be raw adventure, as raw as you could get in North America on a bike with road tires. It was sure to be our greatest adventure on wheels.

And it was.

On September 8, 1985, Marc and I left from Anchorage on Mission: Vancouver, named in honor of the jewel-like city on Canada's Pacific coast, 130 miles north of Seattle. We planned to camp all the way—until we started freezing at night, despite wearing all the clothing we had. Luckily, we were saved a few times when people invited us into their homes. But when we searched for lodging—and found that many of the lodges had shut down for the season—we became desperate, breaking into shuttered lodges, frantically seeking out unlocked windows and doors.

As we headed east for a thousand miles and south for a thousand more, it was a race against the clock—I had three and a half weeks to get back to work—and a race against the sun, for the days grew shorter and colder as sunset arrived ten, fourteen, eighteen minutes earlier each night. The brilliant red and gold splashes of the early northern fall made the white-capped mountain scenery stunning, but it also brought a frightening chill. Usually freezing in the shade until 10:00 A.M., days often didn't go above fifty degrees. Though mountains were all around us, we often begged for hills on the surprisingly flat-to-rolling valley route—just to warm up.

Though Mission: Vancouver was exciting, I'd recommend cycling in the Great North-Northwest only in the middle of summer. In the late spring or early fall, even though the cold weather isn't life-threatening during the day, sub-zero nighttime temperatures and the chance of freezing rain make camping a risk before June 15 and after August 30. In fact, staying in hotels off season may be even less advisable than camping, as many of the lodges are closed until June 1 and after September 1.

Bike riding in Alaska in the summer means sunny, pleasant temperatures, the midnight sun, lots of mosquitos and a mess of soggy tundra. Although roads crowd with Winnebagos and tourist buses, a summer trip eliminates the dangerous cold and converts our life-threatening challenges into scenic cycling adventures.

All three trips of the Final Frontier bike ride series are routed through the pristine, natural scenery that is turning this region into a tourism gold mine.* Several bike-touring companies have flocked to Alaska, too, most of them doing mini-loops from Anchorage to Valdez via Glennallen, then ferrying back to Anchorage. If you run into some groups on the state's few roads, don't let their support vans and tour guides fool you: Willie's Loop is the *only* way to see the state, since it goes to Denali Park, Alaska's main attraction. Once you know about Denali, it is not to be missed.

If you take any of these trips—even in the sunny, warm summertime—you'll experience the kind of adventure that is possible nowhere else on this continent.

---

*With the crowds, many hotel operators in Alaska and the Yukon recommend reservations *months* in advance, a bit extreme. But given a bicyclist's inability to ride an extra thirty miles for open accommodations, call hotels on the route at least several days before expected arrival. Several managers recommended carrying a sleeping bag even if you are not camping, as some would allow sleeping on the lobby floor or hallways for minimal charge if the place is crowded. This way, at least you have a roof over your head.

# CHAPTER 8

## WILLIE'S LOOP AROUND ALASKA

LASKA IS BIG. THE FORTY-NINTH STATE IS BY FAR THE BIGGEST in the Union, over twice the size of Texas and about a fifth the size of the rest of the country. Appropriately, *Alyeska* means "the Great Land" in Aleutian.

My partners and I were constantly reminded of Alaska's vastness as we traveled in a loop from Anchorage into the interior and back by train, bicycle, bus, and boat. Heading north by train. Bob and I passed through the Matanuska Valley, home of the nation's largest cabbages, then got a long look at North America's highest mountain, 20,380-foot Mount McKinley. By bus, we traversed Alaska's vast National Park land and wildlife refuges—larger than all other states have combined—seeing moose, grizzly bears, elk, caribou, and Dall sheep on a tour through Denali National Park. By bicycle, I headed north to Fairbanks with Bob, then southeast toward the Canadian border and southwest to the sea with Marc. We crossed beautiful mountains and came face-to-face with the controversial Alaska Pipeline, the world's longest above-ground pipeline. From Valdez, a half-day ferry cruise took us past the immense Columbia Glacier and some of Alaska's beautiful coastline—of which it has more than the entire continental United States. Finally, a ten-mile train trip and forty-nine-mile bike ride led back to Anchorage.

But there was more to Alaska's enormity than nature. There were also big prices. Since everything must be flown in, costs for food are higher than anywhere else in the country. There were also big dreams:

most of the people we met in Alaska were immigrants—like Willie, who came from Wisconsin fourteen years earlier. There were also big bodies: many Alaskans themselves are oversized, protected by extra layers of fat to ward off the cold winters.

When Secretary of State William Seward paid the Russians $7.2 million for it in 1867, the territory, separated from the rest of the country by Canada and thought worthless by most, was known as "Seward's Folly." Although Russians had hunted for fur and fished there since 1728, most Americans seemed to agree with the critics who said Alaska was all "polar bears and Eskimos."

Then, in the 1880s, gold was struck. Thousands rushed up to Alaska and the Yukon, departing just as fast when the gold was gone. Population returned when the United States military arrived during World War II and surged again with the oil boom beginning in 1957 and the construction of the 800-mile-long Alaska Pipeline in the seventies. Alaska today is home to a little over 500,000 people, clustered in and around Anchorage. The rest of the state remains what it has always been—a frontier.

Even though the bike trip described here took us through the most "civilized" places of Alaska, the lack of population meant that the road itself was often the only thing separating us from total wilderness. In fact, Alaska is so undeveloped that the route here encompasses over half its highway mileage!

Willie's Loop can be ten or thirteen days long, depending on whether you pedal or train to Denali Park. Either way, there's a mandatory ten-mile train ride on the last day from Whittier to Portage, as there is no road from the ferry landing.

If you pedal all the way, the 868-mile route includes three days over ninety miles each and three days over a hundred miles—long riding to be sure, but unavoidable given the spread of accommodations. Despite rugged scenery, the riding isn't difficult, as the highways are mostly flat or rolling and comfortably nestled in valleys. The few big climbs aren't all-morning or all-afternoon affairs. Best of all, the cool, clean summertime air and long hours of sunlight (up to midnight) make the riding sheer pleasure. While summer daytime temperatures can reach eighty-five degrees, the skies can turn rainy and freezing in a matter of a few hours, so don't skimp on protective clothing.

Good weather or bad, I'm sure you'll agree with me on one thing: For variety, for nature, for beauty, for sheer adventure, this trip is BIG.

# DAY 1

Arrival in Anchorage
Terrain: Flat
6 miles

It was a shock to touch down at the airport at 11:00 P.M. and see remnants of daylight! Still, it was pitch dark by the time Bob and I

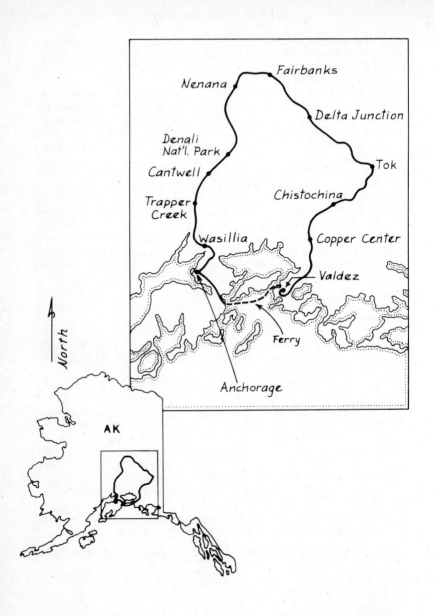

North

Fairbanks
Nenana
Delta Junction
Denali
Nat'l. Park
Tok
Cantwell
Chistochina
Trapper
Creek
Wasillia
Copper Center
Valdez
Ferry
Anchorage

AK

*ROUTE SLIP*
*Total of 868 miles in 13 days*

| Day | Ending Point | Terrain* | Sights | Mileage |
|---|---|---|---|---|
| 1 | Anchorage, Alaska | Easy | Anchorage Museum, Alaska Railroad Depot | 6 |
| 2 | Wasilla, Alaska | Easy | Iditarod Trail Headquarters | 46 |
| 3 | Trapper Creek, Alaska | Easy | | 75 |
| 4 | Cantwell, Alaska | Easy | Best view of Mount McKinley (22 miles north of Trapper Creek) | 95 |
| 5 | Denali National Park, Alaska | Easy | Scenic bus tour, riverboat | 27 |
| 6 | Nenana, Alaska | Easy | The Tripod, *Taku Chief;* | 68 |
| 7 | Fairbanks, Alaska | Moderate | Riverboat Discovery Cruise, First Family, Oldfellows Hall | 55 |
| 8 | Delta Junction, Alaska | Easy | North Pole, Alaska Pipeline | 95 |
| 9 | Tok, Alaska | Easy | | 92 |
| 10 | Chistochina, Alaska | Moderate/Difficult | Mentasta Pass | 91 |
| 11 | Copper Center, Alaska | Moderate | Pipeline Exhibit | 62 |
| 12 | Valdez, Alaska | Difficult | Thompson Pass | 107 |
| 13 | Anchorage, Alaska | Easy | Ferry ride, Columbia Glacier, Prince William Sound | 49 |

*Easy = flat to rolling; moderate = hilly; difficult = repeated miles of hills and climbing

★

slapped the bikes together and pedaled into downtown Anchorage, which reminded me of a typical frontier town, jammed with wooden storefronts, bars, and whorehouses.

Of course, there were modern buildings too, but it still seemed like the Old West, only wetter and colder—much colder. Though almost June, snow was still on the shoulders and the overnight temperature dropped below freezing.

---

**Directions:** From Airport, 6 miles on International Airport Road and Minnesota Drive into downtown Anchorage.

**ACCOMMODATIONS: Sheffield Anchorage Travelodge,** 115 E. 3rd Avenue., Anchorage, AK, (907) 272-7561. <u>Rooms</u>: $90, double $65. Visa, MC, AMEX, DINERS, DIS.

**Anchorage International Hostel,** 700 H. Street, (907) 276-3635.* <u>Amenities</u>: dorms. <u>Cost</u>: $10.

**Camping: Centennial Camper Park,** 8300 Glenn Highway, corner of Muldoon Street, (907) 333-9711.

---

# DAYS 2–5

Since Bob and I were only in Alaska for the weekend, a four-day 243-mile bike ride to Denali National Park was out of the question. We posed for a picture at the eighty-year-old locomotive in front of the Alaska Railroad Depot, then headed for Denali via seven-hour train ride. Much of the way, we had a good view of the road which, like the railway, was flat and slightly uphill along the entire route.

After twenty minutes, all traces of Anchorage disappeared into mountain-framed forests. Swinging west, we soon were in the Matanuska Valley. That's when we met Willie the carpenter.

Ecstatic to have fellow bike riders along, Willie promptly became our tour guide. Matanuska, he explained, is one of Alaska's few productive agricultural areas—despite the short growing season.

"Due to twenty hours of sunlight a day in the summer," said Willie, "Matanuska produces some of the biggest fruit and vegetables in the world. In fact, a farmer friend of mine once gave me a carrot three feet long."

Willie, a Wisconsinite raised on the tall tales of Paul Bunyan, had a

---

*Also information about other Alaska hostels in Willow, Fairbanks, Delta Junction, and Tok. Additional Mission: Vancouver hostels are located in Juneau and Sheep Mountain. Other sources of lodging information included the B&B Association. (Alaska Private Lodgers) at (907) 345-2222 and United States Forest Service Cabins at (907) 345-5700.

story for everything. When the train paused in the historic gold-mining town of Talkeetna, where President Harding drove the "golden spike" that completed the Alaska Railroad in 1923, Willie was telling his tallest one of all: the time he and two Eskimo carpenter buddies began a climb up to the top of Denali, "the High One," or as Americans call it, Mount Mc-Kinley.

"McKinley rises 18,000 feet base to peak, the highest uplift of any mountain in the world, including Everest," he explained. "We were at 16,000 feet when the biggest snowstorm in 132 years hit. It snowed for 64 consecutive days. The only way we could survive was to go underground."

The three climbers lived in an ice cave for seven days until food ran out. With the storm still raging, Willie was left with only one recourse— to eat the other two men.

"It was eat or be eaten," he said sadly. "They were like my brothers. But I'm a big man, and they were starting to look at me like a tasty piece of whale blubber."

Still the storm raged. Forty more days went by. Semi-unconscious, near death, Willie was roused by something tickling the tip of his finger.

"I opened my eyes to see a Dall sheep chewing on my pinky," he said. "Dalls are a special high-altitude sheep, and a family had apparently gotten stranded on the mountain like we did."

After he ate the Dall, he followed a tunnel into a nearby ice cave, where the family had been. It was a graveyard; like the humans, the sheep had eaten each other alive. With enough bones now to fashion a sled, he made it downhill, gave up mountain climbing, and decided to take up bike riding.

How come? we asked.

"It's those big thighs," he said, eyeing mine hungrily. "You never know when they'll come in handy."

Just then, the passengers in our car pointed out the window. It was McKinley—the best view of the High One on the entire trip! About twenty-two miles north of Talkeetna and Trapper Creek, it awesomely towers over the rest of the snowcapped Alaska Range, the tallest of the state's five mountain ranges.

An hour later we rolled through imperceptible 2,300-foot-high Broad Pass, the lowest-traveled pass in the entire Rocky Mountain chain from Mexico to Alaska.

By then, the view of McKinley was long gone, and Willie, who had drained his sixteenth screwdriver and sixty dollars worth of liquor, was completely passed out. For the first time, I noticed Willie's hand. My God! The tip of his pinky was gone!

Bob and I looked at each other with mouths open. No—no way. It was probably a carpentry accident. It had to be. Didn't it?

We arrived at Denali Park, Alaska's number one tourist attraction, just in time to catch a three-hour guided Tundra Wildlife Bus Tour that took us deep into the interior of the huge park, as big as Massachusetts.

As we rumbled over narrow, sharply curving dirt roads out to Polychrome Pass, we saw caribou, wolves, grizzly bears, brown bears, and Dall sheep. When we stopped, moose ambled up to within ten feet. The scenery—mountains, glaciers, tundra, snow-striped peaks and meadows—was like a dream.

But the highlight of the day was the eruption of laughter we got from our guide when we told her Willie's story.

"Nobody for a minute could be fooled by that tale," she guffawed. "It doesn't take a trained zoologist to know that Dall sheep, indigenous to the northernmost latitudes of North America, normally only range as high as 4,500 feet. The highest that one has ever been seen is at 7,000 feet. They would die at anything higher!"

I laughed along with her, looking furtively at my partner. Of course we knew that. Didn't we, Bob?

---

**TAKING THE TRAIN:** The Alaska Railroad leaves daily in the summer at 8:30 A.M. and arrives at 3:20 P.M. in Denali Park. It can also be picked up north of Anchorage in Wasilla and Talkeetna and taken to Fairbanks. Call 1-800-544-0552 or (907) 265-2623. It costs $50 per person plus $10 per bike. Reservations are recommended. By road, it's 243 miles to the north entrance to Denali. Mount McKinley can be seen both from the train and the road. Denali can be toured by helicopter as well as bus.

**TAKING THE FERRY:** The ferry ride from Valdez to Whittier on the state-run Alaska Marine Highway on the last day of the trip is a major highlight. Departing at 7:30 A.M. and arriving at 2:30 P.M., the ferry **does not run on Wednesday or Thursday in the summer.** It costs $54 per person, $6 per bike. 1-800-642-0666. Reservations not usually required. Departure time on the mandatory train from Whittier to Portage is 3:30 P.M. daily. It costs $7.50 for body and bike.

# DAY 2

Anchorage to Wasilla
Terrain: Flat, gentle rollers
46 miles

---

**DIRECTIONS:** From waterfront, northeast 35 miles on 4th Avenue/Post Road/Glenn Highway (SR–1). 4 miles past Matanuska River bridge and Matanuska, turn west 7 miles on George Parks Highway (SR 3) to Wasilla.

**ACCOMMODATIONS: Mat-Su Resort Hotel,** 1.3 miles off SR 3, Wasilla, AK, (907) 376-3228. <u>Amenities</u>: overlooks lake, restaurant, boat rentals. <u>Rooms</u>: $25, deluxe double $95, economy $31. VISA, MC, AMEX, DIS.

**Yukon Don's B&B,** (907) 376-7472. <u>Rooms</u>: 6 units, $40 each. Cash or traveler's checks only.

**CAMPING: Big Lake East & South State Recreation Site,** 10 miles up SR 3, no phone. <u>Amenities</u>: canoe rentals, swimming, no showers.
**Youth Hostel,** near Willow, (907) 276-3635.

# DAY 3

## Wasilla to Trapper Creek or Talkeetna
## Terrain: Slightly uphill
## 75 miles

**DIRECTIONS:** SR 3 all day. For Trapper Creek, cross Susitna River bridge. For last chance of railroad connection to Denali Park, bear right at bridge for 15-mile spur to Talkeetna. There is no bridge across river to Trapper Creek; backtrack required.

**ACCOMMODATIONS: Cash Creek Lodge,** Trapper Creek, AK, (907) 733-2401. <u>Amenities</u>: view of Mount McKinley, barbeques. <u>Rooms</u>: 8 units, 2 cabins; double $45–$65. No credit cards.
**Swiss-Alaska Inn,** near boat launch in East Talkeetna, AK, (907) 733-2424. <u>Rooms</u>: 14, double $90. VISA, MC, AMEX.
**Fairview Inn,** Talkeetna, (907) 733-2423. Historic "golden spike" site. <u>Rooms</u>: 7 units, double $25. No credit cards.

**CAMPING:** Ask at hotels.

# DAY 4

## Trapper Creek to Cantwell
## Terrain: Flat, slight rise
## 95 miles

**DIRECTIONS:** SR 3 all day.

**ACCOMMODATIONS: Reindeer Mountain Lodge,** Cantwell, AK, (907) 768-9262. <u>Rooms</u>: 11, double $65, reservations usually necessary. VISA, MC, AMEX, DINERS, DIS.

**CAMPING:** Ask at Lodge.

## DAY 5

Cantwell to Denali National Park
Terrain: Flat
A Day in Denali
27 miles

---

**DIRECTIONS:** SR 3 all day.

**ACCOMMODATIONS: Denali National Park Hotel,** next to train depot 1½ miles west on Park Road from SR 3, (800) 344-8485 or (907) 276-7234. Rooms: 100 units, double $95; railroad sleeper cars $15. VISA, MC, AMEX.

**CAMPING: Riley Creek Campground,** park entrance, (907) 683-2294.

---

## DAY 6

Denali Park to Nenana
Terrain: Flat
Sights: *Taku Chief,* Tripod
68 miles

In the morning, Willie laughed when Bob and I reported our Dall sheep data.

"I always tell that story when I'm drunk—which is all the time," he said. "I'm an alcoholic, like about half the people in this state."

Indeed, after a slightly uphill rivergrade rise past melting snows, the three of us rolled into Nenana, a little town of 700, to find almost everyone drunk.

The three bars were jammed to the gills with screaming partiers. People were walking rubbery-legged all over the streets. Two of them, a white guy and an Athabaskan Indian who introduced themselves as the Odd Couple (whites and Athabaskans normally don't mix, they said), walked up carrying a six-pack of beer each. When I asked them what was going on, they looked at me as if I was an idiot.

"Why, it's summer!" they exclaimed.

When I turned to Willie for an explanation, he waved me off. "I'll see you tomorrow." He walked off to his room completely sober, leaving us with another mystery to ponder.

We followed the Odd Couple out to a grassy lawn in front of town. There sat a sixty-foot-long red and white wooden tugboat called the *Taku Chief,* which we climbed into and began drinking beer.

"To understand the Alaska interior, ya gotta know that the rivers were our outlets to the world," the white guy explained. "That's why the *Chief* is the second most famous thing in this town. It brought prospectors in the 1890s Klondike Gold Rush and was the last working tug to ply the Yukon and Tanana River basin."

What was the first most famous thing?

"The Tripod," he said, pointing to a twenty-five-foot-tall Tinkertoy of steel tubes down the street. "Eighty years ago, twenty Nenanans awaiting the spring thaw decided to have a contest. First, they set a giant tripod on the frozen Nenana River and rigged it to a blaring siren and a huge clock. Then they each wagered two dollars on the date when the ice would break and set off the siren. The closest estimate won the pot of forty dollars." Since then, the annual "Ice Classic" pot had grown a bit— $156,000 that year.

Our next stop was the Odd Couple's favorite bar, The Beaver Hut. At midnight, even though it was still light and warm (since we were further north than before), we finally went to sleep. Our pals were still going strong.

When we awakened six hours later, they were still partying! In fact, half the people from the night before were drinking away.

The Odd Couple explained that the lack of sunlight in the winter and the wealth of it in the summer does funny things to Alaskans—like turning them into a bunch of manic-depressives. Gloomy in the dark days, they go to bed early and drown their sorrows in alcohol. When the sun finally comes out, they become so overwhelmed with joy that they stay up all night getting drunk.

---

**DIRECTIONS:** SR 3 all day.

**ACCOMMODATIONS: Corner Bar,** Front and A Streets, Nenana, AK, (907) 832-5489. <u>Rooms</u>: 8 units, double $43, hostel $26. Cash or traveler's checks only.

**Nenana Inn,** 623 A. Street, (907) 832-5238. <u>Rooms</u>: 4 units, $50 each. VISA, MC.

**CAMPING:** Lawn of *Taku Chief.*

---

# DAY 7

Nenana to Fairbanks
Terrain: Hilly
Sights: Riverboat Cruise, First Family, Oldfellows Hall
55 miles

After a vigorous, mountainous workout, Bob, Willie, and I arrived in another famous river city, Fairbanks, an old gold rush boom town of 25,000 known as the "Capital of the Interior."

Willie explained that the nickname comes from its position on the Chena River, which gave the local steamships easy access to the mighty

Yukon at the turn of the century. Since riverboats are to Fairbanks what railroads are to Chicago, Willie invited us to join him on an afternoon riverboat cruise, which would take us upriver to the lands of trappers, fishermen, dog mushers, and natives.

We wanted to go, but our three-day adventure was over. At Fairbanks International Airport, we bid farewell to both Willie and the Odd Couple, who followed us into town. I figured that this trip would shut the book on Alaska.

Just before we left, however, I asked how come Willie, an alcoholic, didn't drink with us the night before?

"Yesterday I started taking my anti-alcoholic pills," he answered, reaching into his pocket for a small vial. "They'll cause me to get violently sick if I drink alcohol. This bike trip I'm taking around the state is filled with so much natural beauty that I want to appreciate it cold sober."

With that testimonial, even from a storyteller like Willie, I knew the trip must be great. If I ever got the chance, I vowed, I'd be back.

---

**DIRECTIONS:** SR 3 all day.

**ACCOMMODATIONS: Tamarac Inn Motel,** 252 Minnie Street, Fairbanks, AK, (907) 456-6406. <u>Rooms</u>: 18, double $50. VISA, MC, AMEX, DINERS, DIS.

**CAMPING: Road's End RV Park,** 6½ miles south on SR 2, (907) 488-0295.

---

# DAY 8

Fairbanks to Delta Junction
Terrain: Flat, rolling
Sights: North Pole, view of the Alaska pipeline
95 miles

I got the chance eleven months later, courtesy of more cheap airline tickets. But when I stepped off the plane at 10 A.M. on May 4, 1985, it was a whole different bike trip.

This time I had an entire week—and a new partner. But Marc wasn't the same "I'll never stop" 2,000-mile-a month cycle-maniac of the Big Adventure three years earlier. He had mellowed. He only did 500 miles a month now. He had a camera now, and even spoke of seeing the sights. That was good.

But the next change was the weather—and that was bad. We were faced with parka-grade temperatures, a world blanketed by snow, and a journey that had no big cities or reassuring national parks ahead. Shoving off southeast on the Richardson Highway (SR 2), we seemed to be pedaling off into frigid nothingness. The thought was both exhilarating and frightening.

After stopping within the first hour at North Pole, a made-for-souvenirs town that receives thousands of letters at Christmas time, we spent all day alone in the Tanana River basin. Our only companions were lake-dotted meadows, forests of thin trees, and the powder-dusted mountains of the Alaska Range far to the south.

Just before Big Delta came our first look at the famous Alaskan Pipeline. Its fame is well-deserved: eight-hundred-miles long, three and a half years in the building, daily capacity of one and a half million barrels of oil. We got off our bikes and walked up the Tanana River until we were under the pipeline, suspended thirty feet over the river on its own bridge. Although just a big piece of plumbing hoisted aloft by cables and guidewires, it struck an unusual, artistic presence—like a mini-Golden Gate Bridge—that kept us gazing in awe for about an hour.

---

**DIRECTIONS:** Southeast on SR 2 all day.

**ACCOMMODATIONS: Kelly's Motel,** downtown Delta Junction, AK, (907) 895-4667. <u>Rooms</u>: 18 kitchenettes, $55–$85 each. VISA, MC.

**CAMPING: Quartz Lake Recreation Area,** 11 miles north of Delta Junction, milepost 1433. No showers, no phone.

---

# DAY 9

Delta Junction to Tok
Terrain: Flat, rolling
92 miles

Just out of town we saw an immense, fifteen-foot-tall white milepost marking the end of the Alaska Highway, a 1,519-mile road starting in Dawson Creek, British Columbia. When the Japanese occupation of the Aleutian Islands made Alaska a World War II battlefront, the U.S. Army completed the Alcan (Alaska–Canada) in an astonishing eight months and twelve days.

When the first convoy of trucks rolled in late October, 1942, one of the worst-ever winters kept their average speed on the then-gravel road to twelve to fifteen miles per hour—about as fast as we were traveling by bike.

Closer to the mountains now than the day before, their snowy ridges seemed close enough to touch—and their cold, pure breath chilled us. We saw frozen lakes, were briefly snowed on, and ran across fewer than ten people or cars all the way to Tok, a tiny town founded as a construction camp for Alcan workers.

Known as Alaska's Gateway, since it is virtually the last stop before Canada, Tok unfortunately had no open stores when we arrived, so we couldn't buy tights. Thereafter, Marc rode in jeans, which I found uncomfortable. I braved it on bare legs, which were okay if I kept moving. And I rather enjoyed the reaction when people saw a guy walk in wearing a ski jacket, down vest, ski gloves, and cycling shorts.

---

**DIRECTIONS:** SR 2 all day. Do not turn south on SR 4.

**ACCOMMODATIONS: Golden Bear Motel,** mile 124 Glenn Highway, ¼ mile south on Tok cutoff (SR 1), (907) 883-2561. Amenities: pan for gold. Rooms: 41, doubles $60–$70. VISA, MC, AMEX.

**CAMPING: Tok/KOA Campground,** Alcan milepost 1315, 1 mile west on SR 2, (907) 883-2291. Amenities: laundry, restaurant, lounge.

---

# DAY 10

Tok to Chistochina
Terrain: Moderate climbs
91 miles

Turning south, Marc and I began a three-day ride to the sea through a stunning land of mountains, lakes, and rivers. But before we got out of town, we stopped to pose on Tok's mascot, Bucky the Moose, an eight-foot-tall stuffed moose with Dumbo-ear sized antlers. Bucky's size was typical of a 1,400-pound Alaskan bull moose, the largest of its kind on earth.

The Tok Cutoff took us south into the heart of the Alaska Range, rising a not-so-tough thousand feet over 2,434-foot Mentasta Pass. Even though I wasn't sweating a bit, I was pumping out frost like a locomotive and was thankful to have the rugged terrain to warm me up. It was much, much colder in the higher elevation, and my knees began to rattle like ice cubes.

Everything but the road was covered with snow. The frozen rivers had just a hint of thaw, with tiny liquid streams running down the middle. The total lack of traffic gave me the feeling that we were alone in some sort of wintry paradise.

After sixty-four miles, we stopped at the Slana Ranger Station, where we met a tight-lipped handyman. Hesitantly, he revealed that he lived alone in a small cabin back in the woods that had no heat, running water, or electricity. He had moved to Alaska several years earlier from Idaho, where he complained that there were "too many people."

*Idaho?*

"Yeah, and it's gettin' like that here, too," he monotoned menacingly.

Marc and I looked bug-eyed at each other and hastily plunged back onto the snow-banked highway. Occasionally glancing over our shoulders, we rode as fast as we could over the next twenty-seven mountainous miles to the lodge and trading post at Chistochina. The woman at the desk gave us a big hello and a smile, something we both needed more than we'd admit.

---

**DIRECTIONS:** South on SR 1 (Tok Cutoff) all day.

**ACCOMMODATIONS: Chistochina Lodge,** Chistochina, AK, (907) 822-3366. Rooms: 16, double $40. Advises reservations week in advance. Cash or traveler's checks only.

**CAMPING:** Roadside rest 8 miles south.

---

## DAY 11

Chistochina to Copper Center
Terrain: Hills, flat, hills
Sights: The Pipeline
62 miles

The first half of the ride rolled us up and down along lakes and wooded valleys, sandwiched between the Alaska Range to the north and the Wrangell Mountains to the southeast. After a flat stretch, we rode on a hilly forested ridge for the day's last fourteen miles to the Gold-Rush era Copper Center Lodge, the last lodge north of Thompson Pass. But as pretty as the scenery was, it isn't what stands out.

Walking on the Alaska Pipeline—now, that stands out.

The pipeline, which we began shadowing all the way to its seaside terminal at Valdez, came into view in the flat Glennallen area. We could see it zigzagging about fifteen feet off the ground like a massive snake, supported on giant H-shaped building girders.

---

**DIRECTIONS:** South 33 miles on Tok Cutoff (SR 1). Merge with Richardson/Pipeline Highway (SR 4) and continue south.

**ACCOMMODATIONS: Copper Center Lodge,** Copper Center, AK, (907) 822-3245. Rooms: 18, double $50 (reservations recommended by March 1). VISA, MC, DINERS.
**Caribou Motel,** mile 187 Glenn Highway, Glennallen, AK, (907) 822-3302. Rooms: 45, double $39–$48. VISA, MC, AMEX, DINERS, DIS.

**CAMPING: Squirrel Creek State Recreation Area,** milepost 80, 20 miles south of Copper Center.

---

The zigzag, a visitor's display near the pipeline told us, provides flexibility for earthquakes and expansion/contraction under extreme weather variations (from eighty-plus degrees in the summer to minus-eighty degrees in the winter). The aboveground setup keeps the warm oil from thawing the permafrost.

Despite explicit warnings to keep off the pipeline "for your safety," I have a picture in my photo album of Marc posing with his bike *on top* of it. Of course, I always tell people that we rode our bikes on the pipeline—and when they don't believe me, I show the picture. The reaction is worth the full hour we spent to get that one shot.

# DAY 12

Copper Center to Valdez
Terrain: Mountain climb, long downhill
107 miles

Marc's derailleur broke early in the morning, so he had to hitchhike into Valdez. In doing so, he missed the ride of his life.

After a wild downhill in Tonsina at the Copper River, the road headed inland as dark clouds formed overhead. The longer I rode, the colder, darker, and more mountainous it became. As the road began winding and twisting through the Chugach Mountains, the snow on the ground went from patches to blankets.

When I stopped at a tiny store—the last one on the mountain, as it turns out—the cashier was incredulous. "You're climbing Thompson Pass—in shorts?" she asked.

Not for long, as I soon put on my rainsuit in the increasingly dense mist. A long climb led me to a sign reading, "Avalanche Area Next 7½ Miles. Do Not Stop."

In the time it took to shoot a picture of that sign, the weather got colder—so cold that the dense mist turned into ice, which hurt my throat when I inhaled. But my worrying didn't start until several miles later, when the sky suddenly became a howling, wind-blown canopy of grayish white.

Later, I was told I'd passed right by the massive Worthington Glacier, but at the time I couldn't have cared. I was in the middle of a massive white-out; all I could see was a wall of white on each side and about thirty feet of disappearing pavement ahead.

When I made it to the top of Thompson Pass, I felt like it was 27,000 feet, not 2,700. My nose was numb. My kneecaps were numb. My fingers were numb despite the gloves, and got more numb when bared to set up a victory photo. I stepped off the side of the road and sunk three feet in snow. Seeing nothing ahead but a slope, I put on my ski goggles (yes, goggles) and lowered into an aerodynamic tuck. And for the next fifteen bone-chilling miles, I hung on for dear life as the sky cleared and the road switchbacked through narrow canyons, rocky peaks, huge ice flows, and raging waterfalls.

The exhilarating descent bottomed out in Keystone Canyon, a lush green river gorge heading another flat ten miles into Valdez. When it was over, I could understand why some people refer to mountain-ringed Valdez as the "Switzerland of Alaska." Officially, the city calls itself "The Gateway to the Interior," being a main ice-free port that gold diggers steamed through on their way to the goldfields.

I soon found Marc, who had fixed his bike and spent the entire day scoping out the town. Since it was early season, and the next ferry wasn't leaving for thirty-six hours, he guided me the next day to the Valdez Heritage Center Museum and the Pipeline terminal on the south bank of the bay. We posed with the dramatic *Pioneers of the Oilfield,* a statue dedicated to the 65,000 workers who built the pipeline, then watched a supertanker being loaded.

---

**DIRECTIONS:** South on SR 4 all day.

**ACCOMMODATIONS: Westmark Valdez Hotel,** 100 Fidalgo Drive (next to boat harbor), Valdez, AK, (907) 835-4391. <u>Rooms</u>: 97, double $70–$120. VISA, MC, AMEX, DINERS, DIS.

**CAMPING:** none. A number of inexpensive rooms cater to fishermen, oil workers, and, in at least one case, bike riders.

---

# DAY 13

Columbia Glacier ferry ride
Portage to Anchorage bike ride
Terrain: Flat
49 miles

This day, for the only time in my life, I rode four different modes of transport in twenty-four hours: ferry, train, bike, plane.

Leaving at 7:30 A.M., our seven-hour cruise on the Alaska Marine Highway took us by the Columbia Glacier, a twenty-mile-long, 250-foot-high, four-mile-wide river of ice spilling into Prince William Sound from the Chugach Mountains. Our ferry steered up through a minefield of icebergs, 14 million tons of which "calve" (break off) Columbia every day. We could hear the newborns' first cries.

After Columbia, there was nothing to do for several hours but gawk at yelping seals and gab with the other tourists, mostly senior citizens. One of them, an old guy named Griff from Tallulah Falls, Georgia, told me a great bike trip would be a route through the Appalachians near him called the Blue Ridge Parkway, a trip I filed away for future use.

Arriving in Whittier,* one of many Alaska towns without a road con-

---

*Ferries also available to Seward, which adds another 79 miles to the ride into Anchorage.

nection, we took the Alaskan Railroad shuttle ten miles to Portage, then pedaled to Anchorage. The flat ride was pure pleasure, going by snow-capped mountains, rocky mountain walls and the waters of the Cook Inlet's Turnagain Arm, which got its name from Captain Cook's fruitless zigzagging search for the legendary Northwest Passage two hundred years ago. Supposedly, he kept telling his crew to "turn again."

As we turned into the airport, my trip to Alaska came full circle. Using every available means except dogsled, I'd seen the tallest mountain on the continent and rare animals that live nowhere else, walked on the Alaska Pipeline, and survived a sub-zero wind-chill in shorts—all due to a story-telling, potbellied, alcoholic carpenter, who also happened to ride a bike.

---

**DIRECTIONS:** From Portage, SR 1 north 49 miles to airport.

# SIGHTSEEING INFORMATION

ANCHORAGE, ALASKA
**Anchorage Museum of History and Art,** 6th Avenue and A Street: Displays Eskimo art objects. Tuesday–Saturday 10:00 A.M.–6:00 P.M., Sunday 1:00– 5:00. (907) 343-4326.
**Alaska Railroad Depot:** Totem poles and eighty-year-old locomotive in front; 1 (800) 544-0552 or (907) 265-2623.

DENALI NATIONAL PARK, ALASKA
**Tundra Wildlife Bus Tour:** Free three-hour guided tours conducted all day long; inquire at Denali National Park Hotel, next to train depot. (800) 344-8485 or (907) 276-7234.
**Denali Raft Adventures;** (907) 683-2234. **McKinley Raft Adventures;** (907) 638-2392: Scenic and whitewater floats.

FAIRBANKS, ALASKA
**Tourist Information Office,** 550 First Street: Includes unknown First Family statue, Oldfellows Hall, a vintage goldminers' bathhouse, Clay Street Cemetery. (907) 456-5774.
**Gold Dredge No. 8,** Mile 9, Old Steese Highway: Giant gold-digging ship operated 1930 to 1958; tour includes gold panning. (907) 457-6058.

VALDEZ, ALASKA
**Alaska Marine Highway Ferry;** departs 7:30 A.M., arrives in Whittier 2:30 P.M.; $54 plus $6 bike. 1 (800) 642-0066.
**Pipeline Terminal,** Alyeska Pipeline Service Company, south side of bay: Includes Pioneers of the Oilfield monument; bus tour departing from lobby of Westmark-Valdez Hotel; $15. (907) 277-5581.

**Valdez Heritage Center Museum,** Centennial Building at Egan and Chenega drives: Exhibits of pioneers, gold-seekers, pipeline; free. (907) 835-2764.

WASILLA, ALASKA

**Iditarod Trail Headquarters,** just south of Wasilla: Headquarters, starting line for grueling, 1,000-mile Iditarod Trail Sled-Dog Race, held each March; displays of dogsleds, musher's clothing, video highlights of the race; free. (907) 376-5155.

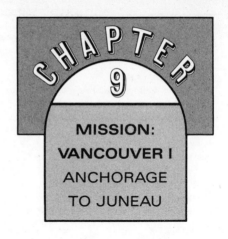

BICYCLING AROUND ALASKA IS ONE THING. BUT BICYCLING *HOME* from Alaska, my brother's bright idea, was a whole different animal. First of all, it's a much bigger animal. Isolated Anchorage lies almost as far west as Hawaii and as far north as Helsinki, Finland. That makes the instructions simple: first go a thousand miles east. Then go a thousand miles south. Add another twenty percent for bends in the road, and you'll end up near the U.S.–Canada border—and civilization. The total, not including 200 miles of gravel roads, is 2,197 miles.

This animal is also a wilder one. Alaska looks civilized next to the Yukon and northern British Columbia. The Yukon Territory, a big piece of frozen real estate just east of Alaska, is shaped like Idaho on steroids and contains only 25,000 people—17,000 of them in Whitehorse. Gargantuan British Columbia, resembling *California* on steroids, isn't much better. Its northern half is empty, save a few Indian tribes and logging trucks.

Mission: Vancouver is not a sightseeing tour like others in this book. There aren't any renowned buildings or promenading actors dressed in seventeenth-century military uniforms. Like Willie's Loop, the natural beauty of the land was astounding—even more so since we rode in September, when the relentless mountains, rivers, and forest were splashed with the flaming yellows and oranges of fall. But unlike Willie's Loop, there are no grand natural attractions—no Mount McKinley, no Columbia Glacier. In fact, we weren't remotely familiar beforehand with anything except Vancouver.

As a result, more than on any other trip, we felt not like tourists or even explorers—but survivalists. Our sole purpose was to get to the end—and hope we'd survive this harsh, vast, cold, beautiful, empty, unknown hunk of the continent. On other trips, I've felt like I was heading out to sea. When we pushed off from Anchorage on September 6, 1985, I felt like we were heading off to outer space.

Though desolate, Mission: Vancouver wasn't difficult because of its terrain—flat and rolling valleys, with occasional moderate climbs over passes and out of river canyons. It was made difficult by life-threatening, late-season cold weather. While the cold did contribute to the adventure, it is something I'd avoid again at all costs.

To make the long tour practical for most people, it's been split into Mission I and Mission II. Divided into two sections, the tour becomes more interesting, adding historic Gold-Rush towns and a scenic ferry ride in Alaska's renowned Inside Passage.

## ROUTE SLIP
### Total of 853 miles in 13 days

| Day | Ending Point | Terrain* | Sights | Mileage |
|---|---|---|---|---|
| 1 | Anchorage, Alaska | Easy | | 6 |
| 2 | Palmer, Alaska | Easy | Russian Cemetery | 42 |
| 3 | Long Rifle Lodge | Easy | Matanuska Glacier | 59 |
| 4 | Tolsana Creek, Alaska | Moderate | Eureka Summit | 71 |
| 5 | Chistochina, Alaska | Easy/Moderate | Alaska Pipeline | 62 |
| 6 | Tok, Alaska | Moderate | | 91 |
| 7 | Beaver Creek, Yukon | Moderate | | 113 |
| 8 | Burwash Landing, Yukon | Easy | | 105 |
| 9 | Haines Junction, Yukon | Easy/Diff. | Kluane Lake, two summits | 75 |
| 10 | Whitehorse, Yukon | Moderate | Klondike II, MV Schwatka | 98 |
| 11 | Carcross, Yukon | Moderate | | 39 |
| 12 | Skagway, Alaska | Easy | Days of '98, Soapy Smith Lives | 64 |
| 13 | Juneau, Alaska (via ferry) | Easy | Inside Passage ferry ride, Juneau Ice Fields, Mendenhall Glacier, Alaska State Museum | 30 |

*Easy = flat to rolling; moderate = hilly; difficult = repeated miles of hills and climbing

★

Mission I, the short section at 853 miles, starts from Anchorage and goes northeast to Tok, repeating a small part of Willie's Loop, then angles southeast into Canada on the Alaska Highway. Stopping at the Yukon capital of Whitehorse, it turns 108 miles due south on the Klondike Highway to the old seaside Alaska Gold Rush town of Skagway.

At this point the bike ride ends and a very scenic ferry ride through Alaska's fjord-strewn Inside Passage begins.* A six-hour cruise down the

*The Inside Passage Ferry to Juneau can also be reached via the Haines Highway to Haines, but a forty-mile stretch of dirt makes it best to continue southeast on the Alcan to the entirely paved Klondike Highway.

panhandle stops in Juneau, where the trip can either end or continue for two extra days to Seattle. A flight to Anchorage will catch the round-trip home.

Next chapter's Mission II has more miles, fewer lodges, and more difficult conditions—including a long stretch of gravel. But let's see if you get through Mission I first!

# DAY 1

Arrival in Anchorage
Terrain: Flat
6 miles

I was more worried about this trip than any I'd done before.

First, I was shocked when I saw Marc. He was fat. His once-granite Frankencycling thighs were jiggling like Jell-O. Four months of working as a telephone operator in the whale-blubber culture of Alaska had added twenty-five pounds to his frame. Our route demanded 110-to-120-mile days if we were going to make it in time for me to return to work. I had hoped to see Mind-Control Marc, the Zen-reading zealot of the Big Adventure—not *this*.

Beyond Marc's weight came a more basic worry: that we'd freeze to death. The trip four months earlier was cold, but dry. Now, we were plunging into the rainy season. This time, there would be no shelter to duck under, and being late in the season, with the midnight sun a distant memory, getting wet could freeze us to death. For the first time on a bike trip, I was plain scared.

We spent the day stocking up: wool socks, wool long-johns, rain suits, whole-leg tights, and mink oil, which we hoped would waterproof our shoes. I got my head together, too, finding a very valuable army surplus item: a World War I Swedish tank helmet. While it made me look like a black leather Conehead, it kept my ears covered and my head warm—an important consideration since much body heat is lost through head, hands, and feet. A normal helmet and regular cycling gloves don't do the trick. Covered from head to toe with wool, polywick and mink oil, I thought I was ready for the elements.

---

**DIRECTIONS:** From airport, 6 miles on International Airport Road and Minnesota Drive into downtown Anchorage.

**ACCOMMODATIONS: Sheffield Anchorage Travelodge,** 115 E. 3rd Avenue, Anchorage, AK, (907) 272-7561. <u>Rooms</u>: 90, double $65. VISA, MC, AMEX, DINERS, DIS.

**CAMPING: Centennial Camper Park,** 8300 Glenn Highway, corner of Muldoon Street, (907) 333-9711.

★

# DAY 2

Anchorage to Palmer
Terrain: Flat to rolling
Sights: Russian Cemetery
42 miles

We started off in a drizzle—exactly what I didn't want to happen. I found out quickly that mink-oiled shoes aren't watertight. Barely out of Anchorage, my feet were already freezing. They wouldn't thaw out until I returned to Los Angeles.

After about twenty miles, it was just forest, mountains, light highway traffic, and increasing gusts of rain. I started to get paranoid. Is this what we could expect for the rest of the trip? Several people had already told us it was nuts to go this late in the season.

Five miles later, we stopped in Eklutna at the 200-year-old restored St. Nicholas Russian Orthodox Church and cemetery. Built above the unstable permafrost soil, the graves resemble bright red, yellow, and white "dog houses," as Marc called them, topped off with three-arm Orthodox-style crosses.

Then, seven miles later, the storm opened up. Miserable from the sweaty rainsuits, drenched and blinded by the downpour, Marc and I looked forlornly at each other. No shelter was in sight.

Suddenly, a van pulled up. A thirty-year-old guy leaned out and shouted, "throw your bikes in." His name was Herman, and in minutes we were in his self-built, half-done log cabin, where his wife cooked a steak dinner for us. That night we slept in their "guest quarters"—an old, broken-down bus next to the cabin.

In the morning, our fears were dissipated in brilliant sunshine. Herman sent us merrily off with a couple of twenty-four-inch-long carrots from his garden—the legendary Matanuska Valley produce that Willie had told me about. As we rode west past the Matanuska River bridge and the picture-perfect, mountain-silhouetted barns and log houses of

---

**DIRECTIONS:** Northeast 35 miles on 4th Avenue/Post Road/Glenn Highway (SR 1). 4 miles past Matanuska River bridge and Matanuska. Turn east with SR 1.

**ACCOMMODATIONS: Valley Hotel,** 606 S. Alaska Street, Palmer, AK, (907) 745-3330. Early-century motif. <u>Rooms</u>: 34, double $47. Owners recommend reservations 2 days in advance in June and July, "weeks" ahead in Aug. VISA, MC, AMEX, DIS.

**CAMPING: Finger Lake State Recreation Site,** 4 miles west. <u>Amenities</u>: swimming, no showers, no phone.

★

Palmer, it was as if all the rain had been used up the day before. In fact, we didn't see rain like that for a long time. But, most of all, the sun somehow gave us faith that a gallant figure, like Herman, would always step out of the shadows to rescue us on this adventure. Illogical as that may seem, it was a comforting thought.

## DAY 3

Palmer to Long Rifle Lodge
Terrain: Slight climb
Sights: Matanuska Glacier
59 miles (plus optional 12 miles to Sheep Mountain)

Climbing gently out of Palmer, the view of the Chugach Mountains to the south was stunning. Mountaintops, white with snow, topped the blazing pallet of fall.

At the fifty-nine-mile mark, Marc pointed to the right. It was the shockingly white Matanuska Glacier, which looked like the whitewater of an immense frozen wave. Though the Long Rifle Lodge (milepost 101) is poised on a hillside just above Matanuska and offers a great view, we rode another twelve miles through Caribou Creek up to the comfy wood cabins of the Sheep Mountain Lodge. Sitting at the foot of Sheep Mountain, we could see white Dall mountain sheep foraging on the steep slopes high above. I fell asleep that night by counting real sheep.

---

**DIRECTIONS:** SR 1 all day.

**ACCOMMODATIONS: Long Rifle Lodge,** (907) 745-5151. Hides hanging on the walls, stuffed trophies, "busy in summer." <u>Rooms</u>: 12, double $50. VISA, MC, AMEX.
**Sheep Mountain Lodge,** (907) 745-5121. <u>Amenities</u>: rustic wood cabins, home-style cooking, hot tub. <u>Rooms</u>: 10, double $62; single beds $8 with your own sleeping bag. VISA, MC.

**CAMPING: Matanuska Glacier State Recreation Site,** milepost 100.

---

## DAY 4

Long Rifle Lodge to Tolsana Creek
Terrain: Climbs, then flat
71 miles

Alaska often remains "freezing in the shade" until late in the morning, as it did the morning after our sheep sleep. Luckily, we had some early hill climbs to warm us up.

After a short climb up Sheep Mountain, we crossed 3,000-foot Tah-neta Pass, swooped downhill, then began a heat-generating climb to the top of 3,320-foot Eureka Summit. Next were forty-three miles of gradually sloping, rolling country leading to a sweeping forested plain. On the horizon emerged the Wrangell Mountains. For me, the day ended too soon.

Not for Marc. He was audibly grimacing with each stroke. When we stopped to talk to a woman who was training a nine-dog sled team (the sled was on wheels), he jokingly asked if he could hitch a ride. Then he turned to me with a dead-serious look and admitted he hadn't ridden since I'd left him last May. His left leg hurt so bad, he said, that it was "useless," a shocking admission from a guy who never admits to pain.

I tossed in bed restlessly that night. Marc obviously couldn't go on for a few days. But if we didn't ride, we'd have to increase future mileage to 150 a day. I could continue solo, but that'd be crazy in this wilderness. I lost sleep thinking about it. Where were those sheep when I needed them?

---

**DIRECTIONS:** SR 1 all day.

**ACCOMMODATIONS: Tolsana Lodge,** milepost 170, Tolsana Creek, AK, (907) 822-3433. Amenities: lakefront dining, trophy display cases, sheep display. Rooms: 6, double $68; reservations necessary. VISA, MC.
**Caribou Motel,** 17 miles west, milepost 187, Glenn Highway, Glennallen, AK, (907) 822-3302. Rooms: 45, $39–$48. VISA, MC, AMEX, DINERS, DIS.

**CAMPING: Tolsana Creek State Recreation Site,** milepost 172.8. No showers or phone.

---

# DAY 5

Tolsana Creek to Chistochina
Terrain: Flat, then hills
Sights: Alaska Pipeline
62 miles

After the pleasant seventeen-mile ride to Glennallen, I experienced a flash of déjà vu: the Alaska Pipeline! Just yesterday, it seemed, Marc and I had climbed on it. A mere photo for months, it reappeared now like a long-lost army buddy.

I got another flash on our ride northwest on the Tok Cutoff, the same 136 miles of Tok we'd done before in reverse. Now splashed with September's flaming hues, not the snow-white of May, it was again a great ride— the Wrangell Mountains to the right, Alaska Range to the left, a road rolling along lakes and wooded valleys. I wondered if there will be any cyclists on Earth besides me and Marc who'll ride the Tok Cutoff twice— even though Marc walked half the way, his face contorted in agony as he pedaled.

But his performance gave me confidence. Only a mind of steel could have pedaled at all in his condition. By comparison, in similar pain a year earlier on the Coast, I'd thrown in the towel. Marc would be okay.

Arriving in Chistochina, I walked into the lodge with a beaming smile, certain the lady at the reception desk—the same one from four months earlier—would be surprised and happy to see me again.

"First time in Alaska?" she asked.

---

**DIRECTIONS:** SR 1 all day.

**ACCOMMODATIONS: Chistochina Lodge,** Chistochina, AK, (907) 822-3366. Rooms: 16, double $40. Advise reservations week in advance. No credit cards.

**CAMPING:** Roadside rest 8 miles south.

★

# DAY 6

Chistochina to Tok
Terrain: Mountainous
91 miles

The ride to Tok wasn't easy, but it went like rote. Climbing and dipping north through the rugged, desolate Alaska Range, I shot over 2,430-foot Mentasta Pass at full speed, powered by autumn's beauty. Refusing my plea to hitch, however, Marc hobbled like an old man, pedaling only with his right leg. The pain of the left wrenched tears from his eyes. For him, our Tok Cutoff reunion has no good memories.

When we arrived in tiny Tok, Bucky the Wonder Moose, the town's stuffed mascot that Marc had once posed on, was tilted to one side and covered with a plastic tarp as if it were sick. When we asked someone what happened, we were stunned.

---

**DIRECTIONS:** SR 1 all day.

**ACCOMMODATIONS: Golden Bear Motel,** mile 124 Glenn Highway, ¼ mile south on Tok Cutoff (SR 1), (907) 883-2561. Amenities: pan for gold. Rooms: 41, double $60–$70. VISA, MC, AMEX.

**CAMPING: Tok/KOA Campground,** Alcan milepost 1315, 1 mile west on SR 2, (907) 883-2291. Amenities: laundry, restaurant, lounge.

★

"Two guys on bicycles came through here about four months ago and were climbing all over this thing," said a local Athabaskan Indian woman. "Some of the kids saw them, and when the riders left they started jumping all over Bucky. As a result, Bucky's foundation got loosened up, and we haven't been able to fix it."

Marc and I looked at each other and cringed with guilt. She must have noticed our reaction. "It wasn't you guys, was it?" she asked.

"No—na-ah," I stammered. "This is our first trip to Alaska."

## DAY 7

Tok, Alaska, to Beaver Creek, Yukon
Terrain: Challenging rolling hills
92 miles plus 34 kilometers equals 113 miles

Now that the familiar terrain of Alaska was behind us, the true adventure began. On our own in a virtually empty land for the next four days and 391 miles to Whitehorse, we headed southeast down the Alcan (Alaskan Highway) knowing there'd be even less traffic than before. That meant less opportunity for help.

This day's ride was a rolling, fatiguing one, despite no major hillclimbs. A store, gas station, and lodge appeared in the first forty miles at Tetlin and Northway junctions, but nothing thereafter. After a semi-long climb up to the Canadian border, ninety-three miles into the day at milepost 1221, we were greeted by a big sign with "Canada" and a red maple leaf painted on it, but no border station; that was thirty hilly kilometers away (nineteen miles) in Beaver Creek.

When we arrived later in the frosty moonlight, the startled customs man flashed a big smile and waved us right through—quite a contrast to our last entry into Canada three years earlier. Apparently, he hadn't heard about us. Or maybe it simply is policy not to turn away any visitors to this mountainous, cold, virtually empty triangle in Canada's far northwest called the Yukon Territory.

---

**DIRECTIONS:** Southeast on Alaska Highway (SR 2 in U.S. and CAN 1) all day.

**ACCOMMODATIONS: Ida's Motel,** on Alcan, Beaver Creek, YK, (403) 862-7223. Amenities: bar, diner. Rooms: 14, double $45. VISA, MC.

**CAMPING: Custom Campground KOA,** milepost 1202, (403) 862-7501.

# DAY 8

Beaver Creek to Burwash Landing
Terrain: Flat to rolling
172 kilometers (105 miles)

Since it kept my head warm, my Swedish tank helmet stayed on twenty-four hours a day when we camped. But after our first night in Canada, when I awoke, stiff and shivering in my sleeping bag, camping in any attire seemed risky. The most telling warning came from my water-bottle: it was frozen solid.

"Hey Marc," I said, "maybe rationing the hotel money isn't worth it."

"You're a wimp," he curtly replied.

That was music to my ears. It meant Marc's knee was almost fully recovered. Still, although he was able to limp along respectfully over the rolling, mountain-framed terrain, it was hardly fast. Muscles kinked-up by frigid sleep and gnarled by the bitter cold of the night and early morning don't move very smoothly.

We arrived in the village of Koidern (milepost 1169) to see inanimate objects gnarled by the cold as well. Some weirdly twisting tree branches pimpled with giant lumps decorated several buildings. These deformities occur when the tree sap freezes during the long winters. We had a good idea of how those tree branches felt.

Fortunately, we tasted a food at Koidern's White River Lodge that made us temporarily forget the cold: butter tarts. A Canadian specialty, these little pie-shaped cinnamon, apple, and pecan tarts became our most sought-after treat, at seventy-five cents each. We'd typically wolf down four or five each at a stop.

I'm convinced that butter tarts have a healing quality. After eating them in Koidern, Marc blazed 116 kilometers (72 miles) without as much as a twitch. By the time I crossed the Donjek River, climbed a big hill, and came down along Kluane Lake to Burwash Landing, he was waiting for me with a lodge room key in hand.

---

**DIRECTIONS:** Alcan all day.

**ACCOMMODATIONS: Burwash Landing Resort,** milepost 1093, Burwash Landing, YK, (403) 841-4441. <u>Amenities</u>: on lake, lounge, small store, glacier flights. <u>Rooms</u>: 35, double $48. VISA, MC.

**CAMPING:** Meadow across from resort. No facilities.

★

## DAY 9

Burwash Landing to Haines Junction
Terrain: Flat, then big climbs
122 kilometers (75 miles)

Passing Destruction Bay, named for the results of a bad storm in the forties, our effortless cruise on the flat shores of idyllic Kluane Lake was soon destroyed as well. For, as we rounded the south end of the lake, we abruptly ran into sheer mountain.

It was the towering Saint Elias Range, Canada's highest. We made two big climbs: over 1010-meter-high (3,394 feet) Boutillier Summit, then a gradual, almost straight-line ascent up 980-meter-high (3,283 feet) Bear Creek Summit.

The climb up Boutillier yielded one of my most vivid pictures: Marc framed by a wall of glistening red-yellow-orange autumn leaves, bracketed by hills of shadowy black-green forests, and topped by pure white mountains. Add the brisk, pure air and I felt a euphoric high that made climbing those mountains pure pleasure.

The long, straight descent from the Bear Creek Summit could have been one of the most fabulous of my life. I say *could* because it was dark as we went down this endless hill—and we froze! I was surprised not to see icicles forming on my elbows as we dropped into the scenic Shakwak Valley and the big town of Haines Junction.

A town of four hundred may not normally qualify as big, but Haines Junction was the first time since Anchorage that we'd seen streetlights.

---

**DIRECTIONS:** Alcan all day.

**ACCOMMODATIONS: Gateway Motel,** first one in town, Haines Junction, YK, (403) 634-2371. <u>Amenities</u>: laundry, bar. <u>Rooms</u>: 8, double $50. VISA, MC.

**CAMPING: Pine Lake,** 3 miles south of town, no phone.

---

## DAY 10

Haines Junction to Whitehorse
Terrain: Flat to rolling
158 kilometers (98 miles)

Our obsession since the beginning of the trip had been Whitehorse.

The Yukon's capital, born as the supply depot of the 1880s Klondike Gold Rush and born again with the construction of the Alcan in 1942 and the tourist boom of the 1980s, had 17,000 people—nearly the entire population of the Territory. It was an oasis of civilization in a desert of forest, our first "real" town since Anchorage.

So, like military men on leave, we planned to paint the town, grab a pizza, see a movie . . . be *civilized*.

Halfway through our ride, joined by a pack of wild horses running free on the open range, we passed through a vast, desolate, treeless area of blackened land covered with burned-out skeletons of fallen trees. An historical marker explained that a massive series of fires swept through the area in 1953. Because of the short growing season, it has taken almost thirty years for the forest to show signs of regeneration, illustrating the delicate balance of nature in the far north.

We soon felt burned-out ourselves. Counting on a fast downhill cruise into Whitehorse, instead we were buffeted by powerful headwinds blowing up Miles Canyon. Forced to *pedal* downhill, it took us two hours to cover those last fifteen miles, which ruined our plans. We were so late and so tired from the last miles that we simply found a room at the barebones Chilkoot Trail Inn, washed our clothes, and fell asleep.

It wasn't a total loss, though, as we did manage to gather a dozen butter tarts, a bag of Canadian-style salt 'n' vinegar potato chips, a couple of Cadbury Rum 'n' Butter candy bars, and a bucket of Kentucky Fried Chicken for a greasy Canadian eat-fest. So much for our big night on the town.

---

**DIRECTIONS: Alcan all day.**

**ACCOMMODATIONS: Chilkoot Trail Inn,** 4190 4th Avenue, Whitehorse YK, (403) 668-4910. Amenities: laundry, close to theaters. Rooms: 37, double $45. VISA, MC, AMEX.

**CAMPING: Sourdough City RV Park,** 4 blocks west on 2nd Avenue, (403) 668-7938. Amenities: laundry.

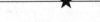

---

While Marc and I continued east, Mission: Vancouver I turns south toward the Alaska Panhandle, the old Gold Rush town of Skagway, and the Inside Passage ferry to Juneau.

## DAY 11

Whitehorse to Carcross
Terrain: Some hills
Sights: Riverboat ride, McBridge Gold Rush Museum
63 kilometers (39 miles)

The easy cruise on the moderately hilled Klondike Highway, the route of the Great Stampede of 1898, allows a half-day cruise on the riverboats S. S. *Klondike II* or M. V. *Schwatka*. The gold miners took boats like these up the Yukon, the river the Indians named *yoochu,* or "great river," for its 2,300-mile route to the Bering Sea. There were once so many riverboats on the Yukon that Whitehorse was briefly a river port to rival any on the Mississippi.

---

**DIRECTIONS:** South 10 kilometers (6 miles) on Alcan to river cruise, south 33 miles on Klondike Highway (Route 2) rest of day.

**ACCOMMODATIONS: Caribou Hotel,** Carcross, YK, (403) 821-4501 Amenities: grocery, café, laundry. Rooms: 11, double $32. VISA, MC.

**CAMPING: Carcross Territorial,** in town at kilometer 106.

---

# DAY 12

Carcross, Yukon, to Skagway, Alaska
Terrain: Flat, hills at end
82 kilometers plus 14 miles equals 64 miles

Today you pass through a territory, a province, and a state—the Yukon, British Columbia, and Alaska. The Klondike highway is scenic and flat until the Alaska border, when it rises to 3,290-foot White Pass Summit. The ride across the border into Skagway, a short-lived boom town of Gold Rush-era buildings, is hilly and scenic.

---

**DIRECTIONS:** South 82 kilometers on CAN 2 (51 miles to U.S. border, plus 14 miles to Skagway.

**ACCOMMODATIONS: Golden North Hotel,** Third Avenue and Broadway, Skagway, AK. Built in 1898 during the Gold Rush heyday. (907) 983-2451. Rooms: 12, double $60—$80. VISA, MC, AMEX.

**CAMPING:** No official sites; try Klondike Gold Rush National Historical Park.

---

# DAY 13

Inside Passage Ferry Trip, Skagway to Juneau
Terrain: Flat
Sights: Mendenhall Glacier, Juneau Icefields, State Capitol
30 miles

Your final day begins with a six-hour boat cruise* through the misty islands, fjords, glaciers, forests, and small towns of the Alaska Panhandle. You dock in the Alaska capital of Juneau, a gold boomtown called The Longest City in the World since it stretches forty miles on a narrow shelf between mountains and water. Its biggest sights are immense glaciers northwest of the ferry landing. Ice views can be had via "flightseeing."

Of course, Marc and I traded the ice show for a harrowing plunge into the wilderness. Though chilled to the bone, we had survived boot camp and were ready to go into battle. Catch up with us in Mission: Vancouver II.

---

**DIRECTIONS:** From ferry landing, 13 miles southeast on SR 7 to downtown, 10 miles back to airport.

**ACCOMMODATIONS: Bergmann Hotel,** 434 Third Street, Juneau, AK, (907) 586-1690. Vintage "old" Juneau. <u>Rooms</u>: 38, double $50. AMEX, DIS. *Youth Hostel:* (907) 276-3635.

**CAMPING: Auke Village,** 3 miles west, or **Mendenhall,** 3 miles east, (907) 789-3111. Neither has showers.

---

## SIGHTSEEING INFORMATION

JUNEAU

**Mendenhall Glacier Visitor's Center,** 10 miles northwest, via SR 7: Vista of 12-miles long, 1-mile wide glacier; access to 1,500 square mile Juneau Icefield. (907) 789-0097.

**Flightseeing,** Glacier Bay Airways: Overflights of Mendenhall Glacier, Juneau Icefields. (907) 789-9009.

**Alaska State Museum,** Whittier Street, one-half block west of Egan Drive. (907) 465-2901.

**Alaska-Juneau Mine:** A producer of over $80 million in gold before 1941 closure, in ruin south of the city.

**St. Nicholas Orthodox Church,** 326 5th Street: Built 1894.

**Alaska State Capitol:** Tours 8:00 to 5:00. (907) 465-4565.

*Ferry Information, Alaska Marine Highway's Inside Passage: daily to Juneau; $22 plus $5 bike; (907) 465-3941 or 1-800-642-0066 for times. Longer ferries are available: 1) Overnight 287 nautical miles to Ketchikan, Alaska's southernmost port; 2) three-day trip from Juneau to Bellingham, Washington; Tuesdays only; $218 plus $33 bike.

PALMER, ALASKA

**Museum of Alaska Transportation and Industry,** Alaska State Fairgrounds, Mile 40.2, Glenn Highway: Features machines that helped develop Alaska, like rare World War II airplane, shepherd's wagon, antique cars. (907) 745-7719.

SKAGWAY, ALASKA

**Klondike Gold Rush National Historical Park,** Broadway and Second Street. In old railroad depot; films, exhibits, walking tours.

**Trail of '98 Museum,** Spring Street between 7th and 8th, City Hall, 2nd floor: More Gold Rush artifacts. (907) 983-2420.

**Skagway in the Days of '98 and Soapy Smith Lives:** True feel of lawless, gambling, whoring, rollicking Gold Rush era; gamble (w/phony money); dance turn-of-century Lambada; watch can-can girls show knickers; gambling at 8:00 P.M., can-can at 9:00 P.M. (907) 983-2420.

WHITEHORSE, YUKON

**SS Klondike II,** south bank of river, east end of town, at 2nd Avenue: Free tours, 9:00 to 6:00: (403) 667-4511.

**MV Schwatka,** docked 2 miles southeast of town, past dam: Two-hour ride through Miles Canyon; 2:00 P.M., 7:00 P.M.; $10. (403) 668-3161.

**Old Telegraph Office and McBride Museum,** 1st Street: Houses Yukon Gold Rush relics such as picks, gold scales, old newspapers. (403) 667-2709.

# MISSION:
# VANCOUVER II
## WHITEHORSE
## TO
## VANCOUVER

F MISSION: VANCOUVER WAS LIKE A TRIP INTO OUTER SPACE, Whitehorse was Pluto, the end of our solar system. Beyond it lay the unknown.

From Whitehorse, 1,551 miles of road separate the frozen northlands of the Yukon Territory from the temperate beauty of Vancouver, just north of the U.S. border. But the great distance isn't the big story of Mission: Vancouver II; it's the sheer desolation, even compared to its sparsely populated predecessors.

There are few stores or lodges, so we always stocked several days of food and sometimes rode 150 miles for shelter. With some lodges out of business or out of season, we sometimes broke in—rather than freeze to death.

Of course, Marc and I made the trip in 1985, in the chill of September. Since then, more lodges have opened, so great distance is required only once, not several times. Otherwise, the pattern established by Mission I remains: ubiquitous mountains, streams, valleys, and forests; a mix of gentle and moderate rolling hills with a handful of long climbs out of river valleys and canyons.

The route of Mission: Vancouver II is totally inside Canada, going east from Whitehorse for three hundred miles on the Alaska Highway, swinging south down the Cassiar and Yellowhead Highways in a thousand-mile arc southeast to British Columbia's interior capital, Prince George, and plunging due south the last five hundred miles to Vancouver.

The rough and tumble Cassiar contains two hundred miles of unrideable gravel road. A couple of tiny, mostly Indian towns crop up only

YUKON

AK

Whitehorse

Jakes Corner

Teslin

Rainbow's Inn

Cassiar Highway
Jct. (37)

North

Dease Lake

GRAVEL ROAD

BRITISH
COLUMBIA

Meziadin Jct.

Kitwanga

Smithers

Burns Lake

Vanderhoof

Prince
George

Quesnel

Lac La Hache

Cache Creek

Yale

Vancouver

U.S.A.

*ROUTE SLIP*
*Total of 1,339 riding miles + 207 hiking miles = 1,551 miles in 17 days*

| Day | Ending Point | Terrain* | Sights | Mileage |
|---|---|---|---|---|
| 1 | Whitehorse, Yukon | Travel Day | | |
| 2 | Jake's Corner, Yukon | Easy | | 50 |
| 3 | Teslin, Yukon | Moderate | | 61 |
| 4 | Rainbow's Inn, Yukon | Easy/Moderate | | 82 |
| 5 | Cassiar Highway Junction, Yukon | Easy/Moderate | | 72 |
| 6 | Dease Lake, British Columbia | Easy/Moderate | | 153 |
| 7 | Meziadin Junction, British Columbia | Hitchike | Bear Glacier | 207 |
| 8 | Kitwanga, British Columbia | Easy/Moderate | World's Oldest Totem Pole | 95 |
| 9 | Smithers, British Columbia | Easy | | 82 |
| 10 | Burns Lake, British Columbia | Easy | | 92 |
| 11 | Vanderhoof, British Columbia | Easy | | 80 |
| 12 | Prince George, British Columbia | Easy | Fort George Regional Museum | 60 |
| 13 | Quesnel, British Columbia | Easy/Moderate | | 68 |
| 14 | Lac La Hache, British Columbia | Moderate | | 113 |
| 15 | Cache Creek, British Columbia | Moderate | | 89 |
| 16 | Yale, British Columbia | Moderate | Fraser Canyon, Hell's Gate | 103 |
| 17 | Vancouver, British Columbia | Easy | | 107 |
| 18 | A Day in Vancouver | Difficult/Easy | Mount Seymour, Stanley Park | 37 |

*Easy = flat to rolling; moderate = hilly; difficult = repeated miles of hills and climbing

★

at its southern end, where you can abort the mission* or ride the Yellow-head Highway east into Prince George.

When the weather got noticeably warmer south of Prince George, we stripped our tights off and zoomed faster and faster through spectacular Fraser River Canyon and rich fruit-growing lands. We were pulled inexorably by Vancouver, the third-biggest city in Canada and the jewel of the Canadian Pacific.

If you're committed to this trip**, be in shape. The average daily mileage, eighty-seven per day (not counting Vancouver sightseeing), is the highest in this book and allows no mistakes. Miss your goal, and there may be no other lodges in between.

If you ever do this trip, even without the weather and lodging problems Marc and I experienced, you'll certainly understand why we called it a Mission.

## DAY 1

Travel Day
Whitehorse, Yukon Territory

---

**ACCOMMODATIONS: Chilkoot Trail Inn,** 4190 4th Avenue, Whitehorse, YK, (403) 668-4910. <u>Amenities</u>: laundry, close to theaters. <u>Rooms</u>: 37, double $45. VISA, MC, AMEX.

**CAMPING: Sourdough City RV Park,** 4 blocks west on 2nd Avenue, (403) 668-7938. <u>Amenities</u>: laundry.

---

## DAY 2

Whitehorse to Jakes Corner
Terrain: Flat, rolling
82 kilometers (50 miles)

Now we felt the pressure.

Taking ten days to get to Whitehorse, Marc and I only had fourteen days left to meet the work deadline my boss had given me. That meant increasing our mileage. And that we couldn't afford bad weather.

Unfortunately, the day we left Whitehorse was a lot like the day we left Anchorage. Stocking up with extra loads of granola and peanut butter

---

*You can arrive in Vancouver a week early by turning west on the Yellowhead Highway and heading to Prince Rupert on the Pacific Coast, 237 kilometers away (148 miles). This leads to a ferry for Vancouver.

**Suggested travel: round-trip to Vancouver, one-way flight to Whitehorse, Canadian Airlines International and Air BC (an affiliate of Air Canada) have flights.

for the empty lands east and south, we headed into the thing we feared most: rain.

Luckily, it wasn't a downpour, and Marc was now in shape. Though soggy and miserable, we slogged east on the Alcan across the steel-girdered Yukon River bridge to Jakes Corner. Feeling the pressure to make distance, we plowed on an extra thirty miles toward Johnson's Crossing.

Groping over the hilly, slick roads in pitch dark the last few miles, getting colder and colder, spooked by the ever-closer sound of thunder, we finally saw a small cluster of buildings. At last, it was Johnson's.

But Johnson's Crossing wasn't much. Just a home and a store. No lodge.

Suddenly, lightning slammed to the ground close enough to make us jump, and a freezing downpour began. We had to get shelter—fast. The store had no overhang to hide under. A dog barked when we approached the darkened house. The only other structure, a flimsy, clapboard garage, had a big lock on it. We were going to freeze to death!

Not knowing what to do, I leaned against the garage wall. *Creeeeak*— it was open! The lock had not caught the bolt.

Shivering, we threw up the tent inside for warmth and listened as the rain turned to hail and sleet. The raging storm pounded that little shack all night long, pounding home the reality of bike touring the Yukon in the middle of September.

---

**DIRECTIONS:** Alcan all day long.

**ACCOMMODATIONS: Crystal Palace Hotel,** on milepost 866, Jakes Corner, (403) 668-2727. <u>Rooms</u>: 9, double $25–$45. VISA, MC.

---

# DAY 3

Jakes Corner to Teslin
Terrain: Moderate hills, then flat
98 kilometers (61 miles)

---

**DIRECTIONS:** Alcan all day long.

**ACCOMMODATIONS: North Lake Motel,** milepost 804, Teslin, YK, (403) 390-2571. <u>Amenities</u>: saloon, restaurant. <u>Rooms</u>: 8, double $49. VISA, MC.
**Morley River Lodge,** milepost 777, Morley River, YK, (403) 390-2639. <u>Amenities</u>: store, laundry, gift shop. <u>Rooms</u>: 6, double $45. VISA, MC. Open mid-April to Mid-October.

**CAMPING: Territory Campground,** 6 miles east, full facilities.

After the hilly ride into Johnson's Crossing, the terrain flattens out along Teslin Lake and River to Teslin, a small community of about five hundred Tlingit Indians. Full services are available here as well as twenty-seven miles further east.

## DAY 4

Teslin to Rainbow's Inn
Terrain: Flat, gently rolling
132 kilometers (82 miles)

"It was Herman," said Marc, a few minutes after we woke up in the shack at Johnson's Crossing.

*What?*

"Herman—the guy who rescued us that first night out of Anchorage in the rainstorm and gave us those giant carrots. He put a "positive curse" on us. That's why we stumbled into this barn last night. Nothing bad can happen to us."

Hmmm, I remembered briefly thinking that same thought myself. But if that was the case, why did I feel so terrible?

My legs felt like slabs of beef in a frosty meat locker. My back and shoulders felt like they were rusted. At 10:00 A.M., it was hard to get up—and I didn't know if I wanted to. After a night in that howling storm, I expected to open the door to see menacing black clouds and drifts of snow thirty feet high.

Instead, sweet sunshine streamed in and the golden leaves of Autumn lay on the ground. The forty-five-degree termperature was hardly T-shirt weather, but there was not a cloud in the sky. The similarity to the morning we left Herman was uncanny.

Maybe our guardian angel cast a spell on the terrain, too, as we made a hundred miles despite the late start. The Alcan follows the Swift River in and out of British Columbia, then heads over the Continental Divide, just three miles before Rainbow's Inn. There are no major hills to speak of over the Continental Divide, just a constant roll to the land.

By nightfall, we were relieved to see the Swift River Lodge. There were storm clouds gathering and we were both developing bad colds. That's why we were unnerved to find the lodge locked.

Desperate for shelter, temperatures plummeting, we knew we'd have to break in. I was a little nervous, having read the James Michener book *Alaska,* in which the penalty for breaking into another man's house in the Yukon goldfields was death. But we had no choice. Marc hoisted me up on his shoulders to check the windows. After checking all but the last one, I prepared to break through the glass when . . . it lifted up.

Inside, we found no water, electricity, clothing, or food. But we did have a good roof—just in time for the storm.

The next day, some store owners down the road told us that the Swift River Lodge had been abandoned for four years.* They knew the former

*It reopened in 1987.

owner, a meticulous old fellow, and couldn't believe he'd leave anything unlocked. Marc looked at me with a raised eyebrow.

"Herman," he said.

---

**DIRECTIONS:** Alcan all day.

**ACCOMMODATIONS: Swift River Lodge,** milepost 733, Swift River, YK, (403) 851-6401. Amenities: laundry. Rooms: 13, double $50. VISA, MC.
**Rainbow's Inn,** milepost 721, (403) 851-6452. Amenities: groceries. Rooms: 6, double $25. No credit cards.
**Rancheria Motel,** milepost 710, (403) 851-6456. Amenities: laundry, groceries. Rooms: 28, double $45–$50. VISA, MC.

**CAMPING: Rancheria Campground,** milepost 718, no phone.

---

# DAY 5

Rainbow's Inn to Cassiar Highway Junction
Terrain: Flat to rolling
116 kilometers (72 miles)

Again the midday temperature topped out in the high forties. Again the gentle rise and fall of the two-lane road was just enough to warm us. And again it would probably drop down into the teens overnight, necessitating shelter. Not to worry though, because the Cassiar Highway Junction, signifying the end of our Alcan trek east, had lodging.

But when we got there, it was all booked up.

With other hotel rooms requiring a seven-to-fifteen-mile detour toward Watson Lake in freezing, pitch-black night, we opted to put on every bit of clothing we owned and sleep in the tent. The night was our low point of the trip—lying there shivering, our noses running, throats raw, praying it wouldn't rain.

---

**DIRECTIONS:** Alcan east to junction of Highway 37.

**ACCOMMODATIONS: Junction 37 Services,** Junction 37, YK, (403) 536-2794. Rooms: 12 units, doubles $35. VISA, MC.
**Liard River Resort,** 10 kilometers east of junction, (403) 536-2271. Rooms: 13 units, double $26. VISA, MC.

**CAMPING:** Same as Junction 37 and Liard River.

# DAY 6

Cassiar Highway Junction, Yukon to Dease Lake, British
  Columbia
Terrain: Some hills, mostly flat to rolling
246 kilometers (153 miles)

Weather was always a topic of conversation. Desperate, we fanta-sized that it would instantaneously get warm as we crossed the British Columbia border. Well, B.C. had no warmth, and even worse, no shelter. Heading south on the Cassiar Highway, there were—and still are—no lodges for 153 miles to Dease Lake.

But at least we had great scenery. Mountains, lakes, and forests were everywhere. Bigger than any American state except Alaska, B.C. is jammed with mountains—the Rockies in the east, the coastal range in the west, and a number of smaller ranges in the interior. Their mineral riches give B.C.'s three million people one of the highest per capita in-comes in Canada. Their beauty makes the area around Good Hope Lake (about a hundred kilometers into the ride) seem like a dream.

Though the sun was setting fast about 7:00 P.M. when we came to the Indian village of Cassiar, which had a campsite and a store, we didn't stop. Seeing no point in pitching a tent and freezing again, Marc and I decided to ride all night to Dease Lake.

It was a good night for it. The sky was starry, the road empty. Past some hilly country south of Cassiar, the terrain flattened out in a long, gradual downhill across the Cottonwood River. I barreled along for an-other hour, wrapped up in the solitude.

Then I realized it was too quiet; I hadn't seen Marc for nearly two hours. Since it was too cold to stop, I turned around and rode north. Eventually, fifteen miles back, I found him—off his bike and crawling on all fours along the highway a few feet up from the Cottonwood River Bridge.

A nut had fallen off his bike somewhere around the bridge, causing his derailleur to drop off. Unable to find the nut in the dark, we had no choice but to camp on the flat bank under the bridge and hope we could find it in the morning.

---

**DIRECTIONS:** South on Highway 37 all the way.

**ACCOMMODATIONS: Northway Motor Inn,** Dease Lake, BC, (604) 771-5341. <u>Rooms</u>: 32, double $51–$54. VISA, MC, DINERS.

**CAMPING: Mighty Moe's Place,** 29 miles south of Cassiar, 53 miles north of Dease Lake. Also has one cabin for rent; rental boats and canoes; no phone; write Box 212, Cassiar, BC, Canada, V0C 1E0.

Not long after we zipped into our bags, a thunderous rainstorm opened up. Though it raged all night long, we stayed dry under the bridge. If we had continued riding, we'd have gotten soaked—and probably ill— in the bitter cold. In the morning, we found the nut on the highway and finished the last sixty miles, ten gravel, into four hundred-strong Dease Lake, an old Gold Rush town now called "The Jade Capital of the World."

While eating dinner in our room at Dease's Northway Inn, I raised my can of V-8 juice to make a toast.

"To Herman," we said in unison. He'd come through again at the Cottonwood River Bridge.


## DAY 7

Dease Lake to Meziadin Junction
A day of hitchhiking
334 kilometers (207 miles)

This stretch had incredible scenery: daunting, forested mountain walls on every side; the biggest hillclimbs of the entire trip, starting with 4,000-foot Gnat Pass Summit.

We might have gotten tired if we had done it by bike.

You see, we enjoyed the scenery from the cab of a pickup truck. After a few miles of pavement south of Dease Lake, it was two hundred miles of gravel all the way to Meziadin Junction—a wet, slippery road jammed with giant, pebble-spitting logging trucks.

After a few short hitches, Marc and I were picked up by a jovial white-haired Scotsman named Jock Maitland, a living symbol of British Columbia's pioneer spirit. A World War II bomber pilot who made forty-eight runs over Nazi Germany as a nineteen-year-old, Jock bought land in British Columbia sight unseen after the war. Still vigorous at sixty years old, he had a wife of twenty-nine and a twelve-year-old son.

Jock took us on a side trip west on Highway 37A to see the most striking sight on the entire tour, the Bear Glacier. The immense blue swath of ice pours out of the mountains into a river just a few startling feet off the highway. It was well worth the detour.

**DIRECTIONS:** Hitchhike south on Highway 37 all day.

**ACCOMMODATIONS: Nechako North Coast Inn and Resort,** 2 kilometers (1.5 miles) west on Highway 37A (10 miles east of Bear Glacier), Meziadin Junction, BC, (604) 636-9222. Amenities: store, restaurant, on glacier-fed Meziadin Lake. Rooms: 35, double $45. VISA, MC.

**CAMPING:** None.

## DAY 8

Meziadin Junction to Kitwanga
Terrain: Rolling hills, general descent
154 kilometers (95 miles)

We were now two hundred miles farther south than the day before, but the weather wasn't any warmer. At least our ride was invigorating, taking us over rolling hills into Cranberry Junction, then a slight downhill into the Kitwanga Valley and the tiny Gitksan Indian settlement of Kitwancool.

Kitwancool, which means "people of the place of reduced number," is famous as the home of the world's oldest standing totem pole, Hole-In-the-Ice. One of over two dozen local totem poles more than a century old, Hole tells the story of how a man saved his village from starvation by fishing through a hole in the ice.

We saved ourselves from freezing ten miles south in Kitwanga ("people of the place of the rabbits") by sleeping in a primitive "bunk house" that night. The only lodging in the region, it seemed a fitting end to our last day on the rugged Cassiar Highway

---

**DIRECTIONS:** Cassiar Highway all day.

**ACCOMMODATIONS:*** **Mina Elsworth's "Bunk House,"** Kitwanga Road near high school, Kitwanga, BC. (604) 849-5843 or (604) 849-5744. Not fancy, but clean. Mina's Place restaurant. <u>Rooms</u>: 4 beds, $15 each. Cash or traveler's checks only.

**CAMPING: Cassiar RV Park,** 5 kilometers (3 miles) north of Junction Highways 37 and 16, (604) 849-5488. <u>Amenities</u>: laundry, showers.

---

## DAY 9

Kitwanga to Smithers
Terrain: Generally flat
132 kilometers (82 miles)

Having conquered the Cassiar, we were starting to get the feeling that the end of the trip was near. Well, a shock was in store with a check

*Closest hotels are 25 miles east on Highway 16 in South Hazelton: **Grandview Inn Hotel,** double $38–$41, (604) 842-5221; **Cataline Motel,** $36, (604) 842-5271; in New Hazelton, **Buckley Valley Motel,** restaurant, $35–$37, (604) 842-5224, **Robber's Roost Lodge,** surrounded by Hazelton mountains, $38–$41, (604) 842-6916.

of the map. We were 808 miles from Vancouver—with just six days to go before I had to fly home!

At least there were signs of civilization now. We passed the cultivated fields, towns, stores, and hotels of the flat Upper Skeena and Bulkley River valleys, the fertile north-central B.C. valleys that Jock had told us about. He'd explained that many American draft dodgers came here during the Vietnam War—so many, in fact, that locals know the Bulkley Valley unofficially as Dodge Valley. The place is so beautiful that hardly any of the expatriates went home after the war, becoming, in Jock's words, "more Canadian than the Canadians."

We passed through Smithers, at 5,000 people the biggest city since Whitehorse, then continued south six miles to Telkwa to visit a familiar expatriate from Scotland. Jock and his wife cooked us dinner, hauled out some rye whiskey and butter tarts, and told us about the uproar that the romance of the retired bomber pilot and the high school girl had caused in the area. Most of all, they made us feel very much at home in their palatial house. No wonder those Americans couldn't leave this wonderful valley.

---

**DIRECTIONS:** South 3 kilometers (2 miles) to end of Highway 37. East at Highway 16 (Yellowhead Highway) rest of day. To take the ferry out of Prince Rupert*, turn west on Highway 16.

**ACCOMMODATIONS: Aspen Motor Hotel,** 4628 Highway 16, Smithers, BC, (604) 847-4551. Amenities: cedar-framed units, whirlpool, sauna, pool. Rooms: 60, doubles $45–$50. VISA, MC, AMEX, DINERS.
**Douglas Motel,** on Bulkley River, Telkwa, BC, (604) 846-5679. Amenities: sauna, whirlpool, cedar-framed units, pool. Rooms: 9, double $41–$50. VISA, MC.

**CAMPING: Riverside Recreation Centre,** on Bulkley River, (604) 847-3229.

# DAY 10

Smithers to Burns Lake
Terrain: Flat to rivergrade
146 kilometers (92 miles)

With easy rivergrade terrain and a pressing deadline ahead, Marc and I plunged back into the cold and started making serious miles—doing in two days what the schedule here outlines in three. The first day, we shot past Burns Lake and rode over rolling, then flat country to tiny

*Prince Rupert is 241 kilometers (149 miles) away. If you can't ride it all in one day, stay in Terrace after 93 kilometers (57 miles).

Fraser Lake, one of the dozens of places in British Columbia named for fur trader Simon Fraser, the first white man to explore here, in 1808. The next day, riding in the level Nechako River valley, we blitzed by Vanderhoof, British Columbia's geographic center, and headed toward "The Hub of the North," Prince George.

Both days were as cold as ever. Cutting into the harsh chill, the riding was never relaxing and carefree, never fluid. I could always feel the air *on* me, pushing against me, stinging me, even with no headwind. The cold was molding our faces into grimaces and embittering our minds as well. We had jokingly called this ride a "mission" at the beginning, but now we believed it.

**DIRECTIONS:** Southwest on Highway 16 all day.

**ACCOMMODATIONS: Burns Lake Inn,** Burns Lake, BC, (604) 692-7545. Amenities: shopping mall access, sauna, whirlpool. Rooms: 44, double $50, VISA, MC, DINERS, AMEX.

**CAMPING: Orange Valley Motel and Campground,** on Highway 16, (604) 699-6350. Rooms: 4, $26–$28. Cash only; campsites $8.

## DAY 11

Burns Lake to Vanderhoof
Terrain: Gentle rollers, flat
128 kilometers (80 miles)

**DIRECTIONS:** Southeast on Highway 16 all day.

**ACCOMMODATIONS: Vanderhoof Hotel,** 2351 Church Street. Vanderhoof, BC, (604) 567-3188. Amenities: dining, big-screen TV pub. Rooms: 32, double $45. VISA, AMEX.

**CAMPING: Vanderhoof Municipal Campground,** on Stony Creek, (604) 567-9393.

## DAY 12

Vanderhoof to Prince George
Terrain: Flat, rolling
97 kilometers (60 miles)

British Columbia's third largest city with 75,000 people, Prince George may as well have been New York after nine days of tiny villages.

Appropriately, we had a New York-style menu in mind as we sailed into town in the thirty-degree darkness. Marc wanted falafel, and I had a craving for Chinese food.

After an hour of hunting, however, it became apparent that no place in town made Marc's falafels. But we found a Wong's just before closing. I quickly ordered fried rice and chow mein, then awaited with glee. Some delectable, steaming hot Chinese food would wipe out the pain of the cold and would make it all worth it.

But it arrived cold and tasted like wood. It was the worst Chinese food I'd ever had!

It figured. This trip wasn't *supposed* to have any luxuries—even as run-of-the-mill as mediocre fried rice.

---

**DIRECTIONS:** Southeast on Highway 16 all day.

**ACCOMMODATIONS: Holiday Inn,** 444 George Street (in midtown), Prince George, BC, (604) 563-0055 or (800) HOLIDAY. Amenities: pool, sauna, casino, lounge, pub. Rooms: 139, double $65–$80. VISA, MC, AMEX, DINERS. **Jacob's Inn,** 1401 Queensway, (604) 563-9236. Rooms: 14, $28–$32. VISA, MC.

**CAMPING: Prince George KOA,** Highway 16 and Kimball Road, (604) 964-7272. Amenities: pool, laundry.

# DAY 13

Prince George to Quesnel
Terrain: Hodgepodge—flat, rolling, hills
109 kilometers (68 miles)

Prince George began our home stretch, a five hundred-mile plunge due south roughly along the Fraser River all the way into Vancouver. On the way, we passed through grass meadows, open cattle rangeland, and steep canyons, an area known as the Cariboo.

The Cariboo is typical of much of Alaska, the Yukon, and British Columbia in that it was brought to the world's attention by gold. A strike

---

**DIRECTIONS:** South on Highway 97 all day.

**ACCOMMODATIONS: Fountain Motor Motel,** 524 Front Street, downtown, Quesnel, BC, (604) 992-7071. Amenities: pool, sauna. Rooms: 34, double $40–$50. VISA, MC, AMEX, DINERS.

**CAMPING: Ten Mile Lake Provincial Park,** 10 kilometers (6.2 miles) north of town, (604) 398-4414.

in 1862 by Billy Barker brought thousands to the area and briefly turned Barkerville into the biggest city on the northwest part of the continent.

The first major town along the hilly yet easy, ride is Quesnel, the main jumping off point for Barkerville. A town of 10,000 bulging with smokestacks and log piles, Quesnel established a pattern we saw with many succeeding river towns: a big downhill into a river valley followed by an equally-long climb on the way out.

## DAY 14

Quesnel to Lac La Hache
Terrain: Many hills
189 kilometers (113 miles)

Climbing out of Quesnel in the morning, we were delighted to find the hard chill gone. For the first time in nearly three weeks, it was above sixty degrees.

Maybe it was just psychological, but my whole body felt better. The riding was smoother and easier than it had been all trip. With a strong wind at our backs, we felt supercharged. Tearing up and down the often challenging Cariboo goldfield trail along the Fraser River, it took us just five hours to ride the seventy-seven miles into Williams Lake, a ranging center of 10,000. Cattle outnumber the people here by a hundred to one; the July 1 weekend brings the Stampede, one of the biggest rodeos in the world.

Turning east from the Fraser River, we rode another fifty miles to 100 Mile House, originally one of a series of gold miners' road houses that existed every twelve to twenty-four miles. The names 150 Mile House, 100 Mile House, etc., refer to their respective distance from Lillooet, the Fraser River town where the Cariboo Wagon Road began.

It had been a good day, one in which we'd discovered a nugget of truth about bike touring: your body works a lot better in warm weather than in cold.

---

**DIRECTIONS:** South on Highway 97 all day.

**ACCOMMODATIONS: Sandman Inn,** 664 Oliver Street, Williams Lake, BC, (604) 392-6557. Amenities: pool, sauna, lounge. Rooms: 50, double $54–$58. VISA, MC, AMEX.
**Fir Crest Resort,** Lac La Hache, BC, (604) 396-7337. Amenities: housekeeping beach cottages, laundry, rec hall. Cottages: 12, double $27. VISA, MC.

**CAMPING:** at both of the above.

# DAY 15

Lac La Hache to Cache Creek
Terrain: Up and down canyon walls
143 kilometers (89 miles)

It got so warm this day that I did the unthinkable: stripped off my full-leg tights and rode without a sweatshirt. The day was as sweet as the crisp apples we tasted here in British Columbia's vast fruit-growing area, an extension of Washington State's.

Toughened by the rigorous weeks in the cold, powered by the sunlight, whipped by the wind, we catapulted over the undulating terrain to Cache Creek, then flung ourselves up the mountain walls of the Fraser River Canyon. Starting in 100 Mile House, we ended up in Boston Bar. That's 150 miles—and we weren't even tired!

More important, we were on schedule. Vancouver was just a day away.

---

**DIRECTIONS:** South on Highway 97 all day to intersection of Trans-Canada (Highway 1).

**ACCOMMODATIONS: Cache Creek Motor Inn,** (nee TraveLodge), junction of Highway 97 and Trans-Canada (Highway 1), Cache Creek, BC, (604) 457-6224. Amenities: pool, coffee shop. Rooms: 37, doubles $65. VISA, MC, AMEX.

**CAMPING: Cache Creek Campground,** 4 kilometers (2.4 miles) north of town on Highway 97, (604) 457-6414. Amenities: pool, laundry, grocery store.

---

# DAY 16

Cache Creek to Yale
Terrain: Challenging, canyon walls
Sights: Fraser Canyon, Hell's Gate Airtram
166 kilometers (103 miles)

Just out of Boston Bar, Marc and I stopped at the Hell's Gate Airtram, which dangles over one of the deepest sections of Fraser Canyon. Although I regret it now, we didn't go. Not only had we enjoyed great views of the canyon already, but the rock 'n roll "psych-up" music and made-for-tourists artificiality turned us off. You see, in our minds, we were no longer tourists. Three bone-chilling weeks of hardship had turned us into crusty survivors who scoffed at the sheer silliness of mere tram rides. We roared out of Yale and Fraser Canyon feeling like Simon Fraser himself, conquering the elements on strength and will alone.

**DIRECTIONS:** South on Highway 1 all day.

**ACCOMMODATIONS: Fort Yale Motel,** on Highway 1 at entrance to Fraser Canyon, Yale, BC, (604) 863-2216. <u>Rooms</u>: 12, double $30–$40. VISA, MC.

**CAMPING: Snow White Campground,** (604) 863-2252, 5 miles south of Yale. <u>Amenities</u>: wading pool, game room, laundry.

# DAY 17

Yale to Vancouver
Terrain: Descent, then flat to rolling
172 kilometers (107 miles)

Marc and I could feel Vancouver inexorably pulling us, like an all-powerful magnetic beam. This place, the third largest city in Canada, meant more than the end of our mission. Vancouver, from what we'd heard, was special. All reports said it was an Eden, a green Oz melding sea, mountains, islands, rivers, and Chinese food. (One-third of the residents are Chinese.) It was known by tour books and travelers alike as "The Jewel of the Pacific."

With no more canyon walls to climb, we shot down the descending Fraser Highway, then hugged Highway 7 all the way west to Vancouver. Warm enough to go shirtless, I rubbed on some sunscreen for the 130-mile trip.

Halfway in, the town of Mission appeared on mileage signs, several of which listed Mission and Vancouver together. That solidified the name Mission: Vancouver in our minds.

**DIRECTIONS:** South 20 kilometers (12 miles) on Fraser Highway (Highway 1) to Haig, then stop. Do not cross Fraser River. Stay on north of river by heading west on Highway 7 for 152 kilometers (94 miles) to Vancouver city limits. Highway 7 splits into Highway 7 and Highway 7A 11 miles west of city, in Coquitlam. Take 7A, around Fraser University into Burnaby. Cross Boundary Road into Vancouver.

**ACCOMMODATIONS: Bosman's Motor Hotel,** 1060 Howe Street, (604) 682-3171 or (800) 663-7840. <u>Amenities</u>: piano lounge, pool, nearby diner. <u>Rooms</u>: 100, double $63–$85. VISA, MC, AMEX, DINERS.
**Kingston Hotel,** 757 Richards Street, (604) 684-9024. <u>Amenities</u>: breakfast, sauna, laundry. <u>Rooms</u>: 54, double $35–$55. VISA, MC, AMEX.

Taking scenic route 7A around Simon Fraser University, we came to the hilly suburban neighborhoods of Burnaby by nightfall. As we were asking a bike rider for the best view of downtown Vancouver, visible to the west, it started to rain.

"Come with me, and I'll show you," he said, dashing off. We followed him higher and higher to his home, where we got a great view, a home-cooked meal from his wife, and an invitation to stay.

At the ideal end of a perfect day coming into our dream city, I realized that we hadn't even asked the fellow his name. "John," he said. "John Herman."

Herman? Did he say *Herman?*

It had to be a coincidence. I don't believe in guardian angels. But if they do exist, having one along sure makes things a lot easier.

## DAY 18

A Day Around Vancouver
Terrain: Major hillclimb, then flat
Sights: Mount Seymour and Stanley Park
60 kilometers (37 miles)

The consummate host, John spent the day leading us on a bike tour of the city.

Our first stop was yet another view of Vancouver, this one from the top of 1,450-kilometer-high (5,000 feet) Mount Seymour. The longest continuous climb of Mission: Vancouver gave us an incredible view of the city, its tall buildings perched on the river- and lake-strewn edge of the continent.

The scenic setting isn't the only thing that gives Vancouver such a fresh feeling. It's a young place. Though visited first in 1792 by English navy captain George Vancouver on a search for the Northwest Passage, it didn't become a city until 1886, when it was a base for gold seekers. Now western Canada's cultural, financial, and trade center, it's mild climate and beauty have made it a tourist magnet.

One of the biggest attractions is Stanley Park, to Vancouver what Central Park is to New York. Located on an islandlike peninsula separated from downtown by a bay, it includes an aquarium, a zoo, a rose garden, and some striking totem poles. Best of all, it's circled by a bike path.

The view from that path was almost surreal: a wall of skyscrapers faced us across a few hundred feet of bay, themselves framed by a backdrop of majestic mountains and the bluest blue sky I've ever seen.

Before heading off to the airport, we also saw the site of Expo '86, the world's fair we'd known about due to thousands of roadside advertising billboards that hit us the moment we entered British Columbia 1,200 miles earlier. We could see construction cranes hovering high in the sky and pavillions nearing completion by the downtown waterfront.

I knew then when my next bike trip would be: nine months later, in

the summer 1986. And I knew where: a trip down the Pacific Coast—
starting at the gates of Vancouver's Expo 86.

---

**DIRECTIONS:** To Mount Seymour from Highway 7A and Boundary Road, west
on 7A a few blocks, turn north over Burrard Inlet bridge, immediate right onto
Dollarton Road. Go left on Seymour Parkway, left at Mount Seymour Road for
a 10-mile climb to top of 1,450-kilometer high (5,000 feet) Mount Seymour.
To Stanley Park from Mount Seymour, 7A west to downtown Vancouver. Bear
right, staying close to harbor, to W. Georgia Street.
To airport from Stanley Park, bike path to English Bay side of peninsula. Hug
shore to Pacific or Beach Streets. Cross Granville Bridge, south on Granville
Street across town to Vancouver International.

---

When Marc saw me off at the airport, he looked a little different than
he did twenty-four days earlier in Anchorage. He had lost twenty pounds!

I wasn't overweight when the trip began. But when I got back to my
apartment that night in Santa Monica and took off my shirt, I was
stunned by what I saw in the mirror: My body was a lean mass of muscle!
I looked like Bruce Lee!

Ten pounds of weight had been stripped away and my pants
wouldn't fit for a week. Mentally and physically, I had never experienced
anything like this before. I never before had endured anything like the
conditions of Mission: Vancouver. And I never want to again.

Unless, of course, another once-in-a-lifetime opportunity arises.

## SIGHTSEEING INFORMATION

HELL'S GATE, BRITISH COLUMBIA
**Hell's Gate Airtram,** 12 kilometers (7.4 miles) south of Boston Bar on Highway 1: Tramway descends 153 meters over narrowest, deepest part of Fraser River Canyon, view of Hell's Gate Fishways, built to aid salmon spawn-
ing; $6.50. (604) 867-9277.

PRINCE GEORGE, BRITISH COLUMBIA
**Fort George Regional Museum,** Fort George Park: Historical exhibits back
to 1807 and Simon Fraser; open 10:00 to 5:00; $1.50. (604) 562-1612.

VANCOUVER, BRITISH COLUMBIA
**Stanley Park:** On downtown peninsula; zoo, totem pole displays, bike path
around perimeter. (604) 681-1141.
**Mount Seymour.** Across Burrard Inlet; 1440 meters high. (604) 929-5212.
**Ferry to Victoria** (Tsawwassen-Swartz Bay Intercity Buses), Pacific Coach
Lines, 710 Douglas Street: British Columbia capitol on Vancouver Island.
(604) 385-4411.

# MARTIN'S TRIPS

## The Pacific Hinterlands

★

---

A BIKE TRIP IS A LOT LIKE LIFE IN THE ARMY. TOGETHER DAY and night, you get to know everything about your partners. Like them or hate them, you share special memories and a bond that can never be broken.

Two trips I took in Oregon and Northern California in the summers of 1986 and 1987 stand out for this quality. They weren't long, but are among my most enjoyable and cherished adventures. They are also the least documented, since I had no time to keep a diary. My partner was Martin Swart.

Martin was a human whirlwind who spent every spare hour of his life drinking, smoking, and carousing. He summarily turned any trip into an around-the-clock party.

Martin couldn't ride by a river without jumping in. He'd talk endlessly with old men and kids in hick-town malt shops, telling jokes, finding out the local gossip, and getting the scoop on local issues. He'd flirt with every woman—young and old—at supermarkets or community pools. This didn't leave much time for riding, but Martin was a slow rider anyway. He'd just hitchhike.

In doing so, Martin conserved his energy for the night—and the bars. "If you want to know a town, you've got to find the people who like to talk about it," Martin would say. "And those types don't sit home watching TV—they hang out in bars."

He was right. Back in the summer of 1982, as I followed Martin across a swath of taverns stretching from Seattle to Minneapolis on the Big Adventure, I learned that a local bar is not only a nice place to unwind; it is a virtual anthropology class of local history, accents, attitudes, and customs.

As we sat in such places, Martin's photographic memory would spit out hundreds of jokes and spin endless yarns. His bottomless wallet would buy nearly everyone a couple of rounds. He could sing every song of Arlo Guthrie or Tennessee Ernie Ford or countless others. He would analyze history with Vietnam vets and trade opinions on everything from welfare to astrology to human motivation. Martin was more interesting, more curious, more alive than anyone I'd ever met.

He also was an entrepreneur. At fifteen, he made extra money by

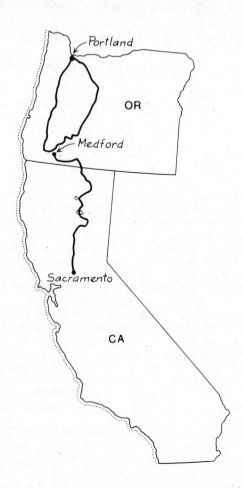

reopening a hamburger joint after hours. At seventeen he started a floor-waxing company that had grown to five employees by the time I met him in 1982.

But by twenty-six, Martin was a nervous wreck, smoking three packs of cigarettes a day. He had relentlessly made his company the biggest of its kind in San Diego. He hadn't ridden a bike in a year. And by May of 1986, when he called me, he sounded desperate. "I need a bike trip," he begged. "I need to clean out my body, to get centered, to get whole again. I need fresh air."

I recommended the Oregon coast—which I'd heard was bike-tour heaven. "Naw," scoffed Martin, "we've got to get away from the coast— that's where all the phonies are." We did settle on Oregon, but instead decided to go inland, off the beaten track, where Martin claimed the people were "real."

The people were indeed friendly and genuine. And the scenery was spectacular, from Mount Hood to Crater Lake, with forests and rivers and even high desert. Crossing back and forth over the Cascades, we saw tiny towns, time-warped, long-haired hippy mountain men and eight-foot-tall llamas. Martin quit smoking the first day and hitchhiked 80 percent at first, but rode it all near the end. By that time, we had ridden through a snow blizzard, slept in a bathroom, and, most important, formed a special bond of friendship. We agreed to try for one trip together every year.

So, in 1987 we picked up where we left off. From southern Oregon through mountainous northeastern California, we pedaled (and hitched) on little-traveled roads, swam in pollution-free mountain streams, stayed in tiny river towns, and visited Indian bars, lava beds, and California's capital. It was another great trip.

In 1988, we got together one day at the end of August. It didn't look like there'd be a trip that year, as I was too busy—and Martin was swamped. His company was expanding crazily and had become nearly the biggest floor-waxing business in the state. Richer by the second, Martin was just moving into a huge new home with his wife of one year.

Over drinks, Martin told me of his plan to expand nationally over the next three years, then retire to raise his kids in Oregon. "But first," he said, "we're going to take that bike trip around the world."

Ah yes, the bike trip around the world. We'd talked about it ever since the Big Adventure. Now we made the commitment. In three and a half years, March 1992, Marc, Martin, and I would fly to Lisbon, Portugal, and ride east. From Japan, we'd fly to Los Angeles, then ride to New York to complete the loop, raising millions of dollars for charity and arriving as heroes. I would have a book and/or movie deal, he prophesied. As always, Martin was thinking big.

"I'll stop smoking," he said. "I'll stop drinking. I won't hitchhike. This will be the greatest adventure of our lives."

We shook on it. I left about midnight with a deep glow of satisfaction. I envisioned me, Martin, and our brothers forty years in the future: old, bald-headed seventy-year-old men, chuckling at the memories of our youthful adventures—and still planning new ones.

But suddenly, twelve hours later, the feeling evaporated.

While driving up to polish the floors of his new house before his family moved in, Martin was broadsided by a truck running a red light at a hundred miles an hour.

It wasn't the way Martin was supposed to die.

I think a lot about Martin. I know no one who lived life as fully. I feel lucky that I got to share a little of it with him up there in the rustic, unspoiled interior of Oregon and northern California, where he and I became friends forever.

# CHAPTER 11

## TOUR DE OREGON

**B**EFORE THIS TRIP, OREGON MEANT ONE THING TO ME: PINE trees. But on the flight into Portland on June 1, 1986, Martin and I saw a variety that changed how we thought about Oregon. At the ridge of the Cascade Range below us was the brilliant blue circle of snow-ringed Crater Lake. Off to the right of the mountains was—no, it couldn't be—what looked like high desert. Then, as the plane veered left to Portland, the massive conical peak of Mount Hood filled our windows. Following the Columbia River gorge, we looked south into the rich farmlands of the Willamette Valley.

Our eight-day, 632-mile D-shaped loop took us to all places we "previewed" by air. Heading east into the cool Cascade forests, we climbed nearly 4,000 feet past the southern shoulder of Mount Hood before dropping southeast into central Oregon's high desert. Moderately easy riding south past the Bend resort area took us through shrub-covered, sunbaked country, complete with mounds of eerie volcanic lava rocks.

Then the scenery changed again. A challenging climb back into the Cascades took us to snowdrift-framed Crater Lake, a stunning extinct volcano full of water. It being early in the season, we had the blue-on-white wonder to ourselves, enjoying its timeless beauty until hit by a snowstorm—not fun with none of the lodges or hotels yet open.

Following an endless downhill southwest into Grants Pass, we rode north through the populous Willamette Valley to complete the loop into Portland.

Along the way, we saw what Martin had hoped to see: "the real people." Bicycle-seat anthropology taught us that the population was a mix of ex-hippies, rugged outdoorsmen, and old-fashioned hard-working types, all bound together by their love of nature and the Portland Trail-blazers basketball team. The "Oregon type" was epitomized one day in a Roseburg supermarket checkout line, where a burly six-foot, seven-inch long-haired mountain man stood buying marijuana rolling papers and talking excitedly about the Blazers.

We also noticed how bicycle friendly the state is. A full one percent of the state's highway funds are devoted to building and maintaining bicycle trails.* Everyone seemed enthusiastic about our trip and strongly

* The Oregon Department of Transportation provides excellent statewide bicycle maps. Write Bicycle Program Manager, Room 200, Transportation Building, Salem, OR 97310, or call (503) 378-3432 or (503) 373-1270.

## ROUTE SLIP
### Total of 632 miles in 8 days or 692 in 9 days*

| Day | End Point | Terrain** | Sights | Mileage |
|---|---|---|---|---|
| 1 | Welches/Zigzag, Oregon | Moderate | Scenic highway, View Mount Hood | 44 |
| 2 | Madras, Oregon | Difficult/Easy | Mount Hood | 78 |
| 3 | La Pine, Oregon | Moderate/Easy | High desert, Lava Caves | 73 |
| 4 | Crater Lake, Oregon | Easy/Difficult | Crater Lake | 80 |
| 5 | Grants Pass, Oregon | Easy | Long downhill | 91 |
| 6 | Sutherlin, Oregon | Moderate | Wineries | 80 |
| 7 | Corvallis, Oregon | Moderate/Easy | Willamette Valley | 94 |
| 8 | Portland (+ airport) | Easy | State capitol, Oregon Trail Center, Old Town | 92 |
| *Option Day 1: | Cascade Locks | Easy | Columbia River Gorge | 42 |
| *Option Day 2: | Timberline | Moderate/Difficult | Mount Hood | 61 |

*(From Timberline, proceed to Madras and resume original route.)*

**Easy = flat to rolling; moderate = hilly; difficult = at least one major hill climb

★

pro-environment. There was virtually no broken glass on the road due to a strict bottle deposit law. Neither of us got a flat the entire trip, another reason why we stayed "pumped up" throughout this great tour of Oregon.

# DAY 1

Portland to Welches/Zigzag
Sights: Scenic highway
Terrain: Flat, slightly uphill
44 miles

Since our purpose was to breathe clean mountain air and "get centered," we didn't waste any time on Portland, where a quarter of Oregon's 2.7 million people reside. Instead, we plunged headlong into the fabled forests of the tenth largest state. With all signs of urbanization ending just minutes from the airport, we started a gradual climb into the Cascade Range that would eventually lead past the highest point in the Beaver State, 11,238-foot-tall Mount Hood.

After twenty-one miles, Martin posed for one of our standard joke pictures—a slack-jawed, glazed-eyed stare at the turn-off sign for the town of Boring. Then he revealed that he felt just like his pose—that he couldn't go on, his unconditioned legs had turned to jelly and his cigarette-clogged lungs were suffocating. So after another twenty-five uphill miles through dense evergreen, I found him waiting at Salazar's Restaurant in tiny Zigzag, his bike in the back of a pickup.

In the restaurant, we were greeted by the logger who'd picked up Martin. He happened to live in Boring and told us, not surprisingly, that "there is nothing to do there."

---

**DIRECTIONS:** From airport, south 7 miles on SR 213. East 39 miles on US 26. Right on Welches Road.

**ACCOMMODATIONS: Rippling River Resort,** 68010 E. Fairway Avenue (¾ mile south of Zigzag on Welches Road), Welches, OR, (503) 622-3101. Amenities: mountain setting, fireplaces, pool. Rooms: 157, double $90–$100. VISA, MC, AMEX, DINERS, DIS.

**CAMPING: Green Canyon,** 1 mile east on US 26, 4½ miles south on FR 2618, (503) 666-0704. Amenities: no showers.

---

# OPTIONAL DAYS 1 AND 2

Portland to Cascade Locks
Cascade Locks to Timberline
Sights: Columbia River Gorge, Mount Hood
Terrain: Hilly, flat, and hill climb
42 plus 61 miles

The Columbia River Gorge, which begins ten miles east of the airport and extends for fifty more, can be included in the Tour de Oregon with an extra day.

**Day 1:** The Historic Columbia River Highway provides a spectacular view at Crown Point before merging with I-84. It passes the Bonneville Dam and fish hatchery before ending in Cascade Locks, which protect river traffic from rapids. Displays along the way describe the Oregon Trail, the great pioneer wagon train route of the mid-1800s.

**Day 2:** Continue upriver to Hood River, an international wind-surfing mecca, before turning south past the east side of Mount Hood. Two passes, 4,700-foot Bennett and 4,200-foot Barlow, are crossed before either a stay in Timberline—elevation, 6,000 feet—and/or intersection with US 26 and the regular route.

---

**DIRECTIONS:** *Day 1,* east 12 miles on Marine Drive to Troutdale. Either merge with I-84 for rest of day or take Historic Columbia River Highway 22 scenic miles east, then merge with I-84. *Day 2,* east 20 miles on I-84, turn south 41 miles on SR 35. To Timberline, turn west 1 mile on US 26, then north 8 miles on steep road.

**ACCOMMODATIONS: Scandian Motor Lodge,** on US 30, Cascade Locks, OR, (503) 374-8417. Rooms: 30, double $45+. VISA, MC, AMEX, DINERS. **Timberline Lodge,** Timberline, OR, (503) 231-7979 Amenities: cozy, rustic, some fireplaces; summer and winter skiing; pool, sauna, spa. Rooms:: 60, double $60–$140. VISA, MC, AMEX, DIS.

**CAMPING: Cascade Locks. KOA,** 1½ miles east off US 30, (503) 374-8668. No camping in Timberline.

---

## DAY 2

Welches/Zigzag to Madras
Sights: View of Mount Hood
Terrain: Steep hillclimb, then moderate road
78 miles

A tough twelve-mile climb took us around the south side of Mount Hood, an immense dormant volcano with a blindingly white year-round snowcap. (A 2,000-foot climb to Timberline leads to slopes and lodging. See details above.)

This section of US 26 is part of the Barlow branch of the Old Oregon Trail, the Indian and pioneer road that Eastern settlers followed to Oregon in the 1840s. The road peaks at Government Camp, where Martin and I, both exhausted, fell dead asleep on the comfy, Old Western-style wooden porch of a store.

We woke up two hours later to find a mostly downhill ride the rest of the day. We climbed a bit at 4,000-foot Blue Box Pass, then dropped into the Warm Springs Indian Reservation, home of the Wasco, Paiute, and Warm Springs Indians. After a four-mile uphill from tiny Warm Springs, a gradual descent led to the town of Madras.

When I rolled in at dusk, Martin was waiting with our itinerary for the evening. Staying with the Paiute who'd picked him up in Warm Springs, we had barbequed rabbit, then went bar-hopping. In Madras, that meant Indian bars, Martin's favorite. The night began with him flirting with the biggest, ugliest available Indian women, the kind he thought were the most fun. It ended with us fleeing from an enraged 220-pound Indian maiden who felt he was getting too friendly with her while doing the Bump.

---

**DIRECTIONS:** East on US 26 all day.

**ACCOMMODATIONS: Master Host Motor Inn,** junction US 26 and 97, Madras, OR, (503) 475-6141. <u>Amenities</u>: pool. <u>Rooms</u>: 48, double $40. VISA, MC, AMEX, DINERS, DIS.

**CAMPING: KOA Madras,** 2435 SW Jericho, 9 miles south on US 97, Haystack Reservation exit, (503) 546-3073.

---

# DAY 3

Madras to La Pine
Sights: Oregon High Desert Museum, Lava River Caves
Terrain: Gently uphill at first, then mostly flat
73 miles

Before we left in the morning, Martin turned to me. "I will not hitch today. No matter how tough the road is, I'll ride it."

Riding south-by-southwest on US 97, I could buy that, since the terrain was fairly mild. Even so, there were surprising scenery changes. From wooded scenery around Madras, we saw a green canopy of grassy, shaded farm country, complete with—of all things—llamas, which we fed and photographed for a good hour. Going through Redmond and Bend, the trees and grassy pastures were often replaced by wheat fields, cattle ranches, and rocky, semi-arid shrubland. It looked suspiciously like high desert, and soon turned into a moonscape of volcanic rock. We looked at each other. "This can't be Oregon."

But it was. A far cry from the evergreens of the Cascades, the eastern two-thirds of Oregon is part of the vast Northern Desert that stretches from Southern California through northern Washington, including Nevada and half of Utah. Central Oregon has dramatic (and inactive) volcanic scenery, including lava flows, craters, and caves. At one point, Martin and I climbed like ants on giant, miles-long mounds of porous rock.

Eight miles south of Bend was the Oregon High Desert Museum,* which featured an outdoor zoo with indigenous desert species, such as porcupines, river otters, eagles, and owls. Since it was getting dark when we got out, I wanted to hurry; it was another twenty miles to tiny La Pine.**

"Go ahead and ride at your own speed," Martin said. "Just wait for me in town."

An hour and a half later, I saw a truck pull behind a building. After another minute, Martin came riding out. I didn't say a word.

After we checked into the hotel and had a few drinks, Martin casually said he'd ride all the way—tomorrow.

"How'd you know I saw you?" I wondered.

"Because if you hadn't, you'd have done something real special for me," he said. "Like buy the drinks for once!"

---

**DIRECTIONS:** South on US 97 all day.

**ACCOMMODATIONS: Sunriver Lodge,** Sunriver, OR, (800) 547-3922 or (503) 593-1221. Amenities: pools, sauna, rafting on Deschutes River, golf, bike trails. Rooms: 325, double $90–$110. VISA, MC, AMEX, DINERS.
**Master Host Motor Inn,** 52560 US 97, La Pine, OR, (503) 536-1737. Rooms: 21, double $40. VISA, MC, AMEX, DINERS.

**CAMPING: La Pine State Park,** 8½ miles north on US 97 and 2½ miles west, (503) 388-6055. Amenities: swimming, fishing.

---

# DAY 4

La Pine to Crater Lake
Sights: Crater Lake
Terrain: Easy, then long, tough climb
80 miles

By noon, Martin and I had polished off forty-four miles of easy terrain over prairie and beautiful tree-lined meadows. Fueling up at the Crater Diner for the long climb to Crater Lake, Oregon's only national park, we were approached by an old man.

"You boys be goin' up to the crater now, will ye?" he asked rhetorically. "Y'know Crater Lake's located at the crest of the Cascades, and the weather's mighty stormy up there right now—especially to be dressed like that."

*Lava River Caves and Lava Lands Visitors Center are just south.
**Closer ACCOMMODATIONS are available at the Sunriver Resort area.

With both of our shirts off in the midday sun, we looked at each other and smiled. A couple of days earlier, we'd climbed over the Cascades and didn't get so much as a chill. We looked southwest in the direction of the lake. Skies were all clear.

"You can't tell from down here," said Gramps. "That's five thousand feet up, y'know."

No big deal, we smirked, turning due west on SR 138 and waving him and the high desert goodbye. By the time we turned left to Crater Lake, having risen 1,500 feet, we saw timber-covered land, clear skies, and highway shoulders covered by several inches of melting snow. I put my head down and pushed slowly up the slope, pedal after pedal. When I finally looked up fifteen miles later, Martin was nowhere in sight—and the snow on the shoulders had grown to a wall eight feet high.

I waited for a while. I put my shirt on, because it was getting cold. I put on my sweatshirt and my jeans when the wind started up. I did jumping jacks and push-ups to keep warm when dark clouds began blocking the sun.

Finally, about three hours after I'd last seen him, Martin arrived in the back of a pickup. "Throw your bike in," he yelled, "we're going to the top." But as I lifted up my bike, the driver shook his head.

"Naw, this is the end of the line for me," he said sharply, craning his neck to see the sky from under his windshield. "From the looks of it, I'd have trouble gettin' down real soon. A storm's ready to kick!"

That was funny. It didn't seem that bad. The driver sped away after we rejected his offer to drive us back down the hill.

Well, the wind soon got stronger, and a few snowflakes started falling, and the snowy walls kept rising until they covered up some of the road signs. But this didn't prevent us from seeing what we came to see. Scrambling up snowdrifts at an elevation of 7,500 feet, we ignored the signs reading, "DANGER—Get Back" and gazed at the treasure below: set into the collapsed crater of an ancient volcano, 1,932 feet deep, deeper than any other crater in North America, the awesome six-mile-diameter circle of brilliant blue known as Crater Lake.

Pictures taken, we merrily set off for the park headquarters, just three miles away. But soon we couldn't see. The sky was now a dark sea of white-gray. The wind whipped snow into our eyes. We couldn't hear each other speak. We couldn't see more than ten feet ahead or at all beyond the shoulders of the road—and narrowly avoided a head-on collision with a groping motorhome. We were plunging blindly into a blizzard!

So we walked and staggered—blown back and forth across the road by the raging storm for the next two hours. When we arrived at the visitor's center, my face was so frozen it took a good minute to speak an intelligible word. When I did, the first thing that came out was, "Damn!"

The lodge was closed until June 15, two weeks away. In fact, Rim Drive, the scenic road that hugs the east side of Crater Lake (we rode the west), doesn't even open until mid-*July*.

Well, we'd both learned from years of bike touring that finding a place to sleep is just part of the adventure. Failing to break into the lodge, we jimmied open an air-raid-shelter door to find a tunnel that led to an unlocked bathroom. On a night like that one, we considered it a four-star accommodation.

---

**DIRECTIONS:** South 44 miles on US 97. West 15 miles on SR 138. South 19 miles on Crater Lake turnoff to Visitors Center.

**ACCOMMODATIONS: Crater Lake Lodge at Mazama Village,** Crater Lake, OR (503) 594-2511. <u>Rooms</u>: 40, double $72. VISA, MC.

**CAMPING: Mazama Campground,** Crater Lake, also (503) 594-2511.

---

## DAY 5

Crater Lake to Grants Pass
No sights on this day
Terrain: Long downhill, then flat
91 miles

At 6:00 A.M. the lights flicked on. A big, square-jawed man in a plaid winter coat, CAT baseball cap, and hiking boots almost tripped over us.

"Well, I must thank you gentlemen for allowing me into your fine home," he deadpanned.

Rudely awakened, we were nonetheless greeted by a beautiful day: the air brisk and pine-scented, the sky bright and peaceful, the lake a royal-blue vision of circular perfection, and, best of all, the breakfast hot. The restaurant was open and filling with a trickle of hardy early-season campers—no doubt only slightly less hardy than the intrepid bicyclists who survived the storm.

We were rewarded for our heroics with a blood-rushing, moderately graded switchback descent, winding west out of the Cascades on US 62 for over thirty miles. Near the small village of Prospect, we picked up the kayak- and canoe-filled Rogue River and rode parallel with it to Shady Cove. Turning southwest through a string of quaint river towns, including the 1860 Gold Rush town of Gold Hill, we entered the Rogue River Valley, a pretty place bracketed by rolling oak and pine-studded hills. Its biggest city is Grants Pass, population 16,000.

Asking drivers, "where's the hottest spot in town?" Martin led us to the aptly named Handle Bar, where he regaled the customers with the story of our bravery on the lake. When I mentioned that he seemed particularly joyous this evening, Martin agreed. "Didn't you notice?" he asked. "This is the first day I didn't hitchhike!"

I did notice. Of course, we'd had a little help, dropping over 6,000 feet from Crater Lake. But he'd ridden it all nonetheless. That's why, though overlooked by Martin in the excitement, *I* had bought the first round.

---

**DIRECTIONS:** Southwest 52 miles on US 62 to Shady Cove. Right on un-named road running south, just west of river for 9 miles. Turn southwest 21 miles on SR 234, west 9 miles on SR 99 to Grants Pass.

**ACCOMMODATIONS: Riverside Inn,** 971 SE 6th Street, Grants Pass, OR, (800) 334-4567 or (503) 476-6873. Amenities: river view, 2 pools, whirlpool, excursions to Oregon Caves (see Sightseeing). Rooms: 174, double $65–$85. VISA, MC, AMEX, DINERS.
**Redwood Motel,** 815 NE 6th, (503) 476-0878. Amenities: pool. Rooms: 24, $40–$46. VISA, MC, AMEX, DINERS, DIS.

**CAMPING: Valley of the Rogue State Park,** 9 miles east of Grants Pass on river, (503) 582-1118.

---

## DAY 6

Grants Pass to Sutherlin
Sights: Wineries
Terrain: Low climbs, rollers and descent
80 miles

Martin truly did have his cycling legs, even with tougher conditions. Steering back toward Portland, we fought prevailing headwinds all the way. There were hills, too, though nothing like Crater Lake.

---

**DIRECTIONS:** North 68 miles on I-5 to Roseburg. Ride the west bank of South Umpqua River (*not* Airport Road) 5 miles to Melrose's Hillcrest Winery, north 7 miles across river. Turn east at Umpqua for 4 miles, turn southeast 1 mile on SR 138. Cross I-5 to Sutherlin.

**ACCOMMODATIONS: Ponderosa Inn,** Junction I-5 and SR 138, Sutherlin, OR, (503) 459-2236. Amenities: pool. Rooms: 60, double $50–$60. VISA, MC, AMEX, DINERS, DIS.

**CAMPING: John P. Amacher,** Winchester, OR, 7 miles south of I-5 exit 129, (503) 672-4901.

---

Riding I-5 north out of Grants Pass, we climbed a thousand feet over Sexton Mountain Pass and shorter heights over two others. Rolling up and down through gradually descending, densely-forested land, we paused in Roseburg, the largest town in the Umpqua River Valley, an area famous for logging, wineries, melons, and fishing.

It was the wineries that interested us the most. Several are scattered in the foothills, including the Hillcrest Vineyard, just northwest in the tiny village of Melrose.

After too many samples in the tasting room, we awakened to find everyone gone. We groggily pedaled to Sutherlin and fell right into bed, too tired to go out. It was our own fault for violating a cardinal rule of bike touring: don't drink during the day.

## DAY 7

Sutherlin to Corvallis
No sights on this day
Terrain: Early hills, then flat valley
94 miles

Well-rested for once, Martin and I powered over moderately tough climbs in the first couple of hours, then sped up as the terrain flattened into grazing land. At Cottage Grove we joined SR-99 for the last, flat miles into Eugene, home to 100,000 people and the University of Oregon—and the start of the Willamette Valley.

The sixty-mile-wide Willamette Valley is Oregon's historical and population heartland. Its fertile soil marked the end of the Oregon Trail and the beginning of the American Dream for 300,000 Americans, mostly New Englanders, who trekked west in the 1840s. We saw several covered bridges in the next few days, testimonies to those Yankee origins.

Crossing through Eugene, we were advised by several cyclists (of hundreds on the road) to take the bike route along the Willamette River. It gave us a scenic, stress-free ride into Corvallis, Latin for "heart of the valley," home of Oregon State University.

When locals informed us that OSU was the "party school" of Oregon, we immediately checked in at the Town House Inn and walked two

---

**DIRECTIONS:** North 36 miles on I-5 to Cottage Grove. North 20 miles on SR 99 to Eugene. North 38 miles on bike path to Corvallis.

**ACCOMMODATIONS: Town House Motor Inn,** 350 SW 4th, Corvallis, OR, (503) 753-4496. Rooms: 104, double $49. VISA, MC, AMEX, DINERS.

**CAMPING: Corvallis-Albany KOA,** 5 miles east on SR 34, 33775 Oakville Road, (503) 967-8521. Amenities: pool, groceries.

blocks to Bar Row. Our evening was spent in two big OSU hangouts, the Squirrel's Tavern and Oregon Museum, interviewing prospective women employees for positions with Martin's company.

"Tell me," Martin would say, grabbing a pencil to make notes, "how were your grades in Mopology and Waxological Analysis?"

## DAY 8

Corvallis to Portland
Sights: State capitol, Oregon Trail Center, Old Town
Terrain: Flat valley
82 miles plus 10 to airport

After a lightly trafficked ride through pretty farmland, we arrived in Salem, the state capital and third-largest city in the state. Salem is a good *old* place, home to the oldest Methodist church west of the Rockies, Willamette University, the oldest college west of the Mississippi, and a water-powered wooden mill. But the best sight was the view from the dome of the unique modern Greek-style state capitol building: a scenic picture of the valley with the mountains on each side of it, the Coast Mountains to the west and the Cascades to the east.

Next stop was Oregon City, the official end of the Oregon Trail and first incorporated city west of the Missouri River. Hearing the hardships of the pioneers at the Oregon Trail Interpretive Center, Martin and I somehow felt like we could relate.

From Oregon City, we rode triumphantly into Portland, 370,000-strong, but with a small-town air about it. An architect we met in Old Town explained that the city is loaded with parks and no building, by law, is over forty stories tall, protecting the view of Mount Hood.

The architect and his wife ended up giving us a tour of the city. They showed us the Yamhill Historic District, with the biggest collection of cast-iron buildings in the West. They showed us the historical statues in Washington Park, Portland's big hangout. They explained that the city,

---

**DIRECTIONS:** North 20 miles on 99W. East 11 miles on SR 51 to Salem. North 38 miles on 99E to Oregon City. North 13 miles on 99E to Portland. To airport: north 6 miles on 99E, east on US 30.

**ACCOMMODATIONS: Red Lion Motor Inn,** 310 SW Lincoln Street, Portland, OR, (800) 547-8010, (503) 221-0450. Rooms: 23, double $80–$100. VISA, MC, AMEX, DINERS, DIS.
**Nendel's Inn,** 9900 SW Canyon Road, (503) 297-2551. Rooms: 139, $45–$60. VISA, MC, AMEX, DINERS, DIS.

**CAMPING:** none in town.

named after Portland, Maine, was founded in 1845 along the Columbia River, then expanded south to the Willamette. Then they invited us home, fed us, and took us out bar-hopping for our final night on the town.

The next day, when they offered to ferry us to the airport, Martin was aghast when I agreed. "Hey," he complained, "I haven't hitchhiked in four days now. You wanna ruin my record?"

So we pedaled to the airport. But before we left, we rode east about ten miles to Troutdale, then rode another fifteen on the Scenic Highway to Crown Point. As we looked at the fantastic view of the Columbia River Gorge, Martin grabbed my hand and shook it. "Now I'm ready for the trip next year," he said.

## SIGHTSEEING INFORMATION

BEND, OREGON
**Oregon High Desert Museum,** 6 miles south of Bend: Includes outdoor zoo and exhibits of Northwest's arid lands; daily 9:00 to 5:00; $3.00. (503) 382-4754.
**Lava Butte, Lava Lands Visitors Center and Lava River Caves,** 10 miles south of Bend: 5,000-foot cinder cone erupted 6,000 years ago; spiral road to top; caves 12 miles south; lantern rentals fifty cents. (503) 593-2421.

BONNEVILLE, OREGON
**Bonneville Lock and Dam, Bradford Visitors Center:** Includes underwater viewing room for fish migrating upstream. (503) 374-8820.

CASCADE LOCKS, OREGON
**Cascade Locks and Aquatic Park:** Riverfront park and museum. (503) 374-8619.

CRATER LAKE, OREGON
**Excursion Boat Tours on the Lake:** Contact Superintendent, Crater Lake National Park, Box 7, Crater Lake, OR 97604. (503) 594-2211.

GRANTS PASS, OREGON
**Hellgate Canyon:** Excursions by jet boat from Riverside Park at south bank of Rogue River; two-hour, forty-mile trip, $12. (503) 479-7204.
**Oregon Caves National Monument:** Largest limestone caverns west of Rockies; guided tours thru illuminated caverns; bus excursions from Riverside Motel. Motel, (503) 476-6873, or Chamber of Commerce, (503) 476-7717 or (800) 547-5927.

OREGON CITY, OREGON
**Oregon Trail Interpretive Center,** 5th and Washington streets: Explains difficult Oregon Trail journey; $2. (503) 657-9336.

PORTLAND, OREGON
**Oregon Historical Society,** 1230 SW Park Avenue: Exhibits provide history of Oregon; Monday through Saturday, 10:00 to 5:00. (503) 222-1741.
**Oregon Institute of Art,** 1219 SW Park Avenue: Complex exhibits European, Early American, and Pacific Northwest Indian art; not open Monday; $3. (503 226-2811.
**Washington Park,** Park Place: 150 acres includes all sports activities, historical statues of Portland's past, free nightly amphitheatre performances in July and August. (503) 796-5193.

ROSEBURG, OREGON
**Hillcrest Vineyards,** 240 Vineyard Lane. (503) 673-3709.

SALEM, OREGON
**State Capitol:** Tours hourly Monday through Saturday; free. (503) 378-4423.

CHAPTER

12

UNKNOWN
CALIFORNIA
MEDFORD,
OREGON, TO
SACRAMENTO

THIS CHALLENGING 548-MILE TRIP GAVE MARTIN AND ME A glimpse of the California that people rarely see—the state's uncrowded, unspoiled, mountainous northeast corner. It's big, open country of green trees and blue skies, jammed with snow-capped peaks, inactive volcanoes, glaciers, waterfalls, white-water rivers, dense forests, alpine lakes, rugged canyons—and hardly any people. The biggest town that we passed through over one three-day stretch was Burney, California, population 3,200.

Starting from Medford, Oregon, and snaking south to Sacramento, the route took us through both the Cascade and Sierra ranges. Starting with a five thousand-foot climb, we briefly dropped onto high desert flatlands, then gradually climbed again, heading through pine-packed valleys and mountains up to eight thousand feet in Lassen Volcanic National Park. After that, we descended along beautiful rivergrade road into the flat Central Valley.

The route had a dazzling mix of nature, culture, and history. The winding Feather River made for a blissful sixty-mile ride. Ashland, Oregon, hosts the world-famous Shakespearean Festival. We saw volcanic activity at the black lava caves of Lava Beds National Monument and boiling lakes, bubbling mud pots, hot springs, and steamers in Lassen. The Lava Beds include battle sites of the Modoc War, the Indian's last stand in California. The last stand for the bike trip comes at Sutter's Fort in California's capital of Sacramento, where the famous Gold Rush began.

This tour was nearly as nature-filled as my Final Frontier trips in Alaska and British Columbia, but didn't require a flight to a remote corner of the world. For over a week, Martin and I were astounded by the peaceful beauty of a place surprisingly close to our own—yet one which might as well have been a million miles away.

---

### ROUTE SLIP
Total of 548 miles in 9 days

| Day | End Point | Terrain* | Sights | Mileage |
|-----|-----------|----------|--------|---------|
| 1 | Ashland, Oregon | Easy | Shakespearean Festival | 14 |
| 2 | Klamath Falls, Oregon | Difficult | | 59 |
| 3 | Tionesta, California | Easy/Moderate | Lava Beds National Monument, Modoc War sites, petroglyphs, ice and tube caves | 60 |
| 4 | Adin, California | Moderate | | 58 |
| 5 | Burney, California | Moderate | Burney Waterfall | 72 |
| 6 | Mill Creek, California | Difficult | Lassen Volcanic National Park | 83 |
| 7 | Belden Town, California | Easy/Moderate | Feather River Canyon | 76 |
| 8 | Marysville, California | Moderate | Feather River Canyon | 76 |
| 9 | Sacramento, California | Easy | Capitol building, Sutter's Fort | 50 |

Easy = flat to rolling; moderate = hilly; difficult = at least one major hill climb

★

---

## DAY 1

Medford to Ashland
Terrain: Flat with slight rise
Sights: Shakespearean Festival
14 miles

Flying toward Medford, the closest link with last year's route, Martin's mission again was to purify his body, to stop smoking, to get "whole." To help him, I brought along a book of my brother's called *Fit for Life*, which detailed a diet regimen. Motivated and armed with sci-

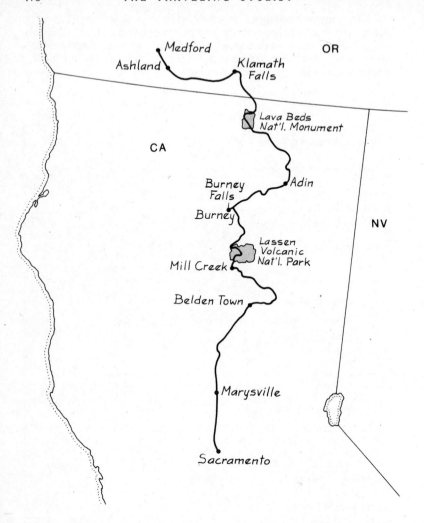

entific analysis, Martin was eager to jump off the plane and start riding into wholeness.

But the airline had mistakenly sent his bike and sleeping bag to Spokane. Since it wouldn't return until 2:00 A.M., we ended up with a free stay at Nendel's Inn.

So instead of attending a play that evening at Ashland's famous Shakespearean Festival, we had an opportunity to explore Medford, the largest city and commercial hub of the Rogue River Valley. With Martin, that meant exploring a bar.

We spent the evening talking with a pear farmer. Medford, it seems, is the pear-growing capital of the United States. Martin and I ended up going back to our hotel room with about a dozen pieces of the bell-bottomed fruit. When I mentioned that *Fit for LIfe* preached an all-fruit diet before noon, the farmer ran out to his truck in the pouring rain and brought us a bag.

---

**DIRECTIONS:** South 14 miles on US 99.

**ACCOMMODATIONS: Nendel's Inn,** 2300 Crater Lake Highway, Medford, OR, (503) 779-3141. <u>Amenities</u>: indoor pool. <u>Rooms</u>: 164, double $50. VISA, MC, AMEX, DINERS, DIS.
**Knights Inn Motel,** 2359 Highway 66, Ashland, OR, (503) 482-5111. <u>Amenities</u>: pool. <u>Rooms</u>: 40, $46. VISA, MC.

**CAMPING: Glenyan KOA,** 5310 Highway 66, Ashland, OR, (503) 482-4138. <u>Amenities</u>: pool, laundry, groceries.

---

# DAY 2

Ashland to Klamath Falls
Terrain: Major mountain climbs
59 miles

After a pit stop in Ashland, we turned east, expecting an easy cruise to Klamath Falls. Well, after an unexpectedly strenuous fifty-nine miles, I wanted to change the name to Klamath Rise and Falls.

Just east of Ashland, we ran into the Cascade Mountains. The next five miles led us up 2,000 feet to the Tub Springs Wayside—me by my own power and Martin via hitchhike. But the climbing was far from over. After a long downhill, we rose gradually to 4,360-foot Parker Summit, then peaked at 4,690-foot Hayden Summit.

Meeting Martin in Klamath Falls after a final, too-short downhill, I didn't realize how beat I was until we sat down after raiding a Safeway. I'd gone seventy-three miles on my first day of riding in a month. Martin looked worse, even though he'd ridden only half my distance. He hadn't been on a bike since our trip to Oregon a year before. We both passed out.

When we woke up, it was dark. "I don't feel like a hotel tonight," Martin yawned, looking up at the cloudless, starry sky. "It's too beautiful to sleep indoors."

Climbing up an eight-foot-high brick fence next to a building, he lifted himself up four more feet onto the roof. "Hey, it's flat up here. Hand me my bike." In minutes, we had our home for the night—on top of a radiator shop with a beautiful view of the Safeway.

**DIRECTIONS:** East 59 miles on SR 66 to Klamath Falls.

**ACCOMMODATIONS: Thunderbird Motel,** 3612 S. 6th Street, Klamath Falls, OR. (503) 882-8864. Amenities: pool, whirlpool. Rooms: 108, double $60. VISA, MC, AMEX, DINERS, DIS.

**CAMPING: Mallard Campground,** 3 miles north on US 97, (503) 882-0482. Amenities: laundry, whirlpool.

# DAY 3

Klamath Falls, Oregon to Tionesta, California
Terrain: Moderate
Sights: Lava Beds National Monument, Modoc Indian War sites,
    lava caves, petroglyphs
60 miles

Heading southeast out of Klamath through flat, increasingly treeless land, we crossed into California and arrived in tiny Tule Lake, the only place in the world whose city symbol is Mr. Potato Head wearing a cowboy hat.

As we rode into Modoc County, the scenery became truly stark, with rocky, high-desert brushlands and mesas. Since it was vaguely reminiscent of the lava rock area south of Bend from the last trip, it was no surprise when we came to Lava Beds National Monument.

While heat-sapped Martin decided to hitch to the Visitors Center, I headed up the rugged monument road to visit the battle sites. Yes, battle sites—the Lava Beds' most striking formations were used for defense purposes by the Modoc Indians, who made a valiant last stand here against the U.S. Army in 1873.

It turned out that I was a casualty here, too. While I was pulling my bike side-to-side as I climbed hilly Hospital Rock, my handlebars broke apart at the spot where an internally run brake wire ran through a hole. Holding up my bloody hand, which had been cut on the jagged edge, I almost laughed at the title of the historical placard a few feet away: "Bad Day at Hospital Rock."

The injury wasn't bad and didn't even hurt my sightseeing. Picked up by Martin in a truck, I still saw the area's giant, eerie mounds of lava and Captain Jack's Stronghold, a natural lava fortress where sixty braves under Modoc Chief Captain Jack held off six hundred U.S. troops for three full months.

I got some first aid at the Visitors Center before we took a bus tour of an area displaying ancient Indian petroglyphs. With no lodging at the Lava Beds, and no knowledge of rooms down the road in Tionesta, we rolled our bags out on the Center's awning-covered porch as darkness fell. The porch protected us from a big rainstorm that night.

---

**DIRECTIONS:** Southeast 23 miles on SR 39 to California border. Continue 8 miles on SR 138 through Tule Lake. Turn south 18 miles on Lava Beds Monument Road to the Visitors Center. Go 12 miles south to Tionesta.

**ACCOMMODATIONS: Park Motel,** 2 miles south of town on SR 139, Tule Lake, CA, (916) 667-2913. Rooms: 12, double $28. VISA, MC.
**Hawks Nest Cabins,** on Lava Beds Road, near Timber Mountain Store, Tionesta, CA, (916) 664-3187. Separate showerhouse. Rooms: 7 cabins, $25; must call ahead. Cash or traveler's checks.

**CAMPING:** At Monument, near Visitors Center, (916) 667-2282. No showers.

---

# DAY 4

Lava Beds National Monument to Adin
Terrain: Some hills plus climb
58 miles

Among the Lava Beds' wonders are giant lava caves that burrow so deeply into the ground that the ice inside never melts. Donning helmets and flashlights, we spent the early part of the day walking them with two dozen other tourists.

We delayed the hilly, 1,000-foot climb over 5,170-foot Adin Pass for a hitchhike to Alturas, the biggest town in the area (population, 3,500) and supposedly the only one with a bike shop. Unfortunately, we arrived to find only a hardware store with a few kids' bikes—but no handlebars. With sundown near, we did the only thing we could do: get a hotel and look for an Indian bar.

Well, we didn't find an Indian bar, but we did find a bar with a half-Modoc in it named Wyoming. The second Martin saw Wyoming, he threw up his hands, gave him a hug and shouted, "Oh, Dad, after all these years, at last I've found you!"

Wyoming looked terrified.

"Oh, Dad," Martin continued dramatically, "I've searched across America, Mexico, Canada for you. And just when I'd given up hope, when I thought I'd be an orphan forever, I saw your nose." Martin knelt down next to the bewildered man so that their faces were side-by-side. "I'm your son," he said. "Look at our noses."

Sure enough, although Wyoming had a round, brown face and black hair, while Martin had red hair and a pink, skinny face, their thin, one-bump, rudderlike schnozzes looked exactly alike.

Martin spent the rest of the night buying Wyoming drinks. He got drunker and drunker, and after much prodding, began calling Martin "son."

Finally, about midnight, Wyoming excused himself and walked out of the room, stumbling back twenty minutes later with a pair of rusty handlebars—kids' old-fashioned Sting-Ray style bars from the 1960s.

"Son," he said, handing Martin the bars, "I'd hate to have you hangin' around here and botherin' me all the time." He gave Martin a big hug and walked off.

---

**DIRECTIONS:** 5 miles south on Monument Road. Southeast 27 miles on SR 139 to Canby. South 22 miles on SR 299 to Adin.

**ACCOMMODATIONS: Juniper Tree Motel,** Junction SR 299 and 139, Adin, CA, (916) 299-3300. <u>Amenities</u>: coffee and cookies in morning. <u>Rooms</u>: 7, double $29. VISA, MC.

**CAMPING: Upper Rush Creek,** 7 miles northeast on SR 299, (916) 299-3215. No showers.

---

# DAY 5

Adin to Burney
Terrain: Flat to rolling, with some climbs
Sights: Burney Falls
72 miles

After a shaky morning on my funny-looking bike, which felt like a turn-of-the-century high-wheeler with its Sting-Ray handlebars, I coasted down into Adin and met Martin, who'd hitched over the pass. We rode together through the flat Big Valley, climbed a fairly steep 500 feet over Big Valley Pass, then whipped down 1,200 feet through the Fall River Valley. By the intersection of SR 299 and SR 89 (forty-six miles from Adin, but eighty-seven for me), I was feeling good; I liked this bike, once I got used to it. Pumped up by the clean air and the forested surroundings, Martin was flying high, too. He'd done fifty already, yet wanted to do more.

So instead of ending the day in Burney, we headed north to see a waterfall that Wyoming had told us was beautiful. Burney Falls, 129 feet high, looked like an alpine Hawaiian waterfall, draping over a stairstep of algae-covered lava rocks into a shimmering emerald pool. Theodore Roosevelt described it as "the eighth wonder of the world." It's a wonder more people don't know about it.

Staying in the campsite, we skipped the backtrack to Burney, a metropolis of 3,000. When we thought about that number later, it amazed us. Since Klamath Falls, the total population of the places we'd been through had been maybe 10,000 people. The traffic was limited mainly to occasional logging trucks. And this was California, of all places, home of 28 million people in search of a parking space.

---

**DIRECTIONS:** Southwest 46 miles on SR 299 and SR 89. North 11 miles on SR 89 to MacArthur-Burney Falls Memorial State Park. South 8 miles on Black Ranch Road to Burney.

**ACCOMMODATIONS: Charm Motel,** 37363 Main Street, Burney, CA, (916) 335-2254. Rooms: 30, double $46–$50. VISA, MC, AMEX.

**CAMPING: MacArthur-Burney Falls Memorial State Park,** on SR 89, (800) 446-7275 (in CA), (916) 452-1950. Amenities: sundries, food.

---

## DAY 6

Burney to Mill Creek Resort
Terrain: All day climbing
Sights: Mount Lassen, bubbling mud pots, volcanic steamers
83 miles

This was the day Martin and I rose to the occasion. Because all day long, we gradually climbed, topping out at 8,600 feet.

Turning south on SR 89, the scenery and the elevation began changing. Vast lava beds appeared as we rose from Burney's 3,130 feet to 5,737 feet at the gates of Lassen Volcanic National Park, where the Cascades join the Sierra Nevada.

The rangers told us that we'd be riding by 10,457-foot-high Lassen Peak, a volcano that erupted three hundred times between 1914 and 1917. Though they were the last eruptions in the continental United States until Mount St. Helens (1980), Lassen is still active, as the boiling lakes, bubbling mud pots, hot springs, and steamers on its slopes testify.

So our ascent began. For the next twenty-one miles, under the gaze of Lassen Peak, we twisted higher and higher, passing 6,000, 7,000, 8,000 feet. I didn't look back, concentrating on developing a rhythm on my gangly bike.

Cresting Lassen Loop Summit, elevation 8,514 feet, I dismounted and got the shock of my life: Martin was a scant 100 feet behind me!

"I know what you're thinking," he said, when he rolled up, "but I didn't hitch. It's the *Fit for Life* diet. I feel so strong—eating those pears every morning, not smoking, not drinking. And watching you on that geeky bike, I figured, 'What the hell—if you can do it on that . . .' "

On the long coast down, which dropped us 2,500 feet out of the park to Mill Creek, I had to laugh: Martin just stopped drinking the night before and hadn't smoked for a grand total of two days. It was all cycle-logical!

---

**DIRECTIONS:** North 6 miles on SR 299. South 74 miles on SR 89 (out of Lassen Park). South 3 miles to Mill Creek.

**ACCOMMODATIONS: Mill Creek Resort,** on SR 172, Mill Creek, CA, (916) 595-4449. Amenities: laundry. Cabins: 9, double $32–$36. Also camping. No credit cards.

**CAMPING: Lassen Park,** 7 sites throughout, including near southwest entrance. Call U.S. Park Service at (916) 595-4444.

---

# DAY 7

Mill Creek to Belden Town
Terrain: Rolling lakeside and riverside grades
76 miles

An incredible day of riding unfolded as Martin and I swept southeast and southwest in a big reverse C, dropping 2,500 feet along the way. Already pretty along Lake Almanor and the Wolf River, the route became stunning next to the North Fork of the East Branch of the Feather River. Curvy and exhilarating, the road wound through the Feather River Canyon, a major gold strike area in the early 1850s. As it dropped the last thousand feet in elevation (to 2,335 feet at Belden), I whipped through that canyon feeling like a Ferrari on Sunset Boulevard.

We entered the spacious Belden Town and Resort abuzz from the great ride. Martin felt particularly triumphant on his second full day of riding without hitching. His legs and lungs healthier by the minute from the exercise and the lack of cigarettes, he now spoke zealously of making a lifelong commitment to the principles espoused by *Fit for Life,* Pritikin, and other health gurus.

Hearing this, the young, red-haired woman who'd served us leaned over the bar and commented, "that doesn't look like much of a diet: chocolate and beer!" Oops—in all the excitement, we'd forgotten. "And," she added, "that doesn't look like much of a bike. Where'd you get those funky handlebars?"

We hit it off right away with Sarah, a Yale philosophy Ph.D. who was renovating this abandoned riverside palace with her brother. With no customers but us, they broke out a game of Trivial Pursuit.

It wasn't wild, but it was just as much fun: after a superb day of riding, just Martin and I discussing life and trivia all night with two friendly strangers in a tiny river town that we'd never heard of before.

**DIRECTIONS:** From Mill Creek, north 3 miles, east 54 miles on SR 89, west 20 miles on SR 70. Cross red bridge into Belden.

**ACCOMMODATIONS: Belden Town & Resort,** on SR 70, P.O. Box 1000, Belden, CA, 95915, (916) 283-2906. <u>Amenities</u>: laundry, river access. <u>Rooms</u>: 11, double $30 + . VISA, MC.
**Pine Aire Resort,** on Feather River, Twain, CA, (15 miles east of Belden on SR 70), (916) 283-1730. <u>Rooms</u>: 7 cabins, $32–$45. No credit cards.

**CAMPING: Belden** (see above). **North Fork,** 2 miles east on SR 70, 2 miles north on FR 274, (916) 283-0555. <u>Amenities</u>: laundry, store.

# DAY 8

Belden Town to Marysville
Terrain: Rolling rivergrade, then flat
76 miles

For the second day in a row, the Feather River Canyon seemed like a dream. Pine trees, sun-bleached rocks, sometimes a wide river, sometimes narrow, but always slightly downhill. Spotting a beach after twenty miles, Martin and I stopped for an hour of swimming in the crisp mountain water—a Huck Finn fantasy for us city boys.

After that, SR 70 broke away from the Feather River, went over some hills, then dumped us down into the flatland of the San Joaquin Valley, California's vast agricultural midsection. We pit-stopped for a pizza in Oroville, a one-time gold and diamond mining center now ringed by mining ghost towns, and shared a table in the crowded parlor with a thirty-five-year-old mother and her four kids: girls Kis and Caresse, and boys Cud (for Cuddle) and Hug (for Huggins).

"I wanted my children to be a beacon of love to the world," mom said when asked about the choice of names. She got her wish: Kis, fifteen, was eight months pregnant. As we rode into Marysville on the freewaylike SR-70, we noted that the differences between small- and big-town America might not be as great as we'd once thought.

**DIRECTIONS:** South on SR 70 all day.

**ACCOMMODATIONS: Oxbow Motel,** 1078 N. Beale Road, Marysville, CA, (916) 742-8238. <u>Amenities</u>: pool. <u>Rooms</u>: 40, double $40. VISA, MC, AMEX.

**CAMPING:** None close by.

# DAY 9

Marysville to Sacramento
Terrain: Flat
50 miles

It was brown farmland as far as the eye could see as we rode along the Sacramento River into Sacramento, California's 300,000-strong capital.

After a picture at the Capitol dome, we headed to Sutter's Fort, the first European settlement in the area. John Sutter changed the course of California history when he found a piece of gold on his land in 1848, causing the famous Gold Rush the next year.

Instead of heading eight miles back to the airport, we decided to stay in town and celebrate at Sam's Hofbrau in downtown. After devouring some greasy German sausage, we moved over to the bar, where I chugged beers and Martin bought drinks for the house.

By the end of the night, it was apparent that the *Fit for Life* experiment had run its course. "It was good while it lasted, eh, Martin?" I commented.

"Yeah, we'll have to do it again next year!" he replied.

I could hardly wait for next year.

---

**DIRECTIONS:** To avoid freeway, go south 1 mile on North Beale Road, south 1¼ miles on Lindhurst, east ½ mile on McGowan Parkway, south 10 miles on Highway 70 to East Nicholas. Go west 32 miles on Markham Road/Garden Highway through Nicholas along the Sacramento River. Turn right 2 miles into Discovery Park Bike Trail. Follow it across the American River. Turn right for 2 miles on Sacramento River Levee bike trail to Old Sacramento and downtown.

**DIRECTIONS:** To airport from capitol, go northeast 15 miles on Garden Highway, east 3 miles on Bayou Road.

**ACCOMMODATIONS: Sandman Motel,** 236 Jibboom Street (on Sacramento River next to bike trail), Sacramento, CA, (916) 443-6515. Amenities: pool, spa. Rooms: 115, double $50. VISA, MC, AMEX, DINERS, DIS.

**CAMPING: Sacramento-Metro KOA,** 4851 Lake Street, 4½ miles west on I-80, exit W. Capitol, (916) 371-6771.

★

# SIGHTSEEING INFORMATION

ASHLAND, OREGON
**Oregon Shakespearean Festival:** One of country's most prestigious; evening and matinee daily performances, exhibit center; reservations needed; $10 to $20. (503) 482-4331.

LASSEN VOLCANIC NATIONAL PARK, CALIFORNIA
**Lassen Park Road:** Thirty-mile drive through park gives access to volcanic mountains, bubbling hot pots, other signs of geologic activity; guide shows highlights, including Hot Rock, Bumpass Hell Trail, Sulfur Works thermal area; $1.75. U.S. Park Service, (916) 595-4444.

LAVA BEDS NATIONAL MONUMENT, CALIFORNIA
Area of cooled molten lava flows; plaques explain role of these formations in Modoc Indian War of 1872–1873; tours of ancient Indian petroglyphs, lava tube caves, ice caves; Visitors Center open 9:00 to 6:00. (916) 667-2282.

McARTHUR-BURNEY FALLS MEMORIAL STATE PARK, CALIFORNIA
Beautiful, stair-stepping falls; 4 miles north on SR 299, 11 miles north on SR 89 from Burney; sundries, food. (800) 446-7275, (916) 452-1950 or (916) 335-2777.

SACRAMENTO, CALIFORNIA
**State Capitol,** 10th and L Streets: Historical exhibits; free guided tours. (916) 324-0333.
**Sutter's Fort,** 27th and L streets: First European settlement in Central Valley; exhibits show 1800s life; $1. (916) 445-4209.

# CHAPTER 13

## REVELATION ON THE BLUE RIDGE
### ATLANTA TO WASHINGTON, D.C.

**B**IKE TRIP AS THERAPY? LIKE FEW OTHER FORMS OF TRAVEL, bike touring's long, solitary hours provide time to reflect, to plan, to think. By October of 1987, I needed that time. As much as I hated riding alone, I felt I had no choice but to fly to Atlanta, Georgia, and begin riding north through the mountains to Washington, D.C.

When I finished eleven days later, I had made a decision that was to substantially change my career, my lifestyle, and my entire outlook on life. That's why I look back so fondly on my tour of the Blue Ridge Parkway, the road that hugs the top of the southern Appalachians along the western backbone of North Carolina and Virginia.

Just before the trip began, I'd reached a crossroads. Eighteen months before, I'd been fired from my job for taking the Mission: Vancouver trip. The time since had been a period of major struggle. I knew I needed to get focused. And one way to do it was to take a bike trip.

That may seem strange, considering that I'd already done thousands of miles from April 1986 to September 1987. I did two trips with Martin, in Oregon and Northern California. I did a tour of Nova Scotia. I flew up to the Vancouver World's Fair, then biked down the Pacific Coast. I even traveled without a bike, visiting Hong Kong, China, Singapore, and Malaysia.

But those were all sightseeing and/or buddy trips. This time, I absolutely needed to go alone, to be free of compromise, to be free to think and analyze my life for hours and days without interruption. This trip would mostly be a journey into my own mind. I knew just the place to go.

While on a ferry in Alaska at the end of Willie's Loop in May 1985, an old man from Tallulah Falls, Georgia, told me about the Blue Ridge Parkway. It rose and plunged 469 miles along the ridges of the Great Smoky and Blue Ridge Mountains, which include forty summits of over 6,000 feet. It topped out at 6,684-foot Mount Mitchell, the highest point in the East. Added to Skyline Drive, winding 105 miles through Shenandoah National Park, there wasn't a stoplight for 574 miles. It was an all-parkway route from the bottom of North Carolina to the top of Virginia.

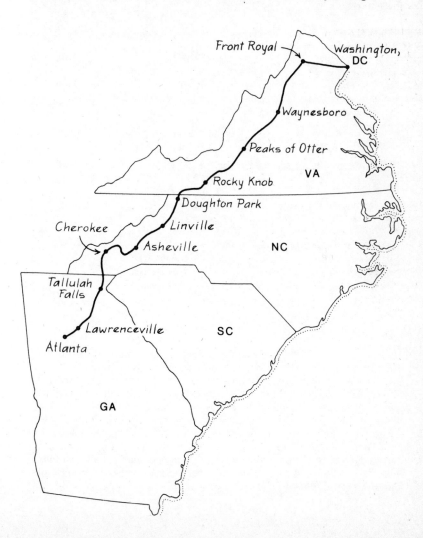

## ROUTE SLIP
### Total of 832 miles in 11 days

| Day | Ending Point | Terrain* | Sights | Mileage |
|---|---|---|---|---|
| 1 | Lawrenceville, Georgia | Easy/Moderate | Sate capitol, Stone Mountain | 36 |
| 2 | Tallulah Falls, Georgia | Moderate | | 79 |
| 3 | Cherokee, North Carolina | Moderate/Difficult | Cherokee Museum | 66 |
| 4 | Asheville, North Carolina | Difficult | | 84 |
| 5 | Linville, North Carolina | Difficult | Mount Mitchell, Linville Falls | 79 |
| 6 | Doughton Park, North Carolina | Moderate/Difficult | Blowing Rock | 75 |
| 7 | Rocky Knob, Virginia | Moderate/Difficult | | 70 |
| 8 | Peaks of Otter | Moderate/Difficult | | 83 |
| 9 | Waynesboro, Virginia | Moderate/Difficult | | 87 |
| 10 | Front Royal, Virginia | Moderate/Difficult | | 105 |
| 11 | Washington, D.C. | Moderate | Manassas National Battlefield, Washington monuments | 68 |

*Easy = flat to rolling; moderate = hilly; difficult = repeated miles of hills and climbing

★

To be sure, it'd be a workout. These mountains were so formidable that Americans like Daniel Boone couldn't even cross them until 1769 (at the Cumberland Gap) — 150 years after colonists had been established on the East Coast. The total trip would be 11 days and 832 miles of climbing, descending, and natural bliss: scenic panoramic overlooks; mountain forest of hickory, oak, and pine; wilderness of deer, bear, bobcat, and turkey; and, in late September, the beginning of fall's brilliant colors.

There would be no distractions, just pure bike riding. No need to figure out a strategy to see the sights. Virtually no need to look at a map. Just stay on the Blue Ridge Highway and head northeast. Just pump up and down. And think.

Before I left, I made a copy of my old *Bicycling* magazine article, "The Principles of Cycle-ology." My gut instinct always told me I ought to be a journalist. Back on the college newspaper, I was the editor of the feature page—and loved it. But that was ten years earlier. Still, that one cycling article always stuck in my mind.

When I packed, I didn't bring any books to read this time. I just brought the article and a couple of notebooks to write in. Then I set off for the Blue Ridge.

# DAY 1

Atlanta to Lawrenceville
Terrain: Flat into town, then rolling, hilly
Sights: Capitol, Stone Mountain
36 miles

I didn't think of this trip as particularly southern. The Blue Ridge was up in the sparsely populated mountains, just a two-day ride from the cosmopolitan melting pot and corporate boomtown of Atlanta.

So I was surprised to see Confederate stars and bars adorning the Georgia state flag at the state Capitol building, along with historical markers about the Battle of Atlanta, old rebel cannons, and a statue of Confederate Governor Joseph Emerson Brown. Later at Stone Mountain, the whole side of a granite mountain was carved with the horse-riding likenesses of Confederate President Jefferson Davis and generals Stonewall Jackson and Robert E. Lee.

---

**DIRECTIONS:** From Hartsfield Atlanta International Airport, go north 5 miles on Stewart Avenue (US 41), east 2 miles on SR 154 to capitol building. Go east 15 more miles on SR 154/SR 10, right 1 mile on Ponce de Leon to Stone Mountain. Then go east 8 miles on US 78, north 5 miles on SR 124 to Lawrenceville.

**ACCOMMODATIONS: Arborgate Inn,** 731 W. Pike Street, junction of SR 120 and SR 316, Lawrenceville, GA, (404) 995-7782. Rooms: 52, double $40–$45. VISA, MC, AMEX, DINERS, DIS.
**Stone Mountain Inn,** 2 miles east in Park, Stone Mountain, GA, (404) 469-3311. Amenities: pool. Rooms: 92, $85. VISA, MC, AMEX, DINERS, DIS.

**CAMPING: Stone Mountain Camp,** (404) 498-5710. Amenities: laundry, groceries.

★

## DAY 2

Lawrenceville to Tallulah Falls
Terrain: Hilly
79 miles

This day took me over rolling rural country that became very hilly after Clarkdale.

That night I got to talking to the waitress at the Hickory Mountain Restaurant in tiny Tallulah Falls, where I'd been writing in my diary for over an hour.

When I told her of my travels, her jaw hung open. "Alaska, Montreal, Nova Scotia—my gosh! The furtherist I been is Atlanta!" she exclaimed. "Don't you work?"

"Lemme show you something," I said, conspicuously ignoring her question and pulling out my *Bicycling* article. After reading it, she ran into the backroom.

"You're a writer, so you gotta write a book someday about all your trips," she said on her return. "I did. It's easy. Look."

She handed me a small hardback book with big print entitled *Firefox,* a story of the people of Tallulah Falls. "That's me," she said, pointing to the author's name. Terry Shead. "And he's in it," she added, pointing to a man, about fifty, two booths away.

"You writin' a book?" he said, not waiting for an answer. "Make sure you put me in there: Honest Bradley Brown, the owner of this place, the wealthy and powerful scion of the industrious Scotch-Irish who came to this region two hundred years ago. We're Presbyterians, and we don't believe in dunkin' in the water like all these Baptists. A little sprinkle'll do us fine.

"My grandfather hauled all the lumber that built this town. My daddy hauled all the iron that built the dam across this beautiful gorge, the second biggest in America next to the Grand Canyon, over twelve hundred feet deep.

"Us Browns got rich when Tallulah Falls was a gambling resort to rival the Catskills in thirties and forties. The Great Wallenda walked the gorge on a wire this big," he held his fingers an inch apart. "Then we got killed by air-conditioning. No one needed to come up from Atlanta anymore for the cool mountain air here at the foot of the Appalachians. Now just got a bunch of retired up here. Rand McNally designated it 'the best place in America to retire,' due to its weather and pretty lakes and woods."

Later, Bradley was haggling with the waitress over his check.

"I thought you said you owned this place," I said, "that you were wealthy and powerful."

He smiled. "Listen, they call me Honest Bradley Brown. I'm known to bend the truth, to stretch the truth, to stick the truth in the closet a while and give it a much-deserved rest. But I've never actually told a lie." Then he walked out.

After the restaurant closed, I found the only motel in town fully booked. The whole region fills with tourists coming to see the autumn changing of the leaves.

Searching for a camp spot, I was stopped by a truck. "Hey, you're the writer, aren't you?" said the driver. "Terry told me about you. If you want, you can sleep at the high school. I got the keys to everything. I'm the janitor."

I followed him up a winding hill to the exclusive Tallulah Falls Boarding School, where he opened the door to the gym and pointed out the showers. Before he left, I got his name, Dale Gibson, to include in that book I knew I'd have to write someday.

That night was the only time I've ever slept on a trampoline in a basketball court. And it was the first time I realized how much I liked the ring of the word *writer.*

---

**DIRECTIONS:** North 10 miles on SR 20, northeast 20 miles on US 23 to Gainesville. Northeast 26 miles on SR 53, north 23 miles on US 441.

**ACCOMMODATIONS: Lakeside Lodge,** on US 441, Tallulah Falls, GA, (404) 754-6022. Near lake, gorge trail. Rooms: 19, double $35. VISA, MC.

**CAMPING: Terrora Park.** Inquire at motel.

---

## DAY 3

Tallulah Falls, Georgia, to Cherokee, North Carolina
Terrain: Big hills plus major climb
Sights: Cherokee Museum
66 miles

Big hills began after Tallulah Falls, the biggest just out of Franklin, North Carolina—two and a half miles of steep grade. It took me an hour to climb against headwinds so strong that I could barely coast downhill.

Scores of "Injun" trading posts appeared as the last miles flattened into a mountain-framed valley. In it was Cherokee, the jumping-off point for the southern end of the Blue Ridge Route and the last remnant of the once-great Cherokee nation.

I was ready for a crazy night at an Indian bar, but it turns out that Cherokee, located within the Cherokee Reservation, has banned bars, lounges, and rock music. I ended up at a McDonald's, where I met a bicyclist.

Like me, Matt Jablonsky was starting the Blue Ridge the next day—but with an unenthusiastic partner.

"She's always complaining about everything," Matt said. "We've been riding for two days already, and it feels like two weeks."

My recommendation was immediate. "Dump her."

I tried to put him at ease by letting him know that, though I always prefer a partner, riding alone can be great. It's certainly better than a bad partner.

He shook his head. "Naw, I couldn't do that to her."

You mean to yourself, I thought. I excused myself. I had my own problems to deal with.

You see, it looked like my Blue Ridge trip might end before it really began. On the ride into Cherokee, I'd called my phone machine and found a call from a corporation I'd interviewed with months earlier. When I phoned the personnel manager, she told me they were about to offer me a job. All I had to do was come in and meet the Vice President of Marketing before he took off on a four-week trip to Asia.

I should have been ecstatic. This was the break I'd been hoping for. The money, the position, the cushy corporate comfort—it was all there. Of course, I'd cut the trip short and fly back to meet him. Heck, being a writer, the book—that was all a fantasy. I set up the meeting for the day before he left, so I'd have a couple of more days to ride.

---

**DIRECTIONS:** North 53 miles to Dillsboro on US 23 (crossing North Carolina border). Then east and north 13 miles on US 441.

**ACCOMMODATIONS: Pioneer Motel,** on US 19S, Cherokee, NC, (704) 497-2435. Amenities: pool, tennis. Rooms: 21, double $45–$55. VISA, MC, AMEX, DIS.

**CAMPING: Double "B" Travel Park,** east 1 mile on US 19, (704) 497-9212. Amenities: groceries, pool.

---

# DAY 4

Cherokee to Asheville (milepost 385)
Terrain: Major climbs all day long
84 miles

I'd resigned myself to wingtips and power ties when I pulled up to milepost 469, the southern terminal of the Blue Ridge Parkway. Then, as if practicing my climb up the corporate ladder, I flung myself into the East's highest mountains and the toughest secton of the Blue Ridge. Almost 20 percent of the climbing of the entire 469-mile route comes in the first 35 miles.

The first three miles jumped 2,200 feet. Then there were similar drops and climbs for the next 35 miles, topping out at 6,053-foot Richland Balsam, the highest point on the highway. A smaller roller coaster took me past Balsam Gap, the scene of a big Cherokee defeat in the

Revolutionary War, as well as Rough Butt Bald and Mount Pisgah. By the end of the day, I cruised down into a By-Lo supermarket just off the Ridge Route in Asheville feeling incredibly macho.

But as dusk descended, my day didn't end. I planned a cool moon-light ascent to Craggy Gardens, the biggest elevation change on the Blue Ridge—2,500 feet. That'd give me 105 miles on the most challenging day of the whole route, allowing me to abort the trip with my head held high, to march happily ever after into the corporate world in my cookie-cutter blue and gray worsted.

On the way up the mountain, I delayed for two hours to drink beer with three local collegians. They mainly talked about the typical hopes, dreams, and fears of all twenty-year-olds. All were ambitious, but afraid of leaving the comfy confines of mother Asheville, population 60,000. One wanted to go to New York, but kept chickening out.

Since I was the veteran of the group, viewed as an oracle of wisdom, I offered some fatherly advice. "You gotta go for it," I implored. "Do you always want to look back on your life knowing that you didn't try?"

Sufficiently rested, I shot up the long, moonlit incline, speeding past hundreds of cars filled with Asheville teenagers making out on the mountainside. And I wondered why I didn't have the guts to follow my own advice.

---

**DIRECTIONS:** Blue Ridge Parkway all day.

**ACCOMMODATIONS: Holiday Inn,** 1450 Tunnel Road, Asheville, NC, (704) 298-5611. Amenities: laundry, pool. Rooms: 111, double $75–$80. VISA, MC, AMEX, DINERS, DIS.
**Four Seasons Motor Inn,** 820 Merriman Avenue, (704) 274-3531. Rooms: 21, $30–$35. VISA, MC, AMEX, DIS.

**CAMPING: Mount Pisgah,** milepost 409, (704) 259-0701. Amenities: grocer-ies, restaurant, no showers.

★

---

# DAY 5

Asheville to Linville (milepost 292)
Terrain: Big climbs plus additional climbs
79 miles

I awoke satisfied, for even though I was aborting the trip, at least I'd knocked off the hardest part of the Blue Ridge. After posing for a picture in front of Mount Mitchell, the East's highest point at 8,884 feet, I planned to drop off the Ridge into the cities below, where I'd catch a bus to D.C. and my flight home.

But when I reached Buck Creek Gap (milepost 345) after a long downhill, I noticed that a strut of my rack had broken—probably from the stress of my climbing those hills like a racer, throwing the bike back and forth instead of puttering up in the granny gear. Supporting the whole load now, the other strut was rubbing against the sidewall of the tire, which wouldn't last long.

Oh well, I was quitting anyway. It would surely last long enough to make it downhill on SR 80 to the town of Marion. Down in civilization, I'd somehow get the thing fixed, then find a bus. I tried to position the broken strut so that it wouldn't move, then took a last look at the Blue Ridge. I'd be back to finish it someday.

The switchback was nerve-wracking. It was so steep, and the drop-off on the sides so severe, that I squeezed my brakes like a Bronx grandmother clutching her purse. Lurching downhill, I wondered what would give out first—my hands or the brake cables. Even though it seemed like I was crawling, I was going fast enough to flip over any moment. I'd have much rather been climbing this hill than descending it.

Then the sound of a gunshot rang in my ears. The rear tire had blown!

Instantly, I was out of control. Despite clamping on the brakes, I was skidding on the rim, picking up speed. The tire sheared through, sparks flew up from the asphalt. I held on like a cowboy on the horns of a wild steer, my feet locked into my toe clips, heading right for the sheer drop-off that would mean certain death.

Terrified, brakes useless, I knew I had to dump the bike. So I leaned lower and lower to my left, like a baseball player sliding into second base. As the bike went horizontal and I felt myself slowing down, I felt a coming sense of relief that I'd survive, that I'd emerge unscathed, that—

*Uuuugggghhhhh!!* My butt was on fire!! My left cheek was grinding into the pavement. And as I skidded downhill, a car barreled toward me, frantically screeching and spinning out on the narrow, twisting road to avoid me. I closed my eyes and gritted my teeth for the impact.

When my eyes opened, I saw the grille of a stopped Ford Bronco two feet away. Shaking like a newborn deer, I got up, took inventory. Surprisingly, nothing broken, but I was scraped up pretty badly.

The driver ran out, screaming, "Are you okay, are you okay?" But when I opened my mouth to assure him I was, I couldn't speak. I was in shock. For the next ten minutes, I could only stammer incoherently.

In that time, the shook-up driver loaded me into his Bronco, turned around, and was halfway to a hospital in Marion. When I finally calmed down enough to speak, I let him know I was okay and said to drop me at the Marion K-Mart, where I picked up a new tube and tire. I would have picked up a new rack, too, but my Eclipse-brand rack and panniers were designed as a unit. Foolishly, each was useless without the other. The only solution was to get the broken strut fixed.

I found the town's only bike shop in the basement of a private home. Outside, a small hand-painted sign read, "Jack's Bicycle Repairs." Inside was a twenty-by-twenty room jammed with new bikes, old bikes, dozens of wheels and frames hanging from the ceiling, and a skinny man about fifty named Jack.

While Jack devised a metal splint to hold my rack together, he told me he'd been a "pretty hot" bike racer as a teenager in the fifties. But since there was no real bike racing in the United States then, he'd have had to go to Europe. Fearing the unknown, he didn't.

"And I always regretted it," he said. "I've always wondered how good I coulda bin. All I know is, I've never in my life enjoyed anything like I did bike racing."

As he said that, I was thinking the same thing about writing.

"And what is it you said you do?" he asked.

"Oh, I've got a job waiting for me in Los Angeles," I said offhandedly. "Marketing management."

"You don't sound too enthused," he said.

"No, it's a good opportunity," I said blandly. "It's a job, anyway."

*It's a job.* Leaving Jack, who didn't charge me a penny, the phrase kept ringing in my ears. Growing up, I never wanted a run-of-the-mill *job*.

On the way to the bus station, I stopped at a phone. I hesitated, then dialed. I told the personnel manager I'd be delayed until the following week. Nothing I could do about it.

"That's too late," she said. "We wanted to hire someone before the vice president left for Japan. You're the number-one candidate."

When I again stated I couldn't make it, the deed was done. She said to call her "just in case" when I returned home. Then I hitched back up to the Blue Ridge Route.

I shot through Linville Falls without stopping at its renowned gorge, was oblivious to the pretty fall foliage, and didn't even notice the heavy auto tourist traffic. I hardly paid any attention to the continuous 200-to-500-foot hills, save a 1,200-footer beginning at milepost 325. I barely felt the scrape on my butt.

I arrived after dark at Holly's Bar in the town of Blowing Rock, where Appalachian State University students from Boone, a "dry" town* six miles north, were running amok. Later on they drove me back two miles, climbed a fence into private property,** and showed me Blowing Rock itself, a breathtaking 4,090 feet above John's River Gorge. Legend has it that an Indian threw a rival over the ledge, only to be stunned when the strong updraft blew him back.

"You're gonna write about this place, aren't you?" one of the guys said on the ride back to the dorms, where I spent the night.

"Huh?" I said, forgetting that I'd showed them my article earlier in the evening.

---

*A referendum in 1989 allows the purchase of liquor in Boone, curtailing the nightly exodus into Blowing Rock.

**Blowing Rock itself is privately owned. It closes at sundown.

"Well, you're a writer, right?"

"Yeah, right, of course," I hesitated, a little scared. I kind of felt like I'd jumped off the ledge at Blowing Rock myself today—and was wondering whether I'd fly.

---

**DIRECTIONS:** North 73 miles on Parkway to milepost 312, northeast 6 miles on SR 181/US 221 to Linville. To Mount Mitchell, take 4.8-mile spur road at milepost 355.4.

**ACCOMMODATIONS: Pixie Motor Inn,** junction of SR 105 and US 221, Linville, NC, (704) 733-2597. <u>Rooms</u>: 25, double $32. Cash or traveler's checks only.
**Chetola Resort,** N. Main Street (milepost 292), Blowing Rock, NC, (704) 295-9301. <u>Amenities</u>: laundry, racquetball, tennis, canoes, pool, sauna, whirlpool. <u>Rooms</u>: 42, $80–$90. VISA, MC, AMEX, DIS.
**Alpen Acres Motel,** north ¼ mile on US 321 at milepost 291, (704) 295-7981. <u>Amenities</u>: scenic hilltop, pool, barbeque. <u>Rooms</u>: 17, $38–$55. VISA, MC.

**CAMPING: Julian Price Camp,** milepost 297, (704) 259-0701. <u>Amenities</u>: rental boats, no showers.
**Linville Falls,** milepost 316, (704) 259-0701. <u>Amenities</u>: no showers.

---

## DAY 6

Linville Falls to Doughton Park (milepost 242)
Terrain: Many short to moderate climbs
75 miles

Twenty million people travel the Parkway every year, and I think all of them were out this day. A ranger at Doughton Park, where I camped after another rolling ride (milepost 276 starts the biggest climb, a thousand-footer), said that crowds come out at different times of the year to see specific flowers bloom: Memorial Day Weekend in May and June for purple and white rhododendrons; June for pink and white mountain laurels; throughout the summer for orange, red, and yellow azaleas. But nothing, he said, compares with the crowds that come out for the colors of fall. And it wasn't even "peak" yet, he said, which comes with the flaming hues of mid-to-late October.

For a Los Angeles boy raised on dull brown, it looked plenty good anyway. Add in the sighting of an occasional white-tailed deer, raccoon, and fox, and it was enough to make me forget the exhaust of the traffic and the haze of career planning. A natural high propelled me across the Virginia state line over two hundred-foot hills, all the way to Spangler's Bed and Breakfast by dark. (See Day 7.)

**DIRECTIONS:** North 4 miles on US 221 to Parkway, north rest of day.

**ACCOMMODATIONS: Bluff's Lodge,** Doughton Park, NC, (919) 372-4499. Rooms: 24, double $56. VISA, MC, AMEX, DINERS.
**Glendale Springs Inn,** milepost 259, ³⁄₁₀ of a mile west of Parkway on SR 16, Glendale Springs, NC, (919) 982-2102 or 982-2103. Amenities: free breakfast. Rooms: 18, $74–$85. VISA, MC, AMEX.
**Lee's Lodge & Restaurant,** 100 yards off Blue Ridge, (919) 982-3286. Rooms: 20, double $32. VISA, MC.

**CAMPING: Doughton Park,** milepost 241, (704) 259-0701. Amenities: groceries, no showers.

## DAY 7

Doughton Park, North Carolina, to Knob, Virginia (milepost 174)
Terrain: Numerous short climbs
70 miles

**DIRECTIONS:** Parkway north all day.

**ACCOMMODATIONS: Woodberry Inn,** 200 feet off milepost 174, Rocky Knob Cabin exit, Rocky Knob, VA, (703) 593-2567. Rooms: 16, double $48. VISA, MC, AMEX, DIS.
**Rocky Knob Cabins,** side road off milepost 174, (703) 593-3503. Open Memorial to Labor Day. Rooms: 7, $40–$60. VISA, MC, AMEX.
**Spangler's Bed & Breakfast,** in view of Parkway on SR 602 at milepost 180, Mayberry, VA, (703) 952-2454. One $50 cabin, one with no water, $20. Cash or checks only.

**CAMPING: Rocky Knob Campground,** (703) 593-3503.

## DAY 8

Rocky Knob to Peaks of Otter (milepost 86)
Terrain: Numerous short climbs with an 800-footer at milepost
  102
83 miles

My legs beat after the long ride the day before, I took it slow. When I stopped for a breakfast of freshly made apple butter at Mabry Mill, a restored water-powered mill at milepost 176.1, I heard the news about an earthquake that hit Los Angeles the day before, October 1. I tried to call my parents all day long, including from Roanoke, Virginia, the biggest city on the Blue Ridge, but the phone lines were jammed.

Since I was looking for meaning in everything at that point, I couldn't help but realize that yesterday was the day I'd have arrived back in Los Angeles. Maybe fate had caused me to wipe out on the mountain and run into Jack the bicycle man.

---

**DIRECTIONS:** Parkway all day.

**ACCOMMODATIONS: Peaks of Otter Lodge,** milepost 86, Peaks of Otter, Bedford, VA, (703) 586-1081. <u>Amenities</u>: restaurant. <u>Rooms</u>: 62, double $64. VISA, MC.

**CAMPING: Loft Mountain,** milepost 79.8, (703) 999-2266. <u>Amenities</u>: coffee shop.

---

# DAY 9

Peaks of Otter to Waynesboro (milepost 0)
Terrain: Numerous climbs, including two big ones
87 miles

After taking the Peaks of Otter Shuttle Bus up to a great view at the top of Sharp Mountain ("You can see both sides from up here," the driver joked, "the Atlantic Ocean over here and California over there"), I polished off the last of the Blue Ridge Route. But it wasn't easy. I made two 1,500-foot climbs before swooping to 649 feet above sea level at Otter

---

**DIRECTIONS:** Parkway all day.

**ACCOMMODATIONS: Deluxe Motor Court,** 2112 W. Main Street, Waynesboro, VA, (703) 949-8253. <u>Amenities</u>: pool. <u>Rooms</u>: 35, double $40–$55. VISA, MC, AMEX, DINERS, DIS.
**Skyline Parkway Motor Court,** junction I-64 and SR 250W, on Afton Mountain, 2½ miles south of Waynesboro, (703) 943-9654. <u>Rooms</u>: 33, $35. VISA, MC.

**CAMPING: Blue Ridge Parkway KOA,** milepost 27, west 1½ miles on SR 56, (703) 377-2795. <u>Amenities</u>: pool, store, laundry.
**Waynesboro North 340 Campground,** 5 miles north on SR 340, (703) 943-9573. <u>Amenities</u>: laundry, groceries, pool.

---

Creek (milepost 62), the lowest point on the entire Blue Ridge. After that, I worked back up to 3,100 feet (at milepost 37), arriving beat at Howard Johnson's on Afton Mountain, two and a half miles south of Waynesboro.

After dinner, I'd written several pages in my diary when my waitress came by with a fourth cup of tea. "You must be a writer," she said.

"Matter of fact," I replied, hoping to reward her sagacity, "check this out." I handed her the copy of "The Principles of Cycle-ology."

By page two, the article had her laughing out loud. I *was* a writer, or so she thought.

# DAY 10

Waynesboro to Front Royal
Terrain: Winding, hilly
105 miles

After a rousing two and a half-mile downhill into Waynesboro, the Blue Ridge was over—just in time to merge with Shenandoah National Park's Skyline Drive, which heads northeast through the Appalachians another 105 miles.

I broke up the long, hilly day with stops at the Skyland Lodge, the highest point on the Drive at 3,680 feet, and three miles south of Front Royal at the Shenandoah Valley Overlook. As I looked at the sweeping view of the valley below, an older fellow I was talking to said, "Y'know, you can see both sides from up here—the Atlantic Ocean over here . . ."

"Yeah," I chimed in, starting to feel like a native, "and California over there."

---

**DIRECTIONS:** North on Skyline Drive all day.

**ACCOMMODATIONS: Constant Spring Inn B & B,** junction 340 and 55 (3 blocks to Skyline Drive), Front Royal, VA, (703) 635-7010. Rooms: 9, double $58. VISA, MC, AMEX.
**Twin Rivers Motel,** 1801 Shenandoah Avenue, Front Royal, (703) 635-4101. Rooms: 20, $36. VISA, MC, AMEX.
**Skyland Lodge,** milepost 41.7, Skyline Drive, (703) 999-2211. Amenities: restaurant. Cabins: 8, $46–$67. VISA, MC, AMEX, DINERS.

**CAMPING: Front Royal KOA,** 2 miles south of Skyline on US 340, (703) 635-2741. Amenities: laundry, pool, golf.

**CAMPING: Matthews Arm,** milepost 22.2, (703) 999-2266. Amenities: no showers.

---

## DAY 11

Front Royal, Virginia, to Washington, D.C.
Terrain: Rolling
68 miles

About midafternoon, as I was wandering around the museum commemorating the two bloody Civil War battles at Manassas, a guy in lycra excitedly ran up. It was Matt Jablonsky of Philadelphia!

"I thought you took that job!" he exclaimed.

I told him the story. Then I wondered where his partner was.

"I dumped her. And I had a great time!"

After riding together the last thirty miles into D.C., Matt and I sat on the steps of the Jefferson Memorial swapping stories for about an hour. After I recounted the story of The Crash in graphic detail, and described my plans for a new career, I finally showed him the old *Bicycling* article.

"Hey, I remember reading this!" he said. "All those people put you up in their homes, right? And your brother has giant legs, right?"

I spent the rest of the night telling him about my other trips and using him for a little market research. Would he buy a book?

"Hey," he summarized, "I've done a lot of bike trips. But you've done more trips than anyone I've heard of. You gotta write it."

---

**DIRECTIONS:** South 2 miles on US 522, east 38 miles on SR 55/US 66 to Gainesville. Go east 28 miles on US 29 (Lee Highway) to Arlington (becomes Washington Street). Turn right on SR 237/Washington Boulevard/SR 27 around Arlington Cemetery to Arlington Bridge and Lincoln Memorial.

**ACCOMMODATIONS: Best Western Executive Inn,** 2480 S. Glebe Road, Arlington, VA, (703) 979-4400. <u>Amenities</u>: laundry, pool, exercise room. <u>Rooms</u>: 20, double $59. VISA, MC, AMEX, DINERS, DIS.

**CAMPING:** None close by.

---

After all the reflection, I still felt compelled to call the personnel manager the moment I got home. But the company had already hired someone else.

Good, I thought. With my mind free, uncluttered by options, only one course of action lay ahead. I immediately bought a Macintosh and started pounding out a story that I thought I could sell to *Bicycling*. A couple weeks later, I took a nonpaying intern job at *Southwest Cycling,* a local cycling publication, so I could get some bylines to shop around. A couple weeks later, *Bicycling* called me to say they wanted to buy the story. About a month after that, another magazine, *California Bicyclist,* called me to do some stories for them. Six months later, I was the editor.

After traveling a meandering road for years, it was exhilarating to have some focus. And fittingly, I'd made my way there by bicycle.

# SIGHTSEEING INFORMATION

ASHEVILLE, NORTH CAROLINA
**Biltmore Estate,** 1 North Pack Square: Opulent French chateâu built by wealthy Vanderbilt family of railroad fame; $17.50. (800) 543-2961.

ATLANTA, GEORGIA
**State Capitol Building,** Washington Street at Martin Luther King Boulevard: Tours Monday–Friday 10:00–2:00; free. (404) 656-2844.
**Stone Mountain Park.** 825-foot-high granite dome w/massive likeness of Confederate heroes carved on sides. (404) 498-5600.

BLOWING ROCK, NORTH CAROLINA
Cliff overhang blows objects up; 2 miles south of town $3.50. (704) 295-7111.

BOONE, NORTH CAROLINA
**Horn in the West:** Amphitheater play depicts struggle of Daniel Boone to settle this area; June through August, 8:30 P.M.; $9. (704) 264-2120.

CHEROKEE, NORTH CAROLINA
**Museum of the Cherokee Indian,** junction US 441 and Drama Road: History exhibits and movies; $3. (704) 497-3481.
**Oconaluftee Indian Village:** "Living" Cherokee museum; $6. (704) 497-2315.

FRONT ROYAL, VIRGINIA
**Skyline Caverns,** US 340, 1 mile south of entrance to Skyline Drive, then 1½ miles south of SR 55 junction: World's only anthrodites ("cave flowers"), upward-growing crystals; $8. (703) 635-4545.

MABRY MILL, NORTH CAROLINA
At Blue Ridge milepost 176.1; old-fashioned water-powered sawmill, blacksmith shop. (703) 952-2947.

MANASSAS, VIRGINIA
**Manassas National Battlefield Park,** junction US 24 and SR 234: Site of two great Civil War battles; museum, slide show, grounds; $1. (703) 368-1873.

# TRAFALGAR SQUARE TO RED SQUARE

## First-Ever Bike Tour to the U.S.S.R.

★

I N MY WILDEST DREAMS, I NEVER IMAGINED *PAYING* TO HAVE someone lead me on a trip. I'd always made my own route, stopped where and when I wanted; traveled as fast as I wanted; drunk in bars with the locals as late as I wanted; and slept in people's homes, in campgrounds, in city parks, in cheap hotels. Through thousands of miles of bike trips, it seems like my buddies and I rode rings around the tour people we'd meet—and had twice as many stories to tell. A tour? A support van? Luxury hotels? Regimented schedule? No way.

But Frank had Russia! In fact, Frank, the tour leader, didn't just have a trip to Russia. He had the first-*ever* trip to Russia—a five-week trip from London to Moscow that he dubbed "Trafalgar Square to Red Square." It was a chance to see *communism,* a chance to meet *them,* to observe the *enemy* from within, to witness the celebrated *glasnost* for myself—and to see it all slowly, methodically, on the *first-ever bike trip to the U.S.S.R.*

I knew about the trip because I'd written a story about it—my first as an intern at a local cycling magazine. It was five weeks. Seven countries. Three of them Communist. One of them, the U.S.S.R., never "open" to cyclists before. It may not seem like a big deal now, but in 1988 Mikhail Gorbachev had only been in power a couple of years. The Berlin Wall remained rock-solid. The term "glasnost" was in use, but not "perestroika." The Soviet Union was still Ronald Reagan's "Evil Empire," still Winston Churchill's "riddle wrapped in a mystery inside an enigma." If I was going to write a book someday—heck, even if I never wrote a book— the first-ever bike tour to Russia would be a great story to tell.

Frank made it clear I'd get no discount as a journalist. No matter. I mailed in my check. I picked up a plane ticket and enough traveler's checks to cover the trip, plus a bike ride back across Europe on the way home. Including $3,650 to Frank, the total was six thousand dollars— more than I'd spent on all my previous trips combined.

Ultimately, the trip was too slow, often boring, and didn't include enough sightseeing or time for socializing with the natives. But it was worth every cent.

I rode by windmills in Holland. Slept in a castle in West Germany.

Saw the magnificent spires of Prague. Drank beer in an illegal bar in Plzen, where beer was invented. Met Solidarity activists in Warsaw. Arm-wrestled with a huge Polish farm woman. Traded dollars for rubles on the black market in Minsk. Ate pickled herring in Pulawy. Queued up for oranges in Mariánské Lázně. Swigged vodka with Russians in the finest restaurant in Moscow. Stood before Lenin's tomb. Got lost in the Metro. And asked everybody what they thought about glasnost.

But most of all, I got a priceless look inside a world that, as events over the next year ensured, would never be the same again. It was com-munism, a way of life that, no matter the nationality, was run-down, dec-ades-behind, yellowed, faded, rain-streaked, peeling, and seemingly universally disliked by the people who lived under it. We all felt very lucky to have been there at such a unique moment in history—just be-fore the hammer and sickle was consigned, as Reagan put it, to the "ash heap of history." It was truly a once-in-a-lifetime opportunity.

## CHAPTER 14

## LONDON TO PRAGUE

THE FIRST LEG OF THE ROUTE I TOOK TO RUSSIA, WHICH crossed five countries in eleven days, is not the 758-mile route I am recommending here. Our leader skirted every big city, and took tiny, untrackable, hilly backroads at every opportunity in an attempt to steer our group of twenty-four from harm's way. As a result, though much of the backcountry route was beautiful, it kept us away from some noteworthy sights and provided us with very little flavor of our host countries.

The bulk of the route here is different from my trip. It starts the same, from London to a Holland-bound ferry at the English coast, then deviates by angling into Belgium for a full day, ending in the 2,000-year-old, Roman-founded city of Maastricht, the oldest in Holland. We didn't see Maastricht or make the next day's stop in Bonn, the German capital and home of Beethoven and some of Europe's oldest universities. While we followed the Rhine River for just twenty miles, this route snakes along its banks through castle-studded mountains all day, including the fabled Romantic Rhine section. Loaded with picturesque wine villages between Koblenz and Mainz, this stretch has the richest artistic and cultural heritage of Germany.

Next come Mainz's many cathedrals from the early Middle Ages; the modern city of Frankfurt, Germany's banking and transportation center, which includes the fully furnished house where Goethe was born and grew up; and the opulent Marienberg castle in the former episcopal town of Würzburg. After riding through Bavaria and linking with our route at

**IMPORTANT:** Visas are required for travel into Czechoslovakia. Contact the Czechoslovak Embassy at 3900 Linnean Ave., Washington, D.C., (202) 363-6308.

For hotel booking in most Czech cities, call **Čedok,** *the Czech national tourist agency in New York at (212) 689-9720. 10 E. 40th St., New York, NY 10016.*

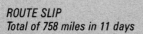

## ROUTE SLIP
### Total of 758 miles in 11 days

| Day | Route End Point | Terrain* | Sights | Mileage |
|-----|-----------------|----------|--------|---------|
| 1 | Arrival in London | | Parliament, Tower of London | |
| 2 | Harwich, England | Easy | | 90 |
| 3 | Breda, Holland | Easy | | 49 |
| 4 | Maastricht, Holland | Easy | St. Servatius Bridge, sixth-century church | 87 |
| 5 | Bonn, Germany | Moderate | Beethoven House, Münster Cathedral | 80 |
| 6 | Mainz, Germany | Easy | Rhine River cruise | 85 |
| 7 | Würzburg, Germany | Easy | Goethe House—Frankfurt, Marienberg castle | 104 |
| 8 | Bayreuth, Germany | Moderate | | 88 |
| 9 | Mariánské Lázně, Czechoslovakia | Easy | Natural mineral water springs | 75 |
| 10 | Plzeň, Czechoslovakia | Easy | Beer—any beer | 44 |
| 11 | Praha (Prague), Czechoslovakia | Easy | Hradcany Castle, U Fleků Beer Garden, Charles Bridge, Jewish Museum, Bona cokolada | 56 |

*Easy = flat to rolling; moderate = hilly; difficult = repeated miles of hills or steep climbing

the Czech border, the trip finishes with the beautiful mineral-bath city Mariánské Lázně, the famous beer-town Plzeň, and the striking gothic capital, Prague. Generally flat, this route avoids the hills we experienced north of Frankfurt.

Even though our route was unsatisfactory in terms of sightseeing, it had the big trade-off of an organized tour: ourselves. Suddenly I had two dozen new friends, several of whom I keep in touch with today.

## DAY 1

Arrival in London
Sights: Big Ben, Parliament, Tower of London, St. Paul's Cathedral

When I entered a London restaurant for our "Welcome" dinner, I was shocked to see the room filled with white hair. Half of the people looked like the only way they'd roll into Russia would be in wheelchairs.

Though some were strong riders, many were veterans of Frank's previous ride-for-ten-miles, eat-for-three-hours tours of Holland, which didn't exactly instill confidence. We had eighteen hundred miles to do. And it didn't help that Frank, a haggard fifty-year-old Dutchman, had procured slow, fat-tired mountain bikes for those who were renting, not easy-rolling road bikes.

One of those was my twenty-three-year-old roommate, who hadn't ridden a bike for years. But he didn't want to wait for the morning to start the ride. "It's just dreadful that we don't have time to see some of London," he said. "Let's see it now."

So, while the senior citizens were in bed, we saw the famous London sights: the gigantic three-hundred-year-old dome of St. Paul's Cathedral, the Parliament Buildings and Big Ben, and Buckingham Palace. We posed for a picture at the ebony mini-Sphinx along the Thames. We looked at the Tower of London, which has housed England's most illustrious prisoners since it was built by William the Conqueror in 1078. Then we crossed Tower Bridge and roamed full-speed all over the southern part of the city.

Crossing back over the Thames, one of our last stops was Trafalgar Square. There Lord Nelson stands high atop a lion-guarded pillar, symbolizing the British fleet's 1805 defeat of Napoleon's armada off the coast of Spain. For us, he symbolized the beginning of one of the most precedent-setting tours in bicycling history.

By midnight, after a final high-speed lap around St. James's Park, I was impressed. My roommate was a pretty fair rider, especially for a guy who didn't even own a bike. And he was funny, too.

"Listen only to God and me, but not necessarily in that order," he deadpanned in a thick Dutch accent, doing a perfect imitation of Frank. In fact, Kent Kzesky, Broadway-bound actor, wit, bike rider, had picked up on half the idiosyncrasies of the people in our group and spent a good hour entertaining me with his impressions before we shut the lights off at 2:00 A.M.

---

ACCOMMODATIONS: **The Cumberland,** Marble Arch, London W1A 4RF, (01) 262-1234, toll-free (800) CALLTHF. Amenities: restaurant. Rooms: 907, double $150–$200. AMEX, MC, DINERS.

**Hotel Europa,** 131–137 Cromwell Road, London SW7, (01) 370-2336. Rooms: 100, double $45–$52. AMEX, MC, VISA.

---

# DAY 2

London to Harwich, England
Terrain: Flat to rolling
90 miles

It was not going to be easy. Just after we left Trafalgar Square in the morning rush hour traffic, heading northeast out of London past the Tower of London, some of the older stragglers almost got run over at the roundabouts. Riding on the left-hand side of the road wasn't their problem; riding a bike was.

Crawling northeast on Highway 12E8 through gently rolling hills covered with glistening yellow rapeweed, we took in all the English culture we could in a single day: a can of half-lemonade, half-beer shandy, plus the bare-busted Page 3 Girl in the tabloid *Sun*. That got me more worked up than our twelve-hour ride to the ferry at Harwich, a pace so slow that I never broke a sweat.

But maybe Frank had the right idea. We'd done ninety miles on our first day, an achievement on any first day of a bike trip—and a miracle for those who hadn't ever ridden this far. No familiar faces were in evidence that night at the ferry's cabarets as it headed for Holland. They were in their cabins recuperating.

---

**DIRECTIONS:** From Trafalgar Square, head east on Fleet Street and contiguous roads past the Tower of London. Then go northeast 113 kilometers on 12E8 Highway to Colchester; northeast 30 kilometers on R 604 to Harwich.

**ACCOMMODATIONS: Sealink Ferry,** Harwich, England. <u>Rooms</u>: Economy cabin double $52, tourist cabin $80. <u>Passage</u>: $30 per person economy, $40 tourist. Booking required. In the United States, call Brit Rail at (212) 575-2667.

---

# FROM HOLLAND TO THE CZECH BORDER

Eighty miles in thirteen hours.

Two dozen of us crawled along at 6.1 miles per hour on our first day in Holland. It had to be the slowest invasion of Russia of all time. The in-shape century-type riders grumbled, and the alumni of Frank's previous tours gasped for breath. But the inch-by-inch pace never changed throughout our five-week trip—probably because our leader just couldn't go any faster.

We uneventfully plodded on along the near-perfect, near-ubiquitous Dutch bike paths. Almost every road had a parallel path, complete with its own signs and bicycle-shaped traffic lights. We could see why: men in suits, old women in dresses, and entire families were riding bikes. One million new bikes a year are bought in Holland, almost twice the per capita rate as the United States.

Burrowing southeast through Holland's Disneyland-cute, windmill-dotted southern countryside, we saw a moated 1509-era castle and perfect storybook brick houses with lace curtains and dolls in the windows. After dipping into Belgium for a couple of hours, we continued crawling due east across the Rhine River and the rolling hills and small villages of West Germany's midsection.

As slow as the pedaling was, it helped our disparate group of twenty-four to fast become a family. With no real huffing and puffing to distract us, we talked all day long. There were divorcees, wives who left their husbands home, husbands who left their wives home, a husband and wife on their tandem, and a blind girl on the back of another. Most had bike toured before, several were daily bikeaholics, and a few had barely ridden. One mid-fifties woman who had never biked (and didn't want her name revealed) took up karate the previous winter as a way to get in condition for the trip. Five months later, she ended up sending two muggers off in an ambulance when they tried to attack her at Denver's Stapleton Airport—where she was catching her flight to London.

Although there were vast differences in ages, which ranged from Kent at twenty-three to Clair Hildreth, a seventy-one-year-old, hundred-miles-per-week Long Islander, we soon found there was very little difference in attitude: nearly everyone was a "do it now" type, itching to be the first American cyclist to trade opinions with Mr. Gorbachev.

One of the most opinionated was Bill Julian, a crotchety sixty-eight-year-old Indiana auto-parts dealer wearing fluorescent green and pink tights who had suffered a heart attack while biking across the United States two years earlier. "My doctor said 'No,' but I said 'The hell with it!' " he crowed every day into his portable tape player, which he'd then play back for everyone, over and over and over. Sixty-eight-year-old Iowa actuary Jack Daniels inexplicably rode in what looked like a cross between a leisure suit and turn-of-the-century golf togs. Dubbed "Mr. Knowledge" by Kent, who dubbed everybody *something*, Jack had a hair-trigger mind that spewed puns, quips, and stories. Once, asked what the letters PDM (a famous Dutch racing team) on his water bottle meant, he thought for a second, squinted his eyes like Clint Eastwood and snarled, "Pretty Damn Macho!"

Underneath those grandfatherly exteriors, Bill and Jack were just like the two "kids" on the tour—me and Kent. We all wanted to see it all.

And taste it all, too. Stopping at a push cart along a tree-lined canal, Kent and I shared Belgian waffles with Hilde "T-shirt Mama" Bly, fifty-six, of Carmichael, California, a century-riding maniac who wore one of her different twenty-five commemorative century T-shirts every day. As we ate *pannekoeken,* a wide-as-a-plate Dutch pancake cooked with apples or other fruit, we met "Wee-wee" Wes Williams, fifty-four, an athletic, joke-a-minute businessman from La Habra, California. Wee-wee got his nickname from an unusual habit: every hour on the hour, he'd pull out of our group and run into the woods to relieve himself.

"It's psychological overcompensation," he explained. It seems in his early days of touring, Wes would go entire days without drinking water, leading to dehydration and, ultimately, kidney problems. Since then, he reflexively drank much more than a waterbottle an hour, a rule of thumb for touring. "Here I go again!" he'd scream to everyone's amusement, prancing through the trees.

Wee-wee Wes had a lot in common with fifty-four-year-old Maureen "Share-me" Schell (dubbed so by Kent because she shared every piece of cheese or chocolate she bought—and made it perfectly clear she expected the same courtesy in return), who frequently left her couch-potato husband home in Chicago to go on adventures like this. Somewhere in Germany, Share-me passed out badges to everyone emblazoned with the slogan: "Enjoy life: this is not a dress rehearsal"—a perfect way to describe the collective attitude of this group as we headed east to the Iron Curtain.

## DAY 3

Hoek van Holland to Breda
Terrain: Flat to rolling
80 kilometers (49 miles)

**DIRECTIONS:** 30 kilometers east to Rotterdam through Vlaardingen, then south 50 kilometers to Breda.

**ACCOMMODATIONS: Novotel Breda,** Dr. Batenburglaan 74, Breda, NL-4837, (076) 659220. <u>Rooms</u>: 81, double Dfl 113–117. AMEX, DINERS, VISA.

## DAY 4

Breda to Maastricht
Terrain: Flat to rolling, then hilly
Sights: St. Servatius Bridge (circa 1280), sixth-century church
138 kilometers (87 miles)

**DIRECTIONS:** South 35 kilometers to Turnhout, Belgium, on R 24, south 73 kilometers to Hasselt, southeast 30 to Maastricht, Holland.

**ACCOMMODATIONS: Hotel Du Casque,** Helmstraat 14, Maastricht, NL-6211, (043) 214343. <u>Rooms</u>: 43, double Dfl 82.50–97.50. AMEX, MC, VISA.

## DAY 5

Maastricht, Holland, to Bonn, Germany
Terrain: Hilly
Sights: Beethoven House, Münster Cathedral (circa 1100)
127 kilometers (80 miles)

**DIRECTIONS:** East 32 kilometers across German border to Aachen, east 30 kilometers on R 264 to Düren, southeast 65 kilometers on R 56 to Bonn.

**ACCOMMODATIONS: Parkhotel,** 1 AM Kurpark, Bonn, D-5300, (0228) 363081. <u>Rooms</u>: 52, double 120–150 DM. EC, MC, VISA.

## DAY 6

Bonn to Mainz or Frankfurt
Sights: The Rhine River
140 kilometers (85 miles)

**DIRECTIONS:** Cross Rhine at Kennedybrücke (bridge), turn south on Haupstrasse, hug Rhine southeast on R 42 140 kilometers along Rhine. To Frankfurt, stay on north bank of Main River 40 kilometers until intersection with Mainzer Landstrasse. Go east into Frankfurt, cut south to bank of Main.

**ACCOMMODATIONS: Central Hotel Eden,** Bahnhofsplatz 8, Mainz, D-6500, (06131) 674001. <u>Amenities</u>: bar. <u>Rooms</u>: 61, double 170–210 DM. AMEX, MC, VISA.
**Hotel City** (central city), Soemmerringstrasse 23, Frankfurt, D-6000/1, (069) 593197. <u>Rooms</u>: 15, double 95–180 DM. AMEX, MC, VISA.

## DAY 7

Mainz to Würzburg or Bamberg
Terrain: Flat, then rolling
Sights: Marienberg castle
170 kilometers (104 miles)

**DIRECTIONS:** From Frankfurt, follow Main 20 kilometers east to Hanau. Turn southeast on R 8 110 kilometers to Würzburg. Go 80 kilometers east on R 22 to Bamberg.

**ACCOMMODATIONS: Hotel Schloss Steinberg,** Auf dem Steinberg, D-8700, Würzburg, (0931) 93061. <u>Rooms</u>: 45, double 160 DM. DINERS, MC, VISA.
**Hotel Die Alte Post,** 1 Heiliggrabstrasse, Bamberg, (0951) 27848. <u>Rooms</u>: 43, double 90–110 DM. AMEX, MC, VISA.

## DAY 8

Würzburg to Bayreuth
Terrain: Gently rolling
140 kilometers (88 miles)

---

**DIRECTIONS:** From Bamberg, go 60 kilometers on R 22.

**ACCOMMODATIONS: Waldhotel Stein,** Bayreuth, D-8580, 1 mile from airport in park, Bayreuth, (0921) 9001. Rooms: 44, 96–196 DM. AMEX, DINERS, VISA.

★

---

## DAY 9

Bayreuth, Germany, to Mariánské Lázně, Czechoslovakia
Terrain: Gently rolling
Sights: Natural mineral water springs
120 kilometers (75 miles)

The biggest "shock" of the trip didn't come from seeing Russia, but from seeing communism. That first happened on May 28, when we pedaled past our last West German *"Gute Fahrt"* (Happy Travels) sign into Czechoslovakia.

The border crossing looked like something right out of 1945. Machine-gun-toting soldiers eyed us suspiciously from barricades and peely-paint-covered guard shacks. Gunnery towers loomed in the distance. We waited for our visa approvals in a border station that was notable for wall slogans made of crooked, childlike styrofoam cutout letters.

We sat in shocked silence as we rode into Czechoslovakia. We seemed to ride back fifty years in time. Nothing was new. The paint on the buildings was yellowed, faded, rain-streaked, and peeling; letters on signs had fallen off or were crooked; traffic signs on the road were cracked and bent; the few cars on the road, Skodas and Ladas, looked like old Ramblers from the Kennedy era.

At first the sheer *unkemptness* of the place reminded me of Mexico, but that was wrong. Mexico, though dirty, is bursting with chaotic life, with color, with noise; Czechoslovakia was drab, lifeless. Eerily, it seemed at times that we saw more poorly painted party slogans than people. It was like the whole country of 16 million was a ghost town—as if a neutron bomb had exploded, leaving the buildings standing, but wiping out the people. We found out later that the western part of the country was depopulated after World War II, when three million resident Germans were expelled. Forty years later, Czechs have only slowly moved in.

The feeling of emptiness continued when we got to Mariánské

Lázně, a once-thriving tourist city set among beautiful tree-covered hills and natural mineral-salt baths that had been a favorite of the aristocracy of Europe. An endless avenue of richly ornate, ultra-classy, ultra-expensive hotels greeted us, now all worn-out and disrepaired. "It used to be Oz," I thought, in awe. Only a classical colonnade and fountain at the center of town were newly refurbished, hinting that an abandoned city was emerging from a long sleep.

Our hilltop Interhotel Esplanade, in earlier days no doubt the ritziest in town, was no different: instead of a shimmery hand-rubbed finish on the cabinets, there was ugly, thick smudge-proof enamel paint; once-bronze drawer handles were now cheap white plastic; the curtains were cheap linen—not fine lace. And, as Kent pointed out, absolutely nothing matched.

Dinner was no better. When I asked the rude, inattentive waiter several times for more butter, he finally brought out one pat, conspicuously labeled "Tourist."

At breakfast the next day, I remarked to Kent that the gritty, thin orange juice I was drinking seemed artificial. He grabbed his glass, tasted it, looked at me, and said dryly, "It's Tang!"

That's it, I concluded. Everything in communism, including what we saw later in Poland and the U.S.S.R., "is Tang." Only not that good.

---

**DIRECTIONS:** Go north 20 kilometers on R 2, east on R 303 70 kilometers to Cheb, Czechoslovakia. Go 30 kilometers southeast on R 21 to Mariánské Lázně.

**ACCOMMODATIONS: Interhotel Esplanade,** 438 Karlovarska (on hillside), Mariánské Lázně, (95) 216214. <u>Rooms</u>: 92, double $52–72. AMEX, MC, VISA.

---

# DAY 10

Mariánské Lázně to Plzeň,
Terrain: Rolling
71 kilometers (44 miles)

Despite the poor quality and sparse quantity of nearly *everything* in Czechoslovakia, the goulash, onion soup, pickles, and chocolate were great. And when it came to beer, we found the best in the world in the town of Plzeň, the original home of Pilsener-style beers, the kind most of the world, including America, drinks today.

Knowing this, I became obsessed with the idea of having a beer in Plzeň. Arriving early for once (since we had only a forty-mile ride that day), our Czech tour guide Elena (dubbed the "Goddess of Love," to put a grin on her stern, unsmiling face) led me, Kent, and Wee-wee Wes on a two-hour hunt for a bar.

On the verge of giving up, we nearly stumbled through a door in a back alley to find ourselves in the middle of what seemed like the locker room of a World Series-winning baseball team. Five beers were only nine crowns, about seventy-five cents. Soon we were arm-wrestling, bear-hugging, and telling jokes with the drunken locals, none of whom had any idea what we were saying—and vice versa.

Then, all at once, the place closed down. What happened? "This was an illegal bar," said Elena. "They steal a keg of beer, serve it until it runs out, and leave before the police show up."

---

**DIRECTIONS:** Go southeast 52 kilometers on R 21 to Stod, then northeast 19 kilometers on R 26.

**ACCOMMODATIONS: Interhotel Continental,** Zhrojnicka 8, Plzeň, CS-30504, (01) 936477. Rooms: 56, double $54–$70. No listed cards.

---

# DAY 11

Plzeň to Prague
Terrain: Flat, easy rolling
Sights: U Fleků Beer Garden, Charles Bridge, Jewish Museum
88 kilometers (56 miles)

Our tour guide didn't pull any punches about her homeland throughout our eight days there, which included two in the beautiful capital, Prague.

"In Czechoslovakia," she'd say sarcastically in her mechanically staccato, shrill-pitched accent, "you can get everything you want."

". . . if you want oranges once a month," added Kent, referring to one day the whole group lined up to buy some rare oranges, which we cleaned the store—and probably the little town—out of. "As you can see, the national sport here is queuing up," Elena happily concluded, without missing a beat. She added that Czechs shop every day, because they never know what will be in the stores.

Still, Elena explained, Czechoslovakia is better off than Poland—so much better that Czech currency is considered "hard" money in Poland and is traded on the black market, just like dollars, pounds and marks. She also claimed the Russians thought Czechoslovakia had the highest standard of living in the world, "because they are told by their government that Russia and the United States have the same standard of living. So when they see all the chocolate and other goods in Prague, they naturally assume Czechoslovakia is enormously wealthy." Elena knew the truth on this score, as she had toured the United States for a month two years earlier.

Prague, a former center of European culture and home of Mozart, Weber, and Kafka, did indeed have chocolate—I ate a dozen unique half-and-half coffee and cream bars called Bona—as well as unique history and beauty. Long a German-speaking city with an influential Jewish population, Prague (Praha) became a Czech-dominated city only in the mid-1800s. Spared the bombing that destroyed other European cities in World War II, all of Prague's landmarks survive: Charles University, one of the oldest in Europe; the statue-lined fourteenth-century Charles Bridge over the Vltava River, where guitar-strumming Czechs were singing Bob Dylan songs; the U Flekû German beer garden; Wenceslas Square, the shopping mecca that filled with demonstrators seventeen months later, prompting the fall of the hardline regime; Hradčany Castle, the 1,100-year-old Bohemian castle high above the city; and even Staronová Synagogue, the only one not damaged in Nazi-occupied Europe.

Planning a macabre Museum of an Extinct People, the Germans left this one synagogue intact and stockpiled Jewish artifacts in it from all over Europe. Ironically, it now actually is a Jewish Museum, housing the chilling drawings of child prisoners knowingly awaiting their turns in the gas chambers. A small contiguous cemetery, its thousands of gravestones eerily shoehorned together, also survived the war.

That visit, one of the few things I did on my own on this trip, tempered the beauty of Gothic, sloganless Prague, seemingly the only thing maintained in the country by the Communists. In a melancholy mood, I sat alone in the freshly painted, colorful Old Town square with a Bona *kombinovana cokolada* bar and reflected on the strange communal bike trip I was on, the first in which I'd had absolutely no control.

It had its bad points. It isn't the way I'd have done it. But it got me here. It was making me some good friends. And it was taking me to Russia.

---

**DIRECTIONS:** Go northeast 88 kilometers on E 12.

**ACCOMMODATIONS: Interhotel Alcron,** 40 Štěpánská (off Wenceslas Square), Prague, CC-11123, (2) 247-094. <u>Rooms</u>: 149, doubles $106–$150. AMEX, DINERS, VISA.

★

# SIGHTSEEING INFORMATION

**British Tourist Authority:** 40 W. 57th Street, 3rd floor, New York, (212) 581-4700

**German National Tourist Office:** 747 Third Avenue, New York, (212) 308-3300.

**Dutch Board of Tourism:** 90 New Montgomery Street, San Francisco, (415) 543-6772.

**CEDOK—Czech National Tourist Office,** 10 E. 40th Street, New York, (212) 689-9720. No visa required in Czechoslovakia for stays of shorter than 30 days; Czechoslovak Embassy at 3900 Linnean Avenue, Washington, D.C., (202) 363-6308.

BONN, GERMANY

**Beethoven's House Museum:** Composer born here on December 16, 1770; Baroque-style townhouse contains his death mask, instruments, portraits, manuscripts. (0228) 635188.

**Bundeshaus (German capital building):** Seat of two houses of German parliament. Appointment required—call (0228) 162152 or go to Hermann-Ehlers-Strasse 29, 5300 Bonn 1.

**Münster Cathedral:** City's oldest church, completed around 1248 but dating back to the Romans and early Christianity on the Rhine, an excellent example of the independent Rhenish transitional style between Romanesque and Gothic; open 7:00—7:00.

**Poppelsdorf Palace and Botanical Gardens:** Richly ornate building in Bonn's historic district completed 1753, surrounded by ten greenhouses and a host of rare plants and trees. (0228) 732259.

**Godesburg Castle Tower:** Built 1210 high on a hill, destroyed in 1500, it remained a picturesque ruin until converted into hotel and restaurant in 1960. Tower visits April to October 10:00—6:00, .50 DM. (0228) 316071.

**Rhine ferry cruise:** Main artery of Europe travels through castle-studded mountains all day, fabled Rhine Gorge with picturesque wine villages between Koblenz and Mainz. This stretch has the richest artistic and cultural heritage of Germany. KD German Rhine Line Information, (0221) 2088-319 + 319.

FRANKFURT, GERMANY

**Goethe House:** House where the poet was born contains paintings, signatures, furniture, and objects from Goethe's era. Open Monday—Saturday 9:00—6:00, Sunday 10:00—1:00. (069) 282824.

**Two-hour walking tour** includes Goethe House as well as the **Römerberg,** the central square of the city; the **Römer,** the city hall since 1405, the **Dom,** the Gothic cathedral where coronation of emperors took place, and **Die Liébfrauenkirche,** the Church of Our Lady originally built in 1308. For map, call (069) 212-8849/51 (train station) or 212-8708/09 (Romer).

LONDON, ENGLAND

**British Travel Centre.** 12 Regent Street. Monday—Saturday 9:00—5:30. Sunday 10:00—6:00. (071) 730-3400.

**British Museum:** Includes relics from Rome, Egypt, Greece, and Babylonia. Free; open Monday—Saturday 10:00—5:00, Sunday 2:30—6:00. (071) 636-1555.

**Buckingham Palace:** Office residence of royalty since 1837; changing of the guard at 11:30 each morning.

**Houses of Parliament and Big Ben:** Victorian Gothic buildings with 320-foot-high Clock Tower and 13-ton timepiece; debates can be heard from Strangers' Gallery.

**Imperial War Museum:** Exhibits of British military history since 1914; open Monday—Saturday 10:00—6:00, Sunday 2:00—6:00. (071) 735-8922.

**St. Paul's Cathedral:** Three-hundred-year-old baroque structure designed by famed architect Christopher Wren features massive dome which once dominated the London skyline; crypt has tombs of Wren, the Duke of Wellington, and Lord Nelson, free, crypt extra.

**Tower of London:** Torturous London prison built by William the Conqueror in 1078; includes oldest church in London, the armor collection and Crown Jewels. Admission charged, extra for jewels. (071) 709-0765.

**Trafalgar Square:** Honoring the British fleet's 1805 defeat of Napoleon's armada off the coast of Spain; 185-foot-high Nelson's Column flanked by four brass lions.

MAASTRICHT, HOLLAND

**Maastricht Tourist Office,** Het Dinghuis Kleine Staat 1, GZ11ED, (043) 252121.

**St. Pietersberg (Mount St. Peter):** Hill includes Fortress of Maastricht, circa 1702, and labyrinth of caves and galleries below the surface, walls covered by paintings and inscriptions, including those of Napoleon. Open daily; admission.

**St. Servatius Bridge and Church:** Oldest church in Holland, first started in sixth century due to initial location on Roman trade route; open daily 10:00—5:00; admission charged.

MAINZ, GERMANY

Obtain maps at the Mainz Tourist Association at Bahnhofstrasse 15 or call (06131) 23 37 41.

**Dom (cathedral).** Premier example of Romanesque architecture, finished in thirteenth century. Museum inside has medieval sculpture. Open all year.

MARIÁNSKÉ LÁZNĚ, CZECHOSLOVAKIA

**Tepla Monastery:** Romanesque church founded in 1197; tours on hour Tuesday—Sunday.

PLZEŇ, CZECHOSLOVAKIA

**Urquell Brewery:** Pilsner beer brewed here since thirteenth century; tours can be arranged.

### PRAGUE, CZECHOSLOVAKIA

**Hradčany Castle:** Eleven-hundred-year-old Bohemian castle and building complex high above the city. Entrance on Hradčanské Náměstí; open Tuesday—Sunday; admission.

**U Fleků Beer Garden:** Outdoor drinking establishment typical of middle Europe, complete with German and Czech live music.

**Charles Bridge:** Fourteenth-century bridge over the Vltava River is lined with thirty religious statues.

**Jewish Museum:** Thirteenth-century temple; once planned by Nazis as "Museum of an Extinct People"; houses drawings of condemned prisoners; includes small contiguous cemetery.

### ROTTERDAM, HOLLAND

**Euromast:** Six-hundred-foot-high revolving restaurant tower in middle of city. Open 9:00 A.M. —10:00 P.M. daily; admission. (010) 436-4811.

**Delfshaven:** Departure port for the English Pilgrims who went to America in 1620. Includes Pilgrim Fathers' Church and a museum. Open Monday—Friday; call local tourist office at (010) 476 4216.

**Netherlands Marine Museum:** Explains history of shipping and the role of Rotterdam, one of world's biggest ports, in sea exploration and commerce. 10:00—5:00 daily; admission. (010) 413-7505

### WÜRZBURG, GERMANY

**Residenz:** Built 1744, is one of Europe's most elaborate baroque palaces. (09) 31-52743.

**Marienberg Fortress:** Dating from 1000 A.D. and changed into a Renaissance palace in 1600, it stands high above the river Main and commands a magnificent view of the city. It houses the Mainfränkisches Museum, which contains Franconian works of art; located across Main River, use Alte Mainbrücke (bridge). (09) 31-44158.

**Two-hour walking tour** includes Marienberg, the Dom, Neumünster, and other sights of this former episcopal town. Obtain map at Würzburg Palais am Congress Ctr. (09) 81-37335.

## CHAPTER 15

## PRAGUE
## TO
## WARSAW

THIS SCENIC 554-MILE ROUTE, WHICH GOES NORTHEAST FROM the Czechoslovakian capital to the Polish capital in a sweeping curve, has the toughest terrain of the entire London-to-Moscow trip. But that doesn't mean it's difficult. Heading east through the Bohemian forest and Carpathian Mountains into Poland, we had only one day of frequent, though short, climbing.

You wouldn't have known it by our speed, though, as the already-slow group slowed to a crawl. As a result, we didn't have time to see the gruesome Auschwitz concentration camp or the magnificent sixteenth-century Wawel Castle of the ancient capital of Kraków, arguably the most famous places in Poland.

In order that your trip doesn't become a scouting report for a future trip, like mine was, the route here jogs through Auschwitz on the way to Kraków, a virtual open-air museum of Polish history whose center remains virtually unchanged since the Middle Ages. An entire day is recommended to tour the striking castle complex of gothic and Renaissance buildings, which house a collection of Flemish tapestries and a burial ground of notable figures in Polish history.

From Kraków, the route stays wholly in the flat Vistula River Valley, making a sweeping curve north through farmland, past the one-time royal retreat of Kazimierz Dolny, and into Poland's capital of *Warszawa* (Warsaw). In contrast to preserved Prague, Warsaw is a completely new city, totally rebuilt after the destruction of World War II.

---

**IMPORTANT: Visas are required for travel into Czechoslovakia and Poland.**
Contact the Czechoslovak Embassy at 3900 Linnean Avenue, Washington,
D.C., (202) 363-6308, and Polish Consulate Division, 2224 Wyoming Avenue.
N.W., Washington, DC 20008, (202) 232-4517.

**Polish Tourism Numbers: Polish National Tourist Office,** 333 N. Michigan Avenue, Chicago, IL 60601, (312) 236-9013 or (312) 787-4466. **Orbis Polish
Travel Bureau, Inc.,** 342 Madison Avenue, Suite 1512, New York, NY 10173.

★

*ROUTE SLIP*
*Total of 549 miles in 8 days*

| Day | Route End Point | Terrain* | Sights | Mileage |
|-----|-----------------|----------|--------|---------|
| 1 | Prague, Czechoslovakia | *Travel Day* | | |
| 2 | Pardubice, Czechoslovakia | Easy | | 72 |
| 3 | Olomouc, Czechoslovakia | Easy/Moderate | Restored castle in Litomyšl | 95 |
| 4 | Cieszyn, Poland | Moderate | | 65 |
| 5 | Kraków, Poland | Moderate/Difficult | Auschwitz concentration camp | 71 |
| 6 | Sandomierz, Poland | Easy | | 99 |
| 7 | Pulawy, Poland | Easy | Kazimierz Dolny | 70 |
| 8 | Warsaw, Poland | Easy | Site of Warsaw ghetto, Lazienki Park with monument to Chopin, rebuilt royal castle | 82 |

*Easy = flat to rolling; moderate = hilly; difficult = repeated miles of hills or steep climbing

# DAY 1

## Arrival in Prague

**ACCOMMODATIONS: Interhotel Alcron,** 40 Štěpánská (off Wenceslas Square), Prague, CS-11123, (2) 247-094. <u>Rooms</u>: 149, double $106–$150. AMEX, DINERS, VISA.

## DAY 2

Prague to Pardubice
Terrain: Flat
118 kilometers (72 miles)

   With Big Red getting closer and closer as we headed east toward
Poland, talk of glasnost was always in the air. Elena flatly predicted that
glasnost would take a hundred years. "That's because the Russian people
have the Czar mentality," she explained, meaning that the Russians have
been conditioned since ancient times to behave en masse, not as individ-
uals, and that they need a strong man or government to tell them what
to do. "So Gorbachev's attempt to turn them into individualists, capital-
ists, and free thinkers actually goes against the Russian character," said
the Goddess of Love. It was a claim we were to hear repeated by East
Germans and Poles, too.

   Of course, the Czechs, Poles, and East Germans had no reason to say
anything good about the Russians, who effectively controlled them at the
time. The Czechs, whose "Prague spring" democratic movement was
crushed in 1968 by the Russians, seemed to have lost some of their will
to move on. Elena used her own mother, who twenty years earlier was a
highly motivated teacher, as a reflection of the malaise of the entire
country. "When she stopped getting raises for doing good work, and
didn't get penalized for doing badly, she slowly stopped working. Now,
she just sits around with her friends, gossiping and smoking."

   If she was like the Czechs Kent and I met in a tavern that night, she
wasn't smoking just any old brand. Offering a pack of highly-sought-after
Marlboros to some young Czechs, we were politely—shockingly—turned
down. They pointed to a little tag at the bottom of the pack: "Made in W.
Germany." They'd only accept the genuine American article.

---

**DIRECTIONS:** Go east on E-12 101 kilometers. Just before entering Hradec
Kralove, turn south 17 kilometers to Pardubice.

**ACCOMMODATIONS: Interhotel Labe,** downtown, Pardubice, CS-53000,
(40) 36711. <u>Rooms</u>: 210, double $40–$60. AMEX, CB, DINERS.

---

## DAY 3

Pardubice to Olomouc
Terrain: Flat, rolling
133 kilometers (95 miles)

**DIRECTIONS:** South 10 kilometers to Chrudim. Turn east 20 kilometers on main highway. Turn south 40 kilometers to Svitawy. Turn east 30 kilometers to Mohelnice. Turn south 33 kilometers to Olomouc.

**ACCOMMODATIONS: Interhotel Flora,** Krapova 34, Olomouc, CS-77200, (068) 23241. <u>Rooms</u>: 230, double $48–$64. AMEX, CB, DINERS.

# DAY 4

Olomouc, Czechoslovakia to Cieszyn, Poland
Terrain: Hilly/moderate
107 kilometers (65 miles)

Halfway through the day, Elena took a train back to Prague and let us fend for ourselves on the final forty miles to Poland. Then all hell broke loose.

Roy Alligretti, a sixty-two-year-old engineer from Soquel, California, was knocked off his bike into a ditch by a drunken tractor driver. While Roy was driven to the hospital, the heaviest rains of the already rainy trip poured down. Then some of my rear wheel spokes broke, warping my wheel beyond rideability.

Damning myself for leaving my indestructible Aero wheels at home on my old Le Tour (my brother had bought me a new bike for this tour), I was stranded out of sight of all the riders except for the "sweep"—the designated final biker, in this case a tandem ridden by "The Odd Couple," six-foot-six-inch David Rasmussen of Santa Barbara and five-foot-one-inch Jody Davis of Cleveland. As we waited for three hours comfortably inside a gas station for our van driver, Bastiàan, and the battered (but not seriously hurt) Roy to rescue us, the others waited for word of our whereabouts in thunderous rain.

It was not a happy group that arrived at the Polish border on June 5.

**DIRECTIONS:** East 107 kilometers on E 7.

**ACCOMMODATIONS: Motel Orbis,** u 1 Armii Ludowej, Cieszyn, PL-43400, (386) 20451. <u>Rooms</u>: 80, double 86–128 DM. No credit cards.

# DAYS 5 TO 9

Roy, Bastiàan, and I wondered if Communist Poland would be as faded, peeling, crooked, and broken down as Czechoslovakia. But we didn't have to set foot in the country to get our answer. As the Polish border guards lifted the border gate for the van to pass, a big piece of metal—big enough to put a severe dent in anybody who might have been under it—fell off the gate and slammed to the ground. Our new Polish guide, Witek (pronounced Vee-tek), picked up the piece, smiled, and said with familiar Communist cynicism, "How appropriate."

Welcome to *Polska*.

What Elena had said about the money was true. We got fantastic zloty rates on the black market for our dollars and dumped our Czech crowns for a nice profit. Food was incredibly cheap. A lunch of onion-covered herring and brown bread was only a hundred zlotys—eighteen cents. (Kent wanted me to write a book: *Seeing Poland on Thirty-five Cents a Day.*) But in other ways, the Goddess of Love was wrong. Poland seemed more affluent than her country. Used to no fruit and vegetables, we now found stooped, weatherbeaten peasant farmers selling cucumbers and strawberries at every roadside. Poland had legalized small-scale private enterprise. Though still backward—we saw hundreds of centuries-old horse-drawn hoes and carts, and store cashiers adding totals by pencil—its auto traffic was heavier and its stores fuller than in Czechoslovakia.

Poland's people seemed as open as its economic policies. Unlike the spirit-sapped Czechs, the Poles were boisterously happy and warm. From her garden, a bra-clad hulk of a woman insisted, in broken English, that I was undernourished and "must come eat big meal right now" in her house. She even brought out her ninety-year-old mother, who spoke English with a perfect *New Jersey* accent, to convince me. When I explained I had to keep up with the group, she put her elbow up on my bike seat and said, "Okay, we wrestle!" For the next five minutes, we arm-wrestled to a draw; while I was straining, veins popping out, she was casually laughing. When I left, she slapped my back and explained that she worked as a "strength coach" at a local university.

Polish children were beyond friendly—they made us feel like a liberating Allied army. Wherever we rode, dozens of children waved and screamed. Wherever we stopped, *hundreds* of children mobbed us. We'd drawn a lot of attention in Czechoslovakia, but nothing like this. They were fascinated by our modern bikes, by our colorful clothing, and by our American culture, which to most was an obsession with Sylvester Stallone's movie character Rambo.

Their enthusiasm could even be a little frightening. Exploring the southern city of Tarnow (bypassed on this route), Kent and I stopped to shoot a picture with a half-dozen kids at a square about a mile from our hotel. Within five minutes, we were surrounded by at least two hundred of them! I could barely move. Little bodies were pressing in all around; little hands were unzipping my tool bag and handlebar bag, grabbing my pump and water bottles. Holding our bikes upsidedown above us, kids hanging on our arms and backs like monkeys, we pushed through the frenzied crowd and made a high-speed escape back to the hotel. A swarm of crazed kids chased us, with a few diehards not out of sight until we were nearly a quarter of a mile away.

Coming back down to get dinner after showering, we found the hotel lobby in a tizzy. The managers were angrily shooing away eight or nine dirty kids who were running in and out.

"You should have been down here about five minutes ago," one said. "There must have been about fifty kids running through here."

Those kids had put two and two together. Only one hotel in town handled foreigners.

This emotion of the Polish people was reflected in other ways, too. First, alcoholism—we saw hundreds of drunken Polish men giddily stumbling along roadsides in broad daylight; and second, a strongly independent political spirit.

In Warsaw, a resident American student whom a group of us met in a bar introduced Marchan, a "radical" nineteen-year-old Polish student who took us into the vortex of Poland's strong antigovernment protest movement. As if on a mission, we traveled by bus to the outskirts of the city, to a church called St. Stanislaus. But like all worship in Poland in the last decade, this church's religion is one part Catholicism and one part politics.

Known as the "Martyr" church, its grounds house an eternal flame to memorialize Jerzy Popieluszko, an outspoken antigovernment Solidarity trade union chaplain who was abducted and killed by the government in 1983. Almost half a million mourners massed for his funeral, and ever since his church has been a sacred shrine—so sacred that even the government was afraid to tread there. As a result, the wrought iron fence surrounding it was covered with radical posters, many from the then-outlawed Solidarity trade union movement, the only place in the country such displays of protest were allowed. "The people are so emotional about this place that they'd go crazy if it were desecrated," Marchan explained.

As we were leaving the martyr church, busloads of Poles were arriving, as if it were a rite of passage for every member of their nationality.

Traveling through Poland was, in a way, a rite of passage for me, too. Often, as I crossed railroad tracks in Poland, I would feel a horrible chill. Forty-five years ago, I would have been on those trains. I'd shudder. Riding through Eastern Europe for me was like revisiting a distant, incomprehensible, unrelenting nightmare—a nightmare I didn't notice while we were riding through West Germany, which seems so modern and up-to-date. But the underdeveloped, agrarian East probably looks a lot like it did back then, and the reminders of what happened here abound: the Museum of the Extinct People in Prague; the Auschwitz concentration camp near Krakow; the Monument to the Fighters of the Warsaw Ghetto; and, most striking of all, a huge wall built of Hebrew-lettered Jewish tombstones just outside the once heavily Jewish village of Kazimierz Dolny, five miles south of Pulawy. To symbolize the destruction of that community, the wall is built with a massive crack splitting the middle of it.

But as gigantic memorials pointed out later on in the U.S.S.R., the Nazi legacy isn't the sole province of the Jews. When asked what Warsaw was like under the Germans, who reduced the city of 3 million to a rubble-heap of 30,000, our normally talkative Polish guide Witek, only thirty-four, sadly looked away and murmured softly, "It was like a dark night."

I found the best way to get to know the Poles was to do what they do—immerse myself in their vodka, which I did about a week later in a hotel room with three Poles in the Soviet city of Smolensk. I learned how to drink the tasteless, smooth-down-your-throat Polish vodka (which my friends, all factory workers, repeatedly assured me was much better than *anything* Russian): one shot every half hour, chased with cucumber soda, goat cheese, salami, and spirited conversation.

"How can you Poles be so proud when you've been so kicked around for centuries—by the Austrian Empire, by the Germans, and now by the Russians," I asked.

"Because," came the answer, "back in the fourteenth century, Poland was a great power. And someday, maybe not next year, maybe not in a hundred years, we will be a great country again. And that is why we feel so good." And we raised our vodka-filled shot glasses to toast to "Polish power," just as we had toasted to "bicycling in Poland," to my "return to Poland," to "Polish vodka," to "freedom for Poland," to "Solidarity," to "Polish women," to "Polish pride," and innumerable other subjects during our five hours together.

## DAY 5

Cieszyn to Kraków via Auschwitz
Terrain: Hilly most of day
Sights: Wawel Castle complex, St. Mary's Church, Renaissance
   Cloth Hall
115 kilometers (71 miles)

---

**DIRECTIONS:** East 40 kilometers on E 7 past Bielsko-Biala to tiny Kety. Turn north 20 kilometers to Oswiecim (Auschwitz). Then go east 55 kilometers through tiny Zator to Kraków.

**ACCOMMODATIONS: Hotel Wanda** (Orbis), u 1 Koniewa, 9, Kraków, PL-30150, (12) 371677. <u>Rooms</u>: 106, double 90–140 DM.

★

# DAY 6

Kraków to Sandomierz
Terrain: Rivergrade flat
160 kilometers (99 miles)

---

**DIRECTIONS:** Go northeast 160 kilometers on highway 217 parallel with Vistula River.

**ACCOMMODATIONS: Pension Cizemka,** Rynek 27, Sandomierz, 27-600, (153) 36-38. <u>Rooms</u>: 32, double $20–$30. No credit cards.

---

# DAY 7

Sandomierz to Pulawy, Poland
Terrain: Flat
Sights: Kazimierz Dolny Memorial and Village
112 kilometers (70 miles)

---

**DIRECTIONS:** Go north 112 kilometers (Kazimierz Dolny 10 kilometers before Pulawy).

**ACCOMMODATIONS: Izbella Hotel,** Dzierznyskiego 1, Pulawy, PL-24100, (6545) 3041. <u>Rooms</u>: 105, rates available on request.

---

# DAY 8

Pulawy to Warsaw, Poland
Terrain: Flat
Sights: Former site of Warsaw ghetto, Lazienki Park and Chopin
  memorial, restored royal castle
130 kilometers (82 miles)

---

**DIRECTIONS:** Go northwest 130 kilometers through Deblin (east side of Wista River).

**ACCOMMODATIONS: Hotel Forum Warsaw,** Nowogrodzka 24/26, Warsaw, PL-00511, (22) 210271, in U.S. (800) 327-0200. <u>Amenities</u>: bar, 2 restaurants. <u>Rooms</u>: 751, double 181–191 DM. AMEX, CB, DINERS.

---

**IMPORTANT: Visas are required for travel into Poland.** Contact the Polish Consulate Division, 2224 Wyoming Avenue N.W., Washington, DC 20008, (202) 232-4517. No visa required in Czechoslovakia for stays of shorter than 30 days; Czechoslovak Embassy at 3900 Linnean Avenue, Washington, D.C. (202) 363-6308.

**Polish National Tourist Office,** 333 N. Michigan Avenue, Chicago, Ill. 60601, (312) 236-9013 or (312) 787-4466. **Orbis Polish Travel Bureau, Inc.,** 342 Madison Avenue, Suite 1512, New York, NY 10173.

# SIGHTSEEING INFORMATION

OLOMOUC, CZECHOSLOVAKIA
Restored castle in Litomyšl.

KRAKÓW, POLAND
**Auschwitz concentration camp,** Oświęcim: Infamous Nazi mass-murder factory. (12)25071.
**Wawel Castle:** Sixteenth-century Polish capital; striking castle complex of Gothic and Renaissance buildings, which house a collection of Flemish tapestries and a burial ground of notable figures in Polish history; full day tours. (12)225155.

KAZIMIERZ DOLNY, POLAND
**Tombstone Memorial:** Crack in wall made of uprooted headstones symbolizes destruction of once-thriving local Jewish community. One mile south of town on highway.

WARSAW, POLAND
**Warsaw Ghetto Memorial,** Jewish Historical Institute. (22)271843.
**Chopin Memorial,** in Lazienki Park.
**Royal Palace, Wilanow:** Reconstructed medieval seat of government. (22)420795.
**Royal Palace Museum.** (22)6353995.

# CHAPTER 16

## WARSAW TO MOSCOW

OUR TRIP INTO THE U.S.S.R. WAS RARE IN 1988, AND REMAINS so as I write this two years later. The border is still not open, and, if it was, travel by bike over the 725 miles from Warsaw would be tough. Seventy years of severely restricted internal travel have deprived Soviets of motels. We often had to bus between big cities since there were no places to stay. In a few cities, it was apparent that a freshly painted, makeshift hotel had been converted from an army building or hospital just for us.

If freedom of travel and accommodations open up in the U.S.S.R. (none are listed here because all hotels must currently be arranged through Intourist, the Soviet travel agency—see numbers below), the riding will be easy. It's literally a flat plain all the way from Warsaw to Moscow, a fact not lost on the invading armies of Napoleon and Hitler in the past, or on the Russians, who are justifiably paranoid.

If the Soviets ever do allow tourists to invade, getting to the major tourist cities that we visited will be simple. Brest, Minsk, Smolensk, and *Moskva* herself are all strung out along 600 miles of Soviet Highway 1, which, when not busing, we rode under the watchful gaze of our round-the-clock police escort. A better plan, passing by small villages as well as the big cities, would be to ride the parallel roads about one kilometer off Highway 1. Unfortunately, we were only allowed a couple of glimpses of these Byelorussian and Russian villages on our highly regulated tour. Still, the narrative that follows will give a good idea of what to expect and what to see in the big cities along this route.

The Soviet Union requires that accommodations be booked before a visa is issued. A travel agent can make the lodging arrangements.

Numbers to know:
   Russia Travel Bureau: 1-800-847-1800
   Soviet Consulate: San Francisco: (415) 922-6642
   Intourist: New York: (212) 757-3884
   American Travel Abroad: New York: (212) 586-5230.

## ROUTE SLIP
### Total of 725 miles in 9 days

| Day | Route End Point | Terrain* | Sights | Mileage |
|---|---|---|---|---|
| 1 | Warsaw, Poland | Travel Day | | |
| 2 | Siedlce, Poland | Flat | | 55 |
| 3 | Brest, Byelorussia | Flat | Fortress Memorial | 65 |
| 4 | Kobrin, Byelorussia | Flat | | 30 |
| 5 | Ivatsevichi, Byelorussia | Flat | | 50 |
| 6 | Baranovichi, Byelorussia | Flat | | 40 |
| 7 | Minsk, Byelorussia | Flat to rolling | First Communist Party Meeting Hall | 85 |
| 8 | Smolensk, Russia | Flat | Katyn Memorial | 190 |
| 9 | Moscow, Russia | Flat | Red Square, Kremlin, Lenin's Tomb, Bolshoi Ballet, Arbat Street, Armoury | 210 |

*Easy = flat-to-rolling; moderate = hilly; difficult = hills or steep climbing.

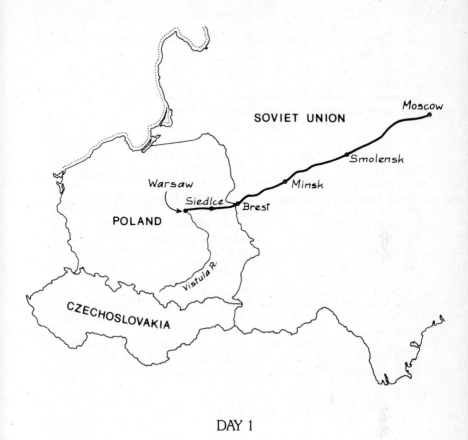

# DAY 1

Warsaw

_____

**ACCOMMODATIONS: Hotel Forum Warsaw,** Nowogrodzka 24/26, Warsaw,
PL-00511, (22) 210271, in U.S. (800) 327-0200. <u>Amenities</u>: bar, 2 restaurants.
<u>Rooms</u>: 751, double 181–191 DM. AMEX, CB, DINERS.

★
_____

## DAY 2

Warsaw to Siedlce, Poland
Terrain: Flat

---

**ACCOMMODATIONS: Guest House**, Street B Prusa 6, Siedlce, 08-110 Poland. Tel: 20-30 <u>Rooms</u>: 46, double $32. No credit cards.

---

As we approached the Soviet border on June 13, riding on the rainy, cold plain that would take us all the way to Moscow, our group of twenty-four had swelled to forty. In Warsaw, we were joined by riders who had opted for Frank's "short" tour. There was grumbling amongst the "family" that the new people hadn't "earned the right" to go into Russia, that they hadn't been tested in the midnight rides of West Germany, the fourteen-hour days of Holland, that they'd just never fit in. The truth was that there simply wasn't enough time to get to know them all; from the moment we hit the U.S.S.R., we rode a lot less, took buses long distances and had activities every moment.

When we stopped for an hour to change our money at the Polish border station, Frank called us together for a speech. "I've gotten you this far," he said dramatically, "but now whether or not they let us in is out of my hands."

With that, we waited for our names to be called. Then we disappeared, four at a time, across the Bug River and the one-mile no-man's-land that separates Poland and the U.S.S.R.

# THE SOVIET UNION

## DAYS 3–9

Terrain: Flat

They didn't search us. They didn't interrogate us. In fact, they joked with us and even posed for pictures. What a letdown!

I was looking forward to something really Cold Warish—gigantic 1950s-style posters of Lenin, hammers and sickles, and toothpicks shoved under your nails. After all, this first-ever bike trip into the Soviet Union could have actually been a CIA trick, right? Kent could have been a chemical weapons expert, fiendishly planning to poison the Kremlin water supply. Yet there was nothing—not even a suspicious Communist eyebrow raised.

As we rode with a police escort three miles into Brest, the million-strong Byelorussian border town, I was struck by how *normal* it all looked; how neat and clean and maintained the wide boulevards were. Sure, it seemed a little dull. There were no Polish-style street vendors, and the buildings—none new—were gray, devoid of neon and colorful displays. But they weren't dilapidated like in Czechoslovakia. Most normal of all were the people. Some mechanically waved, as if they were ordered to do so, but most simply stared at this multicolored horde of riders flying American flags and moved on, as if it were no big deal—as if we were not the *great enemy*.

We had two guides in the U.S.S.R.: Basil, a colorful twenty-three-year-old Muscovite who was with us the entire time, and Alex, mid-forties, who stayed with us in his home republic of Byelorussia. Alex and Basil seemed to confirm what Elena had said, that the Soviets either don't have or are afraid to give their opinions. "What do you think of glasnost?" always drew a response of, "We'll see, we'll see." We speculated that independent thought had been *scared* out of them by hundreds of years of mass murder, imprisonment, and internal exile under the czars and the Communists.

One thing the Russians didn't keep quiet about was their obsession with World War II, the horrors of which seem to have left deep scars of hate and sadness. Books, plaques, tanks, and statues commemorating the "Great Patriotic War" abound. Two major sightseeing stops on our trip were to memorial parks, with the first, in Brest, featuring an eternal flame, a building-sized, grim-faced granite head, and an ominous bell, which bonged sadly every fifteen seconds. This sound, we were told, was the same bong the Russians broadcast by loudspeaker in 1943 to the Nazis, then besieging Leningrad, along with the message, "For every bong you hear, another German soldier has died." Katyn, another vast memorial site in Byelorussia, graphically depicted the Nazi extermination of every member of 186 villages.

Three out of every hundred Russian prisoners of war survived; twenty million Soviets perished. To read about it is one thing; but to go there, to stand where it actually happened, like at Katyn, where the Germans locked an entire village—152 people—into a barn and burned it to the ground, is to feel the sheer monstrosity of the Nazi horror in a way that left us all speechless and angry.

As depressing as Katyn was, riding to it was uplifting. In Minsk, we were joined for the fifty-mile ride to the memorial by a local bicycle club led by 1976 Montreal Olympic road race champion Vladimir Krozinsky. As we rode, a weird phenomenon occurred: Bill and Mr. Knowledge, the slowest riders in the group, started going faster than I! That's because Vladimir and his buddies, tired of the slow pace, were pushing the oldies right up the hills.

As we alternately biked and bused closer to Moscow (Frank said we couldn't ride all the way because the Soviets don't have hotels in cities that have rarely been open to travelers before), a sickness called Ruble-itis set in. Ruble-itis is what Mr. Knowledge called my compulsive trading of dollars to Soviet money-changers, many of whom offered up to ten times the official exchange rate of sixty kopecs (.6 rubles) per dollar. The trade, officially illegal, turned Russia from expensive to cheap. Example: Kent spent $150 to call home at the official rate when we arrived in Brest. For the same ten minutes in Moscow, after I taught him the trade, it was $15.

Actually there was nothing to master. A fifty-yard stroll down the street would bring at least a dozen whispered calls. "Change money?" Rates of four rubles to a dollar were common, with five to one, or six to one, possible with some hard bargaining.

# Moscow

On June 21, we made our long-awaited entrance into Moscow. Actually, it was anticlamactic, as we bused all day and only started riding at the edge of the city. Seven miles later, there it was—the oldest section of the city, its nucleus and site of its finest architecture—Red Square! Despite an orgy of picture-taking, some people were still too sleepy from the bus ride to feel the thrill.

The excitement grew as we roamed the city—a big Russian Disneyland—over the next three days. We marveled at the ornate subways, built deep into the ground to double as air-raid shelters. We saw the lines of shoppers we'd all read about in the papers. We saw soldiers everywhere—blond, swarthy, and Oriental—reminders that the Soviet Union was an empire. We saw Russian heavy metalists wearing "Megadeath" necklaces and other paraphernalia acquired through tourist trades. We walked artsy Arbat Street, where President Reagan and Secretary Gorbachev had strolled together just three weeks earlier. We went inside the Kremlin walls, viewing onion-topped cathedrals, their Russian Orthodox crosses ironically staring into the very offices of Gorby himself, at the very epicenter of the atheist Communist world. We queued up for an hour to walk by the tomb of the man whose face had stared at us from statues throughout the country, Lenin. "He's a little pale," I noted to Nelson Pena, then a twenty-five-year-old *Bicycling* magazine editor. "He doesn't get out much," Nelson explained.

The excitement came to a climax in one mad rush through Moscow. Greg Oxenham (a boisterous thirty-five-year-old Aussie), Nelson, and I found ourselves on our bikes in Red Square, with only twenty-five minutes to go until our bus, several miles away, was to leave for the Moscow Circus. Cutting through hordes of sightseers and shoppers on narrow side streets, we rode maniacally against the crowded, five-lane, rush-hour traffic. Darting in and out between huge buses, dodging opening car doors, riding over unfamiliar streets whose Cyrillic-alphabet names we couldn't read, knowing only the general direction of the hotel, we plunged left, then right, then left. Spotting a familiar landmark, the monolithic, Stalin-era State Department Building, we thought we'd made it with ten minutes to spare. But what we'd found instead was one of the many "copies" of this building that are scattered throughout the capital.

Good thing for us that Nelson remembered the name of our hotel, the Belgrade, which we screamed crazily at dozens of passersby. We pulled up just as the bus was boarding. As Nelson later wrote in his account of the story: "It was the most exhilarating 24 minutes and 30 seconds I've ever spent in the saddle."

I wanted to extend my visa to go to Leningrad, but that wish became a casualty of this system's Red red tape. One must give three days' advance notice to extend a visa, and since I asked at T-minus two-and-one-half days, it was too late. Rush it? They almost laughed.

Two women Greg and I spent an evening with blamed their backward state on the "System," which is built on the redundancy created by full employment. This great ideal results in a traffic cop on every corner (as well as one in a unique glassed-in tower), an elevator sitter on each floor, old women sweeping sidewalks at 11:00 P.M., thousands of officered military personnel walking everywhere, and different lines for order, payment, and receipt of goods. Everything is slow and inefficient, and it takes its toll. The people just aren't productive.

Every night the supply of alcohol ran out. You couldn't buy a single *bivo* (beer) late in the day because the hotel had to ration its supply. We stocked up at lunch.

Even the taxis were inefficient. On June 23, lost near the post office downtown, Nelson, Greg, and I couldn't get a taxi to stop. Hundreds of passengerless cabs passed by, happy with their hourly state wage and seeing no reason to pick anyone up. Diving into the Cyrillic-alphabet labyrinth of the subway, we couldn't tell where we were going and ended up on the other side of town. We arrived halfway through our final send-off dinner with the top brass from Intourist. Our trip was a first for them, too.

The *real* going-away party was to follow in Nelson's room, where we had painstakingly stockpiled sixty bottles of *bivo* for a final blowout. The warm glow everyone left with didn't just come from the beer and vodka. We'd had a great time together.

Everyone left for home or Leningrad the next day, but Kent and I still had one more adventure to go. After hitting Arbat Street and Red Square the afternoon of June 24, Kent, who was staying for a couple of days, bought a ticket at the Bolshoi from some black market scalpers. Flush with rubles from my last trade, I invited the four scalpers to dinner, figuring to get in some good conversation before my train left for Budapest at 10:30 P.M. But the scalpers wouldn't have any of that. "We take *you* to dinner," they countered, and within seconds a cab was hailed. How did they do it so fast? "Because I have *image*. They all know I am richest man in Moscow," boasted the twenty-four-year-old leader, Vladimir, tipping the driver five rubles for the three-ruble ride. We headed across the Moscow River to the Ukrainia Hotel, "the best restaurant in all of Russia."

He was probably right. Kent and I had our finest dinner of the trip—West or East. We still got no opinion on glasnost, but we did see a chorus of dancing girls that would rival the best in Las Vegas. We drank four bottles of "the best Russian vodka." And to top it off, in a place where the ladies wore gowns and the men formal suits, we stripped off our shirts and did what all good tourists in Russia do—traded our T-shirts. The bill came to 221 rubles—nearly what the average Russian makes in a month. I wanted to throw in my 100, but Vladimir waved me off. "I am richest man in Moscow. I have *image*."

And I had no time. It was 10:00 P.M.—half an hour until my train! We had some quick good-bye hugs, grabbed a cab, took a wild ride back to the Belgrade to pick up my bike, made it to the train station by 10:25 and drunkenly ran down the platform to my train. Kent and I only had time to shake hands. "Friends forever," I slurred. "Once a year," he vowed. And the train started.

One and a half days later, the train stopped in the capital of Hungary, which began the next phase of my trip, Budapest to the West. Three-and-one-half weeks later, up the Danube, over the Alps, down the Riviera, and across Iberia, I was in Portugal. I rode it *my* way—breakneck sightseeing and 100 miles a day, with the closest thing to a hotel being an occasional youth hostel. It was great fun, but . . . well, it just wasn't the same.

## SIGHTSEEING INFORMATION

BREST, BYELORUSSIA
**Fortress Memorial:** Featuring an eternal flame, a building-sized, grim-faced granite head and an ominous bell.

MINSK, BYELORUSSIA
**First Communist Party Meeting Hall.**
**Botanical Garden.**

SMOLENSK, BYELORUSSIA
**Katyn Memorial:** Depicts the Nazi extermination of every member of 186 villages. In one case, Germans locked an entire village—152 people—into a barn and burned it to the ground.

MOSCOW, RUSSIA
**Red Square:** Moscow's nucleus and site of its finest architecture, along with Lenin's Tomb. Adjacent is the **Kremlin**, with its onion-topped cathedrals, Soviet government offices, palace towers, and the Armory Museum.
**Bolshoi Ballet Theatre:** Started in 1776, it is the major source of Russian ballet.
**Moscow Tsirk (Circus),** Tsvetnoy Bul'var: World-renowned gymnasts and acrobats.
**Central Lenin Museum,** Revolution Square: Provides Lenin's life history.

# CHAPTER 17

## BUDAPEST TO
## THE WEST
### BUDAPEST TO
### LUCERNE

IT HAS TO BE THE MOST BEAUTIFUL BIKE ROUTE IN THE WORLD. Day-long rides along the Danube. Valley cruises between white-capped Alpine mountains. Grapes ripening in hillside vineyards. Strenuous mountain climbs. Visits to stunning cities loaded with 600-year-old palaces, medieval covered bridges, castle walls, grand gothic parliaments. Every day of this challenging 699-mile, nine-day due-West tour requires a roll of film. Postcards must have been invented somewhere between Budapest and Lucerne.

Strangely enough, I knew none of this beforehand. I simply had a little unfinished business to attend to.

Back in the summer of 1979, when disco was raging and my hair was a giant mushroom cloud, I was in an Austrian train station glancing at a map. In plain letters, there it was near the Salzach River on the town's outskirts: Franz *Wallack* Strasse—a street with my own name on it. In just five minutes, my train would carry me away from Salzburg, the halfway point of my pre-grad-school "take the second-class train around Europe" vacation. It would leave no time for me to cash in the sightseeing chip of a lifetime.

So nearly a decade later, planning my route home from Russia, I knew just two things: I wanted to make it to Lisbon, Portugal, and I had to pass through Salzburg.

And when I got there, I couldn't help but marvel again at this fairy-tale place of Mozart, hilltop castles, and medieval churches, the beauty of which has twice left me speechless. In fact, I marveled at beauty every day on this trip. I felt like it was all a giant movie set—too perfect to be real.

Combining the *Sound of Music* scenery of the Alps with the Old World grandeur, this route starts off in Budapest, "The Queen of the Danube," and follows the legendary river into Vienna, jammed with the imperial pomp of old-fashioned empire. The terrain stays flat until it cuts inland, off the river, to Steyr, then is partly hills, mostly valley into Salzburg. After dreamy Innsbruck, the long easy valleys end and Austria's Tyrol region—otherwise known as the Austrian Alps—begins. But although this stretch in Austria's "tail" is very tough—including a four-mile, thirteen percent grade through the Arlberg area—it had no twenty-mile-long mountain passes. Those are all to the south and east of this ride, going from Switzerland to Italy.

After some more climbing in Swiss hills, the final miles into Lucerne are lakeside and flat. But that isn't the condition this city will leave you in. With its lakeside gardens, covered bridges, and perfect fifteenth-century buildings, Lucerne will send you home or send you further on a euphoric high. It's the perfect way to end The Most Beautiful Bike Route in the World.

**IMPORTANT: A visa is necessary to enter Hungary.** You are permitted to get a visa upon arrival at the airport or if driving a car across the border, but not if you are arriving by train.

Hungarian Embassy, Visa Section, 3910 Shoemaker St. N.W., Washington, DC 20008, (202) 362-6730.
Hungary information: Ibusz Hungarian Travel Co., 630 Fifth Ave., Rockefeller Center, #2455, New York (212) 582-7412.

Austria information: Austrian National Tourist Office, 11601 Wilshire Blvd., Los Angeles, CA 90025.

## ROUTE SLIP
*Total of 699 miles in 9 days*

| Day | Route End Point | Terrain* | Sights | Mileage |
|-----|-----------------|----------|--------|---------|
| 1 | Budapest, Hungary | | Citadella, Castle Hill, Royal Palace, Parliament | |
| 2 | Gyor, Hungary | Easy | | 100 |
| 3 | Vienna, Austria | Easy | St. Stephen's Cathedral, Rathaus, Hofburg, Imperial Crypt | 87 |
| 4 | Krems, Austria | Easy | | 50 |
| 5 | Steyr, Austria | Easy/Moderate | | 79 |
| 6 | Salzburg, Austria | Easy/Moderate/Difficult | Mozart House, Fortress of Hohensalzburg | 85 |
| 7 | Innsbruck, Austria | Moderate/Easy | Hallien salt mine, Berchtesgaden | 99 |
| 8 | Feldkirch, Austria | Difficult/Easy | Arlberg Resort | 105 |
| 9 | Lucerne, Switzerland | Moderate/Easy | Fallen Lion, Musegg Wall, covered bridges over Lake Lucerne | 94 |

*Easy = flat to rolling; moderate = hilly; difficult = repeated miles of hills or steep climbing

## DAY 1

Arrival in Budapest
Sights: Citadella, Castle Hill, Royal Palace, Matthias Church,
   Parliament, Chain Bridge

   Russian soldiers ordered us out of the cabin. They checked the
racks, they probed under the seats with flashlights, they poked the pil-
lows. Glasnost or no glasnost, this was still 1988, and nobody was going
to sneak to the West on this train.
   The West? I was only going to Hungary, another Communist country.
But as we waited at the border for two hours to have our train wheels
refitted for the standard European guage, that was the first sign that
things were different here. The next sign, two hours later when I walked
out of the Budapest East station, was a little more obvious: Arnold
Schwarzenegger, that paragon of capitalism, was staring at me from a
pop-art poster pasted to a marquee across the street. *The Terminator* was
playing.
   Elena, our guide in Czechoslovakia, had told us, "You can get everything in Hungary. It is heaven on earth." In the train station, I got a
hamburger, cooked in something I hadn't seen in weeks: a microwave
oven. Outside were ornate, well-maintained turn-of-the-century buildings along the tree-lined boulevard. Hundreds of tasteful, professionally
appointed displays adorned store windows with bright colors, modern
styles, and fabrics—and even splashes of neon. It could have been Paris!
Budapest indeed is known as "The Paris of the East."
   But there was a price to pay for all this: the black market was barely
gray. When a man furtively slinked up to me and asked, "Change
money?" just like in the other Communist countries, then refused to pay
more than fifty forint for a dollar, I knew something was wrong. Having
heard the *official* rate was 50, I naturally asked for 200, a conservative
4-times rate typical in Poland or Russia. But he laughed, and kept laughing as I went to 150, to 100, to 75. When the bank opened, the official
rate was 47.5 to one, so I called him back for the 50—a whopping 5
percent gain over market. Just as in South America, Israel, and other
places, dollars here were simply a money changer's hedge against infla-
tion.
   Hungary, you see, was an "open" country. In 1988, 7 percent of the
economy had already been privatized. Travel to the West was allowed. As
I crossed the Duna River (the Danube), which separates flat, noisy Pest
and hilly, peaceful Buda—the ancient twin cities united in 1872—I saw
other western influences, like Levi's, Swatch watches, a few BMWs and
even "For Sale" realty signs. No wonder Elena thought it was heaven on
earth compared to its gray Communist brethren.
   While Budapest was up-to-date, it was also ancient. Looking down
from Gellért Hill's Citadella, I could see grandeur that even predates the
old Austro-Hungarian Empire: over on nearby Castle Hill was the Royal
Palace, the seat of power since the thirteenth century; the stunning roof
mosaic of Matthias' Church, which houses Renaissance and Baroque-era

jewelry and art, including the thousand-year-old jeweled crown of Hungary's first King, Stephen (1001–1038). The ornate Parliament Building lay across the river in Pest.

As I headed across the famous Chain Bridge to see the latter, I met Andrash, a twenty-five-year-old bike-riding Hungarian-American U.S. Embassy intern, who invited me to stay in his place. Before I knew it, he and his Hungarian girlfriend Clara gave me a whirlwind tour of Budapest's cafés and took me to—of all things—a punk rock concert. It could have been the United States a decade earlier: I saw Hungarians kids screaming and "slam-dancing," while a Canadian band pounded out guitar-screeching English lyric songs about the alienation of youth and parental repression: "You're such a bore, I really hate you. But I love you more." Communists? I don't think I saw one there—or in the entire city of Budapest, for that matter.

---

**ACCOMMODATIONS: Margitsziget,** on Margaret Island in middle of Danube, Budapest, (361)111-000. <u>Rooms</u>: 206, double $77-$92. AMEX, DINERS, VISA. **Hotel Metropol,** 58 Rakoczi Ut (on main street of city), Budapest, H-1074, (361)421175. <u>Rooms</u>: 102, double $22–$50. AMEX, DINERS, CB.

---

## DAY 2

Budapest to Gyor
Terrain: Flat
161 kilometers (100 miles)

After visiting parklike Margaret Island in the middle of the Danube, I headed off, closely hugging the river and avoiding the mountainous territory inland. The scenic river route was a sea of German tourists, with D (Deutschland) stickers leaping from every car. The cars themselves—Audis, Fords, and Opels—stood out from Hungary's customary Ladas, Skodas, and Polska Fiats, all of which I'd grown accustomed to in eastern Europe. Andrash told me that a Hungarian is only allowed to have a western car after three years of work abroad.

I also had my eyes peeled for something else. "Young women here are not only the prettiest in Europe," Andrash said, "but they also simply have *not* discovered the bra." As I entered a store, loading up on three cans of delicious Russian sardines in olive oil, two potent Czech Plzen

---

**DIRECTIONS:** North and west 120 kilometers on west bank of Danube River to Komarom. Then west 41 kilometers on E 15/E 5.

**ACCOMMODATIONS: Hotel Raba,** Arpad, u 34, Gyor, H-9021, (36-96) 15-533. <u>Rooms</u>: 196, double 1,170 forint ($25). AMEX, MC, VISA.

beers (12 percent alcohol), and a couple of yogurts, all for about a dollar and a half, I could see it was true. For a young, single man, Hungary was a shopper's paradise.

## DAY 3

Gyor, Hungary, to Vienna, Austria
Terrain: Flat
Sights: St. Stephen's Cathedral, Rathaus, Hofburg, Imperial Crypt
140 kilometers (87 miles)

"I heard the voice in German booming over the loudspeakers at the airport—and it sent a chill through me. I guess it's from watching too many films about the Nazis."

So spoke a blond-haired Swede named Roger whom I met while looking at the caskets, urns, bones, and skulls in the Roman catacombs beneath the landmark St. Stephen's cathedral in Vienna. It was uncanny to hear that, after I'd spent several hours at the Rathaus looking at a widely publicized, guilt-ridden exhibit commemorating the fiftieth anniversary of Austria's *Anschluss* with Nazi Germany in 1938. For years, the German-speaking Austrians have claimed they were forced against their will into the merger. They have even erected a monument to their Russian "liberators." But don't believe it—because they don't believe it themselves. Those films at the Rathaus showed Austrians genuinely excited at the sight of Hitler parading through Vienna and by the prospect of being part of his Reich.

But the Austrians also have a long history of their own. Though now a small country of 10 million, they and their Hapsburg rulers controlled vast sections of middle Europe from 1278 until 1918. The city of Vienna, population 1.6 million, is a monument to the empire's greatness. The Ringstrasse, the circular road in the center of the city that runs where the former walls of the Vienna fortress stood, has most of the city's great monuments on or within it: City Hall, Parliament Building, and Burg theater, all among Europe's finest examples of Baroque architecture; the

---

**DIRECTIONS:** Go northwest 40 kilometers on Highway 1 to Mosonmagyarovar, then northwest 14 kilometers on E 5 to border. Across the border, go northwest 14 kilometers on Highway 10 to Gattendorf, then northeast 6 kilometers on Highway 50. Continue northwest 18 kilometers on road to Altenburg and across Donau (Danube) to Engelhartstetten, then west 50 kilometers on Highway 49.

**ACCOMMODATIONS: Atlanta Hotel,** Wahringerstrasse 33-35, Vienna, A-1090, (1) 421230. Amenities: restaurant. Rooms: 70, double AS 800–1350. AMEX, VISA.

★

Hofburg, the seat of the Austro-Hungarian Empire and home of the Haps-burgs during their 640-year reign; and the Imperial Crypt, complete with crowned skulls of the Hapsburg family. Outside the Ring are two opulent, gardened palaces, Belvedere and Schönbrunn. Vienna, in fact, is jammed with so many palaces and churches that I got a stiff neck from looking up so much.

That wasn't the only thing in pain. I could barely walk when I got off the bike. Yesterday's hundred miles, plus today's eighty-seven, though easy and flat, made me realize that even riding from London to Moscow won't get anyone in shape at five miles per hour.

## DAY 4

Vienna to Krems an der Donau
Terrain: Flat
80 kilometers (50 miles)

After spending most of the day sightseeing, my ride out of Vienna along the pretty Danube bike path was just what I needed: flat, relaxing, and very European. Old couples walked along the river, kids were play-ing, young women sat on benches reading books.

As the last rays of sunset dissipated on the tranquil waters, I pulled up to a little kiosk in the town of Krems. Before finding the local camp-site, I sipped a couple of beers with three Austrians as we bantered in languages neither side could understand. They taught me a few words in German, like the all-important *Wo ist* (Where is . . . ?), and I taught them a few in English—and two hours suddenly flew by. It was much more satisfying than the night before, when I'd fielded questions about my Russian trip for four hours from two Americans I met at a restaurant.

That reminded me to make a corollary to the Principles of Cycle-ology: when you go to local hangouts, try to hang out with the locals, not the tourists. I only had one night in Vienna, and it was spent talking about Russia—not learning about Vienna.

---

**DIRECTIONS:** West on south bank of canal. Follow Danube all day. Cross river to Krems.

**ACCOMMODATIONS: Parkhotel,** Edm Hofbrauerstr 19, Krems an der Donau, A-3500, (02732) 3266, <u>Rooms</u>: 72, double AS 600. AMEX, DINERS.

---

# DAY 5

Krems an der Donau to Steyr
Terrain: Flat, then rolling
126 kilometers (79 miles)

Though the scenery began to change as I headed west on the Danube, with vineyard-terraced mountains plunging into it from each side, I began to get bored with the river. So before Linz, I cut "inland" for Steyr—where a crazy night awaited.

As I rode through town asking *"Wo ist pension?"* a hyperactive, thirty-two-year-old Austrian army colonel on a Cannondale mountain bike rode up. His name was Leo, and when I gave him a Russian cigarette, he went nuts—promising in minimal English to find me a free room for the night, get me fed, and to show me "real Steyr."

Joining Leo and his comely eighteen-year-old girlfriend at a local pub, I watched in amazement as he jumped up on tables and pounded his chest with Tarzan wails and tiger roars. "I Teeeeee-ger!" he thundered, drawing his friends from the other tables with their beer and guitars. Soon they started playing music—American music.

Although it was fun, I soon felt some obvious pressure on me. While they knew all the music perfectly, they'd sing the songs like some sort of comic opera—slurring and mangling words beyond recognition—and they knew it. No one could speak more than a few words of English, so Tina Turner's "Rollin' on the River" became "Rollen und a raybe." Knowing the problem, they expected me to provide all the right words, not knowing that I didn't know them myself. But rather than beg off, I'd just make 'em up as I went along.

I must have sung a warped version of John Denver's "Sunshine on My Shoulders" thirty times. By then, it was 2:00 A.M. Drunk, I followed Leo by bike for about five miles out to a big two-story farmhouse. He banged on the door for ten minutes before a sleepy-eyed twenty-five-year-old named Regina answered. They argued in German for about fifteen minutes before he turned to me and said, "Here hotel—free." When I asked who the girl was, he said, "Girlfriend." When I asked about the eighteen-year-old, he smiled. "Girlfriend—number five."

---

**DIRECTIONS:** West 100 kilometers on Highway 3 to Mauthausen. Cross river, then go 26 kilometers on Highway 123/115.

**ACCOMMODATIONS: Hotel Mada,** Steyr, A-4400, (7252) 23358. <u>Rooms</u>: 55, double AS 920—1020. No credit cards.

# DAY 6

Steyr to Salzburg
Terrain: Big climb, hills and flats
Sights: Mozart House (recitals and tours), Fortress of
   Hohensalzburg.
139 kilometers (85 miles)

Loaded down with a care package of bread and boiled eggs from Regina and her grandmother, I headed for a day of pure enjoyment. Never knowing what to expect around the next curve, I passed through beautiful valleys, hills, geese-filled lakes, and picturesque little towns with names like Bad Hall, Kremsmunsters, and Voitsdorf. A major hill-climb at Steinbach was followed by a hiccupping descent to a long valley that led to the place that I'd thought about for nine years: Salzburg.

This place is special. The celebrated traveler/geographer Humboldt described Salzburg as one of the three most beautiful towns in the world. It has a combination of scenery and Italian-influenced architectural beauty that has led it to be called "The German Rome." It is also a music center, where Mozart was born in 1756.

I immediately walked my bike up the steep Mönchsberg, the big hill that overlooks the Old Town, to catch the fantastic sunset on the Salzach River from the Fortress of Hohensalzburg. Then, as I ate my last boiled egg and gazed at the fairy-tale scene below me, I marveled that I'd see a place this pretty, from this same spot, twice in a lifetime.

---

**DIRECTIONS:** Go east 26 kilometers on Highway 122 to Kremsmunster, then southeast 34 kilometers on Highway 120 to Gmunden. Continue southeast 25 kilometers on unnumbered road to Steinbach. Then go south 5 kilometers to Weissenbach, east 26 kilometers on Highways 153 and 151 to Mondsee. Continue east 9 kilometers on road past Thalgau, south 4 kilometers on connecting road to Highway 158, then east 15 kilometers.

**ACCOMMODATIONS: Best Western Kasererhof Hotel,** Alpenstrasse 6, Salzburg, A-5020. (0662) 21265. Manor house dating from sixteenth century. Rooms: 35, double AS 1,815–2,615. AMEX, MC, VISA.

---

# DAY 7

Salzburg to Innsbruck
Terrain: Hilly, then flat
Sights: Hallien Salt Mine, Berchtesgaden
160 kilometers (99 miles)

Groping my way south along the river in the morning, I snapped the picture that was nine years in the making: the Franz Wallack Strasse sign. Back at the statue of Mozart in the Old City town square, a tour guide told me that Franz was a famous architect back in the 1930s.

My exuberance over getting to know old Franz dissipated as I headed southwest in and out of a tiny finger of West Germany. (I'd skipped Berchtesgaden, Hitler's famous German mountain retreat twenty miles due south of Salzburg, and a visit to the Hallien salt mines, featuring miners' "sliding rails" I'd tried out nine years earlier. Together, they'd constitute an interesting all-day Salzburg loop.) In just twenty-three miles, I was totally worn-out by the hilly terrain. With my unconditioned legs aching, I entered Austria's long tail dreaming of "valley," and soon got my wish. The last seventy-two miles lay in the wide, flat Inn River Valley all the way to Innsbruck, capital of the Tyrol province.

Tyrolia means the Alps, which I'd now weave through all the way to Lucerne. With mountains on each side of me, perfectly coiffed farms at their base, and the air as crisp as fresh lettuce, I felt like I could pedal forever. And when I saw Innsbruck ("bridge over the Inn"), I felt as if I could *stay* forever. Framed by an awesome wall of snow-covered mountains, with narrow, balconied streets, bay windows, 500-year-old arcades, and wall frescoes, some dating to the fourteenth century, this longtime crossroads between Italy and Germany seemed like the most livable place on earth. Just one night there didn't seem fair.

---

**DIRECTIONS:** Head southwest 40 kilometers on Highway 312 through W. Germany to Lofer. Turn west 58 kilometers to Wörgl, then southeast 62 kilometers on Highway 171.

**ACCOMMODATIONS: Austrotel,** B, Hofel-Str. 16, Innsbruck, A-6020, 522/44-333, U.S. (800) 223-1588, CAN (800) 531-6767. Amenities: bar, sauna. Rooms: 137, double AS 1,420–1,570. AMEX, VISA.
**Best Western Maria Theresia Hotel,** 31 Maria Theresien strasse, Innsbruck, (5222) 5933. Rooms: 105, double AS 850–1,650. AMEX, DINERS, VISA.

---

# DAY 8

Innsbruck to Feldkirch
Terrain: Major climbs to 6,000 feet, long descent
170 kilometers (105 miles)

I knew there'd be trouble around Arlberg, where the highway line on the map began to get squiggly. But I had no idea that the terrain would climb up and down all day long from Innsbruck, getting tougher and tougher. And there's no way I could have imagined a seven-kilometer, 13 percent-grade monster hill reaching 6,000 feet in height at snowbound

Arlberg. I actually began to resent the cars on the autobahn, way, way down below me, humming through flat tunnels drilled in the mountains.

But what goes up, must come down. I coasted down kilometer after kilometer seemingly all the way to Feldkirch. When I got into town, I bought myself a foot-long Milka chocolate bar and had a good time rapping with a bunch of boys excitedly lined up to see the movie *Rambo III*. As in Poland, Rambo was every twelve-year-old's hero—even more so than Arnold Schwarzenegger. Rambomania made me realize how incredibly powerful American culture is—and how pleased Sylvester Stallone would be if he found out he bested the Terminator in the latter's own homeland.

---

**DIRECTIONS:** Go west 85 kilometers on E 17 to Landeck, then west 85 kilometers on Highway 197/588/190.

**ACCOMMODATIONS: Schlosshotel,** Schlossplate, Bludenz, A-6700, (5552) 63016. <u>Rooms</u>: 36, double AS 1,100—1,320. AMEX, MC, VISA.
**Weisses Kreuz Hotel,** Altenstadt, Feldkirch, A-6800, (5522) 22209. <u>Rooms</u>: 36, double AS 1,220—1,320. AMEX, EC, VISA.

---

## DAY 9

Feldkirch, Austria, to Lucerne, Switzerland
Terrain: Generally flat, with some climbs
Sights: Fallen Lion, Musegg Wall, covered bridges over Lake
    Lucerne
152 kilometers (94 miles)

After crossing the border at Liechtenstein and again a few minutes later in Switzerland, the first thing I saw was a lady stopping traffic on the highway while herding a perfectly manicured, bell-clanging group of cows across it. Yes, the cows were *manicured*. It was like everything in Switzerland (and Austria, for that matter)—immaculate. I don't think I saw one piece of trash in either country.

That doesn't mean I liked everything. I was cursing Swiss highway planners for forcing bike riders off the flat, river-hugging autobahn onto a ten-kilometer mountain climb, just like in Austria, when a biker climbing from the other side of the mountain approached me. (Note: I have arranged the route to avoid these climbs.) After directing a flurry of angry words at the tiny cars below, I realized the other guy, Franz, hadn't understood a word. He only spoke German.

That didn't stop him from leading me down into an exquisite canyon to the town of Nafels, where his English-speaking wife and in-laws awaited. Though it was midday, that was as far as I got. They wanted to hear all about Russia, what certain Americanisms like the word "bullshit" meant, and how Americans could have elected anyone as "dumb" as

Reagan, who seemed to be universally laughed at by Europeans. I wanted to know why everything cost so much ("Because it is *Swiss*," they'd say proudly.); why the German Swiss didn't join the Nazis ("Some did, but most Swiss feel superior to the Germans."); about their migrant worker "problem" (so many Poles and Yugoslavians are in the country doing the "dirty" jobs that the white-collar Swiss are forgetting how). After a few bottles of Boxer Old Lager beer, it was clear I was staying there for the night.

The next day, I only intended on making a quick stop in Lucerne before moving on to Interlaken, since I was rapidly falling behind my schedule to make my nonrefundable plane flight out of Lisbon, Portugal. After a flat lakeside ride into the city, I quickly located the big sights: the Fallen Lion wall carving, honoring the Swiss Guards slain defending the Tuileries in Paris in 1792, and the Musegg Wall, a fourteenth-century fortification. Having used up my quota of two hours in the city, I rolled down to Lake Lucerne, found the road out of town, and reached to balance myself with one hand on a pole while waiting at a traffic light.

Unfortunately, I was a little too far from the pole. As I leaned over at a forty-five-degree angle, the rear wheel suddenly buckled inward from the side force, bowing like a potato chip. It wouldn't even roll. The only place I was going now was a bike shop.

So I ended up unintentionally stopping to smell the roses for another day and a half in Lucerne—and I'm sort of glad I did. I crossed all five bridges over the Reuss River and the lake, including the famous medieval covered bridges—the zigzag Kapellbrücke, built in 1333, and the Spreuerbrücke, circa 1407. I went to 800-year-old St. Peter's chapel and the pretty Glacier Gardens (Gletschergarten), then walked through the back alleys and promenades of one of the loveliest settings in Switzerland—or the world.

By the time I picked up my $124 wheel ("Why so much?" I complained; "It's Swiss," they answered), I'd not only gotten to know Lucerne, but faced the fact that I couldn't make it all the way to Portugal. Therefore, I took it slow to Barcelona, savoring the Matterhorn, Genoa, Nice, Monaco, and Saint-Tropez along the way. In the end, I bused to Madrid

---

**DIRECTIONS:** Go southwest 11 kilometers on Highway 191 to Schaan, west 42 kilometers on Highway 16 to Wattwil, southwest 28 kilometers on Rapperswil Road. Cross lake, then go 34 kilometers on Highway 8 to Schwyz, south 5 kilometers to Brunnen. Go west 19 kilometers on Vierwald Lake shore road, then west 13 kilometers on Highway 2.

**ACCOMMODATIONS: Hotel Pilatus,** Hergiswil, CH-605, on lakefront, one minute from Lucerne, (041) 951-555. Rooms: 70, double Sfr 110–170. AMEX, DINERS, VISA.

★

and took the train to Lisbon. So, while I didn't conquer Iberia by bike as planned, I did vow to come back some day to do just that.

As this trip had shown me, a little unfinished business can be a good excuse for a beautiful adventure.

# SIGHTSEEING INFORMATION

### BUDAPEST, HUNGARY

**Castle Hill (Várhegy):** Its Royal Palace is the city's most famous site. The Vármúzeum inside recounts the city's history, while the Wine Museum has Gypsy music and wine tasting.

**Gellért Hill (Gellérthegy),** Buda: Overlooks the city; on top is Citadella, a hotel, wine-tasting room, and café. Statue commemorates Russian liberation in World War II.

**Matthias' Church (Mátyástemplom),** Castle Hill: The stunning roof mosaic houses Renaissance and baroque-era jewelry and art, including the jeweled crown of Hungary's first King, Stephen (reigned 1001–1038).

**Parliament,** Pest: Neo-Gothic Inner City building has guided tours.

**Margaret Island (Margitsziget):** Park island in middle of Danube; no cars allowed.

### INNSBRUCK, AUSTRIA

**Old Town and the Golden Roof (Goldenes Dachl),** city center: Fifteenth-century royal residence has gilded copper roof.

**Funicular:** Cable car to top of Patscherkofel provides wonderful view of surrounding Alps.

**Hofkirche (Court Church):** Contains marble tomb of Maximilian I, carved with vivid life scenes; guarded by twenty-eight bronze statues. Daily 9:00–5:00; admission.

**Tiroler Landesmuseum ("Ferdinandeum"):** Displays evolution of art over the centuries and stonework from Roman excavations of ancient Roman town of Virunum.

### LUCERNE, SWITZERLAND

Lucerne Tourist Office: call 517171.

**Fallen Lion:** Wall carving honors the Swiss guards slain defending the Tuileries in Paris in 1792, is oldest symbolic memorial in Switzerland, dedicated 1921.

**Musegg Wall:** Fourteenth-century fortification of nine towers that once enclosed Lucerne. Main tower, added in 1686, was warehouse holding salt and corn.

**Five Bridges** over the Reuss River and Lake Lucerne, including the famous medieval covered bridges—the zigzag Kapellbrücke, built in 1333, and the Spreuerbrücke, circa 1407.

**Glacier Garden (Gletschergarten):** Pretty outdoor museum reviews 20 million years of geology.

SALZBURG, AUSTRIA

Salzburg City Tourist Office, Auerspergstrasse 7, A-5021, (662) 8072-0.

**Fortress of Hohensalzburg,** on Mönchsberg: The big hill that overlooks the Old Town.

**Mozart House:** Where Mozart was born in 1756 and raised; recitals and tours.

**Mirabell Gardens:** Decorated with statues, flowers, and fountains, offers super view of the Fortress; includes Palace of Mirabell, one of Europe's most beautiful concert halls.

SALZBURG EXCURSION TRIPS:

**Hallein Salt Mine:** Tour features trip down "sliding rails" used by miners. *Sound of Music* tour also available. Cost: 250AS. Salzburg Panorama Tours, Schrannengasse 2/2/25, A-5020, (0662) 71618-0.

**Berchtesgaden:** Hitler's mountain retreat; 20 miles due south of Salzburg, in Germany.

VIENNA, AUSTRIA

Vienna city tourist information, Margarntenstrasse 1, 1040. Call 588-660. Most attractions along Ringstrasse.

**St. Stephen's Cathedral (Stephansdom):** Landmark gothic-spired cathedral house, first built in 1147, houses caskets, urns, bones, and skulls in catacombs below.

**State Opera House (Staatsoper):** Originally built in 1869; guided tours each afternoon; daily performances.

**Imperial Vault (Kaisergruft):** A crypt containing crowned skulls of 138 Hapsburg family members; located under the Kapuzinerkirche (Church of the Capuchins).

**Burg theater,** in Ringstrasse: Among Europe's finest examples of Baroque architecture.

**Hofburg (Imperial Palace):** Giant complex of offices and courtyards which was the seat of the Austro-Hungarian Empire and home of the Hapsburgs during their 640-year reign. Open daily 8:30–4:00 (Sun. to 12:30 P.M.); admission.

**Belvedere:** Two palaces linked by terraced gardens, considered among the best examples of baroque architecture; includes museum of Austrian baroque art; gardens have excellent view of Vienna; Russian war memorial is close by.

**Schönbrunn:** 1880-room palace was favorite Hapsburg residence when built in 1695–1749; residence of last Hapsburg emperor in 1918.

# ROLLIN' ON THE RIVER

## The Mighty Mississippi

★

---

THE MISSISSIPPI RIVER, THE FATHER OF THE WATERS, THE BIG-
gest, widest, and longest river in North America,* starts off as a shal-
low, fifteen-foot-wide stream pouring out of Lake Itasca, 180 miles
northwest of Minneapolis. My partner and I followed the river for three
extraordinary weeks in the summer of 1989, riding 1,987 miles through
9 states all the way to the Gulf.

The trip resulted from a conversation I'd had three years earlier with
a guy named Christopher, whom I'd met one day while biking down the
Pacific Coast from Vancouver. An adventurer who had once swum in the
Arctic Ocean "just to say I did it," Christopher told me his favorite journey
of all came on the Mississippi River. He and his father had traveled its
entire length—by raft.

Building a Huck Finn-style raft of logs and a tent, father and son left
from Lake Itasca and floated down the river as far as they could during
a two-week vacation. Storing the raft, they returned there the next year
and pushed off. After six years, they completed their quest, floating into
the Gulf of Mexico.

I was hooked. Rafting isn't my bag, but how about doing it by . . .
bicycle? I'd never heard of anyone cycling The River.

And that's too bad. The River went to places that I'd never been before, like Memphis and New Orleans, Iowa, Missouri, Kentucky, Mississippi. It had interesting history, from seventeenth-century French explorers to nineteenth-century military battles, such as New Orleans in the
War of 1812 and Vicksburg in the Civil War. And it had the sight I'd
dreamed of since the Big Adventure: the Gateway Arch in St. Louis.

The gleaming steel Arch, like The River, symbolizes the dividing line
between new and old, East and West. The states drained by the Mississippi, settled after the Atlantic Coast but before the Pacific, have come to

---

*Actually, the Mississippi is not as long as it was a hundred years ago, having streamlined its
curves by constantly overflowing its banks and cutting straighter channels. The Missouri, a
major Mississippi tributary, is now the longest river in North America.

Lake
Itasca

MN

WI

IA

IL

IN

MO

St. Louis

KY

TN

AR

MS

LA

Venice

represent the heartland, even though the crops, the accents, and the attitudes along the way greatly differ. Only The River, the mighty, muddy, continent-bisecting Mississippi, stays the same.

On June 13, 1989, my brother's roommate Larry joined me at the headwaters for the ride down the nationally designated Great River Road. Ahead, I hoped, was a fantastic route for bicycle touring—and good material for the final chapter of a possible book.

My wishes were granted. We had a party thrown for us in a bar in La Crosse, Wisconsin. We discovered, to our dismay, that Iowa has steep hills. We toured Mark Twain's boyhood home in Hannibal, Missouri. We were invited into St. Louis's Busch Stadium to see the Cardinals play. We ate teriaki chicken wings in an antebellum mansion in Mississippi. We experienced a crazy Fourth of July in New Orleans. We looked *up* to see a cargo ship sail twenty feet above us on a levee near the Gulf. And we learned a lot about relationships—farm to city, black to white, North to South.

We even had two newspaper articles written about us. Of course, that didn't hold a candle to Malcolm Forbes, the late magazine publisher, who led a group of motorcyclists down the same route that summer. Nearly every big-time newspaper and magazine in the country covered his ride, while Larry and I had to settle for *The Herald* of Clinton, Iowa, and the *North County News* of Red Bud, Illinois. But we did top Malcolm in a way: he stopped at New Orleans; we continued seventy-five miles farther to the Great River Road's true end—the tiny oil town of Venice.

# CHAPTER 18

## THE NORTH
### LAKE ITASCA, MINNESOTA, TO ST. LOUIS

T HIS TRIP OF 1,054 MILES TOOK LARRY AND ME FROM THE FAR north of the United States to the very middle. Snaking south through Minnesota, Wisconsin, Iowa, Illinois, and Missouri, we followed the Mississippi from its meager beginnings as a small stream a hundred miles south of the Canadian border to its midpoint as a mammoth mile-wide waterway in St. Louis.

On paper, the ride looked easy. In fact, my supercharged partner figured it'd be hard for us *not* to do at least 150 miles a day. After all, the midsection of the continent is all prairie, so the Great River Road should have been totally flat.

Well, we didn't count on stronger-than-normal headwinds blowing up from the Gulf during the first five days. We didn't consider the incredible prairie humidity. We didn't count on Iowa—yes, *Iowa*—blockading us with relentless corn-covered hills, and additional climbing as the road jutted inland in Illinois and Missouri.

As a result, we had trouble making 100 miles a day, much less 150.

The slower pace, however, allowed more time to enjoy the refreshing mix of urban and country. The two biggest cities, Minneapolis–St. Paul and St. Louis, are small and uncongested compared to Los Angeles or New York. There are many cities in the forty- to fifty-thousand range, plus many tiny farm and river towns. Though rarely more than twenty miles between Coke machines, we were nearly always in farmland. The variety was amazing: Minnesota corn, Iowa corn, Illinois corn.

Mississippi
River

Bemidji
Grand
Rapids
Lake
Itasca
Brainerd
WI
Minneapolis-
St. Paul
Wabasha
MN
La Crosse
Guttenberg
IA
Clinton
Muscatine
Nauvoo
IL
Hannibal
St. Charles
MO
St. Louis

*ROUTE SLIP*
*Total of 1,054 miles in 15 days*

| Day | Ending Point | Terrain* | Sights | Mileage |
|---|---|---|---|---|
| 1 | Itasca State Park, Minnesota | Easy | The Headwaters | 32 |
| 2 | Bemidji, Minnesota | Easy | | 33 |
| 3 | Grand Rapids, Minnesota | Easy | | 71 |
| 4 | Brainerd, Minnesota | Easy | | 98 |
| 5 | Monticello, Minnesota | Easy | | 89 |
| 6 | St. Paul, Minnesota | Easy | Minneapolis Park Loop, Minnehaha Park, State capitol, Hall of Justice | 65 |
| 7 | Wabasha, Minnesota | Easy/Moderate | Lake City Drive-In | 76 |
| 8 | La Crosse, Wisconsin | Easy/Moderate | World's Largest Six-Pack, Old Style brewery tour, Don's Seldom Inn | 63 |
| 9 | Guttenberg, Iowa | Easy/Difficult | Pike's Peak, hills in Iowa, Balltown all-you-can-eat | 84 |
| 10 | Clinton, Iowa | Difficult | | 107 |
| 11 | Muscatine, Iowa | Easy | Rock Island, East Davenport Village | 67 |
| 12 | Nauvoo, Illinois | Moderate | Nauvoo Mormon Settlement | 86 |
| 13 | Hannibal, Missouri | Moderate | Mark Twain's hometown | 65 |
| 14 | St. Charles, Missouri | Difficult/Easy | Scenic Highway | 95 |
| 15 | St. Louis, Missouri | Easy | Gateway Arch, Busch Stadium, brewery | 21 |

*Easy = flat to rolling; moderate = hilly; difficult = repeated miles of hills or steep climbing

Aside from a few giant statues of Paul Bunyan, old-fashioned sight-seeing opportunities were rare until Minneapolis–St. Paul. From that point, we toured two breweries (Heileman's in La Crosse, Wisconsin, and Busch in St. Louis), got religion (a Mormon ghostown in Nauvoo, Illinois), American culture (Mark Twain's home in Hannibal, Missouri), architecture, history, and even some baseball (St. Louis's Gateway Arch, Museum of Westward Expansion, and the Cardinals).

We found an incredible view of the Mississippi at Pike's Peak, Iowa, which also overlooks the spot where French explorers Marquette and Joliet became the first Europeans to see the northern Mississippi in 1673. After the uncolonized Indian lands passed through the hands of the French, Spanish, and English, the United States gained the east bank after the Revolutionary War and the west bank with the Louisiana Purchase twenty years later.

As usual, the best part of the ride was the human touch. Although the accents changed, from a Scandinavian lilt in Minnesota and Wisconsin to the husky, plain accent of Iowa and Illinois and the drawl of the Missourians, the people were incredibly friendly throughout. Nowhere else have I experienced people stopping their cars just to say "Hi." That alone made this a great tour.


# DAY 1

Bemidji to Itasca State Park, Minnesota
Terrain: Flat to rolling
32 miles

On the plane flight into Minneapolis and bus ride to Bemidji, Minnesota, I realized that Larry Lawson was my worst nightmare.

All he talked about was riding 200 miles a day. He didn't care about seeing sights, taking pictures, or meeting people.

Larry was the Frankensteinian result of two years of living with my brother Marc. Once a 230-pound, happy-go-lucky partier, Larry had metamorphosed into a lean, mean, broccoli-eating, triathlon-training, Pritikin-obsessed, 185-pound bike-riding machine. A master's candidate in molecular biology, he took Marc's theories on diet, mind control, and bicycling and applied them with studious obsession. With skin bronzed and hair bleached by hours on the road, he'd become a golden Adonis, part-man, part-machine—a cycling cyborg.

On his only other bike trip, the summer before, he and Marc rode from Seattle to San Diego by doing 200 miles a day, and once did 247. Even worse, Larry was fast. For this trip, he had been training 100 miles a day at a five-hour pace.

Larry had just bought a state-of-the-art, $2,000, 18-pound racing bike with Campagnolo drivetrain, 2.2-pound Klein Quantum aluminum frame, triangular aero wheels, microthin 18-centimeter tires, Look clipless pedals, aerodynamic Scott DH triathlon handlebars, and Flight-Control fingertip shifters. Even his brake handles were ergonomically molded to the shape of his fingers. To reduce aerodynamic drag, he carried no panniers, just a 3-pound athletic bag tightly strapped under the seat. It contained a sleep-sheet, windbreaker, extra T-shirt, and odorless garlic powder.

By contrast, I had been putting in maybe 50 miles a week training. I was riding my trusty, pack muleish twenty-four pound Univega touring bike, bloated with a six-pound tent and another forty pounds of gear, maps, tour books, and clothes.

And Larry was twenty-three years old. I was thirty-three.

But a young thirty-three. A tough thirty-three. I'd do his miles—as long as he did my sightseeing.

We arrived in Bemidji with just enough time to make the virtually flat ride to Itasca State Park before dark. We turned right at the Contact Station and a twisty, tree-shrouded bike path led us through camping areas to what the visitors guide calls "The Birthplace of the Mississippi."

"Here 1,475 feet above the ocean the mighty Mississippi begins to flow on its winding way 2,552 miles to the Gulf of Mexico," read the sign. In the background was Lake Itasca—and a fifteen-foot-wide stream gurgling out of it.

Soon it was dusk and the mosquitos were upon us. Fortunately, some University of Minnesota grad students had invited us to stay in their summer "study cabins" near the lake. They hauled out some tequila they'd smuggled into the park and we toasted.

The first was to our journey. The next was to the one hundredth anniversary of the headwaters, discovered by historian Jacob Brower in 1889. Apparently, we all owed him a debt. Fighting logging companies for preservation of the rare red and white pine forest surrounding the headwaters, he created Itasca State Park two years later.

Before a third shot could be poured, my eyes closed. Languidly, I had drifted off like the mighty Mississippi.

---

**DIRECTIONS:** Go south 28 miles on US 71 to east gate of Itasca State Park, then north 4 miles on bike path to Headwaters.

**ACCOMMODATIONS & CAMPING: Itasca State Park,** 1-800-765-2267 or (218) 266-3656. Various lodges. <u>Rooms</u>: 150, double $29–$39. VISA, MC.

★

# DAY 2

Park Rapids to Bemidji
Terrain: Flat
Sights: The Headwaters
33 miles

After snapping a "dip the wheel in the water" photo as proof we were present at the Mississippi's birth, we set to follow it to adulthood. I aimed my bike north.

"What the hell are you doing?" said Larry.

Oh, no. I had a feeling this might happen.

"I'm following the flow of the river," I explained. "It heads north and east in a big hook before heading south."

"That's stupid," he blurted. "That's not the most direct route to New Orleans. That'll make us double back to Bemidji. And it'll cost us a couple hundred extra miles."

This guy apparently didn't understand my dream—and my bike touring philosophy. I was taking this trip to *follow* the Mississippi, not blitz down to New Orleans. I wanted to see the sights, see what Mark Twain saw. I'd had this trip on my mind for three entire years. I was not about to have it ruined.

"Look," I finally said, "this is not negotiable. Do it your own way." And even though I dread riding alone, I took off.

I turned onto the Great River Road, the name of all those roads throughout the trip which closely follow the Mississippi. I was in a bad enough mood already when the road turned to gravel for the next six miles. Delayed when I was attacked by a dog, then doctored by its apologetic owners, that gravel road took me over two hours.

After the gravel, the route crossed and recrossed the rapidly widening Mississippi. It grew fast because lakes were all over, some a few feet wide, some covering entire fields. Minnesota is the "Land of 10,000 Lakes"—an estimate, I'll bet, made during a drought.

One of those lakes is Bemidji, an Indian word meaning "river [the Mississippi] flowing through lake." I rode by the lakefront gazing at giant statues of Paul Bunyan and his blue ox Babe, whose hoofprints, legend has it, created the lakes. Then I was shocked to see another sight: Larry.

"Maybe you're right about riding along the river," he said. "But if you're this slow the rest of the way, we won't be in New Orleans until Christmas. Let's shoot for Grand Rapids."

*Gulp.* That was nearly seventy miles away.

But reunited, that's exactly where we headed (see Day 3), dutifully following the Great River Road. Ironically, we didn't even see the Mississippi for the next forty-five miles, as often was the case throughout the tour, although we did see an eighty-foot-long trout (a former restaurant) and the Chief Bug-O-Nay-Ge-Shig Elementary School.

By the time we crossed the little Mississippi ten miles before Grand Rapids, we got a shock: It had become *big!* Indian children from the

White Oak Point Reservation were jumping off a bridge into it—and living! Although the river wasn't "mighty" yet, it wouldn't be long at this rate.

I was beat by the end of the day, having ridden an uncharacteristic early-trip century to meet the unspoken wishes of an eager-to-please Larry. In fact, he'd been so agreeable that I casually mentioned we might even consider a shortcut the next day to save time, as the river would be sweeping back and forth in a big backward S.

"Not on your life!" he shouted indignantly. He was a believer now. "We're following every last inch of this baby!"

---

**DIRECTIONS:** North 6 miles on SR 2 past park's north entrance, northeast 27 miles on SR 40, SR 9, SR 3, and SR 7 (Great River Road).

**ACCOMMODATIONS: Edgewater Motel,** 1015 Paul Bunyan Drive NE., Bemidji, MN, (218) 751-3600. On lakefront. Rooms: 73, double $49–$59. VISA, MC, AMEX, DINERS, DIS. CAMPING: **Bemidji KOA,** 5707 US 2, (218) 751-1792. Amenities: groceries.

---

## DAY 3

Bemidji to Grand Rapids
Terrain: Flat
71 miles

---

**DIRECTIONS:** East on US 2 all the way.

**ACCOMMODATIONS: Forest Lake Motel,** 1215 NW 4th Street (on US 2 and swimming beach), Grand Rapids, MN, (218) 326-6609. Rooms: 31, double $40. VISA, MC, AMEX.

**CAMPING: Pokegama Recreation Area,** 2 miles west on US 2. Amenities: no phone, no showers, but Mississippi access.

---

# DAY 4

Grand Rapids to Brainerd
Terrain: Flat
98 miles

At last, the river arced south—right into terrible headwinds. The winds normally blow gently north from the Gulf of Mexico anyway, but locals told us these were the worst in a decade. Yet, as I struggled vainly at six or seven miles per hour on the dead-flat prairie, Larry shot ahead, as if there were no winds at all. When I caught him three hours later in Jacobson, he'd been waiting one-and-a-half hours.

"These winds are a bitch. Maybe you'd better draft off me," he suggested.

What an irony. Here I was, Mr. Tour, having biked all over the world, now reduced to needing a tugboat. Later, as we posed on a forty-foot-long plastic deer in Deerwood, the highlight of an attraction-starved, mosquito-bitten, standing-water day, I had to admit a bigger humiliation: I couldn't even keep up with Larry while drafting.

But this guy couldn't be superman, I thought. It had to be that high-tech bike! If we switched—if *I* was in that aerodynamic position and *he* was riding my Mack-truck-with-pedals—I'd beat him.

"Hey, Larry, whadda ya say we switch for a while, just for variety?"

So we switched. And it *was* easier with those aero-bars. Narrower, lower, I sliced through the wind effortlessly. But Larry still blew me away.

By the time we hit Brainerd, or as a guy at a liquor store told us, "the long form of Nerd," it was 6:30. Making it to this one-time lumber town (like many on the long deforested Minnesota plain) was fine with me. I was set to call it a day. Not Larry.

"I love these 9:30 sunsets," he said. "We can ride another forty-five miles, at least. Let's shoot for Royalton."

---

**DIRECTIONS:** Cross Mississippi on US 169. Go 2 miles south, then turn southeast on SR 3 for 22 miles. Turn east 2 miles across river on SR 200 to Jacobson, then south 30 miles on SR 65. Turn west 14 miles on SR 210, south 8 miles on US 169 to Aitkin. Continue straight (west) 11 miles on SR 210 to Deerwood, then 15 miles to Brainerd. Go on left SR 371 south for hotels.

**ACCOMMODATIONS: Holiday Inn,** 1½ miles south on SR 371, Brainerd, MN, (218) 829-1441. Amenities: laundry, sauna, whirlpool. Rooms: 151, double $60. VISA, MC, AMEX, DINERS, DIS.

**CAMPING: Memorial Park,** Crosby, MN (11 miles north of Brainerd), (218) 546-5021. Amenities: beach, laundry, grocery, museum.
**Crow Wing State Park,** 9 miles south on SR 371, (218) 829-8022.

Mercifully, the wind died down. We made it to runty Royalton, where we met a boxboy at a supermarket who was so impressed by the fact that we were from California that he invited us home.

"Set that alarm for 4:30," Larry ordered the kid.

"What?" I said incredulously.

"Well, we're shooting for St. Paul. So we've got to ride a hundred and eleven miles by two o'clock if we want to give ourselves time to sightsee. Right?"

Right, I nodded dumbly. How could I argue with that?

## DAY 5

Brainerd to Monticello
Terrain: Flat
89 miles

---

**DIRECTIONS:** South 31 miles on SR 371 to Little Falls. Continue south 12 miles on US 10 to Royalton. Turn west 2 miles across river on SR 26, then south 19 miles to St. Cloud. Continue southeast 25 miles on CR 75 to Monticello.

**ACCOMMODATIONS: Comfort Inn,** 200 E. Oakwood Drive, Monticello, MN, (612) 295-1111. <u>Rooms</u>: 16, double $44. VISA, MC, AMEX, DINERS, DIS.

**CAMPING: River Terrace Park,** 1 mile north (turn off CR 75 for ½ mile), (612) 295-2264. <u>Amenities</u>: riverside sites, laundry, groceries.

---

## DAY 6

Monticello to Minneapolis–St. Paul
Terrain: Flat
65 miles

We didn't make it into St. Paul by 2:00. We barely made it into town at all.

More headwinds pounded my fatigued legs. Even drafting behind Larry, I could barely move. It was one of the most drudgery-filled bike-riding days of my life. Larry didn't say a word, but I knew what he was thinking: I was a creampuff.

I'd always thought bicycling was helping me hold back the clock. The boxboy was astounded by my age. "Thirty-three? You look like you're in college!" he exclaimed. But now I knew it was a sham. Larry had the boundless energy of youth; I didn't. Today proved that I was pedaling into middle age.

I couldn't blame my sluggishness on terrain either, as we had flat prairie all the way; no downhill slope to speak of. By St. Paul, the Mississippi drops 700 feet in the 360 miles since Lake Itasca, just two feet a mile. I crawled sheepishly into town behind Larry at 9:00 p.m., happy to end this wasted day.

While we were pausing to look at downtown Minneapolis from across the river, a white van came by and stopped. "Hey, didn't I see you about fifty miles away from here around three o'clock?" asked a young blond-haired guy. "Damn, you guys are fast!"

What he didn't know wouldn't hurt him. Paul, an impressionable nineteen-year-old apprentice electrician, went nuts when told we were from California. "Wow, you gotta meet my friends!" he exclaimed, piling our bikes into the van. He took us to a party at a big, wooden two-story house, which seemed to be the norm no matter the neighborhood. "They're from California," he proudly introduced us, and we were fawned over like movie stars.

Later, Paul drove us aimlessly around the city, pointing out the state Capitol building, the Cathedral of St. Paul, the "nice" part of town, the "funky town" section, and the "hip" spots. We ended in a little park on a bluff with a fantastic view of the lighted Mississippi, now a quarter-mile wide.

Paul left about 3:00 a.m. We unrolled our bags and slept under the stars, amazed to be camping in the middle of a big city and by the friendliness of Minnesotans.

---

**DIRECTIONS:** Cross river northeast 4 miles to Big Lake. Then head south 23 miles on US 10 to Anoka. Continue south on CR 3 (Coon Rapids Boulevard) until it becomes CR 1 (East River Road then Marshall Street N.E.). Turn east a few blocks on Hennepin Avenue. Then go south, then east on University Avenue to state capitol and downtown St. Paul. (For greenbelt loop around Twin Cities, see Chapter 4, Day 1.)

**ACCOMMODATIONS: Radisson St. Paul,** 11 E. Kellogg Boulevard, Minneapolis, MN, (612) 292-1900. Amenities: river view. Rooms: 489, double $56. VISA, MC, AMEX, DINERS, DIS.
**St. Paul TraveLodge,** 149 University, (612) 227-8801. Rooms: 50, $39. VISA, MC, AMEX.

**CAMPING: St. Paul KOA East,** 568 Cottage Grove Drive, 9 miles east of Capitol (from I-94, ½ mile southwest on CR 15, follow signs ¼ mile), (612) 436-6436.

★

# DAY 7

St. Paul to Wabasha
Terrain: Flat plus small hills
76 miles

Stopped repeatedly around town by people who asked about our trip and offered sightseeing advice, we hit the road by 4:00 P.M. I figured we only had time for 35 to 40 miles. Then I remembered who I was traveling with.

"Let's shoot for Wabasha," said Larry.

Starting on the river's edge, we climbed up to US 61, crossed the Mississippi, then rode to Red Wing. There we were stopped by an insurance salesman who actually pulled up in his car and parked solely to talk to us—like he had nothing better to do. Although precious mileage time ticked away, we couldn't get over it. Nobody would ever do this in Los Angeles.

On his advice, we climbed up to the summit of Memorial Park for a ten-mile panorama of the Mississippi, one of the best views along its entire length. We saw the north end of Lake Pepin (Lake of Tears in French), named by Father Louis Hennepin for the nearby Indian burial mounds. Pepin, the widened waters of the Mississippi, is a vacation hotspot anchored by Lake City, "The Birthplace of Waterskiing."

Riding into Lake City, we were surprised to find hills, good ones at that. But our effort was rewarded with some great root beer and onion rings at Lake City's Root Beer Stand drive-in. After departing, we enjoyed a pretty lakeside ride past Lake Pepin to Wabasha, where the historic 1856-era Anderson House Hotel awaited.

"That was a good ride," said Larry, soaking in a cast-iron, clawfoot bathtub. "Let's shoot for a hundred and fifty miles tomorrow."

I was going to have to talk to this guy.

---

**DIRECTIONS:** From Mississippi in downtown St. Paul, go east 3 miles on Warner Road, then south on US 10/61 rest of day.

**ACCOMMODATIONS: Anderson House,** 333 W. Main Street, Wabasha, MN, (612) 565-4524. Restored historic hotel. Rooms: 30, double $35–$60. No credit cards.

**CAMPING: Richard J. Dorer Hardwood Forest,** 5 miles east on SR 60, ½ mile south on CR 81, (612) 345-3216. Amenities: primitive, no showers.

---

# DAY 8

Wabasha, Minnesota, to La Crosse, Wisconsin
Terrain: Flat to rolling
Sights: The World's Largest Six-Pack, brewery tour
63 miles

"Wis-*skon*-sin."

Not Wis-con-sin. The latter pronounciation is how dozens of natives knew immediately that Larry and I were foreigners. But Wisconsinites still sounded and acted like Minnesotans to us, meaning they had that understated, proto-Canadian accent and were super friendly. So friendly, in fact, that they stopped Larry dead in his tracks, something I didn't think possible.

It happened after a very pretty ride on a scenic green-on-green road with a view of striking bluffs lining the river. Soon, we crossed over the two-channel Mississippi into La Crosse, a Wisconsin city of 50,000 with the distinct odor of beer.

This old sawmill and railroad town has been a beer town since the 1880s, a fact we celebrated in style—Old Style, that is—with the biggest beer in town. And I do mean *big*. Across the street from the Heileman Brewery was, as the sign says, "The World's Largest Six-Pack of Beer," six cylindrical towers containing 22,200 barrels of Old Style beer—"enough beer to fill 7,340,796 cans and provide one person with a six-pack a day for 3,351 years."

Developing a taste for Old Style during the factory tour, we headed around the corner for "just one more" at a local bar called Don's Seldom Inn. Dazzled by our trip, the bartender drenched us in free beer, brought out twenty pounds of barbeque'd bratwurst, and fired up a party.

Larry explained the intricacies of his high-tech bike to everyone while they taught us how to pronounce Wisconsin. Despite their friendliness, we were surprised by the reaction when we explained we'd be riding the river all the way.

"You're going down *there*—on *those*?" they asked incredulously, as if

---

**DIRECTIONS:** South 54 miles on US 61, east 3 miles on I-90, south on 4th Street (US 14/SR 35) to brewery.

**ACCOMMODATIONS: Radisson La Crosse Hotel,** 200 Harborview Plaza, La Crosse, WI, (608) 784-6680. <u>Rooms</u>: 165, double $85–$95. VISA, MC, AMEX, DINERS, DIS.
**Guest House Motel,** 810 S. 4th Street, (608) 784-8840. <u>Rooms</u>: 39, $33–$36. VISA, MC, AMEX, DINERS, DIS.

**CAMPING: Goose Island Camp,** south 7 miles on SR 35, (608) 788-7018.

the South was another planet. It wasn't the first time, or last, that we heard Northerners make disparaging remarks about their Southern brethren.

## DAY 9

La Crosse, Wisconsin, to Guttenberg, Iowa
Terrain: Very hilly
Sights: Pikes Peak
84 miles

They said it'd be corn as far as the eye could see. They said it'd be pig poop as far as the nose could smell. They said it'd be flat as a pancake.

But they were wrong. As my throbbing thighs attested, Iowa is *not* flat!

We should have known. A blissful ride to the old fort city of Prairie due Chien, the second-oldest city in Wisconsin, took us to an Eagle supermarket and old Ed Farnell. The seventy-five-year-old explained that this site, which means "prairie of the dog" in French, was named for the Indian Chief Alim ("Dog" in Indian) by French explorers.

Ed also told us that Iowa had hills.

"Yeah, sure it does," I said to Larry a few minutes later, shaking my head. "Senility."

We crossed the Mississippi greeted by a sign proclaiming, "Iowa: Come Explore the Heartland." They ought to change it to "Come Explore Your Heartrate," because in a few minutes Ed was proven right.

Pikes Peak State Park was five hundred feet atop a hill that seemed straight up. But the view was worth it. The Mississippi, interlaced with thick rows of trees and vegetation, looked like hedges in a garden. Directly below, Marquette and Joliet had rowed canoes across on June 17, 1673, to become the first white men to set foot on Iowa soil.

Thereafter, the Great River Road was up-and-down all the way to Guttenberg. A long, wild downhill brought us into town alongside the river and a large system of locks.

If I'd been in control, that would have been the *final* downhill of the day. I was beat, and there was at most an hour before nightfall. But Larry didn't agree. At least he certainly didn't stop.

So I plowed on through the winding, unending waves of green corn stalks, picking up speed in the energizing cool of dusk. It was exhilarating to barrel down those Big Surlike hills in my highest gear, then whip up the next incline without stopping.

But when the sky faded to moonless black, the roller coaster became terrifying. I couldn't see the hilltops, or the bottoms, anymore. In addition, I was becoming more and more light-headed. We hadn't eaten since Prairie Du Chien, forty miles back.

As I blindly chugged up and plunged down, as my stomach walls churned and my sugar-deprived mind drifted, I began fantasizing—

about sight of Larry, about sight of a town, about sight of steaming fried chicken, my favorite food.

Just when I concluded that I could not go on without nourishment, I rolled into a tiny three-building town. Out front, I could barely make out Larry's bike in the shadows. Upstairs, light beamed from a doorway.

As I staggered up the steps, my head spinning, I was stunned by an odor so strong it snapped my neck back. My god, I was losing my mind. It was fried chicken!

I looked down to see Larry sitting in front of a plate piled high with a half-dozen pieces of chicken. "Hey," he garbled between mouthfuls, "this is my third helping in an hour. It's all-you-can-eat! They've got catfish and shrimp, too."

I'll never forget that $5.95 buffet at Breitbach's Restaurant. Tiny Balltown, Iowa, will always be proof to me that, on a bicycle, dreams can indeed come true.

---

**DIRECTIONS:** South 59 miles on SR 35 to Prairie du Chien. Go west across Mississippi on US 18 to McGregor, IA, then south 4 miles on SR 340/X56 to Pikes Peak. Continue south 18 miles on X56 (Great River Road). To hotels, go west 2 miles on US 52, right on Schiller Street. To Balltown, head south 19 miles on C 9Y.

**ACCOMMODATIONS: Great River Inn,** on US 52 (no street address), Guttenberg, IA, (319) 252-3070. Rooms: 14, double $39. VISA, MC, AMEX, DIS.

**CAMPING: Paradise Valley,** 5 miles south of McGregor on SR 340, (319) 873-9632. Amenities: laundry, groceries, swimming.
**Pikes Peak,** 2 miles south of McGregor, (319) 873-2341.

---

# DAY 10

Guttenberg to Clinton
Terrain: Hilly
107 miles

It didn't let up. Our ride down the state's eastern bulge was vintage "coastal" Iowa—long, hot hills of corn-green farmland. It was the Great River Road, but the river was nowhere in sight. Though recommended US 52 is long, it can't be as bad as endlessly undulating county road C 9Y, our route to Dubuque.

Upon arrival in Iowa's oldest city, founded by French miner Julien Dubuque in 1788, Larry went shopping. Convinced that the small athletic bag tied under his seat caused unnecessary wind resistance, he replaced it with a round Tupperware cake container. He cut holes to string it into place.

I didn't really care if he did ride .3 miles per hour faster—he was always too far ahead to see, anyway. After five more hilly hours of suffocating heat, I met him in Clinton, where we'd planned a symbolic dip in the Mississippi before it became too polluted.

Well, by the time I climbed out, my flesh was crawling. It already was too polluted! Luckily, a community pool was just up the waterfront. Since Larry and I had both been college wrestlers, and wrestling is the most popular sport in Iowa, we made friends quickly with the kids by teaching them moves. Then, when they discovered we were Californians, they really went nuts. One kid called his mother, Kate Thompson, a reporter for the *Clinton Herald.* Kate's story, "Two Ride River to Finish Bike Book," appeared on page eleven of the June 26, 1989, issue, sharing space with obituaries and arrests.

Crossing into Illinois, we arrived in the hotel-less town of Cordova feeling ecstatic. After a couple of celebratory beers at a local bar, we pitched our mosquito-screened tent just ten feet from the Mississippi and soon were lulled to sleep by the gentle lapping of the Father of the Waters.

---

**DIRECTIONS:** South 39 miles on US 52 to Dubuque. Continue south 47 miles on US 52, then south 19 miles on US 67.

**ACCOMMODATIONS: Best Western-Frontier Motor Inn,** 2300 Lincoln Way (junction of US 67 and US 30), Clinton, IA, (319) 242-7112. <u>Rooms</u>: 117, double $40–$65. VISA, MC, AMEX, DINERS, DIS.

**CAMPING: Bulgers Hollow,** 4 miles north on US 67, 1 mile east, (815) 589-3229. <u>Amenities</u>: no showers.

---

# DAY 11

Clinton to Muscatine
Terrain: Flat
Sights: Rock Island, East Davenport Village
67 miles

Spooked by Iowa, we'd entered Illinois searching for flatter land. Our plan succeeded as far as the Quad Cities, a four-city, two-state area centered on mid-river Rock Island, an 1800-era trading post, Civil War weapons depot, and railroad hub—immortalized in Hank Williams's country hit, "The Rock Island Line."

Relying on reports from the natives, who claimed Illinois was soon hilly, we crossed back to Iowa. The flat road to Muscatine, where Mark Twain got his first journalism job, made us think Iowa's hills were gone.

But an animated watermelon deliveryman, stacking the area's big cash crop at a store, told us we were wrong.

"As sure as there are watermelon groves in Muscatine, there are hills south of here," he said in that husky farmer's accent. Observing the women entering the store, the word "husky" came to mind again: aside from Alaskans, Iowans could well be the fattest people in the country. When I broached the sensitive subject to the portly meloneer, he simply replied, "Corn-fed beef, corn-fed people."

Fed with our anthropological and hill-avoidance information, we crossed the Mississippi back to The Land of Lincoln at about 4:00 P.M. "It's still early yet," said Larry, in a phrase I'd come to dread. "Let's shoot for Nauvoo."

---

**DIRECTIONS:** Go west 3 miles on US 30 into Illinois, then south 32 miles on SR 84. Turn right 11 miles on SR 92 (4th Avenue) through Moline and Rock Island. Cross Government Bridge to Davenport, Iowa, then head southwest 3 miles on West River Drive (US 61). Turn right on S. Concord Street to stay on river bank. Merge with SR 22 for 18 miles to Muscatine.

**ACCOMMODATIONS: Holiday Inn,** 3 miles north on US 61 at junction of SR 38N, Muscatine, IA, (319) 264-5550. <u>Amenities</u>: pool, laundry, sauna. <u>Rooms</u>: 107, double $49–$53. VISA, MC, AMEX, DINERS, DIS.

**CAMPING: Shady Creek,** 10 miles north on SR 22, Fairport, IA, (309) 537-3653.

---

# DAY 12

Muscatine, Iowa, to Nauvoo, Illinois
Terrain: Flat and rolling
Sights: The Old Mormon settlement
86 miles

"Like you fellows, the Mormons were on a trek," the guide at the Visitors Center told us early the next morning. "Only theirs wasn't for pleasure."

At this pace, who said ours was? With the sun setting earlier than up north, I'd ridden into town last night in darkness. Speedy Larry hadn't experienced the terror.

We stayed long enough to learn about the ostracized Mormons, who fled west from New York to Nauvoo in 1839, only to be beset by riots and the murder of leader Joseph Smith. So they fled again in 1846 to Utah, where their polygamous religion stayed put. We soon headed south to the scene of another American original: Mark Twain.

**DIRECTIONS:** Cross river. Go 3 miles on SR 92, then turn south 15 miles on CR 11 and CR 14 to New Boston. Turn east 3 miles on SR 17, then south 18 miles on CR 3. Turn west 1 mile on SR 164 to Oquawka, then south 5 miles on CR 164. Go southwest 7 miles on US 34 (almost to Gulfport), then south 10 miles on SR 9 to Lomax. Continue south 24 miles on SR 9/96.

**ACCOMMODATIONS: Nauvoo Family Motel,** 150 Warsaw Street, Nauvoo, IL, (217) 453-6527. Rooms: 32, double $30–$33. VISA, MC.

**CAMPING: Breezewood Campground,** south 4 miles on SR 96, (217) 453-6420. Amenities: laundry, pool, grocery.

## DAY 13

Nauvoo, Illinois, to Hannibal, Missouri
Terrain: Rolling, flat
Sights: Mark Twain's boyhood home
65 miles

"If you ask me," I told Larry, "Mark Twain looks kind of like Albert Einstein with his hair combed."

Pondering for a moment the giant bust of Twain before us, my partner held up a placard. "It's better to keep your mouth shut and appear stupid than to open it and remove all doubt," it read, one of thousands of Twainisms before us in the boyhood home of America's first great author.

Getting there took us over occasionally rolling, unmemorable, semideserted highway far from the river in stultifying ninety-six-degree heat. We pit-stopped in rundown, half-abandoned Quincy before entering its pretty stepsister, Hannibal, aglow in the riches of tourist paradise. An entire industry has been born of the fact that Mark Twain spent his 1840s boyhood there and based much of his classics *Huckleberry Finn* and *The Adventures of Tom Sawyer* on the town.

In Hannibal, you can eat at the Mark Twain Dinette; ride the Mark Twain Clopper buggy; drive Mark Twain Avenue (US 36); cruise the river on the Mark Twain Excursion Boat; visit Mark Twain Cave (which he romped in as a boy and wrote of as a man); stay at the Mark Twain Motor Inn, or the Tom 'N Huck Motel; shop at the Huck Finn Shopping Center— "The people pleasers from the people pleasin' place"; or celebrate at National Tom Sawyer Days, June 30 through July 4, featuring fence painting, frog jumping, mud volleyball, and a Tom Sawyer look-alike contest.

In fact, the whole state of Missouri has got Twain on the brain, as there is a Mark Twain Lake, Mark Twain National Forest, and even a Mark Twain Bank.

We made a beeline for the Mark Twain Boyhood Home and Museum Complex, housed in the small, two-story clapboard house built by Twain's father, Judge John Clemens, on Hill Street, in 1844. We learned that Samuel Clemens, fascinated by the intrigue of the Mississippi as a young boy, took the pen name Mark Twain, river lingo for "twelve feet deep." We saw Tom Sawyer's Fence, Becky Thatcher's Home, and other ordinary Hannibal structures that have gained immortality.

By then, it was 7:00 P.M. Two hours of riding time remained at best. The sky looked a little cloudy, too.

"Let's stay here for the night," I suggested.

"Let's shoot for the town of Louisiana," said Larry.

Damn. That was thirty-three miles. And it was over very hilly road, from what we'd heard. It would be Balltown all over again—probably without the fried chicken. I finally agreed to do it only if we took US 61 instead of the Great River Road. It was an extra ten miles, but over well-graded highway.

Ninety minutes later, as we were blowing by the Underwood Deviled Ham headquarters and the town of New London, a black cloud appeared. Then it got windy. More black clouds. Lightning cracked. And, within five minutes, we were caught in a howling, tree-bending, sky-blackening, rain-as-big-as-golfballs storm.

I threw on my rain poncho, but Larry hadn't brought one and was freezing. We tried to hitch either direction, but no one would stop. We tried to ride, but the storm blotted Larry's glasses. Since he couldn't see without them, we huddled on the side of the road under my poncho, hoping this was one of those "flash" Midwest rains. After an hour, we realized it wasn't.

It was night by then, and traffic had died down. We rode for several miles, me directly ahead of Larry to lead him. But the pounding rain made us practically invisible, a frightening thought whenever a car appeared. As Larry shivered, we waited on the shoulder for the rain to slacken, then pushed off again. In seconds I heard a loud crash to my right. The shoulder had run out; Larry had crashed in a pile of gravel.

When he got up, frustrated and agitated, he started to slide around on the rain-slickened road in his plastic-bottomed clipless cycling shoes. I didn't say anything, but that's why I don't like clipless shoes for touring. My stiff, hard-bottomed shoes and toe-clips weren't as efficient, but they provided better comfort and transfer of power than tennis shoes. And they allowed me to walk around comfortably and safely, I thought, grimacing as Larry did a half-gainer into the highway blacktop.

This was nuts. We walked down the road in the still-pouring rain and waved our arms again at headlights. In thirty seconds, a truck heading north picked us up.

We arrived back in Hannibal at midnight, five hours after we'd left.

"What happened to you guys?" exclaimed the clerk at the hotel. Larry's elbow and knee were covered with blood from his fall.

"Nothing, really," said Larry. "We're riding the river and made the mistake of not staying on the Great River Road."

**DIRECTIONS:** South 12 miles on SR 96 to Hamilton, Illinois. Continue south 36 miles on SR 96 to Quincy, then south 5 miles on CR 21, and south 5 miles on SR 57. Turn west 7 miles on SR 336/US 24 and US 36 across to Hannibal.

**ACCOMMODATIONS: Mark Twain Motor Inn,** 612 Mark Twain Avenue, Hannibal, MO, (314) 221-1490. <u>Amenities</u>: pool. <u>Rooms</u>: 45, double $45–$65. VISA, MC, AMEX, DIS.

**CAMPING: Mark Twain Cave Campground,** south 1 mile on SR 79, (314) 221-1656. <u>Amenities</u>: laundry, groceries.

## DAY 14

Hannibal to St. Charles
Terrain: Very hilly, then flat to rolling
95 miles

    Never have hills looked so good.
    We were back on our beloved Great River Road. Iowa-style rollers took us to Louisiana, where Larry bought a rain poncho, then flattened on the way to St. Peters.
    Turning east to St. Louis, I couldn't wait to go up to the top of the Gateway Arch, which I'd dreamed about since the Big Adventure. But the elevator ride would have to wait. The Cards were playing the Phillies in three hours, and Larry wanted to see the game.

**DIRECTIONS:** South 86 miles on SR 79, then east 10 miles on I-70 sideroads.

**ACCOMMODATIONS: Ramada Inn Airport West,** 1425 S. 5th Street, St. Charles, MO, (314) 946-6936. <u>Amenities</u>: pool, sauna. <u>Rooms</u>: 150, double $65–$75. VISA, MC, AMEX, DINERS, DIS.
**Hilcrest Motel,** on SR 79, Elsberry, MO, (314) 898-2121. <u>Amenities</u>: pool, gorgeous view, free coffee. <u>Rooms</u>: 15, double $40. VISA, MC, AMEX, DINERS, DIS.

**CAMPING:** None.

# DAY 15

St. Charles to St. Louis
Terrain: Flat
21 miles

We crossed America's other great river, the mighty Missouri, then forded through suburbs and dreadful inner-city neighborhoods on the way to downtown.

While in the ghetto, stopped to take a picture at an ornate stone "St. Louis City Limit" sign, we were approached by a drug dealer named Norris. "Y'all trespassin' on my *store*," he said with a smile. Norris said his lawyers had found there was a two-foot-wide space between the city of St. Louis and the county that ran through the city limit sign. In this space he was legally immune from arrest.

Surprisingly, nobody in the neighborhood seemed to have any idea how far away downtown was. We got answers ranging from ten to fifty miles, when in fact it was less than five—a telling indication of how alienated the poor people were.

We found our way, however, and when we ran into some of the Cardinals' promotions people near the Busch Stadium ticket booth, they got us free tickets, helped us store the bikes, and arranged to have "St. Louis Welcomes Larry and Roy and Their Bikes" flash on the message board in the seventh inning.

The couple we sat next to at the game, who'd been doubting our tales of adventure, were floored. They invited us down to The Landing, a yuppie/college riverfront hip spot just north of the Arch. When they asked if we'd like to sleep at their place, it was the final touch to a perfect day.

It was the final touch to the first half of our trip, too, as "The Gateway to the West" is also the gateway to the South, our next destination. Getting to this point had been a learning experience for us both. We'd learned to blend our styles. We'd done all my sightseeing and almost all of Larry's mileage. He'd learned a little about touring and rain tarps. I

---

**DIRECTIONS:** From St. Charles, go north on Main Street, east on Clark to Free Bridge over Missouri River to St. Charles Rock Road. Go straight on this road (under various names) 25 miles into heart of St. Louis. To Lambert St. Louis Airport, go west on St. Charles Rock Road, right on Lindberg Boulevard.

**ACCOMMODATIONS: Drury Inn Union Station,** 210 20th Street, St. Louis, MO, (314) 231-3900. <u>Rooms</u>: 180, double $59–$77. VISA, MC, AMEX, DINERS, DIS.

**CAMPING:** None.

learned the benefit of aero handlebars—a month before Greg Lemond won the 1989 Tour de France on them.

Most important of all, I gleefully learned that I wasn't over the hill yet, that I could push myself and still improve. I'd ridden wheel-to-wheel with Larry all day.

Yes, indeed, I was still going strong at the ripe old age of thirty-three.

# SIGHTSEEING INFORMATION

HANNIBAL, MISSOURI
**Mark Twain Cave,** south 1 mile from Hannibal on SR 79: Where Twain played as a boy; surfaced in Twain's books as place where buried treasure was found and Tom Sawyer and Becky Thatcher were lost; $6; last tour 7:00 P.M. (314) 221-1656.

LA CROSSE, WISCONSIN
**Heileman Brewery,** 1100 S. 4th Street: Free brewery tours, product sampling; hourly until 4:00. (608) 782-BEER.

MUSCATINE, IOWA
**Great River Days:** Annual mid-August fest of turtle races, boat parades, concerts, music concerts. (319) 263-8282.

NAUVOO, ILLINOIS
**Old Nauvoo Visitor's Center,** Main and Young Streets: Historical background and self-guided walking tour to restored residences of patriarchs like Brigham Young and Joseph Smith. (217) 453-6648.

PIKES PEAK, IOWA
**State Park,** 4 miles southeast of McGregor: Five hundred-foot palisades above river. (319) 873-2341.

PRAIRIE DU CHIEN, WISCONSIN
**Site of the Discovery,** 12 miles south at Wyalusing State Park: Marquette and Joliet, first Europeans to see northern Mississippi River in 1673. (608) 996-2261.
**Villa Louis,** northwest 1 mile on St. Feriole Island: Opulent mansion with one of nation's best Victorian art collections; built by H. L. Dousman, an agent of John Jacob Astor's American Fur Co. (608) 326-2721.

ST. LOUIS, MISSOURI
**Anheuser-Busch Brewery,** Lynch and 13th Streets: Tour includes Clydesdales, samples. (314) 577-2626.
**Missouri Historical Society,** Forest Park between Kingshighway, Lindell and

Skinker boulevards: Exhibits on Old West and growth of St. Louis. (314) 361-1424.

**Missouri Botanical Garden,** 4344 Shaw Boulevard: World-renowned. 577-5100.

**Gateway Arch,** grounds of Jefferson National Expansion Memorial; 630-foot-high stainless steel; Museum of Westward Expansion below. (314) 425-4465.

ST. PAUL, MINNESOTA

**State Capitol Building,** Aurora Avenue between Cedar and Park: Forty-five-minute tours. (612) 296-2881.

**Science Museum of Minnesota,** 30 E. 10th Street: Programs on space and science. (612) 221-9454.

**St. Paul Hall of Justice,** between St. Peter, Kellogg, Wabasha and 4th streets: Includes monstrous 36-foot-high onyx statue, "Left-handed Indian God of Peace." (612) 298-4131.

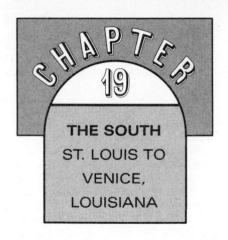

## CHAPTER 19

### THE SOUTH
### ST. LOUIS TO
### VENICE,
### LOUISIANA

**W**E HEARD IT IN CONVERSATION AND EVEN SAW IT ON T-shirts: "American by nationality, Southern by the grace of God." Yes, the people in the South were different. It's Southern Hospitality, they say. Honor. A chivalry that suggests, "If you come into my house, I'll treat you like a king." And, as Larry and I learned, they'll do just that.

But that didn't mean they stopped us on the road just to say "Hi" like the people in Minnesota or Iowa did. Anything but a Southern accent seemed to mean "foreigner" to most. Heck, forget about the accent; we were on bicycles, so they *knew* we were outsiders. "Ain't y'all heard of somethin' called the *car*?" or "Y'all related to Pee-wee Herman?" were typical comments.

This route includes Illinois, Missouri, and Kentucky, and we found out quickly that the South begins north of the old Confederacy. Many say it begins at St. Louis. Missouri is historically half-North, half-South, having joined the Union in 1821 as the last slave state in the Louisiana Territory, yet fighting with the North in the Civil War.

The 931 miles of this fourteen-day, seven-state* trip took us along the mile-wide Mississippi all the way to the Gulf of Mexico. Along the way we saw the pollution-blackened Ohio River splash into it. We saw soybeans, rice, and King Cotton growing alongside it.

*This trip isn't routed into Arkansas, but you can briefly cross into that state with a five-minute ride from Memphis.

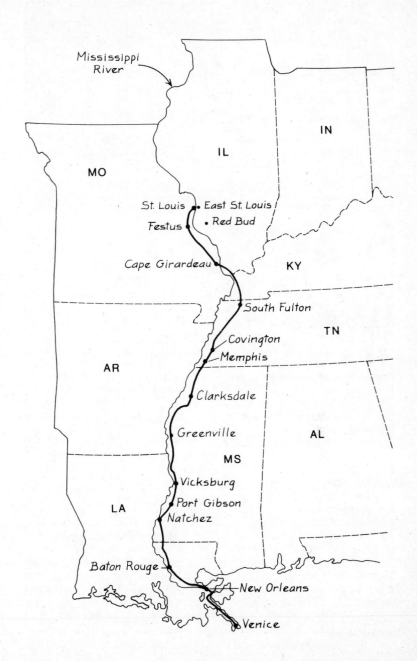

*ROUTE SLIP*
*Total of 931 miles in 14 days*

| Day | Ending Point | Terrain* | Sights | Mileage |
| --- | --- | --- | --- | --- |
| 1 | Festus, Missouri | Easy | Gateway Arch | 55 |
| 2 | Cape Girardeau, Missouri | Easy | Old French homes, Trail of Tears State Park | 87 |
| 3 | South Fulton, Tennessee | Moderate | Ohio River, four states in one day, Whistlin' Pig Restaurant | 87 |
| 4 | Covington, Tennessee | Easy | | 87 |
| 5 | Memphis, Tennessee | Easy | Graceland, Mud Island, Beale Street, Peabody Hotel, Rendezvous Restaurant | 58 |
| 6 | Clarksdale, Mississippi | Easy | | 81 |
| 7 | Greenville, Mississippi | Easy | Winterville Mounds State Park | 73 |
| 8 | Vicksburg, Mississippi | Easy | Mount Holly antebellum mansion | 99 |
| 9 | Port Gibson, Mississippi | Easy/Moderate | Vicksburg National Military Park, city tour | 28 |
| 10 | Natchez, Mississippi | Easy | Natchez Trace, antebellum homes | 36 |
| 11 | Baton Rouge, Louisiana | Moderate | State capitol building | 90 |
| 12 | New Orleans, Louisiana | Easy | French Quarter, Bourbon Street, Musée Conti, Preservation Hall, Pat O'Brien's, Jackson Square | 75 |
| 13 | Venice, Louisiana | Easy | The Levee | 75 |

*Easy = flat to rolling; moderate = hilly; difficult = repeated miles of hills or steep climbing

Cotton, in fact, may be symbolic of both this trip and the South itself. Cotton loves the heat, and we were sweating from morning to night—moving or standing still. It thrives in flat, water-soaked ground, and we saw no Iowa-style hills, only a little rolling country, and mostly flat land. In fact, a long stretch of the Delta area in Mississippi is dead flat. The river's elevation, which dropped nearly 900 feet from Lake Itasca to St. Louis, drops only about 600 as it meanders to the Gulf of Mexico—a thousand miles of hard-to-follow hairpin turns that assured we saw much less of the Mississippi than before.

Cotton dominates the southern Mississippi's history, too. Other than New Orleans, the area was unsettled until the early 1800s, much like the North. After slavery and cotton moved in with the Louisiana Purchase, however, a different world was built: the Old South.

Highlights of our trip included a few peeks inside that world. We saw plush antebellum mansions in Vicksburg and Natchez and toured the historic Vicksburg battlefield, site of a Civil War siege that helped end the Old South forever.

In addition, we made a rare ride of four states in one day, rode by Elvis Presley's Graceland, pedaled on the Spanish moss-shrouded Natchez Trace, heard jazz on Bourbon Street, and sampled excellent samples of southern cooking: fried catfish in Fulton, Kentucky, ribs in Memphis, and Cajun food in New Orleans.

In total, this trip may have more flavor to it than any I've taken in the United States. So when you hear someone, like my friends in Don's Seldom Inn in La Crosse, Wisconsin, ask, "You're going down *there*—on *those*?" don't hesitate to respond, "Hell, yes—and you're going to wish you'd gone with me."

# DAY 1

St. Louis to Festus
Terrain: Flat
55 miles

East St. Louis, Illinois, may be the most notorious city in America. "The armpit of the world," said the guys in Don's Seldom Inn. "The murder capital of the world," said old Ed Farnell in Prairie du Chien. "You will die if you go there," said the truck driver who gave us a hitch back into Hannibal. Asked if they'd ever been across the river, our friends from the Cardinals game looked stunned. "Are you crazy?"

But while up at the top of the 630-foot Gateway Arch, it became obvious that a photo including it and the St. Louis skyline could only be taken from East St. Louis.

So that's where we went.

Although the view from the east levee of the Mississippi was great, I don't recommend anyone's going over there. Please stay in Missouri and ride the flat road to Festus. Because I don't want to be responsible.

East St. Louis looks like a war zone. Vacant, overgrown lots where houses used to be. Abandoned, dilapidated, burned-out commercial buildings and private homes. People standing around listlessly. Young women pushing baby strollers. Old men groggily walking along, occasionally swigging from brown paper bags. All of them poor. All of them black. All glancing suspiciously at two white men riding by with bicycles, camera equipment, and traveler's checks totaling thousands of dollars.

And, just before a boarded-up Church's Fried Chicken, one of the cyclists got a flat.

To save weight, Larry hadn't installed Mr. Tuffy tire liners, or brought a spare tube. Not a wise idea when your tire is worn down to the threads.

"I hope you can patch that thing fast, Larry," I said with rising anxiety, "because the vultures are circling."

Dozens of pairs of eyes were on us. All action seemed to stop. Three young men marched toward us. One was incredibly tall and thin, about six-foot-five, 150 pounds. One was short and fat, about five-foot-four, 200 pounds. The last one, wearing an Arnold Schwarzenegger T-shirt, was six feet tall, 185 pounds of rippling muscle. They walked closer and closer, stopping about ten feet away. My body tensed for the coming onslaught.

The fat man stepped forward, his hand rising up from his hip. I instinctively raised my hands in self-protection. He grabbed my right hand.

And he shook it.

"How ya'll doin'?" he said happily. "First time in East St. Louis?"

We ended up spending a couple of hours with the East St. Louis welcoming committee. The muscle man talked about diet and nutrition. The fat man, an auto mechanic, was fascinated by the high-tech components of Larry's bike. The thin man, a computer programmer, pulled a printout from his pocket showing his analysis of the recent N.B.A. college draft. "My matrix showed the Sacramento Kings choosing Sean Elliott, bad knees and all, over Danny Ferry, due to a higher leadership coefficient. Instead, they surprised everyone and went with Purvis Ellison," he said. "Ain't that a bitch?"

---

**DIRECTIONS:** From airport, go southeast 20 miles on Natural Bridge Avenue to Gateway Arch. Turn south 20 miles on Broadway (SR-231). Merge with US 61. Continue south 15 miles.

**ACCOMMODATIONS: Holiday Inn,** 1200 Gannon Drive, Festus, MO, (314) 937-0700; Amenities: pool, whirlpool. Rooms: 139, double $49. VISA, MC, AMEX, DINERS, DIS.
**Red Bud Motel,** 1103 S. Main Street, Red Bud, IL, (618) 282-2123. Rooms: 12, double $30. VISA, MC.

**CAMPING: KOA St. Louis South,** 8000 Metropolitan Boulevard (north 8 miles), Barnhart, MO, (314) 479-4449.

"This has always been a tough place," the thin man explained as we sipped Colt 45's in the shade at Church's. "In fact, if you've seen a lot of Humphrey Bogart's films, he often says he's from East St. Louis. It was a bad-ass place long before black folk showed up here."

After a commemorative group picture, Larry and I got on SR 3, the Illinois Great River Road. Intoxicated and euphoric, we made the forty-three miles to Red Bud by sundown.

# DAY 2

Festus to Cape Girardeau
Terrain: Flat, rolling
Sights: Old French homes, Trail of Tears State Park
87 miles

The route recommended here stays on the west side of the Mississippi, passing through rolling hills and St. Genevieve, the oldest city in Missouri (founded 1732). We remained on the east side, however, unable to get out of Red Bud.

Larry's tire blew twice in the first hundred yards from the motel, the second one putting a half-inch rip in the tube. That was unfortunate in a tiny town without a bike shop. I rode off to the local auto parts store, but it had only American-style tubes with Shraeder valves, not the French-style Presta valves Larry's rim was designed for.

By the time I got back with the bad news, Larry had become a local celebrity. Gathered around him was a crowd and a reporter named Jana Kueker. Her story, "California Bikers Tell of Adventures on the Road," appeared in the July 6 edition of the *North County News*.

After the interview, Larry built a mega-patch from several small ones and we moved on, stopping every five miles to pump up the tire.

Riding along the river on Highway 3 south of the prison town of Chester, we stopped to ask for water at a private home—and entered a shocking world.

Confederate flags hung on the walls. Pictures of black men with targets drawn on them were pasted on a door. Gus, a white guard at the prison, gave us lemonade as he calmly described "a deadly black conspiracy" called Brotherhood of the Struggle. Their symbol, which he drew on a napkin, was a barbed-wire pentagram dripping with blood. "That's *white* blood," he said.

But, I was more worried about Gus, who surely was KKK, than the so-called Brotherhood. What if he found out I was Jewish?

Later, as Larry pumped up his tire outside, I analyzed Gus as a "paranoid psychotic." When I turned around, I got the chills. He was looking right at us.

About fifty miles later, having ridden solo for the last three hours when Larry dropped back with derailleur problems, I heard a truck suddenly honk from behind. It was Gus. Oh my god, he'd hunted me down! I prepared to have my name in the paper again—in the obituary section.

But then I noticed his passenger: Larry. While running an errand, Gus had picked Larry up and decided to drive him to a bike shop in Cape Girardeau, Missouri, over sixty miles away. He took us all over town to look for bike shops (none were open), then joined us for beer and pizza. Before he left, he gave us a tour of Trail of Tears Park, just north of the city.

"This park includes a section of the route used by the Cherokees on their exile from Tennessee to Oklahoma," Gus explained, shaking his head sadly. "What we did to those Indians is shameful."

Gus, this rabid racist, proved to be a paradox I haven't figured out yet.

---

**DIRECTIONS:** South 77 miles on US 61 to Fruitland. Bear left on CR W. For Trail of Tears State Park, go east 12 miles on SR 177 to park, then south 9 miles to Cape Girardeau.

**ACCOMMODATIONS: Holiday Inn,** junction of I-55 and William Street, Cape Girardeau, MO, (314) 334-4491. <u>Amenities</u>: pool, whirlpool, sauna. <u>Rooms</u>: 187, double $65–75. VISA, MC, AMEX, DINERS, DIS.

**CAMPING: Trail of Tears State Park,** (314) 334-1711.

---

## DAY 3

Cape Girardeau, Missouri, to South Fulton, Tennessee
Terrain: Flat, rolling, hilly
Sights: Ohio River confluence, four states in one day, Whistlin'
  Pig catfish
87 miles

After spending all morning getting Larry a new tire, derailleur, tubes, and Mr. Tuffies, we began one of the best days of our trip. Jam-packed with four states, a landmark, and great food, it included tree-shaded, gently hilly terrain perfect for bicycling. And it also removed all doubt that we'd entered the South.

The day before, Jana Kueker didn't have a Southern accent, but Gus did. Today, as we crossed the Mississippi from Missouri into Illinois, everyone did—even if a woman we met in Cairo didn't think so.

"No, we don't talk Southern here in *Karo*," she said in her twang. Since the area's fertile, cotton-growing soil reminded the first settlers of the Nile Delta, many towns have names like Cairo, Thebes, Karnak, and . . . Pulaski?

Before leaving "Little Egypt," we stopped to see "the great convergence," where two of America's biggest rivers, the Ohio and the Mississippi, flow together. From the viewing platform at Fort Defiance, where

General Grant launched a Union attack that led to victory at Vicksburg, a turning point in the Civil War, we watched the black, mucky, polluted waters of the Ohio collide with the blue waters of the Mississippi. It's clear the Ohio won; the Mississippi emerges the color of dark gook.

We crossed the ugly Ohio, chalked up our third state, Kentucky, and entered a world of beauty. Whip-sawing over a rippled plain, we bobbed and weaved through lush forests and tree-lined farmlands. The energizing ride was topped off by a prize waiting at the Kentucky–Tennessee border in Fulton: the Whistlin' Pig restaurant, where $4.95 bought an immense catfish dinner plus all-you-can-eat fried chicken and salad bar. Larry and I were amazed at the bargain and proceeded to clean the place out.

Still, we apparently weren't in the South yet. According to a student we met at the Pig, that would come on the two-mile ride into South Fulton, when we crossed into our fourth state of the day: Tennessee.

"At first glance, Tennessee seems a lot like Kentucky," he said. "The people sound a lot alike. The states cover similar turf, from the Appalachians to the Mississippi. Both were settled at the same time, and both populations were torn between the North and South during the Civil War. But they seceded. We didn't."

---

**DIRECTIONS:** East 4 miles across river on SR 146, south 27 miles on SR 3 to Cairo. For confluence, go south on US 60/62 West, turn 1 mile on Fort Defiance dirt road. For Kentucky, go north on US 62 East across Ohio River bridge, 41 miles on US 62/51 to Fulton, then south 2 miles on SR 43/US 45E to Tennessee.

**ACCOMMODATIONS: Fulton Plaza Motor Inn,** 1019 W. Stateline, South Fulton, KY, (901) 479-3040. Amenities: not fancy. Rooms: 18, double $22, VISA, MC, AMEX, DINERS, DIS.
**Quality Inn,** Highway 51, exit 1, Buchase Parkway, Fulton, Kentucky, (502) 472-2342. Rooms: 80, $40–$46. VISA, MC, AMEX, DINERS, DIS.

**CAMPING:** None in area.

---

# DAY 4

South Fulton to Covington
Terrain: Flat
87 miles

In Tennessee, we hit day-long rain. It didn't slow us down, though, as the shoulder on US 51 was wide and the terrain was just slightly rolling. We made our goal 125 miles away in Memphis at the place everyone called the best rib joint in the South: the Rendezvous.

The ribs were great. The boisterous jazz band atmosphere was even better. To beat the two-hour wait, we ate at the bar and were served immediately.

Getting a hotel wasn't as easy. Everything in America's fifteenth largest city (650,000 people), named after another Nile Delta town, seemed booked. We finally borrowed a lesson learned from the Big Adventure: ask for a damaged room. The downtown Days Inn gave us one for twenty dollars off.

---

**DIRECTIONS:** South 87 miles on US 51.

**ACCOMMODATIONS: Best Western Inn,** on US 51, Covington, TN, (901) 476-8561. <u>Amenities</u>: pool. <u>Rooms</u>: 75, double $39–$45. VISA, MC, AMEX, DINERS, DIS.
**Best Western Inn,** US 51 (22 miles south), Millington, TN, (901) 873-2222. <u>Rooms</u>: 77, $45–$55. VISA, MC, AMEX, DINERS, DIS.

**CAMPING: Meeman-Shelby State Park,** (901) 876-5201, 10 miles west of Millington.

---

## DAY 5

Covington to Memphis
Terrain: Flat
Sights: Graceland, Mud Island, Peabody Hotel, Beale Street,
   Rendezvous Restaurant
38 miles plus 20 sightseeing

Looking at the calendar that morning, Larry estimated that we were going to miss Fourth of July in New Orleans by two days at our current rate.

"We ought to go for it," he said.

Even though I could keep up with Larry by now, I knew this idea was dumb. "I don't think you realize what this entails," I said. "It's 480 miles to New Orleans. We've got some major all-day sightseeing ahead in Vicksburg, Natchez, and Baton Rouge. There's no more 9:30 sunset. The heat is getting worse and worse. It's July 2 today, so it'd be three days at 160 miles each—with sightseeing."

"Listen," he argued, "it's dead-flat all the way now. And it's Fourth of July in New Orleans, for god's sake! It's got to be the biggest 'sight' on this trip! We gotta go."

So, we checked out Beale Street, the "Birthplace of the Blues," went halfway across the I-40 Mississippi River bridge just to say we'd been in Arkansas (this route doesn't go there), browsed the lobby of the legendary Peabody Hotel, with its fountains, flocks of ducks, player pianos, and bronze greyhounds, and cruised by Elvis's grave at Graceland.

Then, as crazy as it seems, we took off for New Orleans.

---

**DIRECTIONS:** South on US 51 to downtown Memphis.

**ACCOMMODATIONS: Peabody Hotel,** 149 Union Avenue, Memphis, TN, 1-800-PEABODY, (901) 529-4000. Rooms: 375, double $120–$159. VISA, MC, AMEX, DINERS, DIS.
**Days Inn,** 164 Union, (901) 527-4100. Rooms: 110, double $40–$65. VISA, MC, AMEX, DINERS, DIS.

**CAMPING: T. O. Fuller State Park,** toward Graceland, 3rd Street (US 61) to Mitchell Road, turn west to park, (901) 785-3950.

---

# DAY 6

Memphis, Tennessee, to Clarksdale, Mississippi
Terrain: Rolling, flat
81 miles

Enjoying mostly flat terrain with gentle rolling hills, we shot out of Memphis into Mississippi with the river nowhere in sight. Not that we missed the Great River Road. It's just that the Mississippi River had long started to loop back and forth in hairpin-turn switchbacks. There is no way a road could follow it.

State borders can't even follow it. As it has cut new, straighter channels over the years, parts of Arkansas have ended up on the east side of the river and parts of Tennessee and Mississippi on the west. Whole towns have been wiped off the map, a phenomenon Mark Twain described in his short story, "A Dying Man's Confession." Since Minnesota's Itasca State Park was established in 1891, the river has shrunk by 222

---

**DIRECTIONS:** All day south on US 61.

**ACCOMMODATIONS: Best Western Regency Inn,** on US 61, Clarksdale, MS, (601) 627-9292. Amenities: pool, whirlpool, exercise room. Rooms: 93, double $50. VISA, MC, AMEX, DINERS, DIS.

**CAMPING: Great River Road State Park,** 39 miles south of Clarksdale on SR 1.

miles, now making it 2,330 miles—the *second* longest in America, next to the Missouri's 2,465 miles. Due to concrete mattes and levees placed in the last half-century, it probably won't get much shorter.

Clarksdale, the official stop on the tour, is located west of the spot where Spanish explorer Hernando De Soto reportedly saw the Mississippi River for the first time in 1541. We stopped just long enough to find that out, then kept pressing on.

## DAY 7

Clarksdale to Greenville
Terrain: Flat
74 miles

While pausing in Rosedale, thirty-nine miles south of Clarksdale, we considered staying at the Great River Road State Park. "We've ridden 120 miles already today," I said. "It might be the last time we get the chance to camp with a view of the river."

"No," Larry said unequivocally. "It's only 5:00. Over three hours more of sunlight. Let's shoot for Greenville."

So we blitzed on through farmland and teeny-weeny towns on the flat, boiling hot Mississippi Delta, the great floodplain between the Mississippi River and the Yazoo River to the east. It was a vast place of rice, soybeans, and cotton, the state's staple crop, as far as the eye could see. Mississippi has been the country's number one producer of cotton since the days of slavery, a major reason why it became the second state to secede from the Union in 1861.

Strangely, when Larry and I hit the port city of Greenville, which almost disappeared in 1927 when the Mississippi flooded it for two months, our roles reversed. As the sun dropped, I wanted to keep going. Now Larry was hesitant.

"Don't you think we've gone far enough?" he said meekly.

"No way, dude," I said, half-ignoring him, pumped with adrenaline.

Twenty-five miles south, the sun was long gone, but I kept pushing. I simply couldn't stop. I was wired. The ground was dead flat, the sky was clear, there was some moon, and I felt stronger and stronger as the air cooled.

"Larry, let's ride all night."

"The hell with that!" he suddenly screamed, his brakes squealing. "We've already ridden a hundred and eighty miles today. I'm stoppin' right now!"

That's when it dawned on me: while I was used to riding in the dark, Larry wasn't. That was Larry's Achille's heel: he couldn't see at night!

So there we stood on this little road, with a lake on one side and a big antebellum mansion on the other, wondering where we'd sleep. Just then, a big GM Surburban four-door wagon-truck pulled up. A pink-faced man popped his head out.

"You boys know yo' loiterin' in front mah prop'ty?" the driver said.

We quickly explained who we were and what we were doing, and T. C. Woods, landowner, power-broker, entrepreneur, and all-around self-made man, warmed up.

We spent the next two hours driving all over the swampy Mississippi Delta with T.C. ("Top Cat," he claimed), an immaculately coiffed pseudo-aristocrat who knew everybody and everything.

T.C. explained that the mechanized harvesting of cotton and soybeans is the reason why the population from Clarksdale to Vicksburg has the lowest per capita income in the country. Field hands aren't needed, so welfare in the overcrowded rural black neighborhoods was rampant. He also showed us abandoned wooden shacks that used to be sharecroppers' homes littering the fields.

But not everyone was poor. White neighborhoods of beautiful spacious homes on one side of the highway stood in stark contrast to the black neighborhoods of shacks on the other. It was like going from Beverly Hills to Watts.

When we drove back to his mansion, T.C.'s wife had dinner waiting for us. When we told the Woodses we planned to hit the road early, they put us up in their mosquito-net house on Lake Washington, one of many "slivers" of the Mississippi that had been cut off when it changed direction.

---

**DIRECTIONS:** South 15 miles on US 61. Turn west 7 miles on SR 444, then south on SR 1, the Great River Road, 52 miles to Greenville.

**ACCOMMODATIONS: Hampton Inn,** 2701 US 82E, Greenville, MS, (601) 334-1818. Amenities: pool, whirlpool. Rooms: 120, double $40–$50. VISA, MC, AMEX, DINERS, DIS.

**CAMPING:** No official sites. Try **Winterville Mounds State Park,** 6 miles north of Greenville on SR 1.

---

# DAY 8

Greenville to Vicksburg
Terrain: Flat
99 miles

Another long, flat, boiling ride on the Delta led us to Vicksburg, the scene of one of the most decisive battles of the Civil War.

Since Vicksburg controlled the Mississippi from a high bluff, it became a major war objective of President Lincoln and General Grant. When the Confederates surrendered Vicksburg on July 4, 1863, after forty-seven days of siege, giving the Union control of the Mississippi River and cutting the Confederacy in half, more than a war was lost.

Locally, spirits were so demoralized that the city of Vicksburg refused to celebrate the Fourth of July for over a hundred years. Many historians agree that the fall of Vicksburg brought an end to the antebellum way of life.

But the relics remain in the form of many antebellum mansions, a Mississippi paddlewheel ride, even a 130-year-old tide-making machine (a remnant of an Army Corp of Engineers flood-control project). But after spending three hours and sixteen miles roaming over the memorial-strewn battlefields, Larry and I didn't have time for any of that.

For us, a bigger battle remained. It was only twenty-nine hours to the fireworks in New Orleans. And we had 230 miles to go.

---

**DIRECTIONS:** South 43 miles on Great River Road (SR 1). Pass Lake Washington, Mount Holly, small Mayersville. Continue south 31 miles on US 61 to Vicksburg.

**ACCOMMODATIONS: Comfort Inn-East,** 3959 E. Clay Street, Vicksburg, MS, (601) 634-8438. <u>Amenities</u>: pool, sauna, whirlpool. <u>Rooms</u>: 61, double $45. VISA, MC, AMEX, DINERS, DIS.

**CAMPING:** None.

---

## DAY 9

Vicksburg to Port Gibson
Terrain: Flat to rolling
Sights: Battlefield, antebellum homes, first Coke bottling plant
28 miles

Minutes after we had climbed out of the Mississippi Delta and entered rolling terrain, it began pouring rain. We were stopped dead in our tracks at the Port Gibson Country Store.

Hanging out with the owner Irving Errington and his wife, Miss Rren (yes, two r's) another rainy two hours, we listened to them talk about Civil War personalities like they were neighbors, something T.C. had done also. "That ole Ulysses [S. Grant] knew what he was doin' when he come 'a through here in '63," said Irvin, as if he'd seen him in person. "But Sherman [William Tecumseh, the notorious Union general who burned the South], now, he was a bastard."

Started by the South for the South and mostly fought in the South, the War Between the States remains a daily part of life down here.

When the rain stopped, it was after 9:00 P.M. We planned on at least making it to Natchez. "You oughta take the Trace," said Irvin.

He meant the Natchez Trace Parkway, the historic 400-mile road that we hadn't even heard of until then. Loaded up with free beer, pretzels, and assurances from Irvin that "no one beats the South for hospitality," we set off in the dark.

---

**DIRECTIONS:** South 28 miles on US 61.

**ACCOMMODATIONS: Gibson Landing,** antebellum mansion, on US 61 past 2nd traffic light, Port Gibson, MS, (601) 437-3432. <u>Amenities</u>: breakfast. <u>Rooms</u>: 5, double $48–$65. VISA, MC.

**CAMPING: Rock Springs.** From Vicksburg, go east 24 miles on US 80/SR 467, then southwest 20 miles on Natchez Trace. No phone; 17 miles to Port Gibson next day.

---

# DAY 10

Port Gibson to Natchez
Terrain: Rolling
Sights: Natchez Trace, antebellum homes
36 miles

The Trace, originally built in 1801 to link isolated Natchez to Nashville, the closest "civilized" point of the United States at the time, cut a narrow, deep swath through towering forest that made us feel like we were riding in the bottom of a canyon. With a thick canopy of mist above us and the rolling road almost invisible beneath us, the trafficless night ride became a surreal free-fall into a black abyss.

The sensation was enhanced by the din of billions of crickets, reverberating in eerie, rhythmic unison. It was a macabre sensation, to hear a thing we could not see, to ride semi-inebriated through the body of a living, pulsating forest, its heartbeat pounding in our ears and keeping us on the edge between fascination and terror. I was almost waiting for the throbbing cadence to take physical form and attack us, as if we were infringing on some sacred, hidden, primeval insect ritual.

While I reveled in the intrigue, Larry was freaking out. Because of his poor night vision, made worse by the heavy mist, he was riding blind, using me as his eyes. Suddenly, he bumped his front wheel on my back one and tumbled into the highway at fifteen miles per hour. He didn't get up quickly.

"I'm so tired," he pleaded. "Please, let's stop."

That's how, in the morning, we actually got to see the Trace, and it was stunning: beautiful pine forests delicately veiled with Spanish moss.

The beauty was matched by a different sort in Natchez. The oldest city on the Mississippi, founded in 1716, it's jammed with 500 stately eighteenth-century mansions. It'd take a whole day to look through them, but we didn't have time to do more than shoot a picture and shoot back onto US 61.

After riding the first twenty miles before breakfast, we still had another 165 to go to New Orleans. The date was July 4. The fireworks were set for twelve hours.

---

**DIRECTIONS:** South 2 miles on US 2, south 26 miles on Natchez Trace Parkway, merge 7 miles with US 61.

**ACCOMMODATIONS: Burn Mansion,** 712 Union Street, Natchez, MS, (800) 654-8859 or (601) 442-1344. Circa 1832. Rooms: 6, double $75–$125. VISA, MC, AMEX, DINERS, DIS.
**Days Inn,** 2 miles south on US 61, (601) 445-8291. Rooms: 123, $40. VISA, MC, AMEX, DINERS, DIS.

**CAMPING: Natchez State Park,** north of city off US 61, (601) 442-2658. Amenities: no showers.

---

# DAY 11

Natchez, Mississippi, to Baton Rouge, Louisiana
Terrain: Rolling and hilly
90 miles

By 12:30 in the afternoon, after a number of hills, we hit the Louisiana border. It was the last state on our trip, the seventh from St. Louis, the tenth from Minnesota. And it was the only one named after a king, Louis XIV, who ruled when the explorer La Salle claimed the entire Mississippi for France in 1682.

By 5:00 P.M., we were in Baton Rouge, Louisiana's second-largest city with 220,000 people. We glanced at the state capitol, skipped the other attractions, like the Old State Capitol and the Louisiana Naval War Memorial, then did some figuring.

We had just seventy-five flat miles to go to New Orleans. The fireworks were set for 10:00 P.M. That gave us five hours, putting a smile on my face. At fifteen miles per hour, we could make it! The improbable goal of riding nearly 500 miles in three days, of arriving in time to see the fireworks explode over the Mississippi in New Orleans, was ours!

Then Larry spoke.

"Roy, let's hitch."

*What?*

"This means we're going to have to ride at night," said Larry apologetically. "I can't handle the riding at night. I can't see."

I knew it was true.

"Listen Larry," I said. "We can hitch to see the fireworks if we have to, anyway. Let's just ride as far as we can and see what happens. Something always has on this trip, right?"

---

**DIRECTIONS:** South 92 miles on US 61 to capitol. Bear left off US 61 (business route) to Riverside Drive. Turn left on Capitol Lake Drive.

**ACCOMMODATIONS: Ramada Hotel,** 1480 Nicholson Drive, Baton Rouge, LA, (504) 387-1111. <u>Rooms</u>: 280, double $57–$89. VISA, MC, AMEX, DINERS, DIS.
**Comfort Inn,** 10445 Rieger Road, (800) 228-5150. <u>Rooms</u>: 120, $34–$39. VISA, MC, AMEX, DINERS, DIS.

**CAMPING: KOA Baton Rouge,** 7628 Vincent Road (12 miles east on US 190 in Delham Springs, 1 mile south on SR 3002, ½ mile west on SR 1034), (504) 664-7281. <u>Amenities</u>: laundry, pool.

---

# DAY 12

Baton Rouge to New Orleans
Terrain: Flat
75 miles

Larry was manic, blazing nearly twenty-five miles per hour at times down US 61. Even drafting off him, I could barely keep up. But it was in vain. The sun was gone by 8:00 P.M. at this latitude; a good hour of darkness lay ahead. Somehow, I hoped he wouldn't notice.

He did.

"Well, I guess we hitch," I said matter-of-factly. "Unless . . ."

"Unless what?"

"Unless we get lights!" I screamed. "Look!"

Off to the right, small lights wiggled along the ground. It was a bunch of kids with flashlights! Larry and I jumped off the highway, ran over and negotiated with them. We could barely communicate since they were Cajuns, offspring of the French who settled in Louisiana 250 years ago, and spoke the pidgin Creole language. But they sure understood money. We paid the five of them twenty dollars for all their flashlights.

We strapped three of them on Larry's handlebars, and two on my panniers. And almost two hours later, we rolled into the biggest city in Louisiana and one of the craziest in all the world—New Orleans. Or, as I was quickly corrected by a bar tender: *N'aw-lins.*

The French, who founded it in 1718, called it Nouvelle-Orleans. Although gone for nearly two centuries, their spirit has remained in the French Quarter, the original settlement of the city. It's the place where anything goes. We walked jammed, narrow Bourbon Street, past the soulful wailings of blues singers, the bebop of jazz musicians, parading homosexuals, drunken conventioneers, black kids tap dancing for money, and reams of confetti snaking down through the air from the partiers up on the wrought-iron balconies above. Finally, we made our way out to the Mississippi, where a crowd of thousands had gathered.

At exactly 10:00 P.M., the skies lit up. We'd done it!

We spent the next couple of hours with Dave and Mike, two black twenty-eight-year-olds. They became our tour guides, showing us Jackson Square, the Cathedral of St. Louis, Pat O'Brien's, and other famous New Orleans sights. But as we went into place after place, sampling gumbo soup, black-fried crawfish, Cajun rice, and hurricanes, it became clear that neither of them had any money. Despite the fact that they had university-caliber intelligence and verbosity, they were homeless.

About 1:00 A.M., we stopped at the French Quarter A&P for cookies, peanuts, two six-packs of beer, and a gallon of milk for Dave, who had an ulcer. Then we headed out to their "home" on the benches facing the Mississippi, where we talked excitedly into the wonderful, warm *N'awlins* night.

---

**DIRECTIONS:** Southeast 29 miles on SR 30 to Brittany. Continue southeast 52 miles on US 61 past airport into French Quarter.

**ACCOMMODATIONS: Le Richelieu Motor Hotel** in the French Quarter, 1234 Chartres Street, New Orleans, LA, 1-800-535-9653 or (504) 529-2492. Amenities: pool. Rooms: 87, double $80–$90. VISA, MC, AMEX, DINERS, DIS.
**Chateau Motor Hotel,** 1001 Chartres Street, (504) 524-9636. Amenities: pool. Rooms: 44, $59–$70. VISA, MC, AMEX, DINERS.
**La Qunita Inn West Bank,** 50 Terry Parkway, Gretna, LA, (504) 368-5600. Amenities: pool. Rooms: 154, double $44. VISA, MC, AMEX, DINERS, DIS.

**CAMPING: Bayou Segnette State Park,** 6 miles west of ferry landing in Westwego, junction of US 90 and Drake Avenue, (504) 436-1107.

---

# DAY 13

New Orleans to Venice
Terrain: Flat
75 miles

Next morning Larry and I set out, once and for all to take the Great River Road as far as it could go: to Venice, a tiny oil refinery town dangling out in the Gulf of Mexico. The almost dead-flat ride turned out to be the easiest of the entire trip. Sometimes, the road even dropped below the level of the river itself. Held in place by levees, the Mississippi is often higher than the land. We'd look *up* to see ships going by.

We celebrated our sighting of the Gulf of Mexico that night in Venice at the little bar next to our hotel, the Black Gold Lounge. It wasn't more than a few barstools and a pool table, and the beer came in runty little eight-ounce bottles. But a party is a party. We ordered twice as many bottles and let loose.

In the morning before hitching back to New Orleans, we looked for a sign saying "Congratulations! This is the end of the Great River Road." But a long hunt around the harbor yielded only a small, faded, peeling stop sign at a boat landing near the Chevron terminal. After three weeks on the road, at the end of an incredibly interesting adventure, Larry and I broke into uncontrollable laughter as we read the sign.

It said, "Stop. Drop-Off."

After the hectic pace of this trip, that summed up my feelings quite nicely.

---

**DIRECTIONS:** Ferry to Gretna. Turn left on 5th Street, then right on Lafayette Street, which becomes SR 23. Take SR 23 rest of way to Venice. To New Orleans International from Canal Street, go east 13 miles on Tulane Avenue/ Airline Highway (US 61).

**ACCOMMODATIONS: Venice Inn,** near end of SR 23, Venice, LA, (504) 534-7424. <u>Rooms</u>: 93, double $39.75. VISA, MC, AMEX.

**CAMPING:** None.

---

# SIGHTSEEING INFORMATION

BATON ROUGE, LOUISIANA
**State Capitol,** Capitol Lake Drive: Thirty-four stories of statues and murals, Governor Huey Long garden grave; free. (504) 342-7317.

GREENVILLE, MISSISSIPPI
**Winterville Mounds State Park and Museum,** 6 miles north of Greenville: Describes local Indian culture of a thousand years ago. (601) 334-4684.
**Mount Holly:** Restored antebellum mansion, twenty-four-inch-thick brick walls; possible B & B. (601) 442-3718.

MEMPHIS, TENNESSEE
**Mud Island:** On island in river; theme park depicting life on the Mississippi; museum, 1870 steamboat, live entertainment; $6 admission. (901) 528-3595.
**Graceland Mansion,** 3717 Elvis Presley Boulevard, 10 miles south of downtown: Elvis Presley's residence, place of death; grave site, museum of Gold Records, motorcycles; $6.50. (901) 332-3322 or (800) 238-2000.

## NATCHEZ, MISSISSIPPI
**Grand Village of the Natchez Indians,** 400 Jefferson Davis Boulevard: Artifacts of long-destroyed local tribe; free. (601) 446-6502.

**Natchez Pilgrimage Tours:** One- to three-house tours; $4–$10. (800) 647-6742 or (601) 446-6631.

**Self-Guided Tours:** Maps available at Chamber of Commerce, 205 N. Canal Street. (601) 445-4611.

## NEW ORLEANS, LOUISIANA
**Pat O'Brien's,** 718 St. Peter Street: Home of legendary Hurricane drink.

**Preservation Hall,** 726 St. Peter Street. Traditional old-time jazz band every night; $2; 8:30 P.M. to 12:30 A.M. (501) 522-2238.

**St. Louis Cathedral,** Jackson Square: One of nation's oldest churches; open until 5:00 P.M. (504) 861-9521.

**Musee Conti's Louisiana Legends,** 917 Conti Street: Life-size wax replicas of New Orleans' important historical figures, Huey Long to Napoleon; extra two-hour home tour; $4 plus $3 for tour. 525-2605.

## ST. GENEVIEVE, MISSOURI
**Historical Museum,** Merchant and Third streets: Oldest Missouri city; French homes walking tour. (314) 883-5750.

## VICKSBURG, MISSISSIPPI
**Vicksburg National Military Park:** Visitors Center with movie, displays; hilly 16-mile road through battle areas. (601) 636-0583.

**Martha Vick House,** 1300 Grove Street: Built by daughter of city's founder, Newit Vick. (601) 638-7036.

**Balfour House,** corner of Cherry and Crawford streets: Post-siege Union army headquarters; considered one of state's finest Greek Revival structures; built 1835; three-story elliptical staircase; Civil War artifacts. (601) 638-3690.

**The Vanishing Glory,** 500 Grove Street: Multimedia description of forty-seven-day siege; 9:00 to 4:30; $2. (601) 634-1863.

**Biedenharn Candy Company Museum,** 1107 Washington Street: Where Joe Biedenharn bottled Coca-Cola for first time in 1894; 9:00 to 5:00; $2. (601) 638-6514.

**Spirit of Vicksburg:** One-and-a-half-hour paddlewheel ride on Mississippi; $6. (601) 634-6059.

**Waterways Experiment Station,** south 2 miles at Halls Ferry Road: Tide-making machines, scale models of city; 7:45 to 4:15; $4. (601) 634-1863.

## WHITE CASTLE, LOUISIANA
**Nottoway Plantation,** 2 miles north of SR 1: Considered to be most palatial antebellum home on Mississippi; 64 rooms, 200 windows; $6. (504) 545-2730.

CHAPTER
20
BICYCLING IN
PARADISE:
HAWAII

**H**IGH OVER THE EASTERN PACIFIC IN SEPTEMBER OF 1989, MY stewardess was flabbergasted. "You're bringing a *bicycle* to Hawaii?" she exclaimed, eyes bugging out in disbelief. "What in the world are you doing that for?"

The conventional wisdom is that you go to Hawaii to lie on the beach and get a tan. Exercise, if any, will come during the Samoan fire-dancing segment of your nightly luau, when you reach repeatedly for another helping of *tako-puku* (marinated octopus). If you're real energetic, you'll put on a snorkeling mask and float around in the coral at Hanauma Bay. After all, Hawaii is for honeymoons, not athletic activity—right?

Wrong! Hawaii is a great place for sports. For one thing, it is the birthplace of the Ironman Triathlon. And the 112-mile cycling segment of the Ironman was originally staged as the annual Oahu Around-the-Island Bike Race, pointing out that bicycling has a long history on the islands.

I came to Hawaii as a result of a phone call from Bully Kapahulehua, the organizer of Cycle to the Sun, an incredible thirty-eight-mile race from the sea to the top of Maui's 10,023-foot-high Mount Haleakala, one of the world's largest inactive volcanos. Would I like to cover it for the magazine, all expenses paid? he asked.

Would I? My first bonafide press junket—to Hawaii! When I told my girlfriend about it, she naturally wanted to come along and make a romantic vacation out of the affair. But I had a different idea: another chapter for the book!

*ROUTE SLIP*
*Maui, 158 miles + Haleakala option, 86; Oahu, 160 miles + Hanauma*
*   option, 24*
*Total of 428 miles in 9 days*

| Day | Route End Point | Terrain* | Sights | Mileage |
|---|---|---|---|---|
| 1 | Kaanapali Beach, Maui | Easy | Lahaina | 29 |
| | OPTION: Climb up Haleakala | Difficult | Crater | 86 |
| 2 | Kahului, Maui | Moderate/Difficult (dirt) | The "Rocks" | 27 |
| 3 | Hana, Maui | Moderate/Difficult | Hana Highway | 52 |
| 4 | Makena/Kahului, Maui | Moderate/Difficult (dirt) | Seven Pools of Kipahulu | 50 |
| 5 | Waikiki, Oahu | Easy | War Memorial, Waikiki Beach | 20 |
| | OPTION: Hanauma Snorkling | Easy | Hanauma Bay | 24 |
| 6 | Kuilima Point, Oahu | Easy/Moderate | Polynesian Cultural Center | 64 |
| 7 | Waikiki, Oahu | Easy/Difficult (dirt) | North Shore beaches | 76 |

*Easy = flat to rolling; moderate = hilly; difficult = repeated miles of hills or steep climbing

Adding a stop in Honolulu to my itinerary, I mapped out routes around the islands of Maui and Oahu. Then I called my brother Marc.

When it was over, our shortest bike trip had been one of our best. The same things that make Hawaii great for vacationing make it super for bike touring. The sunny, tropical weather includes eighty- to ninety-degree temperatures all year long. While that includes frequent rain, it typically ends quickly. The often-challenging terrain—some of it unpaved*—took us through a spectacular variety of scenery.

We climbed along pristine, windswept rocky shorelines that hardly ever see cars or people; wove through the hustle-bustle excitement of

*Consider riding mountain bikes. It may be wise to ride mountain bikes in Hawaii—especially if you own a very expensive, delicate road bike. But, although we marvel that our road bikes are still functional, we wouldn't have done it any other way.

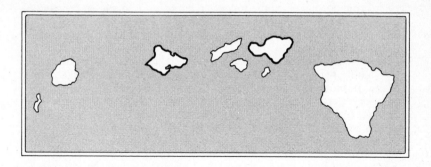

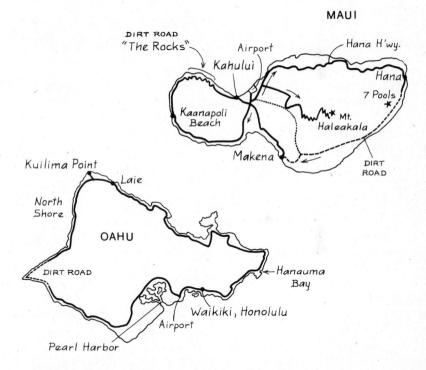

MAUI

DIRT ROAD
"The Rocks"

Airport

Hana H'wy.

Kahului

Hana

7 Pools

Kaanapoli
Beach

Mt.
Haleakala

Makena

DIRT
ROAD

Kuilima Point

Laie

North
Shore

OAHU

DIRT ROAD

Hanauma
Bay

Waikiki, Honolulu

Airport

Pearl Harbor

glitzy Waikiki Beach; snaked through incredibly dense jungle on the Hana Highway; chugged through barren fields of volcanic rock on Mount Haleakala; cruised along the world-famous surfing spots of Oahu's north shore; made a somber visit to the sunken USS *Arizona* in Pearl Harbor.

This variety came neatly packaged on two islands: Oahu, "The Gathering Place," and Maui, "The Valley Isle."

Oahu, despite being the congested home of Honolulu, 80 percent of Hawaii's one million people, subdivisions, freeways, and thirty-eight McDonald's restaurants—the highest Mac-per-capita ratio in the world— is mostly rural. The ride is easy, too. Except for the hilly southeast corner and a stretch of dirt in the far west, the coastal roads are fairly flat.

Maui, the second-largest Hawaiian island and slightly bigger than Oahu, has a rougher, longer ride. A sparsely populated agricultural island of sugarcane, pineapple, and cattle that is fast becoming the "in" spot for tourists, Maui's perimeter roads cross over mountainous shoulders of the two volcanos that give the island its rough figure-eight shape. Long stretches in the northwest and east are dirt, but are ultimately rideable, even on road bikes. Virtually vehicle-free, they showed us a striking jumble of canyons, crests, gorges, and isolated beaches that few see on Maui.

Circumnavigating two of Hawaii's eight main islands took us nine days and 428 miles. That left plenty of time for the "can't miss" things everyone else does—snorkeling at Haunama Bay, sunbathing at Waikiki, and eating shaved ice in Lahaina. It also allowed us to attempt what Bully Kapahulehua claims is the longest, highest, steepest hillclimb in the world: Mount Haleakala. Our misadventure on the volcano was unquestionably *the* memorable incident of the trip and maybe of my bike-touring career.

# Maui

## DAY 1

Kahului Airport to Kaanapali Beach/West Maui
Terrain: Flat
Sightseeing: Lahaina
29 miles

Is it possible to start first in a race and finish last—without having anyone pass you?

And is it possible for heaven on earth to become hell on earth in just a few hours?

As I discovered to my own personal dismay, the answer to both questions is yes.

The heaven, of course, was Hawaii. And the race, to my surprise, was Cycle to the Sun. I had no plans to take the thirty-eight-mile road up to the summit of breathtaking Haleakala Crater—no plans to climb *10,000 feet*. This, after all, was supposed to be a vacation. I stepped off the plane in Maui on September 6 looking forward to my first stress-free bike tour in a quite a while. I wasn't unemployed. I wasn't on a mission. I wasn't trying to break a curse. I wasn't going solo. I wasn't anticipating any personality battles. I wasn't trying to figure my life out. I was just going to enjoy this island paradise, the first bike trip of the rest of my life.

Then I met Tom Resh.

A licensed bike racer, Resh had come both to compete in Cycle to the Sun and write about it for another cycling publication. Running into each other at Kahului Airport, we discovered that we were to be roommates for the next five days at the Kaanapali Beach Hotel—an inconvenience since both of us were flying in unscheduled roommates the next day: retired bike racer Patty Peoples and Marc. Needless to say, Room 107 got a little crowded, but we fast became one big happy family.

While Tom was there to win the race, Patty, Marc and I were there to enjoy the good life. While he practiced on the roads, we snorkeled in the fish-laden coral reef of Kaanapali Beach's Hanakao'o Point and did "cannonballs" off forty-foot-high Black Rock. While Tom did a test climb on Haleakala, we roamed the neighborhood's luxurious beachfront hotels, traipsing across the swinging wood-and-rope bridge at the Hyatt Regency and speeding down the two-story triple-loop water slide at the Maui Westin. As Tom massaged his legs and meditated, we merrily cruised the tourist shops of funky-spunky Lahaina, the one-time "Whaling capital of the Mid-Pacific" and the capital of eighteenth-century Hawaii ruler King Kamehameha the Great. While Tom religiously stuck to his spartan carbohydrate diet, we sat down under the acre-wide Banyan Tree to gulp down handfuls of chocolate-covered macadamia nuts and chomp on banana, papaya, and bubblegum flavored shaved ice.

The day before Cycle to the Sun, at a spaghetti-packed Carbo Party held on the hotel lawn just in front of the beach, Tom informed us "there was absolutely no doubt" he would win the race. "In fact," coolly assured the veteran top-ranked racer, "I will probably set a record." Breaking the old record of two hours, fifty-six minutes and six seconds would bring him the top prize of $2,500.

At the Carbo Party we met Rob Tubbs, a manager of Maui Downhill, one of three companies that drive helmeted tourists up to the top of Haleakala, then let them cruise down on specially outfitted, disk-braked mountain bikes. Tubbs claimed he owned the downhill record of one hour and seven minutes.

"This is one event where I'm built for speed," laughed the aptly named 300-pounder. He invited Marc and me on a complimentary trip *down* the mountain. We looked forward to it.

At ten that night, Patty's bike arrived from the airport after being lost for two days. Since she had retired for a year, her bike was strictly for pleasure riding. That is, until a race official in the lobby saw her, told her the field was weak, that a slot was open, and that she could win four hundred dollars.

By midnight, Patty had paid her twenty-dollar entry fee, was ready to race, and planned to win.

This got Marc and me thinking: here we are in Maui, our roommates are doing the climb, one of them is a woman who hasn't been on a bike in a week and hasn't trained in a year, and it's probably the one time we'll ever have a chance to ride up this incredible road. I was here to cover the race, right? What better way to cover it than to do it!

We'd once climbed 6,000 feet on a bike trip through Granite Pass in Wyoming's Bighorn Mountains. Marc climbed 7,000 feet up Hurricane Ridge on Washington's Olympic Peninsula with Larry the preceding summer. But those were nothing compared to *10,000 feet*. This would be something we'd never forget.

And after what happened, I assure you we won't.

---

**DIRECTIONS:** From airport, go southwest 1 mile on Keolani Place (Highway 36A). Continue 7 miles on Kuihelani Highway (H 380), southwest 16 miles on Honoapiilani Highway (H 30) to Lahaina. After 3 more miles, turn left on Kekaa Drive to Kaanapali resort hotels. For cheaper hotels in Kahana, Napili, and Kapalua, turn left off H 30 onto Lower Honoapiilani Road.

**ACCOMMODATIONS: Kaanapali Beach Hotel,** Kekaa Drive, Kaanapali Beach, (808) 661-0011 or (800) 367-2603. Amenities: pool. Rooms: 431, double $105. VISA, MC, AMEX, DINERS.
**Maui Sands Resort,** 3559 Lower Honoapiilani Road, Napili, (808) 669-4811 or (800) 367-5037. Rooms: 78, $55. VISA, MC.
**Pioneer Inn,** 658 Wharf Street, Lahaina, (808) 661-3636 or (800) 657-7890. Rooms: 48, $39. VISA, MC, AMEX, DINERS.

## OPTION*

Kahului to the top of Haleakala Crater
Terrain: 10 miles flat, 38 miles up, and 38 miles down
86 miles

Marc and I got up at 4:00 A.M. and drove to the Cycle to the Sun starting line at the seaside town of Paia. Since Tom was scheduled to start his climb at 7:30 A.M. and promised he'd set a record of under two hours and fifty minutes, I figured we'd better leave by six if we were to make it up the mountain in time to take his picture at the finish line.

We left in a light rain as the race's organizers were setting up. While we technically weren't allowed to drink the Exceed and eat the bananas and oranges at the course's five aid stations, a volunteer explained that no one would hassle us.

---

*To fit a climb of Haleakala within the tour, stay in Kahului for one extra day following Day 2. Begin and end the day at your hotel. Lighten your load by leaving most gear behind. The grade is only about 7 percent, doable with adequate food and water.

"Hardly any unregistered riders are crazy enough to do this road on their own," he told me, "so you probably won't have any problem getting food."

The early morning air was still cool and misty as I plowed up the gradual incline, feeling strong. By mile eight, I was way ahead of schedule. Only forty-five minutes had expired, and I wasn't even breathing heavy. At this rate, I'd be at the top in under four hours!

Then the road got steeper—*a lot* steeper.

Just after the eight-mile marker, the road jumped from 6 percent grade to 11 to 12 percent. Right away, I had to stand up out of the saddle and agonizingly grind it out in slow motion, my knees and quads straining under the pressure of every stroke. I had to traverse the slope sideways in looping switchbacks instead of riding straight up. I was pulling up on the handlebars so much that my upperarm triceps muscles felt as if they were going to burst.

Eventually, mile ten went by—after half an hour! *Two miles in thirty minutes!* This was nuts. My god, I thought in amazement, how in the world could anyone do this hill in less than three hours? They must be some kind of supermen.

Mile fourteen went by—and I looked at my watch. Dammit! This can't be! The last four miles had taken *one hour*! I'd been riding for almost two-and-one-half hours now, and had only gone fourteen miles.

Not only was I behind schedule, not only were my knees throbbing and my triceps aching, but no one had passed me yet. I may be a good hill climber, but Tom and the other top guys should have passed me by now if they were going to make it in under three hours. Something was wrong.

I got to the top at mile fifteen, then began an exhilarating descent down the other side. What relief! The wind in my face, leaning into the turns, going down, down, down for nearly three miles from the top until . . . I stopped.

Wait a minute, I said to myself. The *top*? What the hell? The top—the Haleakala crater—was supposed to be at thirty-eight miles. And that thirty-eight miles was supposed to be all *uphill*. This had to be the wrong way!

So uphill it was yet again. Back the three miles. Then a long, frightening, brake-squealing descent down that hellishly steep, winding road. Mile fourteen, mile twelve, mile ten—they all ratcheted by. A truck with a Cycle to the Sun sticker on it drove up.

"Oh geez, you were supposed to turn right at mile eight," the driver lamented, slapping the side of his face. "We didn't have a guy out there early in the morning, and a few riders kept going straight. We thought we'd caught them all. You didn't go all the way to the top of Olinda Road, did ya?"

Wordlessly, I hung my head yes.

"Then you're a better man than I'll ever be."

With that, he handed me a cookie and a Coke. "Take this—you'll need it. All the aid stations are closed down by now. The last riders made the turn nearly an hour ago."

It was now 9:45. My plan to take a picture of Tom was now a joke, as he'd be done within an hour. When I turned the corner at the eight-mile mark, I was thirty miles from the summit, under normal conditions about three hours away. But this wasn't exactly normal. After climbing ten extra miles, most of them extra-difficult ones at that, I was hungry, hurting, frustrated, and demoralized. I had gone from first to last without anyone passing me.

Back on a normal slope now, the climbing should have gone easier. But it didn't. I crawled along—and seriously considered quitting. I had no water or food. I could feel my kneecaps beginning to scrape against my thighbones due to the over-torqueing of Olinda Road. My triceps muscles were starting to twitch uncontrollably. And the once-misty skies had cleared a path for the blazing beams of the midday tropical sun. My visibility diminished as stinging rivers of sweat flowed into my eyes.

At the eighteen-mile mark, about 11:30, I thought I was dreaming. I saw a market—the only market on Haleakala Crater. I was saved! I'd eat a big lunch, get my strength back, and be at the top by 2:30.

Then I discovered that I'd left my wallet in my car. All I had was eighty cents—at the inflated prices of the Sunrise Market and Protea Farm, good enough for a 1.25-ounce Tiger's Milk Protein Bar.

That was it. I decided to quit.

Hanging out in the shade for forty-five minutes, reading from a rack of Maui tourist maps before getting ready to coast back to Paia, I ran across a description Mark Twain made of Haleakala when visiting Hawaii about 120 years ago. "It's the sublimest spectacle I've ever witnessed, and I think the memory of it will remain with me always," he wrote. Now, it just so happened that I was reading Twain's *Adventures of Huckleberry Finn* on this trip. This coincidence had to be a sign from heaven.

In minutes, I was on the road again. Going up.

Over the next seven miles, I got off the bike twice because I could no longer hold my handlebars. As I frantically deep-massaged my triceps, which felt as if they were detaching from my arm bones, I felt so alone. I'd seen no other riders in over seven hours. Then, at mile twenty-five, at one-thirty in the afternoon, I saw a sight that shocked me: Marc.

True, my brother is not a great hill climber and was way out of shape for a hill like this. But this scene was truly sad: he was riding a groggy three miles an hour, weaving back and forth, ashen-faced, drenched in sweat, totally wasted.

And he had an all-too-familiar story to tell: Olinda Road. Officials had turned him around after about four miles. The first aid station had just closed up when he rode by. Marc had a little over a dollar in his pockets and bought two bananas at the store.

As we talked, an old couple in a car pulled up. "Do you have any food?" I immediately asked. No food, but Coca-Cola mercifully appeared from the window—two cans.

As Marc inhaled his soda, he revived. "Com'on, man, only thirteen more miles," he commanded me, that mind-over-matter look in his eyes. For ten years now, Marc had been a student of Mind Control. In Alaska, remember, he'd pedaled for a week with only *one* leg. Now he bolted off.

When I reached the entrance to Haleakala National Park Headquarters three miles later, I was walking. I could no longer lean on my shredded triceps, which were randomly going into painful spasms. At this rate, I wouldn't make it up to the crater before dark.

The three rangers at the entrance hut seemed to get a real kick out of my predicament. They huddled for a second, then instructed me to lie on the ground.

"You're in luck," one of the two lady rangers said. "Jean and I happen to be taking a massage therapy class." And, believe it or not, the two of them kneeled down and alternately massaged my arms, working on them for a good half hour. And when they were done, my triceps felt as good as new.

When I stopped at the Visitors Center at mile thirty to get some water, it was 3:00 P.M. Just then, a bus pulled up. And who jumps out but Patty!

"I wondered where you guys were!" she screamed. "We've had the ceremonies, eaten lunch, and everything. I came in second. And Tom won—setting a new record!" Tom's time was 2 hours, 45 minutes, and 32 seconds; Patty's 3:47:33.

Before she hopped back on the bus with all the other riders for the ride downhill, I asked Patty if she'd seen Marc on the road uphill.

"No," she looked surprised, "I didn't."

That's funny, I thought as I waved to her and rode off. This is only a two-lane road. Up here at 8,000 feet, there aren't even any trees to hide under. It's all volcanic rock. A guy on a bike should have been in plain sight. I figured Marc probably made it to the top already and Patty just missed him. Still, the top was eight miles away, and Marc doesn't usually ride uphill that fast. Oh, well.

Rounding the twenty-fourth of twenty-eight switchbacks on the way to the crater, I felt my body running low on carbohydrates, so I flagged down a car and asked for food. The driver gave me some crackers, an apple, and two cans of Coke. He also gave me some mysterious information: he also hadn't seen a bike rider. Hmmm.

At 3:50 P.M., about two miles from the top, a metallic glint on the ground caught my eye from up the road. The closer I got, the more and more it looked like a . . . bike. And sure enough, behind a giant lava rock, sound asleep, was Marc.

I could barely wake him, and when his eyes did blink open, he was a zombie, babbling unintelligibly. As he staggered over to his bike, I handed him a Coke. "You don't have anything in your body," I warned him, grabbing my bike. "You'll kill yourself if you try to ride. Now stay here and hitchhike—and meet me at the top."

In twenty minutes, I became the last 1989 finisher of the thirty-eight-mile Cycle to the Sun. It'd taken me ten hours and forty-eight miles, five-and-one-half hours and ten miles more than I'd planned. Light-headed from the altitude and lack of food, I weakly raised my arms in triumph at the crater's 10,000-foot-high edge.

Unfortunately, the crater itself was a real letdown—mainly because I couldn't see it.

At 4:15 P.M., the 3,000-foot-deep, 21-mile-circumference crater, big enough to swallow New York's Manhattan Island, was filled in with late afternoon clouds. In fact, the whole mountain was now surrounded by clouds, so there was no view of Maui at all. The best view comes before noon on Haleakala.

But I did have a good view of some food. Ernie and Cherie Lou, honeymooning newlyweds from Denver, were picnicking on Hawaiian sweet bread, chicken sandwiches, grapes, and extra-thick Maui potato chips when I invited myself over. A few minutes later, Marc stumbled out of the station wagon of Dr. Steve Moser, a Cycle to the Sun volunteer. Citing the Hippocratic Oath, Moser refused to let us get our retribution on Haleakala by riding down it. Claiming we'd either freeze in the ever-colder mountain air or be too weak to control the bikes, he ferried our bikes and us back down to Paia.

And that was a bummer. The thrill of zipping full-speed down Haleakala was the only way to justify the ordeal of crawling up it.

Then we remembered our old friend Mr. Tubbs. At 4:30 the next morning, Marc and I and two dozen other tourists piled into the vans of the Maui Downhill company and headed back up to the top of the Haleakala Crater. After witnessing the spectacular world-renowned sunrise over Haleakala, "The House of the Sun," we put on our mandatory crash helmets and rainsuits and hopped on the mountain bikes.

"I'm gonna beat Tubbs's record of one hour and seven minutes," Marc said to me, pinching a couple inches of his belly for emphasis. "I'm gonna go crazy. This'll make it all worth it."

And that's why going down Haleakala in *three* hours, forced to ride our oversized brakes all the way down to satisfy Maui Downhill's insurance policy, left us a little bored. It was exciting for the sixty-five-year-old couple who hadn't been biking since they were kids, though.

---

**DIRECTIONS:** From Kahului to Paia, go west on Kaahumanu Avenue (H 32) to Hana Highway (H 36) to Baldwin Avenue (in Paia). Turn right 8 miles on Baldwin (stop when it changes to Olinda Road). Turn right 1½ miles on a small, un-marked road (Makawao) 1.6 miles up Haleakala Highway (H 37 then six miles on H 377). Past small market, turn left 20 miles on H 378 to edge of crater. Reverse for home.

**CAMPING: Haleakala National Park,** (808) 572-9177. Amenities: 2 sites, no showers, no water in 1, no permit needed, no fee.

★

Despite going down Haleakala so slowly, it was weirdly satisfying. You see, I probably won't be back in Maui for a long time, so I eventually just sat back and enjoyed the breathtaking view of the entire island. It was also rather nice to be able to ride in front of the pack and hear the reassuring squeal of brakes just behind me. Because, if I got lost this time, I sure as hell was going to take everyone with me.

# DAY 2

Kaanapali Beach to Kahului
Terrain: Mountainous, much dirt
Sights: The "Rocks"
27 miles

The ordeal on Haleakala shocked me. After 28,000 miles of bike tours, I'd forgotten two basic rules: bring a map; bring money. At least we did pack plenty of water before taking Highway 30 around Puu Kukui, the smaller, older volcano at Maui's largely unexplored west end.

The road became hilly and winding as it hugged the edge of rugged mountains and lush canyons, and there soon were no cars or people in sight. Just thousands of cattle, keeping the plunging mountain walls as neatly manicured as a putting green. About fifteen miles into the ride, we saw something even more striking: The Rocks—big ones, small ones—balanced precariously on top of each other, three, four at a time. It looks so natural, yet it's eerie—as if beings from another planet had left them.

Before we finished pondering The Rocks, our hilly paved road became a hilly, deeply rutted *dirt* road, which is why there were no cars. But since the dirt was hardpacked, we didn't have much trouble riding over it. And best of all, it took us to Mokolea Point, with its face-slapping winds and scenery of blue waters and deep canyons.

Eventually, paved road led to Kahului, Maui's main seaport and population center. The hotels perched on pretty Kahului Harbor aren't

---

DIRECTIONS: From Kaanapali Beach, go north 12 miles on H 30/Lower Hon-oapiilani Road. Continue loop east and south 14 miles (2 dirt) on H 340. Go 1 mile more on Highway 3400/Kahului Beach Road to hotels.

ACCOMMODATIONS: **Maui Beach Hotel,** 170 Kaahumanu Avenue, Kahului, (808) 877-0051 or (800) 367-5004. <u>Rooms</u>: 156, double $55. VISA, MC, AMEX, DINERS, DIS.
**Maui Palms,** 171 Kaahumanu Avenue, (808) 877-0071 or (800) 367-5004. <u>Rooms</u>: 112, $38. VISA, MC, AMEX, DINERS, DIS.

★

fancy, but prevent a backtrack to Kaanapali Beach and allow an early rest for the big day to follow: either a climb up Haleakala or the ride down the Hana Highway.

# DAY 3

Kahului to Hana
Terrain: Slick, curvy road
Sights: The Hana Highway
52 miles

It's called the Hana Highway. But the unofficial name of the winding, hilly, pockmarked, and crowded two-lane northeast Maui highway that holds a natural wonder behind every bend is "The Highway to Heaven." Along with 617 curves and 56 bridges comes a nonstop array of waterfalls, rain forest, steep cliffs, sheer drops into the ocean, and other stunning visual pleasures.

We got off our bikes often to comb through the dense forest, filled with hanging vines, wildly twisting branches, lush overgrowth, bamboo forest, and thick groves of monkeypod and mango trees. We each left our bike once unexpectedly, too, leaning too fast into a road slickened by frequent ten-minute rains and smashed mango fruit.

By the time we got to Hana, we were beat—and famished. There had been no food stops all the way from Paia.

We feasted our eyes on beautiful Hana Bay much as King Kamehameha must have in the 1780s, before he conquered all the islands a decade later. After fighting one of his battles here in his early years, he found his "favorite" wife, Kaahumanu, who was raised in a cave in Hana (marked by a plaque near the lighthouse) at the foot of Kauwiki hill. Since Marc and I refused to pay $300 for a hotel room and weren't allowed into the jammed campsite without reservations, we know that cave well. It was our home for the night.

---

**DIRECTIONS: Go west on Kaahumanu Avenue (H 32) to Hana Highway (H 36).**

**ACCOMMODATIONS: Hotel Hana Maui,** Hana, HA, (808) 248-8211. Plush, bay view. Rooms: 105 units, doubles $300. VISA, MC, AMEX, DINERS.
**Hana Kau Maui Resort Condominiums,** (808) 248-8426. Rooms: 9 units, $75. VISA, MC, AMEX, DINERS.

**CAMPING: Waianapanapa State Park,** 4 miles northwest of Hana on H 36. Call (808) 244-4354 in advance for permit, or go to office in Wailuku; on-site caretaker (808) 248-8061.

---

★

# DAY 4

Hana to Makena or Kahului
Terrain: Terrible road, then much dirt road
Sights: Highway to Hell, Seven Pools of Kipahulu
50 miles

The pristine southeast side of Maui is hardly ever seen, due to a large stretch of dirt after the Seven Pools of Kipahulu. But getting to the pools via concrete on Highway 31 is much, much worse. I consider H 31 to be the worst road in all of recorded history, which is why I call the Piilani Highway the "Highway to Hell."

The narrow, ten-mile paved road is composed entirely of a crazy quilt of pothole-filler blobs. While car drivers were merely vibrated, we bikers were jarred out of our minds for seven hilly, brain-rattling miles. It slowed our pace to a crawl and loosened anything on our bikes that was not securely tied down, as I found out when I turned around to see only *one* of my running shoes remaining on my rack.

The locals say they prefer this road because it discourages tourists. The Highway to Hell isn't nearly as crowded as the highway to Hana. This relative isolation and beauty may be why this area is popular with celebrities.

Fortunately, the Seven Pools made up for the jarring ride. Sculpted by nature out of volcanic rock, the pools of pure river water stairstep down from a waterfall as they head to the ocean. It was a great place to refresh ourselves and prepare for the next challenge: eight miles of dirt road.

Maps label this stretch of the Piilani Highway "impassable" or "four-wheel drive only." But as bad as the rutted, uneven, muddy dirt road is, we traveled at a slow but decent pace on our thin-tired road bikes. Picturesque views of a cattle-grazed countryside plunging into the sea made the ride worth it.

---

**DIRECTIONS:** Go west 10 miles on H 31 to Seven Pools. Go 25 more miles (first 8 dirt) to your choice of 1) Makena—right 6 miles on dirt road, 2) Kahului—follow H 31 right to Highway 37 (Kulu Highway/Haleakala Highway), 27 paved miles.

It is 21 miles from Makena to Kahului. From Wailea, go north on Wailea Alanui Drive to Piilani Highway or Kihei Road in Kihei. Then take Mukulele Highway (H 350) back to Kahului.

**ACCOMMODATIONS: Wailea Condominiums,** 3750 Wailea Alanui, (808) 879-1595 or (800) 428-3088. 150 units, $110+. VISA, MC, AMEX, DINERS. In Kihei, 7 miles north, **Maui Lu Resort;** 575 South Kihei Road, (808) 879-5881 or (800) 922-7866. Rooms: 158, $63+: VISA, MC, AMEX, DINERS. Many others.

★

When H 31 became paved again, we skipped the dirt road to Makena, where Maui's beautiful south coast begins, for a ride back to Kahului airport. We had a date with a 27-minute, 101-mile flight to the best-known of the Hawaiian islands: Oahu.

# Oahu

## DAY 5

Honolulu Airport to Waikiki Beach
Terrain: Flat
Sights: USS *Arizona* War Memorial
20 miles

Before tourism came to Oahu, the Japanese did, bombing Pearl Harbor and pushing the United States into World War II. Strangely enough, while visiting the site memorializing the thousand slain sailors entombed in the sunken hull of the battleship *Arizona* on December 7, 1941, I had a strange feeling that Japan had won the war.

The film about the attack was conciliatory, explaining that Japan was "forced" to action by an American economic stranglehold. It seemed as if it didn't want to offend the many Japanese in the audience—or all over Oahu. For as we cruised down to Waikiki, crowded with restaurants, shops, food stores, McDonald's, hotels, and dancing Hare Krishnas, it was clear that 75 percent of the tourists were Japanese!

---

**DIRECTIONS:** From airport to USS *Arizona* National Memorial, go west on Nimitz Highway (H 92), Kamehameha Highway (H 99) to Visitors Center. To Waikiki Beach, retrace route to airport, then take Nimitz 10 miles into Honolulu (heavy traffic) or parallel streets, back east on H 92 (Ala Moana) to dead end. Turn right at Kalakaua Avenue to Waikiki.

**ACCOMMODATIONS: Hawaiian Regent,** 2552 Kalakaua Avenue, Waikiki, (808) 922-6611 or (800) 367-5370. Amenities: tennis. Rooms: 1346, double $86–$155, VISA, MC, AMEX, DINERS, DIS.
**Hawaiian Monarch Hotel,** 444 Niu Street, (808) 949-3911 or (800) 922-7866. Rooms: 300, $43. VISA, MC, AMEX.

**CAMPING: Sand Island State Recreation Area,** H 92, south right to end of Sand Island Road.
**Keaiwa Heiau State Recreation Area,** 3 miles northeast of H 720, end of Aiea Heights Drive. Reach both at Division of State Parks, (808) 548-7455.

---

With Diamond Head in the background, hordes of young Japanese girls walked arm-in-arm along Kalakaua Avenue, all carrying plastic shopping bags, as if they were on a bargain-hunting spring break from college. Many signs and tourist booklets were in Japanese. The *Honolulu Star* was filled with stories, many angry, of Japanese buying up the island.

Adhering to the "When in Rome, do as the Romans do" philosophy, I walked into one of the ubiquitous tourist shops and bought a rice ball. Seeing my confusion, three Japanese girls laughingly instructed me in the proper use of seaweed paper.

It then struck me that Hawaii may be an even greater bargain for Americans than for Japanese. You get tropical beaches and a trip to Japan, all in one.

## OPTION

Waikiki to Hanauma Bay
Terrain: Some hills
Sights: Hanauma Bay
24 miles

After visiting the state Capitol building, the Iolani Palace State Monument, and the statue of King Kamehameha in Honolulu, we headed east. A twenty-four mile (out-and-back) bike ride led to Hanauma Bay State Underwater Park.

Hanauma's protected coral is home to thousands of species of fish. I've snorkeled all over the world, including Jacques Cousteau's favorite spot, Ras Mohammed in the Red Sea, but I've never seen such variety and quantity of sea life.

---

**DIRECTIONS:** Go east 2 miles on Kalakaua Avenue through Kapiolani Park, name changes after 1 mile to Diamond Head Road (seaside climb around volcano). Name changes again after 1½ miles to Kahala Avenue. At Waialae Park, turn left on Kealaolu Avenue for 1 mile. Turn right, go 6½ miles on H 1/Hwy 72 (Kalanianaole Highway) to Hanauma Bay.

---

## DAY 6

Waikiki to Kuilima Point
Terrain: Short climb, mostly flat
Sights: Polynesian Cultural Center
64 miles

This day, we headed as far away as we could from Honolulu: Kuilima Point, the northernmost reach of Oahu.

After passing Hanauma Bay and Sandy Beach, a climb at Makapuu turned the corner onto the island's north side. We immediately felt the winds change—from in-our-face to at-our-back—then descended along the edge of cliffs high above perfect beaches, small islands, and deep blue waters.

After groping through the cities of Mokapu and Kaneohe, the Kamehameha Highway provided flat, breezy coastline views and sparse traffic to Laie Bay. Awaiting there was the Polynesian Cultural Center and histories of the Pacific's island peoples.

Since the sun sets at 6:30, the famous Polynesian show starts at 7:30, and we weren't aware of the local lodge, we rode on to the North Shore. There, the only accommodations are beach hovels rented by surfers who come to battle the biggest waves in the world.

Luckily, we found room in the normally booked bungalows. As our surfer roommates explained in Australian, New Zealander, and European accents, the sea was flat.

---

**DIRECTIONS:** Retrace route to Kalanianadle Highway (H 72) past Hanauma Bay and Sandy Beach. Stay on H 72 to dead end at Pali Highway (Highway 61). Next through urban area turn right 2 miles on H 61 (Kailua Road) to beach. Go 1.5 miles on Kalaheo Drive past Kaneohe Marine Station and Kaneohe Beach Park. Turn right 2 miles on H 65, then right on H 836/H 83 (Kamehameha Highway) for rest of day. To Hilton, go 6 miles up road at Kuilima Point; after 5½ miles, turn right, ½ mile private road.

**ACCOMMODATIONS: Turtle Bay Hilton,** 57-091 Kamehameha Highway, (800) 445-8667 or (808) 293-8811. 800-acre North Shore resort. Amenities: tennis, restaurants, horseback riding, golf. Rooms: 486, double $156. VISA, MC, AMEX, DINERS, DIS.

**Laniloa Lodge Hotel,** 55-109 Laniloa, Laie, next to Polynesian Center, (808) 293-9282 or (800) 367-8047. Rooms: 47, $60–$110. VISA, MC, AMEX, DIS.

**CAMPING: Malaekahana State Recreation Area,** 1 mile north of Laie on H 83.

**Waimanalo Bat State Recreation Area,** in Waimanalo on ocean side of H 83.

---

## DAY 7

Kuilima Point to Waikiki
Terrain: Flat with long dirt road
Sights: North Shore beaches
76 miles

With our good memories of the muddy, rock-strewn dirt roads of Maui, we considered ourselved blessed after leaving the North Shore.

About twenty-three miles into this day's route, Farrington Highway became dirt.*

Better yet, to prevent vehicles from entering, it was blocked off by a rock wall. So we had the dirt all for ourselves to Kaena Point, the uninhabited west end of Oahu. Alternately riding, hiking, and carrying the bikes over the remnants of a road wiped out by storms several years ago, we were alone, seemingly light-years away from paved and peopled Waikiki. It was the one place of solitude on an island bloated with tourists, and made us feel like swashbuckling explorers.

After turning southeast and emerging back onto paved road at Yokohama Bay Beach, civilization came fast. The forty-five-mile ride back to Waikiki headed along Oahu's "McDonald's Coast," with one virtually every mile.

Back in urban Honolulu, the contrast to desolate Kaena Point was striking. But still, as I lay on the beach the next day with thousands of others, gazing at the swaying palm trees, the clear blue sea, and the tanned Japanese girls walking by, I realized that Waikiki was much nicer than anyplace I'd ever been—except for Maui. And when I noted how I got there, I had to chuckle out loud. There's no way to measure how much bike touring has enriched my life. And here I was, being paid to take a bike trip.

I looked over to check on my bike. Yeah, I thought—Hawaii and my bicycle. This truly is paradise.

---

**DIRECTIONS:** Go 13 miles on Kamehameha Highway (H 99). Turn west just past Waialua Bay onto Route 821. Turn right on Waialua Beach Road, then right when Waialua dead-ends at Farrington Highway (H 930). Ride 30 miles on H 93 around Pearl Harbor until merge with (H 99) near Pearl City. (Do not slip onto H 1 at 20-mile mark.)

Save 28 miles with non-coast option. Stay on Kamehameha Highway 17 miles to Farrington Highway.

---

*To avoid the dirt, and save twenty-eight miles in the process, see below.

# SIGHTSEEING INFORMATION

HONOLULU, OAHU

**USS *Arizona* Memorial,** Pearl Harbor: Film of events leading to attack, shuttle boat trip to offshore memorial and sunken hull; free; 8:00 A.M. to 3:00 P.M. (808) 422-0561.

**Waikiki Aquarium,** 2777 Kalakua Avenue: Has over 300 species of Pacific marine life, some unique to Hawaii, world's most-isolated island group.

**Hawaiian State Capitol,** Beretania and Richards streets: Unique modern rectangular structure decorated with volcanic rock; 9:00 to 4:00, Monday through Friday.

LAHAINA, MAUI

**Whale Watching.** Between December and April.

**Lahaina-Kaanapali Railroad,** H 30: 6-mile narrow gauge line travels along coast, canefields; restored nineteenth-century sugarcane line; departs Lahaina all day; $7.50. (808) 661-0080.

**Banyan Tree,** town center on Front Street behind courthouse: Largest tree in Hawaii; covers an acre.

LAIE, OAHU

**Polynesian Cultural Center,** next to Brigham Young University: 35-acre waterway/lagoon reconstruction of old South Sea island villages of Hawaii, Tahiti, Fiji, Tonga, Samoa, Maori New Zealand; exhibits, water pageants, live shows, hula classes, coconut cracking, staple island foods like poi; music show, 12:30 P.M.; canoe pageants hourly, 1:00 to 4:00; "This is Polynesia," 7:30, ninety-minute show; cast of 125, war dances, songs; admission $25. (800) 367-7060 or 293-3333.

★　　　★　　　★　　　★　　　★

# ABOUT THE AUTHOR

BELIEVING THAT "YOU LEARN MORE, SEE MORE, TALK *to more people, get in better shape, and get a better tan while riding a bike then by any other means of travel," Roy Wallack toured sixteen countries, thirty-eight states and seven Canadian provinces and territories in an eight-year period from 1982 to 1989. He has ridden across North America from Pacific to Atlantic, down both coasts, along the Mississippi River from beginning to end, down from Alaska, through the Blue Ridge Mountains, and around Hawaii. He also was a member of the landmark first-ever bicycle tour into the Soviet Union in 1988.*

*Describing his 25,000-mile odyssey as "My Bike Trip, Myself," Roy jeopardized jobs and relationships in the pursuit of world-famous sights, different accents and cultures, and the sheer adventure of the road. Ultimately, as he began writing about his adventures, he became a journalist. A former editor of* California Bicyclist *magazine, his travel and fitness articles have appeared in* Bicycling, Fitness Cycling, Men's Fitness, Pacific Sport, *and* Triathlon Today. *Now the West Coast Lifestyle Editor of* SportStyle *magazine, be resides in Santa Monica, California, just fifty feet from the beach bike path.*